Human Capital versus Basic Income

Human Capital versus Basic Income

Ideology and Models for Anti-Poverty Programs in Latin America

FABIÁN A. BORGES

University of Michigan Press
Ann Arbor

Copyright © 2022 by Fabián A. Borges
Some rights reserved

Note to users: This work is licensed under a Creative Commons Attribution-NonCommercial-NoDerivatives 4.0 International License. A Creative Commons license is only valid when it is applied by the person or entity that holds rights to the licensed work. Works may contain components (e.g., photographs, illustrations, or quotations) to which the rightsholder in the work cannot apply the license. It is ultimately your responsibility to independently evaluate the copyright status of any work or component part of a work you use, in light of your intended use. To view a copy of this license, visit http://creativecommons.org/licenses/by-nc-nd/4.0/

For questions or permissions, please contact um.press.perms@umich.edu

Published in the United States of America by the
University of Michigan Press
Manufactured in the United States of America
Printed on acid-free paper
First published February 2022

A CIP catalog record for this book is available from the British Library.

Library of Congress Cataloging-in-Publication data has been applied for.
ISBN 978-0-472-13292-8 (hardcover : alk. paper)
ISBN 978-0-472-03897-8 (paper : alk. paper)
ISBN 978-0-472-90277-4 (OA)

DOI: https://doi.org/10.3998/mpub.12001219

To Rebecca,
None of this would have been possible without you

CONTENTS

Figures	ix
Tables	xi
Acronyms and Abbreviations	xiii
Acknowledgments	xv
1. Introduction: Conditional Cash Transfers and Latin America's Left Turn	1

Part 1: The Political Origins of the Two Models of CCTs

2. Presidential Ideology and CCT Adoption Revisited: Uncovering the Relationship	21
3. Lula and Brazil's Left Learn to Love CCTs: From Rejection to Acceptance and Transformation	46
4. Human Capital vs. Basic Income: Models of Cash Transfers in Mexico and Brazil	69

Part 2: Ideology and the Diffusion of CCTs

5. The Effect of Presidential Ideology on CCT Scope and Design: A Quantitative Test	95
6. Diffusion Revisited: Presidential Ideology and the Two-Track Diffusion of CCTs	119
7. Presidential Ideology's Effect on CCT Adoption and Design: The Cases of Costa Rica, Bolivia, and Argentina	135

Part 3: Ideology and the Future of CCTs

 8. Conclusion: The Future of CCTs   169

  Notes   197

  References   215

  Index   263

Digital materials related to this title can be found on the Fulcrum platform via the following citable URL https://doi.org/10.3998/mpub.12001219

FIGURES

1-1 CCT Coverage in Latin America, 1996–2015 (Percentage of the Total Population and Millions of People)   3
1-2 Number of Countries with CCTs and Left-Wing Governments in Latin America (1996–2015)   7
1-3 Left-Wing Governments in Latin America by Country and Year (1995–2015)   9
2-1 Estimated Effect of Time on Probability of CCT Adoption at Different Levels of Regional CCT Adoption   34
2-2 Number of CCTs Adopted by Presidential Ideology   35
3-1 Brazilian CCT Coverage by Households (1996–2015)   48
3-2 Inflation Adjusted Value of CCT Stipends (July 2001 = 100)   64
4-1 Mexico and Brazil: CCT Coverage as a Percentage of Population Minus Share of the Population Living in Poverty (Earning Less Than $4.00/day) (1997–2015)   88
5-1 Average CCT Coverage in 18 Countries (1996–2015)   98
5-2 Unweighted Average of CCT Coverage for 18 Countries (1996–2015)   99
5-3 Unweighted Average of Main Dependent Variables by Presidential Ideology (1996–2015)   100
5-4 Marginal Effect of Having a Left-Wing President on CCT Coverage at Different Poverty Levels   110
5-5 Marginal Effect of Having a Left-Wing President on CCT Coverage at Different Inequality Levels   111
5-6 Marginal Effect of Having a Nonleft-Wing President on CCT Coverage at Different Child Labor Levels   112
5-7 Influence of Left Government on CCT Design   116
6-1 Number of Entries on International Financial Institution Websites for Brazilian and Mexican CCTs (up to 2010)   123

7-1 Avancemos: Evolution of Coverage (2005–2015) 137
7-2 Avancemos: Stipend Purchasing Power by Grade over Time (2007–2016) 143
7-3 Bono Juancito Pinto: Evolution of Coverage (2006–2015) 146
7-4 Bolivian Cash Transfer Programs: Stipend Purchasing Power (2006–2015) 153
7-5 Argentine Cash Transfer Programs: Evolution of Coverage (2005–2015) 155
7-6 Asignación Universal por Hijo: Stipend Purchasing Power (2009–2015) 164
8-1 Share of Students Scoring "Low" on 2013 TERCE Exam (by Grade and Subject) 190
8-2 PISA Score (Average of Reading, Math and Science) and Income per Capita (2015) 192

TABLES

1–1	Models of CCTs	5
1–2	Spending on CCTs	11
2–1	Presidential Ideology and CCT Adoption	28
2–2	Event History Analysis of CCT Adoption (1995–2010)	32
4–1	Contrasting Mexican and Brazilian CCTs (circa 2015)	87
4–2	Mexican vs. Brazilian CCTs: Penalties for Noncompliance	89
5–1	Preliminary Time-Series Cross-Section Analysis of CCT Coverage (as % of Population) (1996–2015)	103
5–2	Time-Series Cross-Section Analysis of CCT Coverage (as % of Population) Minus Poverty Rate (1996–2015)	105
5–3	Time-Series Cross-Section Analysis of CCT Scope (1996–2015)	106
5–4	Estimated Effect of Having a Left-Wing President on CCT Coverage by Country	107
5–5	Predicted CCT Type of Post–Bolsa Família Programs	113
5–6	Ideology and CCT Design	114
6–1	Comparison of Country Cases (circa 2012–2013)	130

ACRONYMS AND ABBREVIATIONS

AUH	Asignación Universal por Hijo (Universal Child Allowance)
BJP	Bono Juancito Pinto (Juancito Pinto Bonus)
CEPAL	Comisión Económica para América Latina y el Caribe (Economic Commission for Latin America and the Caribbean)
CCT	conditional cash transfer
FAO	United Nations Food and Agriculture Organization
IDB	Inter-American Development Bank
IDH	Ingreso para el Desarrollo Humano (Income for Human Development)
IFI	international financial institution
IMAS	Mixed Institute for Social Assistance
ISI	import substitution industrialization
Jefes	Programa Jefes y Jefas de Hogar Desempleados (Unemployed Heads of Households Program)
MAS	Movimiento al Socialismo (Movement Toward Socialism)
MDS	Ministério do Desenvolvimento Social e Combate à Fome (Brazil's Ministry for Social Development and the Fight against Hunger)
OECD	Organization for Economic Cooperation and Development
PAN	Partido Acción Nacional (National Action Party)
PETI	Programa de Erradicação do Trabalho Infantil (Program for Eradication of Child Labor)

PGRM	Programa de Garantia de Renda Mínima (Guaranteed Minimum Income Program)
PISA	Programme for International Student Assessment
PRD	Partido de la Revolución Democrática (Party of the Democratic Revolution)
PRI	Partido Revolucionario Institucional (Institutional Revolutionary Party)
PRO	Propuesta Republicana (Republican Proposal)
PROGRESA	Programa de Educación, Salud y Alimentación (Education, Health and Nutrition Program)
PRONASOL	Programa Nacional de Solidaridad (National Solidarity Program)
PRT	power resource theory
PSDB	Partido da Social Democracia Brasileira (Brazilian Social Democracy Party)
PT	Partido dos Trabalhadores (Workers' Party)
RPS	Red de Protección Social (Nicaragua) (Social Protection Network)
SEDESOL	Secretaría de Desarrollo Social (Mexico's Social Development Ministry)
SNTE	Sindicato Nacional de Trabajadores de la Educación (National Union of Education Workers)
TERCE	Third Comparative Regional and Explicative Exam
UBI	universal basic income
UNESCO	United Nations Educational, Scientific and Cultural Organization
UNICEF	United Nations Children's Fund

ACKNOWLEDGMENTS

This project has been nearly a decade in the making and would not have been possible without the many institutions, colleagues, friends, and family members who helped me along the way. Their support and contributions have improved this work and enriched my life in more ways than I can express. To them I am deeply grateful.

First and foremost, I owe a large debt of gratitude to Gerry Munck, who helped transform my vague desire to study social policy in Latin America and the politics of conditional cash transfers into a doctoral dissertation at the University of Southern California (USC), a multiyear research agenda and, ultimately, this book. Gerry was accessible and good humored, yet uncompromising in his commitment to quality scholarship—everything I could want from a mentor. His tireless work ethic pushed me to work harder every day and not settle for less. I am proud to call Gerry a mentor, a role model, and a friend. Gerry has continued to support this project long after his formal responsibilities to it ended.

I was also helped greatly by Carol Wise, who was a supportive mentor and a tireless advocate on my behalf since the day I first set foot on USC's campus. Carol encouraged me to submit my work to journals early on, an experience that, although initially frustrating and discouraging, toughened me up early in my academic career. The great friends I made at USC were perhaps the best part of the graduate school experience. The companionship and support of dear friends played a crucial role in getting me through that long process. I am particularly grateful to Justin Berry, Mariano Bertucci, Juve Cortés, Nic de Zamaroczy, Parker Hevron, Deniz Kuru, Jess Liao, Jillian Medeiros, Mike Perez, Cintia Quiliconi, Simon Radford, Mariana Rangel, Mauricio Rivera, Bárbara Zárate Tenorio, and Christina Wagner Faegri. I am also grateful to Jefferey Sellers, Nick Weller, Ben Graham, and Diana O'Brien for their insightful comments and critiques of early versions of what eventually became this book. I am also grateful to Robin King at Georgetown University for getting me interested in CCTs and encouraging me to pursue a PhD in political science.

At Cal State University, San Bernardino I have been lucky to be part of a collegial, no-drama department that provided a supportive environment for my research. Brian Janiskee has been a fantastic department chair and a strong advocate for the interests of junior faculty. Meredith Conroy has been a particularly supportive colleague and a good friend. I am grateful for her help in navigating the book publication process and for serving as a sounding board for my ideas and occasional frustrations. I am also grateful to Steven Childs, Mark Clark, and Tony Field for their support.

Despite the occasional bout of altitude sickness, field research in Latin America proved to be a much more valuable and rewarding experience than I could have ever imagined. I came out of this experience thoroughly convinced that, far from an outdated practice, field research remains an invaluable asset in an era when cross-national data can be easily downloaded. I was consistently humbled by the willingness of busy people to share their valuable time with me. In Argentina, Cintia Quiliconi, a close friend and fellow Trojan, helped me find housing in Buenos Aires on short notice. Cintia and Diana Tussie graciously provided me with office space at FLACSO (Facultad Latinoamericana de Ciencias Sociales)–Argentina's International Relations Department. I am particularly indebted to the World Bank's Rafael Rofman, who exposed me to the idea that the goals of CCTs in Argentina and Bolivia might be different from those of CCTs in Mexico and Costa Rica. That insight blossomed into this book's central argument. Valeria Loira and Ezequiel lo Valvo granted me full access to ANSES (Argentina's National Social Security Administration) and with good humor answered my obscure questions regarding the functioning of Asignación Universal por Hijo. Mercedes Botto welcomed me into her home and was kind enough to put me into contact with several former policymakers.

In Bolivia, I was lucky to count on the support of Tatiana Vargas, Costa Rica's chargé d'affaires, who, in addition to being a gracious host, allowed me to work out of the Costa Rican Embassy in La Paz. I am also indebted to Orlando Murillo for providing me with documents on Bono Juancito Pinto that I would not have been able to access otherwise given much of the government's reluctance to talk to a student from a US university.

In Costa Rica, Katherine Stanley-Obando put me in touch with former president Oscar Arias and Education Minister Leonardo Garnier. Over drinks, Carla Valverde, a dear friend and former Avancemos staffer, provided a firsthand account of the political intrigue that surrounded that program during its first years in operation. Olga Sonia Vargas and the staff of Avancemos showed great interest in my research and did everything in their power to help me see it to fruition.

This book would not have been possible without generous funding and support. Portions of this study were made possible by the funding received from USC through the Judith Grayson Manning Memorial Fellowship, Gold Family Fellowship, Zilpha R. and Joan A. Main Dissertation Completion Fellowship, and the Dornsife College of Letters, Arts and Sciences Field Research Grant. At Cal State, San Bernardino, reassigned time from the Political Science Department and the School of Social and Behavioral Science lightened my teaching load and allowed me to focus more time on research and writing.

I am also grateful to the three anonymous reviewers at the University of Michigan Press. They provided detailed and constructive criticism that was instrumental in sharpening the book's argument and helped me avoid a few embarrassing mistakes, particularly in the conclusion. I am also grateful to Elizabeth Demers for supporting this project and guiding it to fruition.

Finally, I would like to thank my family for instilling in me the desire to learn about the world and encouraging me to make academia my profession. I thank my mother, Iris, and father, David, for their love and support in every phase of my life, this project being no exception. I thank my aunts Pilar and Libia and cousins for providing me with a home in Costa Rica even though I have not lived there for 15 years. Finally, words cannot convey the gratitude I owe Rebecca Kimitch, my wife, part-time editor, and full-time cheerleader. She encouraged me to come to the United States for graduate school and supported my plan to pursue a doctorate. She worked tirelessly to build homes for us in Washington, DC, Los Angeles, and later Claremont, bent over backwards to cheer me up when I occasionally "lost my smile," and was a pillar of support during periods of uncertainty surrounding my health. I also thank her for bringing into my life Gaby and Sam, our two wonderful and energetic children. I dedicate this book to Rebecca.

[Brazilian President] Lula [da Silva] has tried to compensate for his macroeconomic orthodoxy with innovative social initiatives.... At the end of the day, however, perhaps his most important achievement on this front will be the generalization of the Bolsa Familia initiative, which was copied directly from the antipoverty program of [right-wing] Mexican Presidents Ernesto Zedillo and Vicente Fox. This is a successful, innovative welfare program, but as neoliberal and scantly revolutionary as one can get.
—Jorge G. Castañeda, former Mexican foreign minister and expert on the Latin American left

Despite its absence of ample, general and unrestricted universality, the Bolsa Familia program, because of characteristics such as its search for equality, its breadth of coverage, its attention to children and women and its non-contributory nature can be classified as a social democratic policy for the contemporary period.
—Déborah Thomé, Brazilian social policy scholar

CHAPTER 1

Introduction

Conditional Cash Transfers and Latin America's Left Turn

Covering 56 million people or slightly more than a quarter of Brazil's population in 2015, Bolsa Família (Family Scholarship) is one of the world's largest and most heralded anti-poverty programs. It is perhaps the most famous example of a conditional cash transfer (CCT) program, a homegrown Latin American social policy innovation that seeks to simultaneously reduce poverty and increase educational attainment by awarding poor families regular stipends on the condition that their children attend school. In the immediate term, cash transfers relieve poverty by boosting family incomes. In the long term, the requirement that beneficiary children remain in school is expected to increase their human capital, which should, in turn, improve their earnings prospects and thus prevent them from growing up to be poor adults.

The intellectual authorship of CCTs remains contested. Brazilians would disagree with Jorge Castañeda's statement above, noting that by the time Mexico adopted the world's first nationwide CCT, Progresa/Oportunidades (To Progress/Opportunities), in 1997, several Brazilian cities had been operating their own subnational CCTs for almost two years.[1] What is not contested, however, is the overwhelming popularity of CCTs—among governments, international institutions, and, most importantly, beneficiaries. In a clear example of policy diffusion, these programs spread quickly, first across Latin America (Sugiyama 2011) and later around the world (Brooks 2015). In 1997, 1.5 million Brazilians and Mexicans, roughly 0.3% of the region's population, were enrolled in CCTs. By 2015, 131.8 million people across Latin America, or about one in five people, were enrolled in such programs (see fig. 1–1). Their success in the region prompted governments in settings as diverse as sub-Saharan Africa, Southeast Asia, and even New York City to enact their own programs. By 2015, 40 countries around the world operated CCTs (Morais 2017, 29).[2]

Returning to the quotes above, there is evidence supporting both of these seemingly contradictory statements. In line with Castañeda's observation, Bolsa Família, like Progresa/Oportunidades, constitutes a market-based or "neoliberal" approach to combating poverty. Both programs target the poorest members of society. More specifically, they focus on the so-called deserving poor—those who are poor through no fault of their own (children)—and are conditional on beneficiaries actively taking steps to overcome their situation (by staying in school). Their ultimate goal is to equip beneficiaries with the tools needed to "lift themselves up by their bootstraps." Both assume that families, as units made up of rational actors, understand their needs better than the government ever could and thus award cash rather than in-kind benefits. And, in line with neoliberal concerns over budgets and deficits, these programs are cheap, especially when compared to growing pension expenditures (Cecchini and Atuesta 2017).

Yet not all CCTs are created equal. Brazil and Mexico's CCTs differ significantly with regard to targeting, conditionality, and stipend structure. In terms of targeting, whereas Mexico relies on a stringent means test, Brazil enrolls beneficiaries based on self-reported incomes. With regard to conditionality enforcement, whereas in Mexico noncompliance immediately leads to the loss of that month's benefits, initial noncompliance in Brazil merely leads to a warning. A second violation within six months of that warning leads only to a one-month delay in benefits. Only after a third violation are benefits lost for the month. Mexico's program expels beneficiaries for the remainder of the school year if they violate conditionality three times or accumulate 12 unexcused absences. In Brazil, expulsion for noncompliance occurs after five violations but is in practice uncommon. In general, whereas Mexico adopts a strict (critics would say punitive) approach to conditionality enforcement, noncompliance in Brazil is treated as a sign that a family faces an additional vulnerability. A social worker is dispatched to help the parents overcome the difficulties preventing them from sending their children to school.

The programs also differ in terms of stipend structure. Because the opportunity costs associated with choosing school over work increase as students become older, Mexico's stipends increase with each grade. And, because women have historically received less schooling than men, they

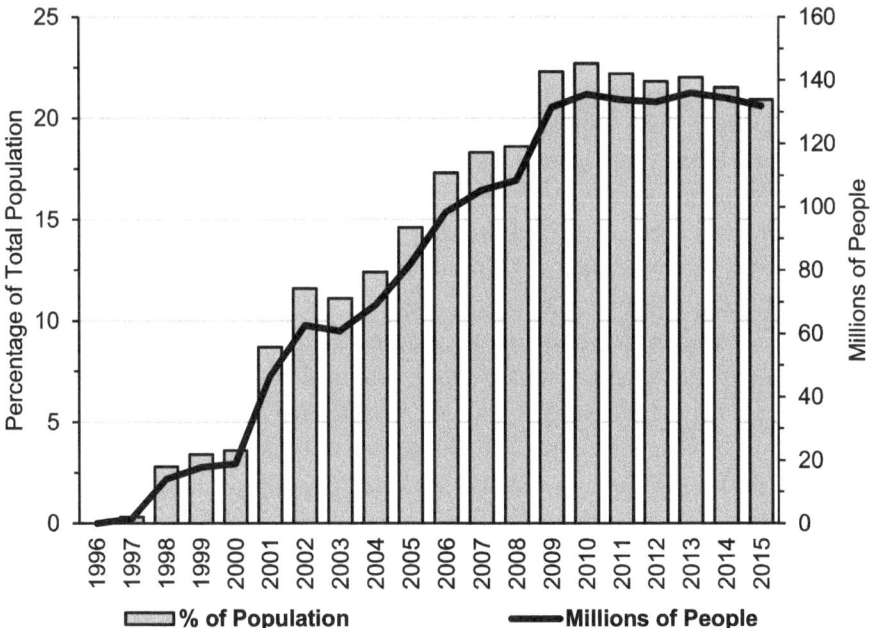

Figure 1-1. CCT Coverage in Latin America, 1996–2015
(Percentage of Total Population and Millions of People)
Source: Cecchini and Atuesta (2017, 22), based on Non-contributory Social Protection Programmes Database (CEPAL 2018).

receive larger stipends. Bolsa Família, in contrast, provides a flat stipend for each child under 15, though 16 and 17 year olds do receive a more generous stipend. The program also provides a supplemental subsidy determined on a case-by-case basis for families that remain in extreme poverty despite receiving Bolsa Família. Furthermore, with the intent of providing a minimum income floor for all Brazilians, Bolsa Família provides an unconditional base stipend for all households living in extreme poverty, even if they do not have children.

These differences reflect the contradiction at the heart of the twin goals of reducing poverty in the short term and increasing human capital over the long run (Soares, Ribas, and Osório 2010). If the priority is to reduce poverty as much as possible, it is counterproductive to revoke the benefits of noncompliers, as they tend to be the most vulnerable members of society. In contrast, given the effectiveness of conditioning benefits (Schady and Araujo 2008; Baird, McIntosh, and Özler 2011; de Brauw and Hoddinott

2011; Baird et al. 2014; Paiva et al. 2016), strict enforcement makes sense when building human capital is the main priority. CCT design can be tailored to prioritize one objective over the other. Whereas Mexico chose to emphasize human capital through strict conditionality, Brazil chose to emphasize poverty reduction and consciously took steps toward guaranteeing a minimum income floor. In that sense, Bolsa Família constitutes a step (albeit a modest one) toward shielding Brazilians from the market. It can, therefore, be considered, as Déborah Thomé argues in the quote above, "a social democratic policy."

In a nutshell, this book argues that there exist two distinct models of CCTs in Latin America and the choice of model is determined by government ideology. Whereas the right was attracted to CCTs for their potential to boost human capital, the left was attracted to their potential to reduce poverty and saw them as a step in the direction of providing an universal income floor (see table 1–1). The "human capital" model, pioneered by Mexico's right, focuses on using conditionality to incentivize school attendance among a narrowly targeted segment of the population. The more expansive "basic income" model, pioneered by Brazil's left, focuses on relieving poverty by providing a minimum safety net for a broad segment of the population. This pattern was not unique to Mexico and Brazil. Drawing on cross-national quantitative analyses covering the entire region and in-depth case studies of Argentina, Bolivia, and Costa Rica based on original field research, this book will show that, across the region, left-wing governments enacted more expansive and universalistic CCTs than their centrist and right-wing counterparts.

This finding addresses a major gap in the recent literature on the politics of social policy in the region. Past research has produced substantial evidence that left-wing governments are more likely to expand social policy and, as a result, have reduced poverty and inequality more than their centrist or right-wing counterparts (Birdsall, Lustig, and McLeod 2012; Huber and Stephens 2012). Surprisingly, however, no relationship was found between presidential ideology and the adoption of CCTs (Díaz-Cayeros and Magaloni 2009; Sugiyama 2011), the most progressive policy available to Latin American governments (Goñi, López, and Servén 2008, 20; Lindert, Skoufias, and Shapiro 2006, 71).

In highlighting the existence of two models of CCTs, the book clarifies the relationship between the widespread election of left-wing leaders in the 2000s (the so-called left turn) and the diffusion of CCTs, two of the most important developments in Latin American politics during the 2000s. This relationship was not straightforward or mechanical. Precisely because of its programmatic commitment to universalism and distaste for narrow targeting, Latin America's left was initially hesitant to embrace what turned out to be the most effective policy in its arsenal. Given this initial opposition, the left turn might well have put a brake on CCT diffusion. Prominent left-wing politicians in Brazil and Mexico, the two countries most closely associated with these programs, originally opposed CCTs. Left-wing presidents in Argentina and Bolivia were among the last major political actors in their countries to support CCTs. Moreover, the cases of Venezuela and Nicaragua show that the left's rise could spell the end for existing programs. The spread of CCTs in countries governed by the left during the second half of the 2000s was contingent on Brazilian center-left President Luiz Inácio Lula da Silva (2003–10), who was originally skeptical of CCTs, ultimately embracing the CCT programs he inherited and adapting them in a basic income direction. Only once CCTs had been shown to advance their programmatic goals did left-wing politicians truly embrace them.

More broadly, the book demonstrates that government ideology continues to be a major factor in shaping social policy in Latin America. The diffusion of CCTs and the basic income model in particular offer strong evidence against the claim that globalization, which pits developing countries against one other in competition for foreign investment, has sparked a social policy "race to the bottom" (Rudra 2008). It would be a mistake to

Table 1-1. Models of CCTs

	Human Capital CCTs	Basic Income CCTs
Central Goal	Conditionality to promote human capital accumulation and, over the long run, prevent intergenerational poverty	Transfers as a tool to relieve short-term poverty and, over the long run, create a basic income floor
Targeting	Narrower (focused on groups with human capital deficiencies)	Broader (aiming to build universal safety net)
Stipend Structure	Variable (compensates for opportunity cost of not working)	Uniform across beneficiaries
Conditionality	Strictly enforced and punitive	Less rigorously enforced, non-compliance seen as evidence of vulnerability
Ideology of Proponents	Right and center	Left

argue (as the Latin American left initially did) that the diffusion of CCTs constitutes an example of convergence toward a "neoliberal bottom" inasmuch as it involves the spread of means-tested, targeted programs. CCTs are rules-based entitlements that *extended* social policy to Latin America's neediest populations, which have historically been excluded from government benefits.

By demonstrating that diffusion of CCTs was mediated by government ideology, this book also warns against making excessively sharp distinctions between domestic and international drivers of policy change. Yes, the spread of CCTs was an example of policy diffusion: over the span of little more than a decade, the vast majority of the region's countries came to possess a similar policy that had not even existed years earlier. But diffusion occurred along two tracks. Ideology determined which foreign actors were seen as credible and which policies were perceived worthy of emulating. The center and right were eager to copy Mexico's program and work with the World Bank and the Inter-American Development Bank. The left was skeptical of the Mexican right's policies and international financial institutions but highly receptive to ideas emanating from Lula's Brazil. Thus, both international influences and domestic politics mattered.

1.1 Two Transformations: CCT Diffusion and the Left Turn

Latin America underwent two major transformations during the 2000s: the diffusion of CCTs and the left turn (see fig. 1–2). The basic facts are as follows: starting with Mexico in 1997, most of the region's countries came to adopt their own CCTs. These programs have significantly boosted the incomes of the poorest Latin Americans and in the process caused significant reductions in poverty (Stampini and Tornarolli 2012) and inequality (Soares et al. 2009; Lustig, López-Calva, and Ortiz-Juarez 2013) all while boosting school enrollment and attendance (Baird et al. 2014; García and Saavedra 2017; Bastagli et al. 2019). The spread of highly progressive CCTs constitutes a pathbreaking development in the region's social policy, which has historically neglected the poor in favor of the better off (Lindert, Skoufias, and Shapiro 2006; Haggard and Kaufman 2008).

As Latin American social policy was undergoing this "quiet transformation," the region's electoral politics underwent a much louder (and at times strident) transformation. In arguably the most important leadership shift in

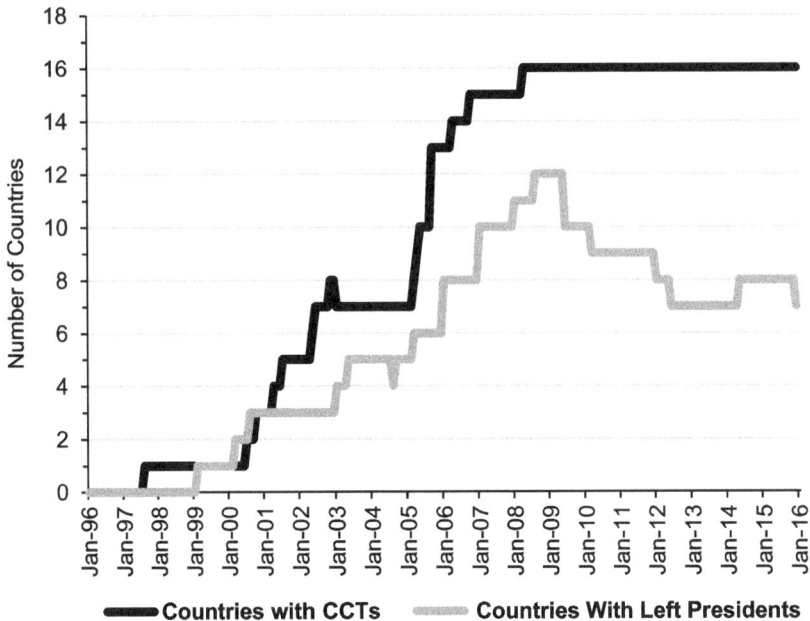

Figure 1-2. Number of Countries with CCTs and Left-Wing Presidents in Latin America (1996–2015)
Sources: News reports and Dataset on Political Ideology of Presidents and Parties in Latin America (Murillo, Oliveros, and Vaishnav 2010).

Latin American politics since democratization in the 1980s, the left, which many believed had become irrelevant in the aftermath of market reforms and the collapse of communism, experienced a resurgence. Beginning in 1998 with the election of Hugo Chávez (1999–2013) in Venezuela, voters across the region elected left-of-center governments that campaigned on promises of higher social spending and income redistribution. By 2009, at the peak of the left turn, nearly two-thirds of Latin Americans lived under a leftist government (see fig. 1–3).

This naturally raises the question—*what is the relationship between the diffusion of CCTs and the left turn?* In answering that question, the book tackles a broader question: *What is the effect of government ideology and, more specifically, leftist governments on social policy under globalization?*

Political science research provides a priori reasons to expect a relationship between these two trends. The election of left-wing and labor-backed governments was central to the emergence and expansion of social policy in both industrialized (Stephens 1979; Korpi 1983; Esping-Andersen 1985; Hicks 1999; Huber and Stephens 2001) and Latin American countries (Segura-Ubiergo 2007; Haggard and Kaufman 2008; Huber and Stephens 2012) during the previous century. However, there is evidence that the constraints of globalization and economic liberalization have since weakened or even completely eliminated ideology's effect on social policy in both industrialized (Pierson 1996; Huber and Stephens 2001) and Latin American countries (Madrid 2003; Kaufman and Nelson 2004; Weyland 2004; Brooks 2009).[3] Some scholars have gone so far as to argue that globalization sparks a social policy "race to the bottom" (Rudra 2008), whereby pressure to attract and retain footloose global capital leads governments to cut social spending (Garrett 2001).

Research on Latin America has pushed back against these claims, finding that left-wing and labor-allied governments continue to enact more egalitarian social policies than their nonleft counterparts (Castiglioni 2005; Huber and Stephens 2012; Pribble 2013; Martínez Franzoni and Sánchez-Ancochea 2016). Further, left-wing governments during the 2000s outperformed center and right governments in terms of reducing poverty and inequality (Cornia 2010; Birdsall, Lustig, and McLeod 2012).

At first glance, that the diffusion of CCTs coincided with the left turn appears to support the view that ideology continues to influence social policy (Lavinas 2013a). It is thus puzzling that past research has consistently found no relationship between CCT adoption and government ideology (Díaz-Cayeros and Magaloni 2009; Sugiyama 2011; Brooks 2015). The seeming absence of a relationship between left governments and the most progressive policy available to Latin American governments (Goñi, López, and Servén 2008, 20; Lindert, Skoufias, and Shapiro 2006, 71) is the central puzzle that this book seeks to explain.

1.2 Conditional Cash Transfer Programs

CCTs marked a pathbreaking development for Latin American social policy for two reasons: their progressivity and their use of transparent rules to select beneficiaries. With regard to the former, CCTs provide safety nets for groups that have traditionally been excluded or, at the very least, underserved by the region's social policy, namely the rural poor, urban shanty-

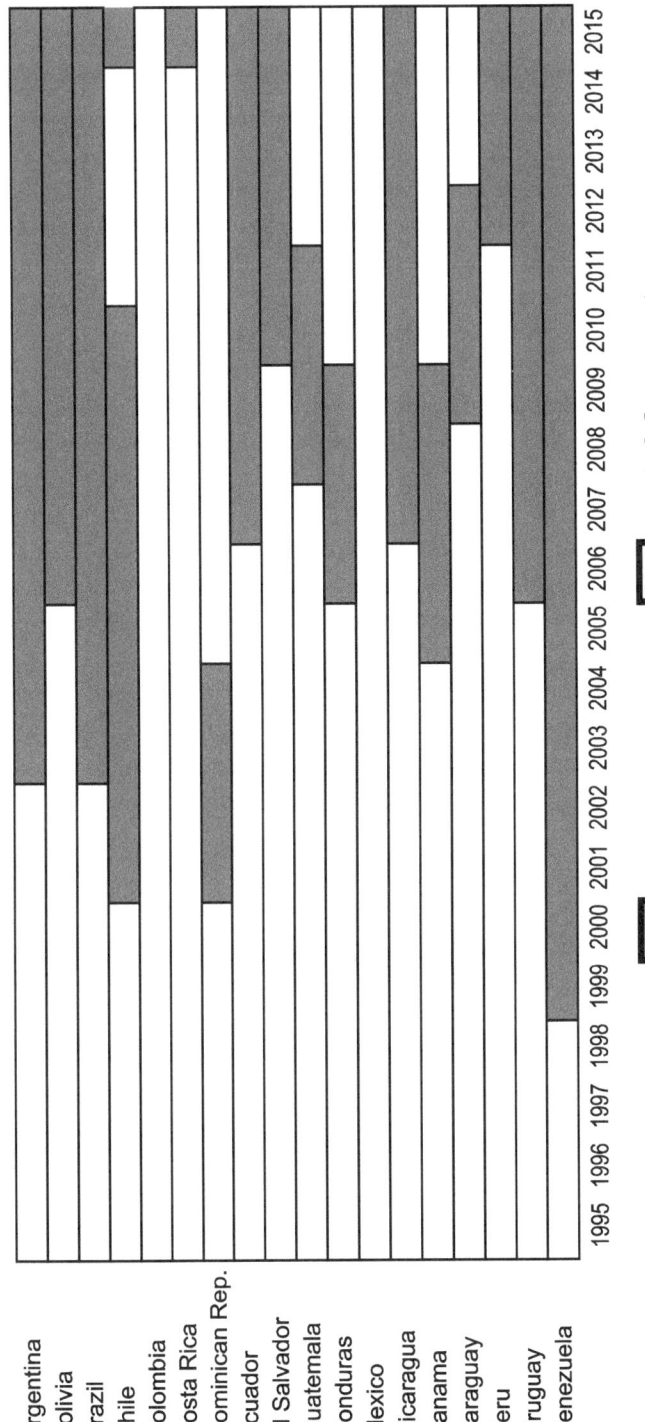

Figure 1-3. Left-Wing Governments in Latin America by Country and Year (1995–2015)
Sources: News reports and Dataset on Political Ideology of Presidents and Parties in Latin America (Murillo, Oliveros, and Vaishnav 2010).

town dwellers, and informal-sector workers. On the latter point, rather than a privilege dependent upon support for a particular politician or party, CCTs constitute entitlements targeted to individuals based on predetermined objective criteria such as age, poverty, and gender.

Not only has the region historically been the world's most unequal, its governments have pursued social policies aptly described as "reverse Robin Hood" (Lindert, Skoufias, and Shapiro 2006, 13) in that they primarily benefit the economically well off and politically organized (Mesa-Lago 1978) at the expense of the neediest.[4] This regressivity stems from a mismatch between the region's labor markets and the way in which social policies are organized and paid for, the region's welfare regime. In enacting welfare policies, such as healthcare and pensions, most of the region's countries emulated Southern Europe in establishing systems in which a family's benefits were financed primarily through deductions to a presumed (male) breadwinner's salary. This model clashes with the reality of the region's labor markets, which have historically had high levels of informality (Barrientos 2004, 2009). This mismatch worsened following the 1980s debt crisis and subsequent market reforms. Trade liberalization, the elimination of subsidies for domestic-oriented firms, and massive public-sector layoffs dramatically increased the share of the region's population employed in the informal sector and thus excluded from contributory government benefits.

In contrast to traditional social policy, CCTs explicitly target low-income households regardless of labor market status. Whereas about 80% of contributory pensions and 65% of unemployment benefits are spent on the richest 40% of the population, about 75% of CCT stipends go to the poorest 40% (Goñi, López, and Servén 2008, 20). In contrast to traditional policies, which reflect the interests of urban groups (Haggard and Kaufman 2008), CCTs exhibit a rural bias (Robles, Rubio, and Stampini 2019).

Still, these policies are no panacea. While highly progressive, they represent only a small fraction of the region's social spending. Despite covering one-fifth of Latin Americans (Cecchini and Atuesta 2017, 22), CCT spending in 2015 represented just 0.35% of the region's GDP or 3.01% of its total social spending (Cecchini and Atuesta 2017, see table 1-2). As Hunter (2021, 100) notes, "Innovations are layered upon the old model but do not displace it. In other words, they have begun to address the needs of poorer segments of society but not at the expense of the occupational categories privileged by the old system." Thus, the old "narrow but deep" welfare state coexists with and dwarfs these new "broad and thin" policies.

The selection of beneficiaries through transparent, well-publicized rules and the actual application of said rules—the two hallmarks of programmatic policy—also represent a break with the past. The limited funds spent on poverty relief were often distributed clientelistically: politicians (patrons) used handouts to buy the poor's (clients) political support. At the expense of their political autonomy, beneficiaries became captive constituencies for corrupt political machines. Management of CCTs tends to be centralized under newly created social development ministries or even under the office of the presidency precisely to reduce the power and minimize the discretionary authority of corrupt subnational politicians. Most programs deposit stipends directly to beneficiaries' bank accounts, further minimizing the role of local officials and reducing opportunities for diversion of funds. Clear eligibility rules and national hotlines for resolving disbursement problems have all but eliminated the need for intermediaries (brokers) between beneficiaries and the state. Surveys of Mexican (De La O 2015, chap. 6) and focus groups of Brazilian (Sugiyama and Hunter 2013) CCT beneficiaries confirm that they "know that these programs cannot be traded in a *quid pro quo* fashion for votes" (Hunter 2017, 11).

Table 1-2. Spending on CCTs

	CCT Spending as % of GDP (around 2015)[1]	CCT Spending as % of Public Social Spending (around 2015)[2]
Argentina	0.59%	4.0%
Bolivia	0.20%	1.6%
Brazil	0.50%	3.9%
Chile	0.15%	0.9%
Colombia	0.27%	3.9%
Costa Rica	0.17%	1.5%
Dominican Republic	0.43%	5.2%
Ecuador	0.66%	7.7%
El Salvador	0.24%	3.2%
Guatemala	0.06%	0.9%
Honduras	0.20%	2.2%
Mexico	0.23%	2.2%
Nicaragua	No CCT	No CCT
Panama	0.10%	1.1%
Paraguay	0.22%	1.9%
Peru	0.18%	3.3%
Uruguay	0.39%	2.6%
Venezuela	No CCT	No CCT
Weighted Average[3]	0.35%	3.01%

Sources: [1] Cecchini and Atuesta (2017, 31); [2] Cecchini and Atuesta (2017, 34); [3] Weighted as a share of the population of the 18 countries listed based on World Bank (2018).

1.2.1 Policy Effects of CCTs

Touted by the United Nations as "one of the most significant developments in global social policy since the expansion of social security in industrialized countries" (Fajth and Vinay 2010, 1), CCTs are considered an overwhelming success. They are credited with pulling 15.5 million Latin Americans—13% of the region's population—out of poverty (Stampini and Tornarolli 2012) and reducing income inequality at a time when it was increasing in the rest of the world (Lustig, López-Calva, and Ortiz-Juarez 2013, 130). More recently, CCTs have helped shield poor families from a regionwide recession following the end of the global commodity boom. After declining steadily for a decade, income inequality has been stagnant since 2010. And, after declining to its lowest recorded levels in 2014, poverty increased only slightly in 2015 and 2016 (CEPAL 2017, 88).

With regard to education, the overwhelming majority of studies find that cash transfers increase school enrollment, attendance, and grade completion, as well as lower the dropout rate (Baird et al. 2014; García and Saavedra 2017; Bastagli et al. 2019). These effects are generally larger for girls and at the secondary school level. Programs with stronger conditionality enforcement tend to produce larger effects (Baird et al. 2019). In contrast, these same studies concur that transfers have little (if any) effect on learning outcomes (i.e., how much children are learning). This issue will be revisited in the book's conclusion.

But are these programs succeeding at their long-term goal of breaking the intergenerational transmission of poverty? Much less is known about the long-term effects of CCTs. This type of research has been hindered by the relative newness of most programs and the challenges of tracking beneficiaries over several years. Only recently—now that the first generations of long-term CCT beneficiaries are entering the labor market—has it become possible to rigorously test these predictions. Disappointingly, however, the handful of studies of long-term effects conducted describe their findings as "inconclusive" (Molina-Millan et al. 2016, 25) or, at best, "modest" (Araújo, Bosch, and Schady 2016, 16).

Iliana Yaschine (2015), evaluation director early in the history of Mexico's Progresa/Oportunidades, attributed the disappointing results to the region's poor-quality public schools. It should be stressed that CCTs are, at best, a minor component of overall education policy. Some CCT skeptics have even expressed concern that these programs may have actually distracted governments from the crucial and politically difficult task of improving education. As Reimers, DeShano and Trevino (2006, 7) note:

> CCTs provide government officials the option to appear to address human capital objectives in a national development strategy, even as they avoid difficult reforms to significantly improve education. . . . Investing resources which could have been invested in significant improvements in the quality of teaching in CCTs has the double political advantage of avoiding the political costs of the former, while capturing the political benefits of distributing cash directly to the poor, an opportunity that many government officials and politicians perceive as yielding political support.

1.2.2 Political Effects of CCTs

That CCTs are awarded programmatically and are (largely) shielded from political manipulation does not mean that these programs have no political consequences. In a clear example of retrospective economic voting, research from across the region utilizing diverse methodologies finds robust evidence that CCTs increase electoral support for presidential candidates from incumbent parties (De La O 2013; Zucco 2013).[5] These effects hold even for governments that did not initiate the program in question (Díaz-Cayeros, Estevez, and Magaloni 2009; Zucco 2013). CCTs may even have tipped the balance in close presidential elections, most notably Mexico in 2006 (Díaz-Cayeros, Estevez, and Magaloni 2009) and, more speculatively, Brazil in 2014 (Zucco 2015).[6] More broadly, CCT beneficiaries are also more likely to support the current government (Manacorda, Miguel, and Vigorito 2011) and incumbent presidential candidates (Layton and Smith 2015).

CCTs may also improve the quality of democracy. Mexican states with higher levels of CCT coverage in 2000 had lower corruption levels five years later (Grimes and Wängnerud 2010). Programs are also associated with increased political participation and voter turnout among beneficiaries (Hunter and Power 2007, 16; De la O 2013; Layton and Smith 2011). In fact, evidence from Brazil reveals that CCTs foster a sense of personal autonomy and citizenship rights among beneficiaries (Sugiyama and Hunter 2013).

1.3 The Resurgence of the Latin American Left

The wave of left-wing governments that swept into office across the region at the turn of the century came as a surprise to many analysts of Latin American politics. In retrospect, it probably should not have been all that surprising. Latin America has a long history of left-wing politics dating back to the early twentieth century. The world's most unequal region, it has long offered fertile ground for socialist and communist ideologies as well as for more ideologically flexible populist movements.

In the aftermath of the 1959 Cuban Revolution, the region's left was torn between two competing strategies for achieving control of the state and enacting policies to address inequality and ultimately liberate workers from the tyranny of markets: ballots (e.g., Chile's Salvador Allende) and bullets (e.g., Cuba's Fidel Castro). Three global trends—the spread of democracy across the region starting in the late 1970s, the widespread adoption of neoliberal market reforms in the aftermath of the 1980s debt crisis, and the fall of communism and subsequent collapse of the Soviet Union after 1989—appeared to close off both paths, prompting many to dismiss the left as a historical anachronism. With regard to bullets, the spread of democracy and its widespread acceptance as "the only game in town" (Linz and Stepan 1996, 15)—the only legitimate means of obtaining and exerting political authority—delegitimized armed insurgency as a path to power. With regard to ballots, although democracy allowed the left to compete for office without fear of repression and substantially reduced the likelihood of a military coup against it if elected, the new consensus in favor of free-market policies and the failures of centralized planning meant that few voters were interested in what the left was selling. Indeed, between the resounding electoral defeat of the Sandinistas in Nicaragua in February 1990 and election of Hugo Chávez in Venezuela in December 1998 the region had no left-wing governments.[7]

Yet the end of the Cold War also presented an opportunity. The left no longer faced severe hostility from the United States or had to defend the Eastern Bloc's undemocratic practices (Angell 1995, 231). At the same time, the extreme income inequality that originally gave birth to the left had not disappeared (Castañeda 1993). In fact, inequality increased steadily during the 1990s, peaking at its highest reported level in 2002 (Cornia 2014, 5). Similarly, a higher share of the region's population lived in poverty in 2000 than on the eve of the 1980s debt crisis (CEPAL 2014, 16). Further, growth following the debt crisis was modest and prone to reversals. The opening of capital accounts contributed to painful financial crises, most notably in Mexico in 1994–95, Brazil in 1999, and Argentina in 2001–02. Average incomes in the region declined during the so-called lost half decade (1998–2002) that immediately preceded the left turn (Ocampo 2004, 68).

1.3.1 The Left in Power

Poor economic performance ushered in the left turn and good economic performance ensured its consolidation (Weyland 2009; Murillo, Oliveros, and Vaishnav 2011; Kaufman 2011). Specifically, starting around 2003, just as the left turn was gathering momentum, the prices of the region's main export commodities, most notably oil, metals, and soy, rose sharply in response to growing demand from China's booming economy. This global commodity boom fueled a decade-long "golden era" in the region marked by fast growth without inflation and declining poverty and inequality (Kingstone 2018), which, in turn, contributed to the reelection of left-wing incumbents.[8]

It was at this point that the trajectories of left governments started to diverge, with some following a more moderate promarket path and others a more radical path marked by significant state intervention in the economy.[9] The former tended to come from long-standing, institutionalized parties of the left, which, ironically, traced their roots to Cold War Marxist parties. The most notable examples of this were Brazil's Workers' Party, Chile's Socialist Party, and Uruguay's Broad Front. The radical left consisted of new and highly personalistic movements, most notably Venezuela under Chávez, Bolivia under Evo Morales (2006–19), and Ecuador under Rafael Correa (2007–17) (Madrid 2010).[10] The latter also tended to adopt a more confrontational foreign policy toward the United States.

The general consensus is that governments of the left outperformed their centrist and right-wing counterparts in terms of reducing poverty and inequality (Cornia 2010; McLeod and Lustig 2011; Birdsall, McLeod, and Lustig 2012; Huber and Stephens 2012) and possibly social spending.[11] Research attempting to tease out differences in the performance of the two lefts, however, has been inconclusive.[12] For that reason, in analyzing the relationship between CCTs and government ideology, this book's theory and empirical analysis rely on a dichotomous classification.

Throughout this book, the ideology of politicians and political parties will be measured in accordance with the Dataset on Political Ideology of Presidents and Parties in Latin America (Murillo, Oliveros, and Vaishnav 2010). Ideology is assessed based on the economic policies a president implemented in office, as opposed to the platform they campaigned on, and is coded on a five-point scale, where one is left and five is right.[13] The original dataset covers the period up to 2009. It has been extended to 2015 based on news reports from Reuters and *Latin America Weekly Report*.

1.4 Structure of the Book

This book argues that there exist two distinct models of CCTs in terms of target population, conditionality enforcement, and stipend structure, and the choice of model is determined by government ideology.

Chapter 2 demonstrates that, although countries with left-wing presidents were no more likely than those governed by the center and right to enact CCTs, across the region these programs, counterintuitively, were initially *proposed* by governments of the right and center and *opposed* by the left. This was true in Mexico and Brazil, the countries that popularized these programs, as well as in Argentina and Bolivia, where left-wing presidents ultimately adopted CCTs but did so reluctantly. Left-wing presidents in Nicaragua and Venezuela actually dismantled existing programs upon taking office. This ambivalence and, at times, outright hostility toward CCTs is explained by the left's preference for universal policies over narrowly targeted ones, worries that their opponents would use CCTs to buy the poor's support, and the initial association between those programs and the right and institutions such as the World Bank and the Inter-American Development Bank.

Chapter 3 details how the left overcame these initial misgivings. Brazil's experience under center-left President Lula da Silva proved crucial. Originally critical of the CCTs he inherited, Lula embraced them only after his preferred and more ambitious anti-poverty program failed. But Lula went beyond continuing his centrist predecessor's programs. He expanded and transformed them in the direction of providing a universal income floor. Charismatic, politically popular, and respected among the region's left, Lula widely publicized the merits of his country's CCT. His credibility and the adaptation of CCTs to better match the left's universalistic agenda made cash transfers palatable, indeed desirable, to other leftist presidents. Thus, the book argues, in the absence of Lula's adaptation, the left turn might well have put a brake on the spread of CCTs, just as it did in Nicaragua and Venezuela.

Chapter 4 demonstrates that there came to exist two distinct models of CCTs: a "human capital" model based on means-tested targeting and strict enforcement of conditionality, exemplified by the program launched by Mexico's right, and a more universalistic "basic income" model with more permissive enforcement of conditionality, exemplified by Brazil's program under Lula.

Chapter 5 relies on quantitative tools to confirm the existence of these two distinct types of CCTs and their relation to ideology. A quantitative analysis of 18 countries finds that left-wing governments operate CCTs that come closer to covering the entirety of the poor population, cover a larger share of their countries' populations, and cost more than the programs of their center or right-wing counterparts. Beyond coverage, a subsequent analysis of the 10 national programs adopted after Lula's embrace of CCTs confirms that program design—evaluated in terms of the scope of the target population, strictness of conditionality enforcement, and stipend structure—is heavily influenced by government ideology.

Chapter 6 argues that the diffusion of these models to the rest of the region was filtered through ideology. Right and center governments, with international financial institution assistance, enacted CCTs based on the human capital model, while the left, with assistance from Brazil, enacted CCTs based on the basic income model. Whereas the Mexican model emphasized cash transfers as a means of reducing poverty over the long term by ensuring that poor children stayed in school, the Brazilian model envisioned transfers as an end in themselves, a stepping-stone toward the creation of a universal income floor.

The prior quantitative findings and the claims regarding diffusion are then fleshed out in chapter 7 through case studies of the political processes that culminated in the adoption of a human capital CCT by a centrist president in Costa Rica and of basic income CCTs by left-wing presidents in Argentina and Bolivia. In Costa Rica, President Oscar Arias (1986–90; 2006–10) openly campaigned on enacting a CCT to reduce the country's high secondary-school dropout rate. Arias enacted a program similar to Mexico's but exclusively targeting low-income secondary-school students. In contrast, Bolivia's Morales and Argentina's Cristina Fernández de Kirchner (2007–15) were originally skeptical of CCTs. The programs they ultimately adopted were presented in terms of reducing poverty and providing a universal income floor much more so than on building human capital. The programs they enacted went even further in the basic income direction than Brazil's pioneering program.

The book concludes by analyzing how recent shifts in government ideology have affected CCT design. Following in the footsteps of Brazil's Lula, Costa Rica's left-wing governments reformed the human capital CCT they inherited in a basic income direction. In Mexico, left-wing populist Andrés Manuel López Obrador (2018–present), replaced the country's iconic human capital CCT with a series of broadly targeted unconditional transfers. In contrast, right-wing governments in Argentina and Brazil, the latter more so, gradually retrenched the basic income CCTs they inherited. In neither country did coverage keep up with rising poverty rates. More worryingly, there is evidence that López Obrador and his right-wing populist Brazilian counterpart, Jair Bolsonaro (2019–present), utilized cash transfer policy clientelistically during their first year in office. The chapter concludes by assessing the future of CCTs and anti-poverty policy in the region. Although CCTs have increased school enrollment and relieved poverty, the ability of beneficiaries to escape poverty as adults is hampered by low-quality public education. Reforming education, however, is a complex and politically difficult issue.

PART 1

The Political Origins of the Two Models of CCTs

CHAPTER 2

Presidential Ideology and CCT Adoption Revisited

Uncovering the Relationship

Latin American politics underwent two major transformations during the 2000s. Starting with Mexico in 1997, governments across the region adopted large-scale conditional cash transfer programs. The spread of these highly progressive programs constituted a pathbreaking development in the region's social policy, which has historically neglected the poor in favor of the middle class and the better off (Lindert, Skoufias, and Shapiro 2006; Haggard and Kaufman 2008). The widespread adoption of CCTs coincided with the resurgence and subsequent electoral dominance of left-wing governments across the region. Beginning in 1998 with the election of Hugo Chávez (1999–2013) in Venezuela, voters in country after country elected left-of-center governments that campaigned on promises of higher social spending and income redistribution (Castañeda 2006; Weyland 2010; Levitsky and Roberts 2011; Flores-Macías 2012). In sum, the 2000s saw CCTs implemented in nearly every country in Latin America and left-of-center presidents elected in a majority of the region's countries. How were these two transformations related?

Past research on the determinants of social policy adoption and design have emphasized the role of government ideology. Power resource theory (PRT), the dominant explanation for social policy among industrialized countries (Korpi 1983; Stephens 1979; Esping-Andersen 1985; Huber and Stephens 2001) as well as Latin America (Segura-Ubiergo 2007; Haggard and Kaufman 2008; Huber and Stephens 2012), attributes the expansion of and cross-national variation in social policy to the relative strength of the left and its allies in organized labor. Thus, there were strong a priori reasons to suspect that the left turn played a role in the widespread adoption of CCTs. Yet past cross-national research uniformly fails to find a relationship between government ideology and CCT adoption in the region (Díaz-Cayeros and Magaloni 2009; Sugiyama 2011) and across developing countries more broadly (Brooks 2015). Indeed, Latin American governments from across the ideological spectrum adopted CCTs.

This chapter challenges the view that, despite occurring parallel to each other, the left turn and CCT adoption were unrelated. Although a statistical analysis of the determinants of CCT adoption confirms prior research in finding that governments of all ideological persuasions were equally likely to *adopt* these programs, a closer look at the political process behind the adoption of CCTs in six countries reveals that governments of the right and center *introduced* CCTs to the political agenda. The left in fact initially *resisted* and even *opposed* these programs. Left-wing leaders today closely associated with the expansion of CCTs, most notably Brazil's Luiz Inácio Lula da Silva (2003–10) and Argentina's Cristina Fernández de Kirchner (2007–15), were initially deeply critical of these types of programs. Furthermore, in Nicaragua and Venezuela the left's ascension to power led to the cancellation of existing CCT programs.

What explains this counterintuitive outcome? Given their programmatic preference for universalistic policies, left-wing politicians opposed CCTs' narrow targeting of beneficiaries and strict conditionality enforcement, which they associated with neoliberalism. Left-wing politicians were also reflexively skeptical of policies endorsed by centrist and right-leaning politicians and multilateral banks—the very actors that years earlier spearheaded the so-called Washington Consensus market reforms (Williamson 1990) that led to a retrenchment of the region's social policy (Huber 2006).

2.1 What We Know (or Think We Know) about CCT Adoption

A large body of in-depth single-country case studies and a handful of cross-national quantitative analyses have sought to explain why, starting in the late 1990s, Latin America, a region with a history of severe income inequality and "reverse Robin Hood" social policies, innovated the use of highly progressive poverty-reduction policies, the most notable of which were CCTs.[1] Existing explanations can be categorized as political, economic, and related to policy diffusion.

2.1.1 Political Explanations

Explanations based on politics encompass both the incentives faced by politicians and the policy preferences of the broader population. PRT predicts that left-leaning governments will be more likely to both adopt new social policies and make existing policies more generous and universal. Thus, some scholars have assumed a connection between the region's left turn and the adoption of CCTs (Lavinas 2013a). However, none of the prior cross-national quantitative analyses has found evidence of such a relationship (Díaz-Cayeros and Magaloni 2009; Sugiyama 2011; Brooks 2015).

Given its initial focus on industrialized countries, PRT takes the existence of a democratic government as a given. Yet democracy cannot be assumed in developing countries. Having a democratic government is a necessary precondition for PRT. Democracy affects social policy through two channels: electoral competition, which provides politicians with incentives to deliver popular social programs, and interest group freedom, which allows groups to lobby and protest on behalf of their preferred policies (Haggard and Kaufman 2008).

Several studies find a positive relationship between democracy and adoption. Analyzing 114 developing countries, Brooks (2015) finds that more democratic countries are more likely to adopt CCTs. Relatedly, Díaz-Cayeros and Magaloni (2009) find that long-standing regimes are also more likely to adopt such programs. Given the sample they study, which consists of 21 Latin American and Caribbean countries during the 1990s and 2000s, regime duration serves mainly as a proxy for cumulative years of democracy, a factor associated with higher levels of social spending among Latin American countries (Huber and Stephens 2012).

Both cross-national quantitative research and case studies have found that political competition influenced adoption. Brooks (2015) finds that countries with divided governments—those in which the legislature is controlled by a party different from that of the president—are more likely to adopt CCTs.[2] Case studies of Mexico and Brazil, both of which adopted programs during periods of increasing political competition, emphasize the importance of elite competition for votes. Research on Mexico's pioneering program stresses the importance of growing electoral competition during the final years of the Institutional Revolutionary Party (PRI) regime (Dion 2009, 2010; De La O 2015; Díaz-Cayeros, Estévez, and Magaloni 2016; Garay 2016). In Brazil, increasing competition from the left-wing Workers'

Party (PT) may have pushed the centrist Fernando Henrique Cardoso (1995–2002) to enact federal funding for municipal CCTs in 1997 and launch the Bolsa Escola Federal CCT in 2001 (Melo 2008; Coêlho 2012a, 2012b; Garay 2016).

It is worth noting that the widespread adoption of CCTs followed two decades of sharply increasing income inequality (López-Calva and Lustig 2010; Cornia 2014). The median voter theory predicts that in a democracy redistribution will increase in line with income inequality (Meltzer and Richard 1981). The more unequal a society is, the lower the pivotal median voter's income will be relative to the mean income level and, thus, the more the median voter stands to gain from redistribution. Single-mindedly focused on getting elected (and thus pleasing the median voter), politicians could thus be expected to respond to rising inequality through increased redistribution in the form of a CCT, which, as noted, is among the most redistributive policies available to Latin American policymakers (Lindert, Skoufias, and Shapiro 2006; Goñi, López, and Servén 2008). In line with this argument, there is evidence that more unequal countries were more likely to adopt CCTs (Diaz-Cayeros and Magaloni 2009; Osorio Gonnet 2018, chap. 4).

PRT also predicts that redistributive policies will be the result of popular mobilization. Thus, governments facing high levels of protest could be expected to adopt CCTs as means of diffusing social tensions and expanding their electoral support.[3] In a related argument, Britto (2008, 187) speculates that increasing urban violence could explain CCT adoption. In her words, "fear encourages elites to favor public policies that tackle poverty directly and, in particular, that keep poor children and adolescents in school." This provocative claim has not been tested systematically.

2.1.2 Economic Explanations

CCT adoption has also been interpreted as a response to market reforms enacted during the 1980s and 1990s, which significantly increased economic vulnerability in the region (Dion 2010; Barrientos 2013) and, in turn, increased demand for safety net policies (De La O 2015). Vulnerability increased demand for social assistance through two channels. First, increased labor-market informality, a product of trade liberalization, de-industrialization, and public-sector downsizing, increased the share of workers excluded from traditional contributory social insurance. Second, slow growth and periodic financial crises during the 1990s increased the need for emergency safety nets.

Economic stagnation and financial crises that disproportionality hurt the poor increased public demand for safety nets. Mexico's CCT is widely seen as a response to the country's 1994–95 Tequila Crisis (Cortés and Rubalcava 2012; Díaz-Cayeros, Estévez, and Magaloni 2016, 163). Similarly, Brazil's federal CCTs were, at least in part, a response to the economic hardship caused by the country's 1999 currency devaluation (Melo 2007, 39; Fenwick 2009, 111). Several early CCTs, most notably those in Colombia (Brearley 2011) and Honduras (Moore 2008), were originally meant as temporary responses to downturns. Though envisioned as permanent, Argentina's Asignación Universal por Hijo (Universal Child Allowance) was enacted in response to the 2008–9 global financial crisis (see chapter 7). Still, although the first CCTs emerged during the region's so-called lost half decade (1997–2002), half of Latin America's CCTs were enacted during 2005–8, in the middle of a once-in-a-generation economic boom fueled by high international commodity prices. Cross-national statistical research on this question has been inconclusive. Díaz-Cayeros and Magaloni (2009) do find a negative relationship between growth and adoption. Looking at a wider sample of countries, however, Brooks (2015) finds a positive, though not robust, relationship.

In an argument that combines political and economic factors, Barrientos (2013, 12) posits that the spread of cash transfers in the developing world may be explained by a shift in the composition of government revenues away from payroll and corporate taxes toward consumption taxes, which fall heavily on the poor. This echoes earlier work by Timmons (2005), who argues that government spending tends to reflect the interests of those who pay for it. As such, countries highly dependent on consumption taxes should spend more on policies benefiting the poor. CCT adoption could be an example of this.

2.1.3 Diffusion Explanations

The rapid spread of similar anti-poverty programs across the region raises the possibility that, in adopting CCTs, governments were responding not only to domestic pressures but also learning from or emulating neighboring countries, or both. Policy diffusion offers an explanation as to why neighboring countries facing different conditions sometimes adopt strikingly similar policies and institutions. Shared political, economic, and cultural traits, as well as constant interaction at the governmental and societal levels, make Latin American governments keenly aware of policies innovated by their regional peers. Thus, it should be no surprise that Latin American governments emulate successful or politically popular policies, or both, that have been enacted by neighboring countries, CCTs among them.

There are strong a priori reasons to suspect that the spread of CCTs constitutes a diffusionary process. Weyland (2006, 18–19) defines policy diffusion as having three characteristics: an S-shaped curve pattern, geographic clustering of policies, and commonality among diversity. First, the black line in figure 1–2, which provides a tally of the number of CCTs operating in the region, resembles the famous S-shaped curve. Second, it constitutes an example of geographic clustering whereby, over the span of little more than a decade, the vast majority of the region's countries came to possess a similar policy that had not even existed years earlier. Third, given that CCTs were adopted by governments of the left (Bolivia and Guatemala) as well as the right (El Salvador and Mexico) and by the region's richest (Argentina and Chile) as well as its poorest (Bolivia and Honduras) countries, their proliferation offers a clear example of commonality among diversity.[4]

This is not be the first time Latin America has been at the epicenter of a wave of social policy diffusion that ultimately went global. The widely studied diffusion of Chile's private pension system during the 1990s placed Latin America at the forefront of the debate between domestic and international explanations of social policy adoption (Madrid 2003; Weyland 2006; Brooks 2009).[5]

Prior quantitative research on Latin America (Sugiyama 2011; Osorio Gonnet 2018, chap. 4) and developing countries more broadly (Brooks 2015) finds that countries become more likely to adopt CCTs as the share of neighboring countries with such programs increases. Furthermore, the case study literature provides substantial evidence that, in adopting CCTs, late adopters were emulating the pioneering experiences of Mexico and Brazil (Brearley 2011; Lana and Evans 2004; Martínez Franzoni and Voorend 2011). These experiences were widely publicized by the media, academics, and international financial institutions. The latter, most notably the World Bank and Inter-American Development Bank (IDB), provided substantial technical and financial support for the adoption and operation of CCTs across the region (Lana and Evans 2004; Martínez Franzoni and Voorend

2011; Sugiyama 2011; Ancelovici and Jenson 2013; Brooks 2015; Osorio Gonnet 2018, chap. 5). These institutions funded 44 CCT-related loans and projects in the Americas between 2000 and 2011 (Sugiyama 2011, 247–77) and hosted dozens of seminars and workshops on the topic (Osorio Gonnet 2018, 289–90).[6]

Garay (2016, 14) outright rejects diffusion as an explanation for the recent adoption and expansion of propoor social policies in Latin America, CCTs included, based on three arguments. First, adoption was not the result of direct pressure or strong incentives by an international actor. Additionally, there exist important cross-national differences in the design of the programs that were adopted. And, finally, some countries in the region did not adopt the policies in question, most notably Venezuela.

On the first point, Hunter (2021, 95) argues that, although IFIs did not take the lead in promoting CCTs, let alone impose them, "the 'first mover' cases of Mexico and Brazil commanded the attention of policy makers from other countries within the region," and their example was crucial in explaining the rapid spread of these programs. With regard to the second point, Garay's definition of diffusion is excessively restrictive. Diffusion need not entail the spread of a "neat, concrete, well-defined blueprint, largely replicating the original model" (Weyland 2006, 71). Imitator countries may simply follow the original policy's general guidelines or principles. Indeed, as the remainder of this book will demonstrate, there exist systematic design differences between CCTs operated by left-wing and nonleft governments. Yet, despite these differences, all of the region's CCTs are based on the same general principle: relieving today's poverty through regular cash stipends and in the process "nudging" families receiving them into keeping their children in school with the ultimate goal of preventing tomorrow's poverty. Finally, nothing in the existing diffusion literature implies that all peer countries will ultimately adopt a particular policy innovation.[7]

2.2. Testing the Determinants of CCT Adoption

Focusing on the role of presidential ideology and policy diffusion, this section conducts a statistical test of the hypotheses and findings discussed in the previous section. The analysis will test the generalizability to the region as a whole of the case study literature's findings and assess the robustness of the results of prior cross-national analyses of CCT adoption. Table 2–1 pro-

Table 2-1. Presidential Ideology and CCT Adoption

Year	Country	Program Name	President in Power	Ideology[1]	CCT%[2]	IFI Debt[3]
Oct. 1997	Mexico	Progresa/Oportunidades/Prospera	Ernesto Zedillo	Center-Right	0%	4.32%
July 2000	Costa Rica[4]	Superémonos	Miguel A. Rodríguez	Center-Right	11.76%	6.33%
Oct. 2000	Honduras	Programa Asignación Famíliar/ Bono 10,000/Bono Vida Mejor	Carlos R. Flores	Center	11.76%	23.42%
April 2001	Brazil	Bolsa Escola/Bolsa Família	Fernando H. Cardoso	Center	23.53%	2.76%
July 2001	Colombia	Familias en Acción/ Más Familias en Acción	Andrés Pastrana	Center-Right	23.53%	5.13%
May 2002	Chile	Chile Solidario Programa Puente/ Ingreso Ético Famíliar	Ricardo Lagos	Center-Left	41.18%	0.82%
June 2002	Ecuador	Beca Escolar/Bono de Desarrollo Humano	Gustavo Noboa	Center-Right	41.18%	9.18%
Nov. 2002	Nicaragua[5]	Red de Protección Social	Arnoldo Alemán	Right	41.18%	15.23%
Oct. 2004	Argentina	Programa Familias/ Asignación Universal por Hijo	Néstor Kirchner	Center-Left	41.18%	16.94%
March 2005	El Salvador	Red Solidaria	Antonio Saca	Right	70.59%	10.65%
April 2005	Uruguay	PANES/Asignaciones Famíliares	Tabaré Vázquez	Center-Left	70.59%	16.37%
Sept. 2005	Dominican Rep.	Red Solidaria	Leonel Fernández	Center	70.59%	5.79%
Sept. 2005	Paraguay	Tekopora	Nicanor Duarte	Center-Right	70.59%	11.49%
Sept. 2005	Peru	Juntos	Alejandro Toledo	Center-Right	70.59%	9.05%
April 2006	Panama	Red Oportunidades	Martín Torrijos	Center-Left	82.35%	5.97%
Oct. 2006	Bolivia	Bono Juancito Pinto	Evo Morales	Left	82.35%	20.47%
Jan. 2007	Costa Rica	Avancemos	Oscar Arias	Center	82.35%	2.61%
April 2008	Guatemala	Mi Família Progresa/ Mi Bono Seguro	Álvaro Colom	Center-Left	88.24%	5.50%

Sources: [1] Dataset on Political Ideology of Presidents and Parties in Latin America (Murillo, Oliveros, and Vaishnav 2010); [2] Percentage of countries in the sample with CCTs (excluding country in question) during adoption year; [3] World Bank and Inter-American Development Bank loans as a percentage of GDP during adoption year; [4] Program was cancelled in 2002 by centrist President Abel Pacheco; [5] Program was not renewed by left-wing President Daniel Ortega, a leftist.

vides a summary of the adoption of the CCT programs analyzed and the main explanatory variables at the time of adoption.

2.2.1 Hypotheses and Measurement

Dependent Variable: CCT Adoption
Adoption is measured dichotomously and is defined as taking place during the year a country's government announces the launch of a nationwide anti-poverty program that provides monetary transfers conditional on school attendance. This excludes subnational CCTs, pilot versions of programs, and CCTs without an educational conditionality.

In several instances, incoming governments changed the name and even altered the design of CCTs they inherited. For the purposes of the statistical analysis, adoption occurs *only* when a government adopts a CCT in a country that at the time did not have a program in place. For example, the decision by Chile's right-wing President Sebastián Piñera (2010–14; 2018–present) to replace the country's Chile Solidario with Ingreso Ético Familiar in 2012 is not treated as an "adoption." In contrast, centrist Costa Rican president Oscar Arias's (1986–90; 2006–10) decision to adopt Avancemos in 2007 is treated as an adoption because the country had not had a CCT in place since 2002, when the Superémonos program was shut down.

Key Explanatory Variables
Presidential ideology. The logic of PRT leads to the expectation that *countries with left-leaning governments will be more likely to adopt CCTs than those with nonleft governments*. Ideology is operationalized using a dummy variable coded one if the president is center-left or left as coded by the Dataset on Political Ideology of Presidents and Parties in Latin America (Murillo, Oliveros, and Vaishnav 2010).[8]
Regional CCT adoption. If CCT adoption has in fact been a case of policy diffusion, *the probability that a country will adopt a CCT should increase as the share of countries in the region with such programs increases*. Following past studies (Sugiyama 2011; Carnes, and Mares 2014; Brooks 2015), diffusion is operationalized as the share of countries in the region with CCTs (excluding the country in question).[9]
IFI influence. Although CCTs were a homegrown Latin American innovation, the World Bank and IDB heavily promoted them across the region and the world (Lana and Evans 2004; Martínez Franzoni and Voorend 2011;

Sugiyama 2011; Ancelovici and Jenson 2013; Brooks 2015; Osorio Gonnet 2018, chap. 5). Thus, *countries closely linked to IFIs should be more likely to adopt CCTs*. Depth of ties to IFIs is measured as the sum of outstanding World Bank and IDB loans as a share of a country's GDP lagged by one year. World Bank loan data were obtained from its World Development Indicators (World Bank 2020). IDB loans were compiled from the institution's annual reports (IDB 2018). This is the first study to test the effects of IDB lending.

Other Explanatory Variables

Objective need for CCTs. These programs serve two objectives: reducing poverty over the short run and increasing human capital over the long run. The models will test to what extent those goals explain CCT adoption.

Poverty reduction motive. *Countries with higher poverty levels and more unequal income distributions should be more likely to adopt CCTs.* The objective need for programs to address poverty is measured in terms of both level of poverty, measured as the share of a country's population living in poverty (defined as an income of less than $4.00 a day), and the level of income inequality, measured in terms of the Gini coefficient. The poverty data was compiled by SEDLAC (2018).[10] The inequality data comes from the Standardized World Income Inequality Database (Solt 2016).

Human capital motive. *Countries with lower educational attainment and higher rates of child labor should be more likely to adopt CCTs.* Educational attainment is measured as average years of schooling among 15–24 year olds as reported in the Education Attainment Dataset (Barro and Lee 2013). Child labor is measured as the share of 5–14 year olds in the workforce as compiled by the United Nations Children's Fund (UNICEF 2018).

Number of protests. Politicians facing mass mobilizations may be able to use social policy to assuage or even co-opt protestors. Protests are measured as the total number of riots and demonstrations in a country lagged by one year as reported by the Cross-National Time-Series data archive (Banks 2011).[11]

Crime levels. If CCTs are, as Britto (2008, 187) speculates, a response to crime, countries with higher levels of crime should be more likely to adopt them. Crime is measured as a country's homicide rate per 100,000 inhabitants lagged by one year as reported by the United Nations Crime Trends Surveys (UNDOC 2018). This is the first study to systematically analyze the effects of crime and popular protest on CCT adoption.[12]

Control Variables

The models incorporate a battery of control variables. To control for intensity of political competition, models incorporate dummy variables measuring whether a given year is an election year and whether the president's party or legislative coalition lacks a legislative majority. Both were obtained from the Database of Political Institutions (Scartascini, Cruz and Keefer 2018). Governments with stronger technical capabilities should be more likely to adopt complex programs like CCTs. Following Sugiyama (2011), the models control for government effectiveness as reported in the World Bank's World Governance Indicators (World Bank 2020).

Barrientos's (2013, 12) supposition regarding the politics of indirect taxation is tested by including a measure of taxes on goods and services relative to GDP lagged by one year as reported by Organization for Economic Co-operation and Development (OECD 2018). The models also control for GDP growth and GDP per capita as reported by the World Development Indicators (World Bank 2020).

2.2.2 Analytic Techniques

To systematically test the determinants of CCT adoption during a given year, I conducted an event history analysis (also known as survival-time analysis) covering 18 Latin American countries during the years 1995 through 2010. This technique explores the factors that affect the probability that a country will adopt a CCT during a given year. This type of analysis considers a set of cases as being "at risk" (of adopting a program) until they experience the event under study (CCT adoption). At that point, the case is removed from the sample as it is no longer "at risk." The event history analysis is conducted as a time-series-cross-sectional logit analysis (Beck, Katz, and Tucker 1998; Carter and Signorino 2010).[13] Most independent variables are lagged by one year to avoid endogeneity issues and temporal ordering (Box-Steffensmeier and Jones 2004, 111).

2.2.3 Statistical Findings

The results of the event history analyses presented in table 2–2 confirm past research in finding that CCT adoption is driven by policy diffusion and unaffected by presidential ideology. As more of their regional neighbors adopted CCTs, Latin American countries that had not adopted their own

Table 2-2. Event History Analysis of CCT Adoption (1995–2010)

	(1)	(2)	(3)
Left President	−0.223	−0.304	−0.281
	(0.909)	(0.659)	(0.676)
% of Countries with CCTs	2.582*	3.225*	5.251*
	(1.309)	(1.504)	(2.781)
IFI Loans	2.999	−3.801	12.948
	(5.480)	(11.013)	(10.147)
Gini Coefficient	—	−0.121	—
		(0.135)	
Poverty Rate	—	—	0.026
			(0.041)
Avg. Yrs. of Schooling	—	0.127	—
		(0.373)	
Child Labor	—	—	−0.120
			(0.116)
Number of Protests	—	0.100	0.130
		(0.112)	(0.131)
Homicide Rate	—	—	0.028
			(0.039)
Election Year?	—	−0.490	−0.049
		(0.706)	(0.677)
Minority Government?	—	0.203	0.854
		(0.985)	(1.114)
Government Effectiveness	—	2.113*	3.527*
		(0.914)	(1.768)
Indirect Taxes	—	0.122	—
		(0.200)	
GDP Growth	—	0.162*	0.212*
		(0.072)	(0.100)
GDP per Capita	—	−0.756	−1.028
		(0.491)	(1.044)
Constant	−6.904*	−5.037	−9.963+
	(3.178)	(7.916)	(5.346)
N	181	163	120
Wald Chi2	13.28	172.18	465.16
Log Likelihood	−47.17	−40.471	−31.67

Standard errors in parenthesis. +p <=0.1 *p <=0.5; ** p <=0.01; *** <=0.001 in two-tailed test.
Note: +Cubic polynomial approximations are used to model time dependence but not presented.

program became more likely to do so, regardless of whether they were governed by presidents of the right, center, or left. These results are robust across a wide range of model specifications.

The analysis begins with a bare bones model of CCT adoption that includes only presidential ideology, the share of countries in the region with CCTs, and IFI loans as a share of GDP (model 1). The goal in doing this is to demonstrate that the effects of these variables are not dependent on the inclusion or exclusion of any particular control variable (Achen 2002). With regard to ideology, the model finds that having a left-wing president, though negatively signed in this and other models tested, has no effect on the likelihood of adoption. With regard to diffusion, the share of countries with CCTs has a positive and statistically significant effect on the probability of adoption. IFI loans, however, do not influence CCT adoption.

Model 2 incorporates average years of schooling and the Gini coefficient, which, respectively, capture the "objective" need for a policy that increases educational attainment and redistribution, as well as the number of protests during a given year and a battery of control variables.[14] Most importantly, the effects of diffusion and ideology remain unchanged. The share of countries with CCTs retains a positive and statistically significant effect on likelihood of adoption. Having a left-wing president and reliance on IFI loans again fail to achieve statistical significance.

Neither of the variables measuring an "objective" need for a CCT influence the probability of adoption. Nor does protest activity. In line with Sugiyama (2011), however, countries with more effective governments are more likely to adopt CCTs. Contrary to the pioneering experiences of Mexico and Brazil, which adopted their programs in response to economic crises, GDP growth has a positive and significant effect on likelihood of adoption. Counter to Barrientos's (2013) expectations, reliance on consumption taxes does not make countries likelier to adopt these programs. None of the other variables achieve statistical significance.

Based on model 2, figure 2–1 plots the probability of CCT adoption as a function of time and level of CCT diffusion, assuming the remaining variables are held constant. The different lines plotted estimate the likelihood that a country would have adopted a CCT at a given point in time assuming different levels of regional CCT adoption (0%, 25%, 50%, and 75% of countries in the sample). The figure also shows that the probability of CCT adoption increased in two distinct bursts, first from years four to seven (roughly 1998–2003) and again from year 11 on (roughly 2005 onward).[15]

Model 3 incorporates the rates of poverty and child labor in lieu of the Gini coefficient and levels of schooling, and, at the cost of a quarter of the observations (n = 120 instead of 165 in model 2), tests the effects of the homicide rates.[16] None of these variables is statistically significant. The results from previous models hold—share of countries with CCTs, government effectiveness, and GDP growth have positive and significant

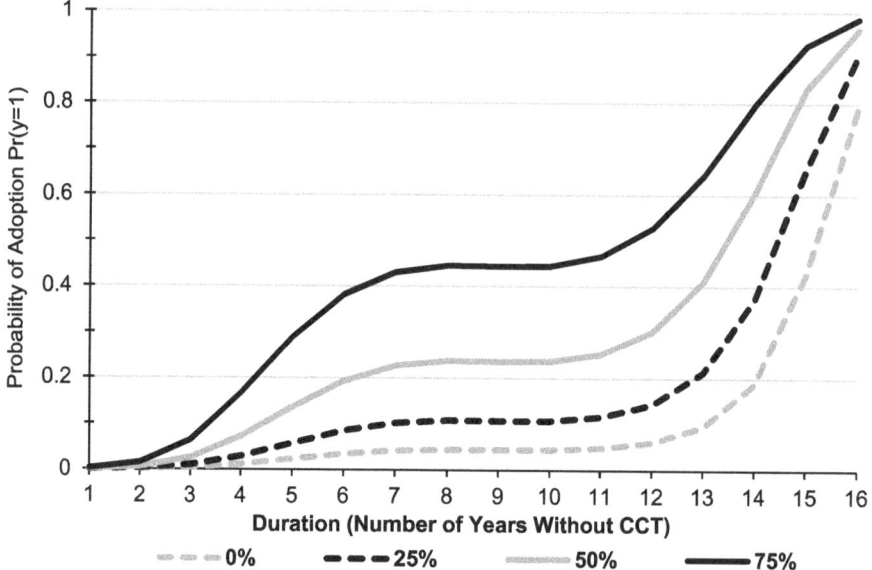

Figure 2-1. Estimated Effect of Time on Probability of CCT Adoption at Different Levels of Regional CCT Adoption
Source: Model 2-2 (see table 2-2).
Notes: Assumes all binary variables at their modes and continuous variables at their mean levels.

effects on the likelihood of adoption. Once more, ideology fails to achieve significance.

2.2.4 Taking Stock of the Findings

The main findings of the event history models with regard to ideology should not be all that surprising. Although the leftward shift in politics and the adoption of CCTs ran parallel to each other, a closer look at the ideologies of the presidents who adopted CCTs presented in table 2-1 reveals that, among 16 CCTs currently operating in the region, a comparable number were adopted by right-leaning (eight) and left-leaning (six) presidents (see fig. 2-2). It is for that reason that cross-national statistical analyses find no effect of ideology on the probability of adopting a program.

As a ex post facto explanation of this robust finding, scholars have noted that CCTs offered "something for everyone"—left, right, or IFI (Sugiyama 2011, 257; Brooks 2015, 553). The left could get behind broad-based pro-

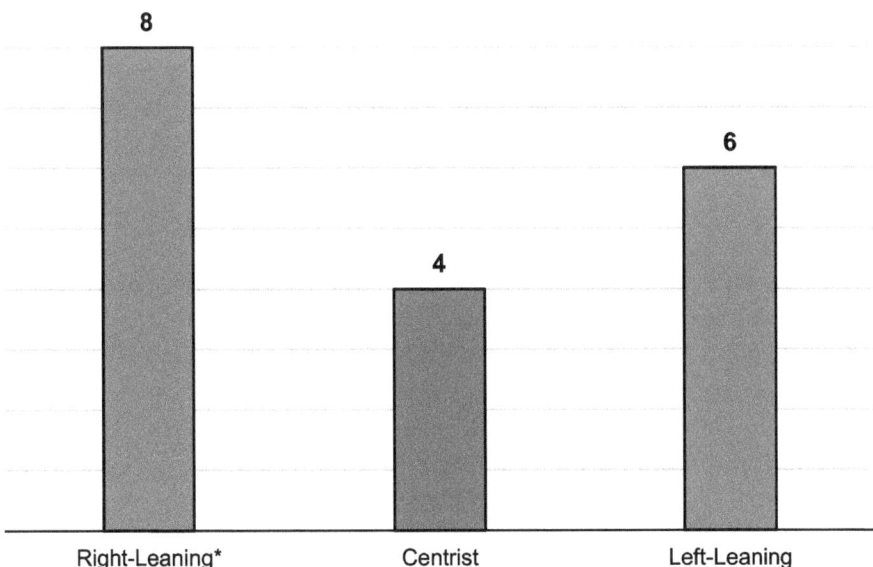

Figure 2-2. Number of CCTs Adopted by Presidential Ideology
Source: Dataset on Political Ideology of Presidents and Parties in Latin America (Murillo, Oliveros, and Vaishnav 2010).
*Includes Costa Rica's Superémonos CCT, which operated during 2000–2002 and was enacted by center-right President Miguel Angel Rodríguez.

grams that reduced poverty while expanding access to education and healthcare. The right could support these programs because they were market-oriented, cheaper than the alternatives, targeted toward the "deserving poor" (i.e., children are poor through no fault of their own), and geared at improving the country's stock of human capital. And, as a wide range of studies have shown, CCTs are widely popular among beneficiaries who, in turn, have been willing to reward incumbent politicians of all ideological stripes at the ballot box (Díaz-Cayeros, Estévez, and Magaloni 2009, 2016; Layton and Smith 2015; Manacorda, Miguel, and Vigorito 2011; De La O 2013; Zucco 2013).

CCTs were also appealing to the IFIs that later helped to fund and promote them. In the aftermath of market reform, IFIs came to accept that growth alone was insufficient for reducing poverty and that permanent targeted anti-poverty programs—rather than short-term safety nets—were necessary (Birdsall and de la Torre 2001; Birdsall and Székely 2003). IFIs came to adopt a holistic understanding of the causes of poverty that emphasized the links between food consumption, nutrition, health, and education. Providing any of these benefits in isolation, it was argued, would likely be insufficient to pull families out of poverty. CCTs offered an affordable means of accomplishing these goals simultaneously (Levy 2006).

CCTs were compatible with three emerging "economic-ideological" trends in the international policy community at the time: the shift away from a rights-based view of social entitlements toward an obligations-based conception, the move toward market and incentive-based anti-poverty policies, and the increased acceptance of narrow poverty targeting (Adato and Hoddinnott 2010, 13–14). Additionally, by addressing concerns such as female empowerment, human capital, and community participation, these programs fit well with the "current mainstream discourse on poverty reduction" (Britto 2008, 185).

2.3. Delving Deeper: The Left's Initial Skepticism of CCTs

Granted, the left, right, and IFIs all had good reasons to back CCTs. However, *the left in most countries did not in fact support these programs until well after they had become widespread.* While valuable, cross-national statistical studies tell only part of the story. Reducing CCT adoption to a dichotomous yes/no decision obscures the dynamic give-and-take of political debates and the complexity of the policymaking process. The same can be said about evidence in support of diffusion. That the ideas behind CCTs were available to and ultimately influenced politicians and technocrats throughout the region tells us little about the timing and politics surrounding adoption.

For starters, the policies that get adopted are not always the sitting government's idea. Governments may co-opt the opposition's most promising proposals. Policies may also be adopted under duress or in response to public opinion or mobilization, or both. Lavinas (2013a, 13–14) has used this logic to argue that it was actually the left that put CCT programs on the political agenda. Even in defeat, it forced centrist and right-wing incumbents to seriously address poverty. This statement, however, clashes with the available evidence. Centrist and right-wing governments were the main initiators of cash transfers to the poor (Reygadas and Filgueira 2010, 175). In fact, the first CCTs—those adopted by Mexico (1997), Honduras (1998), and Costa Rica (2000), which then set in motion the diffusion process—were adopted by market reforming governments that at the time faced little competition from the left.

More tellingly, a closer look at the political processes behind CCT adoption across the region reveals that left-leaning politicians, including some who have come to be seen as intimately linked to the regional and global diffusion of CCTs, most notably Brazil's Lula, were initially skeptical of if not outright opposed to these policies.

2.3.1 Evidence from Across the Region

As the following discussion of six cases shows, the left's opposition to CCTs can be well documented.

Mexico. The left-wing Party of Democratic Revolution (PRD) opposed the first national-level CCT, Progresa/Oportunidades, at the time of its 1997 launch (De La O 2015, 76). Both the PRD and the right-wing National Action Party (PAN) were concerned that the long-ruling PRI would use the program clientelistically, as it had with the National Solidarity Program (PRONASOL), an earlier anti-poverty initiative (Dresser 1994; Molinar and Weldon 1994; Bruhn, 1996; Dion 2000; Díaz-Cayeros, Estévez, and Magaloni 2016). The program's timing did little to assuage these concerns: center-right President Ernesto Zedillo (1994–2000) announced the program one month after the 1997 midterm elections, which marked the first time that the PRI had lost its legislative majority since coming to power in the 1930s. The left criticized the decision to replace inefficient food subsidies with cash transfers, accusing the government of doing the World Bank's and the IDB's bidding. In fact, the Zedillo administration purposefully chose not to seek financial support from IFIs (Levy and Rodríguez 2004, 257; Dion 2010, 204).[17]

Forced to negotiate, Zedillo succeeded in bringing the PAN on board by establishing an impartial evaluation mechanism and guaranteeing that transfers would not be disproportionately targeted toward PRI strongholds. These assurances were insufficient for the PRD (De la O, 2015, 8). The party remained a vocal critic of the expansion of targeted programs at the national level, advocating instead for universal social insurance (Teichman 2008, 563; Dion 2009, 76; Garay 2016, 244–45; Tomazini 2019, 38). At the local level, successive PRD governments of Mexico City criticized the national-level CCT for its reliance on "targeting and surveillance" (i.e., conditionality) while simultaneously implementing a universal non-contributive pension for seniors (Luccisano and Macdonald 2014, 334).

Given the success and resounding popularity of CCTs among voters and the PRD's perceived antipathy toward them, the party's presidential candidates—Cuauhtémoc Cárdenas in 2000 (González Rodríguez 2000) and Andrés Manuel López Obrador in 2006 and 2012 (Nieto and Gómez 2012)—went out of their way to assure voters that they would continue the program if elected. That is, only for political reasons did the left mute its ideological opposition to CCTs.

Brazil. Most of the Brazilian left was initially unimpressed by cash transfers. In 1991, Eduardo Suplicy, a senator from the left-wing PT, proposed an unconditional cash transfer for all Brazilians over 25. In contrast to the proposal made that same year by Mexican economist Santiago Levy that became the basis for Progresa, Suplicy did not envision a direct link between transfers and education. Despite its universalistic design, segments of the PT refused to back Suplicy's proposal (Hunter 2010, 71).

Arguing in 1993 that a basic income would be ineffective at combating intergenerational poverty, economist José Márcio Camargo instead proposed that transfers target families with school-age children and be conditioned on school attendance. These ideas formed the basis for a series of subnational CCTs that quickly spread throughout Brazil starting in 1995 and culminated in the creation of the Bolsa Escola Federal (Federal School Scholarship) CCT in 2001 under centrist president Cardoso.

Local- and national-level *petistas* were divided on CCTs. Faced with the need to deliver tangible results to their electorates, pragmatic PT mayors enacted CCTs. Indeed, left-leaning mayors were more likely to adopt such programs than other mayors (Melo 2007; Sugiyama 2008, 2012b; Coêlho 2012b). However, many national-level PT leaders continued criticizing both subnational and national-level CCTs (Hunter 2010, 155). In the run-up to the 2002 elections, Lula criticized Cardoso's policies on television for being a new form of *assistencialismo* (Ansell 2014, 30–31), that is, social policy based on handouts rather than universal rights (Hunter 2010, 155). While campaigning for the presidency, Lula derisively called the program "Bolsa Esmola" (Charity Scholarship), criticizing it for being too modest to tackle the country's poverty (Aith 2001; O Estado de S. Paulo 2001b). He remained critical during his first months in office. In a March 2003 speech,

Lula explicitly criticized Cardoso's CCTs as a distraction from much-needed "structural reforms" to Brazilian social policy (Azevedo 2013).

Lula went on to fully embrace CCTs after the failure of his own, more ambitious, anti-poverty initiative (see chapter 3). Even then, far-left PT members derided his program for being "paternalistic and demeaning" and following the targeted approach advocated by IFIs. They dismissed the program as a palliative and criticized its "efficient capacity to placate the poor and thereby facilitate the 'politics of adjustment'" (Hunter 2010, 155). In the words of a long-time PT legislator, "We didn't struggle for two decades in the opposition for this!" (quoted in Hunter 2010, 155).

Bolivia. While not openly opposed to CCTs, left-wing President Evo Morales (2006–19) did not include them in his 2002 or 2005 campaign platforms (McGuire 2013, 9). Cash transfers were first proposed in Bolivia in 2002 by center-right politician Gonzálo Sánchez de Lozada (1993–97; 2002–3) during his campaign for a second nonconsecutive presidency. Sánchez proposed using transfers to increase female school enrollment and healthcare usage among young children (Pardo 2003, 46). He won the election but was forced to resign in October 2003 before the programs could be implemented.[18]

Although education-linked cash transfers failed to materialize at the national level, they were implemented locally in El Alto, a primarily indigenous city on the outskirts of La Paz. In September 2003, the city's center-right mayor Luis Paredes launched Bono Esperanza. The program's popularity prompted Jorge "Tuto" Quiroga (2001–2), the centrist who Morales defeated to become president in 2005, to promise a national Bono Esperanza (McGuire 2013, 10). Morales went on to adopt the Bono Juancito Pinto (Juancito Pinto Bonus) CCT in late 2006 (see chapter 7).

Argentina. Presidents Néstor Kirchner (2003–7) and Cristina Fernández de Kirchner (2007–15) of the left-wing Front for Victory faction of the Peronist Party were openly disdainful of the targeted programs spreading across the region. As Peronists, the Kirchners firmly believed that poverty should be tackled through the creation of formal employment, which in turn would universalize traditional contributory social insurance (interviews with Laura Golbert and Pablo Vinocur; Arciádono 2016, 103). And, indeed, despite a commodity boom that allowed for rising minimum wages and pensions and an expansion of pension coverage, Kirchner failed to invest in anti-poverty programs (Levitsky and Murillo 2008, 28). Opposition to CCTs was strongest from Alicia Kirchner, Néstor's sister and social development minister during much of the Fernández administration. Alicia repeatedly derided CCTs as "neoliberal," "impositions from international institutions," and "prepackaged (*enlatados*) programs" not suited for Argentina's reality (Kirchner 2010, 10).

Establishing an income floor for children was the central campaign plank of centrist Elisa Carrió, the runner-up in the 2007 presidential elections. Opposition legislators proposed multiple cash transfer bills during 2007–9 that languished due to lack of government support (Repetto, Díaz-Langou, and Marazzi 2009). *Thus, the Kirchners were the last major political actors to join the consensus in favor of cash transfers.* Fernanández adopted the Asignación Universal por Hijo (AUH) CCT in October 2009 (see chapter 7).

Venezuela and Nicaragua. Venezuela has the distinction of being the only major Latin American country to have never adopted a national-level CCT. Centrist Rafael Caldera (1994–99) experimented with small-scale CCTs in the mid-1990s as a way of compensating those negatively affected by structural adjustment (Penfold-Becerra 2007, 67). Having criticized these programs for their lack of ambition and subordination to economic stability, Caldera's left-wing successor Hugo Chávez (Chávez Frías 2014, 49–50) summarily dismantled them upon assuming office (Penfold-Becerra 2007, 70). Flush with resources from an oil boom, Chávez invested heavily in social policy starting in 2003. However, his *misiones (missions)* awarded benefits largely on political criteria (Penfold-Becerra 2007; Hawkins 2010, chap. 7; Corrales and Penfold 2015, chap. 4).

Nicaragua's Daniel Ortega (2007–present) "openly opposed" the country's much-heralded Red de Protección Social CCT while in opposition and discontinued it upon being elected, even though international funding was available for its continuation (Hanlon, Barrientos, and Hulme 2010, 173). Enacted under the center-right administration of Arnoldo Alemán (1997–2002), RPS was acknowledged as one of the region's better designed CCTs and credited with achieving most of its poverty and school enrollment objectives (Maluccio and Flores 2005; Moore 2009). Yet Ortega replaced RPS with in-kind food transfers for poor rural households (Flores-Macías 2012, 46; Martínez Franzoni 2013, 20).

Thus, as the cases of Venezuela and Nicaragua show, the left not only opposed CCTs when in opposition. When it came to power, it could dismantle existing programs. It is telling that the two countries in the region where the left has faced the least political opposition are the only two countries where CCTs failed to take hold.

2.3.2 The Right and the Center's Reasoning

At first glance, it is counterintuitive that the right pioneered these highly redistributive programs while the left largely opposed them. After all, as Bobbio (1996) argues in his seminal work on the topic, the key distinction between left and right is their stance on inequality. The left sees inequality as artificial, "a product of customs, laws and coercion by the stronger" and therefore "socially modifiable" through government action (Bobbio 1996, 70). In line with this view, there is a vast literature showing that left-wing politicians have been more supportive of the expansion of social policy in both industrialized (Stephens 1979; Korpi 1983; Esping-Andersen 1985; Hicks 1999; Huber and Stephens 2001) and Latin American countries (Segura-Ubiergo 2007; Haggard and Kaufman 2008; Huber and Stephens 2012).

The right, in contrast, is by definition skeptical about the possibility (and often the desirability) of correcting inequality through government action. At best, those on the right believe "such interventions will be ineffective. At worst, they will create perverse incentives or be captured by special interests seeking privileges" (Noël and Thérien 2008, 19). Yet this explanation is incomplete. Bobbio's definition implies that the right is pro-inequality. This is problematic as, at various times and places, right-wing governments have been responsible for social policy expansion, as was originally the case with national-level CCTs. Thus, "the right is not simply a welfare-skeptic mirror image of the left" (Jensen 2014, 2). Noël and Thérien (2008, 18) push back against Bobbio, arguing that the right is not "anti-egalitarian" but rather has different concepts of equality and fairness.

On this point, Lakoff (2016, 181) argues that for the right "there is a world of difference" between assistance for those who are not responsible for their misfortune and the able-bodied poor, who have no one but themselves to blame for their situation. Under this logic, the right's support for CCTs is justified. CCTs help children who are poor through no fault of their own remain in school rather than work to help support their families. Armed with an education, it is hoped, CCT beneficiaries will go on to be productive adults who will sink or swim based on their own abilities and effort. Furthermore, policies that promote human capital such as CCTs constitute "a collective good" that increases "the competitiveness of the economy in international markets" (Kaufman and Segura-Ubiergo 2001, 557) and thus potentially benefits the private sector, a key member of the right's political coalition.

Centrist parties tend to be cross-pressured on social policy. Research on industrialized countries distinguishes between secular centrist and Christian Democratic parties. Long-term governance by the former is associated with residual welfare states (Huber and Stephens 2012, 19). The latter, in contrast, are associated with social policy expansion, albeit in a more modest and less universalistic direction than under the left. Turning to Latin America, secular centrist parties, which have been the norm in the region, have not emphasized income redistribution but have been strong proponents of public education (Huber and Stephens 2012, 19). Thus, they could be expected to be highly supportive of the human capital objective of CCTs. It is more difficult to theorize about the region's Christian Democratic parties, which have been successful only in a few countries and display more heterogeneous social policy preferences than their European counterparts (Mainwaring and Scully 2003). Regardless, centrist parties played a major role in enacting market reforms in the 1980s and 1990s and thus could be expected to support social policies that promoted education, were compatible with the tenets of market reform, and were supported by IFIs.

2.3.3 The Left's Reasoning

The left, for its part, had justifiable reasons to be wary of CCTs when they first appeared. The 1980s debt crisis and subsequent market reforms strongly advocated by IFIs resulted in an overhaul of the region's development model. Reforms led to significant cuts in social spending and, ultimately, to sharp increases in poverty and inequality (Huber 1996). The Washington Consensus called for governments to scale back their social policy ambitions and focus instead on the neediest sectors (Williamson 1990), a difficult proposition for the left to accept given its preference for universalistic policies and commitment to reducing inequality. Simply put, means-tested anti-poverty programs were not the left's preferred approach to social policy.

Although regressive in that it largely excluded those outside the formal labor market, the "Latin American model" (Haggard and Kaufman 2008) of social protection pursued prior to market reform embodied universalistic aspirations. Such policies were inspired by Southern European welfare regimes in which social insurance benefits are linked to the employment of a (male) breadwinner (Esping-Andersen 1990; Barrientos and Santibáñez 2009). The architects of these policies had assumed that, as the region modernized, agricultural and informal workers would be absorbed into industry and, therefore, qualify for the full range of contributory benefits (Lo Vuolo 2008). However, the import substitution industrialization (ISI) strategy pursued during the period from the 1940s through the 1970s failed to create the number of jobs needed to achieve near-universal coverage. Furthermore, the 1980s debt crisis and subsequent dismantling of ISI and the downsizing of public bureaucracies in the 1980s increased the share of the population employed in the informal sector and thus excluded from traditional social policy.

Concerns over the growing social crisis and the threat it constituted to their popularity prompted governments throughout the region, with support from IFIs, to experiment with targeted anti-poverty programs. The first generation of these programs, so-called emergency social funds, financed small-scale economic development projects proposed by communities. These programs, however, largely bypassed the poorest communities (Huber 2005; Siri 2000; Tendler 2000). Furthermore, there was widespread evidence from across the region that governments distributed these funds clientelistically (Graham 1992; Molinar and Weldon 1994; Roberts 1995; Bruhn 1996; Graham and Kane 1998; Schady 2000; Díaz-Cayeros, Estévez, and Magaloni 2016).

Evelyne Huber (1996, 181), one of the foremost authorities on the relationship between the left and social policy, captures the Latin American left's concerns:

> Caution has to be exercised lest they [targeted programs] become mere palliatives. Such programmes can be very helpful, as long as they do not detract from the basic task of building permanent universalistic programmes and institutions. The danger is that such programmes lead to a diversion of resources and to duplication because of the creation of new institutions to administer them.... A second danger is that such programmes, by virtue of

being targeted, increase the discretion of political leaders and bureaucrats with regard to the allocation of resources and thus the incentives for patronage and corruption.

In this context, marked by a recognition of the need to boost the incomes of the poor and the failure of social funds, technocrats in Mexico and Central America began implementing CCTs at the national level in the late 1990s. Led by the IDB and the World Bank, IFIs wholeheartedly embraced and promoted this new policy. From the left's perspective, CCTs were just another technocrat-designed, IFI-backed policy aimed at doing just enough to defuse popular mobilization in favor of redistribution (Teichman 2008). Furthermore, the left feared that the right and center would manipulate the new programs in order to remain in power.

Moreover, the left's initial antipathy toward cash transfers was not a uniquely Latin American phenomenon. Prominent left wingers derided South Africa's cash transfer programs for being "neoliberal" attempts at "providing 'talk left' ideological cover for . . . 'walk right' policies" by the ruling African National Congress (Barchiesi 2011; Bond 2014; Ferguson 2015, 28).

In sum, the left's objections can be categorized based on three criteria: (1) programmatic opposition to narrow targeting and concern that CCTs would detract from the construction of universal policies, (2) concerns that CCTs would be used clientelistically as was the case with earlier programs, and (3) association of CCTs with right-wing governments and IFIs.

2.4 Conclusions

This chapter problematized and challenged the prevailing conventional wisdom regarding the relationship between government ideology and CCT adoption. Past research has found that, although the diffusion of CCTs across Latin America coincided with the left turn, CCT adoption was unrelated to the left turn and presidential ideology more broadly. Granted, it is true that during the 2000s these programs were adopted by presidents of all ideological stripes. And, as past research and the statistical analysis conducted in this chapter show, left-wing governments were no more likely to adopt these programs than their centrist and right-wing counterparts (Díaz-Cayeros and Magaloni 2009; Sugiyama 2011). However, a deeper analysis of the political debates surrounding CCT adoption in six countries across the region reveals that left-wing politicians had serious doubts about these programs and many even opposed them outright. The left initially opposed CCTs in Mexico and Brazil, the two countries most associated with CCTs. Even in Bolivia and Argentina, two countries where left-wing presidents ultimately adopted national-level programs, those leaders were late converts responding to proposals issued by rivals from other parties. Left-leaning leaders in Nicaragua and Venezuela went so far as to dismantle existing programs upon taking office.

This surprising finding seemingly runs counter to PRT, the dominant explanation of social policy development in Latin America (Segura-Ubiergo 2007; Haggard and Kaufman 2008; Huber and Stephens 2012). The left opposed CCTs' narrow targeting of beneficiaries, worried that they would foster clientelism, and was generally unwilling to support policies backed by right-leaning governments and multilateral banks, the very actors that years earlier had pushed for Washington Consensus market reforms. From the left's perspective at the turn of the century, CCTs carried the stench of neoliberalism.

In short, presidential ideology influenced the spread of CCTs, though not in a straightforward or mechanical manner. Given the left's initial attitude toward CCTs, the left turn might well have put a brake on their diffusion. But the story did not end there. The proven effectiveness and political popularity of CCTs gradually won over left-wing leaders. The Brazilian experience under Lula marked a major turning point in this regard. Originally dismissive of the CCTs he inherited, Lula embraced them following the failure of his ambitious Fome Zero (Zero Hunger) program. Charismatic, popular, and widely respected, Lula went on to sell the rest of the Latin American left on the benefits of CCTs.

The next chapter analyzes how Lula went from being skeptical toward CCTs to becoming one of their most vocal advocates.

CHAPTER 3

Lula and Brazil's Left Learn to Love CCTs

From Rejection to Acceptance and Transformation

Described as "likely the most important government anti-poverty program the world has ever seen" (Rosenberg 2011), Brazil's Bolsa Família is the world's largest conditional cash transfer program. By the end of 2015, the program covered 56 million people, 28% of Brazilians, and paid more than $8 billion in monthly stipends (CEPAL 2018). Bolsa Família is now ubiquitous in the poorest parts of Brazil, such as the semiarid Northeast, where as many as half of residents are enrolled (Thomé 2013). The program's results have been equally dramatic. During 2004–11, it was responsible for pulling 22.2 million Brazilians out of extreme poverty (Morais 2017, 125), helping to reduce the country's traditionally high levels of income inequality (Soares 2012, 20).

As Luiz Inácio Lula da Silva, Brazil's center-left president from 2003 to 2010, tells it, he was an iconoclast who, in creating Bolsa Família, challenged social policy experts and international financial institutions. In his own words "experts did not accept the idea. They preferred to give the poor dietary staples, or to do things for them" (cited in Tepperman 2017, 34). Bolsa Família is today synonymous with the figure of Lula and his Workers' Party (PT). The program won over Brazil's poor, transforming them into a loyal constituency for the PT (Zucco 2008) and Lula earned a near-saintly reputation as a "father of the poor" (Hunter 2014).[1] This paid off handsomely for Lula and his successor Dilma Rousseff (2011–16), helping them win elections and govern the country for 13 consecutive years (Hunter and Power 2007; Zucco 2013).[2] Internationally, Lula came to be seen as a global ambassador of CCTs, in no small part because he made Bolsa Família a central plank of his administration's ambitious foreign policy agenda (Boultinghouse 2015).

That Lula, who clawed his way out of poverty to become a union leader and ultimately Brazil's president, possessed unique insights into poverty relief that learned "experts" could not grasp and that those insights, in turn, explain Bolsa Família's dramatic success makes for a great story. That story, however, falls apart upon further inspection. First, Lula, like many left-wing Latin American politicians, was reflexively opposed to CCTs when he first learned about them (see chapter 2). In fact, in 1990 he rejected a proposal that would have legitimately made him the father of Brazilian CCTs (Buarque 2013) and instead backed antihunger policies that would "give the poor dietary staples" (Bourne 2009, 81). Second, this aversion to CCTs continued despite early evidence of their potential. Starting in 1995, mayors across Brazil, including many from Lula's own PT, began implementing successful CCTs (Aguiar and Araujo 2002; Sugiyama 2012b). By 1997, centrist President Fernando Henrique Cardoso (1995–2002) was experimenting with CCTs at the federal level. This culminated in the 2001 launch of Bolsa Escola Federal (Federal School Scholarship), the country's first nationwide CCT. Lula criticized the program for not being generous or universal enough, dismissing it as a palliative that failed to address the root causes of poverty (Aith 2001; O Estado de S. Paulo 2001b; Ansell 2014). Third, by the time Lula launched Bolsa Família, right-leaning governments in Mexico, Colombia, and a handful of other Latin American countries had already been operating CCTs for several years, often with funding and technical assistance from IFIs and other "experts" (Sugiyama 2011; Ancelovici and Jenson 2013; Osorio Gonnet 2018).[3]

Thus, by the time Lula assumed the presidency in January 2003, CCTs were considered "best practice" by Brazilian and foreign "experts" alike. Yet Lula remained wedded to the idea that relieving hunger offered the most effective means of reducing poverty. Lula embraced CCTs only after it became clear that Fome Zero (Zero Hunger), his government's flagship antihunger strategy, was destined to fail. At the suggestion of IFIs (Lindert et al. 2007, 13–14; Reid 2007, 234; Lustig 2011, 12; Morais 2017, 126), Lula reprioritized the CCTs he inherited, merging them to create Bolsa Família. Ironically, the cash transfers Lula long opposed are now his most widely recognized legacy.

This has led some scholars to dismiss Lula's social policy as a mere continuation of Cardoso's policies (Câmara Neto and Vernengo 2007, 73–74; Costa 2009, 704). But Lula and later Rousseff did much more than that. Brazil's left gradually expanded and reshaped the programs it inherited in

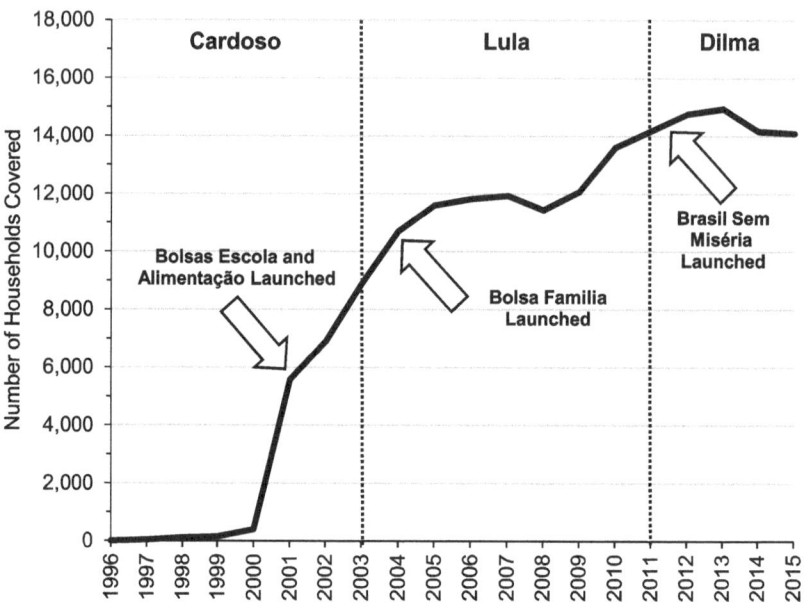

Figure 3-1. Brazilian CCT Coverage by Households (1996-2015)
Sources: Rocha (2013, 150) and Non-contributory Social Protection Programmes Database (CEPAL 2018).

the direction of establishing a basic income floor for needy Brazilians. The number of households covered by federal CCTs more than tripled from 3.60 million when Bolsa Família launched to 12.79 million when Lula stepped down in 2010. Expansion continued under Rousseff (2011–16), peaking at roughly 14.09 million households (see fig. 3–1). For better or worse, Bolsa Família distinguished itself from CCTs elsewhere in the region in adopting a less punitive approach to conditionality that prioritized reducing poverty in the short term over the uncertain promise of reducing it in the long term through human capital formation.

The previous chapter demonstrated that, although governments from across the ideological spectrum adopted CCTs, left-wing politicians were seldom the ones that first put them on the political agenda. In fact, in several countries, Brazil included, the left initially opposed CCTs. From the left's perspective, targeted programs were a neoliberal idea and a distraction from the urgent task of enacting universal social policy. This chapter further explores these claims through an analysis of how Lula and the Brazilian left came to embrace and ultimately transform CCTs.

3.1 Cash Transfers Enter Brazil's Political Agenda

The story of Brazilian CCTs begins in 1990, 13 years before the launch of Lula's universally lauded Bolsa Família. That year, independent of one another, two economists associated with Lula's PT—Eduardo Suplicy, a senator representing São Paulo and one of the party's founders, and Cristovam Buarque, a future governor of the Federal District of Brasilia and education minister under Lula—presented two distinct proposals for national-level cash transfer programs targeting the poor. Although their proposals initially failed to attract much interest at the national level, by 1995 programs based on their ideas were being adopted at the subnational level. These programs, which proved successful and politically popular, quickly spread across the country. The Cardoso administration would take note and gradually establish a series of national-level CCTs that Lula would, begrudgingly, combine to form Bolsa Família.

3.1.1 Suplicy and Buarque: The Fathers of Brazilian CCTs

Although the idea of cash transfers targeting the poor was first discussed in Brazilian policy circles as early as the 1970s (Suplicy 2004; Buarque 2013; Rocha 2013, chap. 1), serious discussion did not begin until 1990 with the release of Suplicy's and Buarque's proposals.[4] Despite obvious similarities, these two norm entrepreneurs significantly disagreed on the purpose and thus the design of cash transfer programs. Suplicy envisioned cash transfers as a means of providing every Brazilian with a minimum standard of living regardless of employment status. Buarque envisioned transfers as a tool with which to incentivize school attendance and thus equip children with the human capital needed to escape poverty. Whereas Suplicy's books justify transfers using the language of rights and guarantees, Buarque writes of conditionality and incentives.

Both proposals received significant pushback from within the PT. In Suplicy's (2004, 127) words, "It has not always been easy to persuade, above all, the PT economists or other party mates, that the minimum income guarantee was a proposal that was fully compatible with the objectives of greater equality and eradication of poverty defended by the party." Buarque (2013, 17) is blunter: "In the PT, the majority said that, instead [of] making a social revolution, it was a compensatory program to trick the poor."

In response to his narrow loss to the populist Fernando Collor de Melo

(1990–92) in the 1989 presidential elections, Lula created a "shadow government" to propose alternatives to the new administration's neoliberal policies.[5] Lula appointed Buarque, who had only recently joined the PT, to head the "office of education." Based on his earlier work, Buarque (2013, 15) proposed the awkwardly named Renda Mínima Vinculada à Educação (Minimum Wage Linked to Education), which would have awarded poor families regular stipends conditional on school attendance. Lula and the PT summarily rejected the proposal and, in Buarque's (2013, 15) words, "lost the chance to be linked to the origin" of CCTs. Lula chose instead to back a poverty relief strategy centered on relieving chronic hunger that would ultimately evolve into Fome Zero (Bourne 2009, 81; Ansell 2015, 1268).

That same year, Suplicy, freshly elected as PT's first senator, authored a bill proposing an unconditional cash transfer for all Brazilians over 25 via a negative income tax. The benefit would have been rolled out gradually over 10 years starting with those over 60. The Senate unanimously approved the proposal, formally called Programa de Garantia de Renda Mínima (Minimum Income Guarantee Program) the following year. Cardoso, then a senator, described it as "a realistic utopia with its feet on the ground" (Suplicy and Buarque 1997, 85). The bill, however, languished in the Chamber of Deputies, where PT deputies were among its opponents (Hunter 2010, 71).

The gap between the two proposals was narrowed following a 1991 meeting of PT-affiliated economists. Poverty specialist José Márcio Camargo criticized Suplicy's decision to target adults and start with the elderly. He proposed instead that the program target families with school-age children and link transfers to school attendance. Doing this, Camargo argued, would, in addition to reducing current poverty, improve productivity and tackle intergenerational poverty (Melo 2007, 41; Morais 2017, 11). Although still committed to an unconditional income floor for all Brazilians, Suplicy was open to starting with children. After much effort and against the wishes of many in the PT, the modified Renda Mínima policy was incorporated into the PT's 1994 platform (Suplicy 2004, 127–29). But, at least according to Suplicy (2004, 130), it "did not receive the importance it deserved."

3.1.2 Pioneering Subnational CCTs

While Suplicy continued fighting for Renda Mínima in the legislature, Buarque, who was elected governor of the Federal District of Brasilia, took matters into his own hands, implementing his proposal in January 1995 under the catchier Bolsa Escola name. The policy was not endorsed by the PT's central leadership (Tomazini 2019, 30) and faced resistance from local party officials (Buarque 2013, 17). Other critics included teachers, who demanded that Bolsa Escola's funding be spent on higher salaries, and conservatives, who derided the program as both unworkable and an electoral ploy. Others worried that paying families to keep their children in school "would pervert the nobility of education" (Buarque 2013, 17).

Also in early 1995, urged on by Suplicy (Coêlho 2012b, 80; Suplicy in Tomazini 2019, 30), José Roberto Magalhães Teixeira, mayor of the city of Campinas in São Paulo state from Cardoso's centrist Brazilian Social Democratic Party (PSDB), implemented a subnational version of Renda Mínima. In contrast to Bolsa Escola, which rigorously enforced attendance and revoked the cash transfers of noncompliers, the Campinas program was unconditional in all but name (Aguiar and Araújo 2002, 42; Buarque 2013, 20–21). Despite this more rights-based focus, local PT officials initially voted against the policy. Suplicy (2004, 126) had to personally visit Campinas to convince them to change their minds (see also Melo, Ng'ethe, and Manor 2012, 147).

Surprisingly, there appears to have been very little cross-pollination between the two programs (Morais 2017, 12). Despite their many similarities, the two programs differed in terms of priorities and in their diagnosis of school absenteeism and desertion. Bolsa Escola sought to use stipends to incentivize school attendance among the poorest children and thus increase their human capital. As it was premised on the belief that strict conditionality enforcement was necessary to keep the poor in school, payments were discontinued if children were absent more than two days a month (Suplicy and Buarque 1997, 86; Aguiar and Araújo 2002, 42). Furthermore, to ensure only the neediest benefited, families had to be recertified as poor every year (Rocha 2013, 29).

In contrast, Renda Mínima was primarily an anti-poverty program. Absenteeism was not monitored, let alone punished. It was assumed that all families *wanted* to send their children to school but the poorest ones were *prevented* from doing so by their reliance on the income their children generated. By boosting incomes, cash transfers would improve attendance and increase human capital without the need for costly enforcement. Renda Mínima's emphasis on poverty reduction was exemplified by Teixeira's decision to house the program in the Department of Family, Children, Adolescents and Social Action. Bolsa Escola, in contrast, was overseen by the Department of Education (Aguiar and Araújo 2002, 42; Buarque 2013, 20–21).

Thus, already in 1995, there existed two types of cash transfer programs in Brazil (Aguiar and Araújo 2002, 41–42; Paulics 2004, 15; Buarque 2013). These contrasting philosophies would continue to influence the design of CCTs in Brazil and across Latin America for years to come (see next chapter).

3.1.3 Subnational Diffusion of CCTs

Word of these two pioneering programs spread quickly across Brazil as well as internationally. The programs were recognized in national and international media and received several high-profile awards (Buarque 2013; Sugiyama 2013, 91–92). Eleven programs were in place by the end of 1996. At the end of that year, Brasilia's Bolsa Escola received the Public Management and Citizenship award for innovative local policies from the Getúlio Vargas Foundation and the US-based Ford Foundation as well as the United Nations Children's Fund's (UNICEF) Child and Peace Prize (Aguiar and Araújo 2002, 43). The number of cities with CCTs continued growing. Nearly 50 cities had their own programs by the time the Cardoso administration launched Bolsa Escola Federal in 2001 (Sugiyama 2008, 201).[6]

Counter to the cross-national findings, municipalities governed by the PT and other left-wing parties were in fact more likely to adopt CCTs (Melo 2007; Sugiyama 2008; Coêlho 2012a). PT mayors were responsible for 61% of the 90 municipal CCTs proposed during 1995–2001 (Coêlho 2012a, 64). This presents a puzzle. During the first half of the 1990s, PT members dismissed policies targeting the poorest of the poor, such as CCTs, as little more than "a smokescreen to disguise an abandonment of any serious commitment to redistribution of wealth or extension of universal benefits via a comprehensive welfare state" (Macaulay and Burton 2003, 147). And, as noted above, PT's national leadership was uninterested in Suplicy's and Buarque's proposals and PT municipal councilors in both Brasilia and Campinas initially opposed their cities' pioneering programs.

This change in attitude toward CCTs, which was initially limited to PT mayors, was part of a broader evolution by the PT in response to the challenges and responsibilities of governing.[7] As the party started to win control of mayoralties across the country during the 1990s, it was forced to moderate its positions almost to the point of resembling a traditional catchall party (Hunter 2010). The need to deliver tangible improvements in the quality of life of their constituents forced PT mayors to behave more pragmatically than their legislative counterparts (Couto 2003).[8] To get elected, mayoral candidates need to secure absolute majorities and therefore appeal to a larger and more diverse bloc of voters than is needed to enter Brazil's highly proportional legislature, which allows parties with relatively low vote shares to win seats (Mainwaring 1999).[9] Once in office, the need to negotiate with other parties and the desire to secure reelection forced mayors to seek a balance between the PT's long-term national-level ideological project and addressing constituents' day-to-day concerns. CCTs proved compatible with both goals.

Furthermore, the kinds of long-term structural changes the party wanted simply could not be achieved at the local level. As Hunter (2010, 80) explains, "The development of signature programs such as participatory budgeting and the Bolsa Escola reflected a commitment to honoring and furthering the party's basic values of participation, transparency, and redistribution yet within the confines of the extant political and economic order." While cash transfers were compatible with the party's "preferential option for the poor," their reliance on targeting represented a "radical" shift from PT orthodoxy (Macaulay and Burton 2003, 147). Though far from their ideal, CCTs provided PT mayors with a feasible, effective, and popular way to deliver on their promises to voters.

3.1.4 Cardoso's National-Level CCTs

As subnational CCTs were spreading across Brazil, Buarque and Suplicy continued advocating for nationwide CCTs in line with their respective visions. Both unsuccessfully reached out to Cardoso (Buarque 2013, 32–33; Morais 2017, 12–13) and Paulo Renato Souza, education minister during the administration's eight years (Sugiyama 2013, 93; Morais 2017, 13). Buarque described his experience with Souza as being "snubbed," noting that "the feeling I had was that he laughed in my face" (O Estado de S. Paulo 2001c).

Despite this, momentum was growing. PT and PSDB partisans were competing over the "paternity" of CCTs: "PT partisans would emerge as strong advocates for cash transfers for the poor and critique the Cardoso government for failure to address social needs. PSDB partisans would respond that their mayors had also enacted CCTs in cities throughout Brazil" (Sugiyama 2012a, 35). On the legislative front, six federal cash transfer bills were proposed during 1995–96, the majority of them authored by centrist legislators (Suplicy 2004, 132; Melo, Ng'ethe, and Manor 2012, 148).

By 1996, Cardoso had become "convinced" that his party needed to enact a federal program (Melo, Ng'ethe, and Manor 2012, 148). Still, he proceeded in a cautious, piecemeal fashion, beginning in late 1996 with the small and highly targeted Programa de Erradicação do Trabalho Infantil (Program for Eradication of Child Labor, PETI). The program provided monthly stipends to poor families living in parts of the country where children were considered most at risk of working in dangerous activities, such as charcoal making and sugarcane harvesting. Benefits were conditional on school attendance and attending an after-school remedial education program that would prevent them from combining school with work (World Bank 2001; Rocha 2013, 69). Like the Brasilia program it was modeled after (Coêlho 2012a, 69), PETI was more about keeping children in school and out of work than reducing poverty per se. The program's beneficiary population peaked at 1.01 million in 2005 before being folded into Bolsa Família (CEPAL 2018).

Facing a reelection campaign against Lula at the end of 1998, Cardoso saw CCTs as a tool with which to counter the PT's reputation as a champion to the poor (Rocha 2013, 47). December 1997 saw the launch of Programa de Garantia de Renda Mínima (Guaranteed Minimum Income Program, PRGM), which offered to cover half the stipend costs of subnational CCTs. The program was to roll out gradually over five years beginning in cities with low human development.[10] PRGM was plagued with operational problems at both the federal and municipal levels (Rocha 2013, 52–57). At its peak in 2000, the program reached only 1,350 of the country's 5,500 municipalities (Coêlho 2012a, 69).

Given PRGM's disappointing results, Cardoso finally enacted a large-scale CCT in April 2001. Although the bill was baptized as the Magalhães Teixeira Law in honor of the PSDB creator of the Campinas program, the program itself was named and modeled after Brasilia's program.[11] Bolsa Escola Federal provided monthly stipends to poor children between six and 15 conditional on maintaining an 85% attendance rate. Like its subnational namesake, it was controlled by the Ministry of Education and conceptualized primarily as a tool for boosting school attendance among the poor and keeping children out of the workforce (Hevia 2011, 355). While data on the program is scarce, conditionality appears to have been strictly enforced, though there was significant variation across municipalities (de Janvry et al. 2005; Rocha 2013, 56). Bolsa Escola Federal reached 5.11 million families or about 13% of Brazil's population at the end of Cardoso's presidency (CEPAL 2018).

The PSDB saw CCTs as crucial to extending its rule beyond Cardoso's second (and final) term. Competition over the presumed political spoils from cash transfers influenced PSDB's internal politics. In part due to concern that the increasing visibility Bolsa Escola Federal provided Education Minister Souza would allow him to clench PSDB's nomination for the 2002 elections, Health Minister José Serra launched his own CCT, Bolsa Alimentação (Nutrition Scholarship), in September 2001 (Melo 2008, 170; Rocha 2013, 66). The new program sought to improve nutrition and reduce infant mortality by providing cash transfers to poor expectant mothers and poor children under six conditional on mothers attending pre- and postnatal medical checkups, ensuring their children's vaccinations remained up to date, and attending seminars on nutrition and education. Stipends were equal to those offered by Bolsa Escola Federal. The program reached 966,000 families or about 2.5% of Brazil's population at the end of Cardoso's presidency (CEPAL 2018).

Equally important was the launch that same month of the Cadastro Único (Single Registry), a unified database of poor Brazilians that sought to improve efficiency and coordination and reduce the duplication of administrative costs among the government's safety net programs (de la Briere and Lindert 2005; Rocha 2013, 64–65). By the end of the Cardoso administration, the database covered 70% of the country's poor (IPEA 2003, 38; Hall 2006, 696). This database, which the Lula administration would greatly improve and expand upon, was crucial to Bolsa Família's eventual expansion.

By this point PT mayors had been operating CCTs across the country for years, but this did not stop the PT's central command from criticizing Cardoso's programs. In 2000, Lula criticized Cardoso's policies on television for being a new form of *assistencialismo* (Ansell 2014, 30–31): social policy based on handouts rather than universal rights (Hunter 2010, 155). The following year, while attending a seminar on Fome Zero, Lula mockingly called Bolsa Escola Federal "Bolsa Esmola" (Charity Scholarship), criticizing it for being too modest to tackle the country's poverty (Aith 2011; O Estado de S. Paulo 2001b). Similarly, José Genoíno, PT's president, simultaneously dismissed the program as an "esmola" and accused Education Minister Souza of "making the Ministry of Education his campaign committee" (O Estado de S. Paulo 2001a). In contrast, both Suplicy (O Estado de S. Paulo 2001b) and Buarque (O Estado de S. Paulo 2001c) applauded the program.[12]

Cardoso's embrace of CCTs appears to have been the product of a domestic diffusionary process rather than the international one described in the previous chapter. There is little evidence that Cardoso or other federal-level Brazilian policymakers were influenced by the experiences of Mexico or other countries.[13] In fact, Sugiyama (2012a, 42) states that Brazilian policymakers took great pride "in their belief that the municipal Bolsa Escola programs were 'proof' of their country's ability to innovate and provide creative solutions for poverty alleviation." Further, these officials deny that their decision was a response to pressure or inducements from IFIs.

By the end of his final term, Cardoso had launched three federal CCTs and in the process set in motion a dramatic transformation in Brazilian social policy. The programs enacted by the centrist Cardoso more closely resembled Buarque's conditional human-capital-focused program than Suplicy's unconditional basic income proposal. Bolsa Escola Federal, like its subnational namesake, was designed to keep children in school. The more narrowly focused PETI, which combined transfers with remedial education, was even more education-focused. While not conditioned on education, Bolsa Alimentação was also focused on human capital formation with benefits conditioned on health interventions targeting expectant mothers and young children.

3.2 Lula Learns to Love CCTs

Lula finally won the presidency on his fourth attempt in 2002, defeating Serra by a wide margin.[14] Despite the emerging consensus behind CCTs, Lula's views on social policy had evolved remarkably little since 1990, when he dismissed Buarque's original proposal. He remained wedded to the now outdated idea that relieving hunger was the most effective means of reducing poverty. Lula was forced to reconsider the merits of CCTs following the spectacular failure of Fome Zero, his overly ambitious and complex hunger eradication and poverty reduction initiative. The realities of governing forced Lula, like PT mayors before him, to act more pragmatically and embrace programs he had previously dismissed as not ambitious enough. But Lula did more than just continue the programs inherited from Cardoso.

He expanded them and reformed them in a direction more akin to Suplicy's universalistic and unconditional basic income proposal.

3.2.1 Fome Zero's Rise and (Spectacular) Fall

Perhaps influenced by memories of the hunger he personally faced growing up poor in Brazil's Northeast during the 1950s, Lula remained convinced that hunger constituted Brazil's most urgent problem. Thus, he began his historic administration with a vow to eradicate hunger. In an impassioned inauguration speech on January 1, 2003, Lula vowed:

> If, by the end of my term, all Brazilians are able to eat breakfast, lunch and dinner, I will have fulfilled my life's mission. While there remains one Brazilian brother or Brazilian sister going hungry, we have more than enough reason to be covered in shame. (cited in Economist 2003)

Fome Zero was an ambitious effort to transform that promise into reality. Infinitely more complex than Cardoso's Bolsas, Lula's flagship initiative was to consist of more than 30 hunger-related programs ranging from food distribution to land reform, and was to require coordination between half a dozen federal ministries, subnational governments, local citizen committees, and even large businesses.[15] Fome Zero was designed by 45 researchers from the Citizenship Institute, a PT-affiliated think tank, and coordinated by incoming Food Security Minister José Graziano de Silva, an agronomist and long-time advisor to Lula (Yasbek 2004; Tavares 2005; Costa 2009).[16]

The program combined emergency measures to relieve current chronic hunger as well as local development projects and structural reforms aimed at preventing future hunger (Graziano, Del Grossi, and Galvão 2010, 20). The two emergency programs were Cartão Alimentação (Nutrition Card), an unconditional monthly food stamp program, and food baskets for the poor.[17] At the local level, food security would be improved through microcredit for farmers, community food banks and gardens, nutrition and literacy classes, and the opening of affordable "popular" restaurants, among many other initiatives. Finally, Fome Zero's structural reforms were to include investments in irrigation, sewage, and electrical infrastructure, land reform, and federal crop purchases. Complexity was further increased by the PT's commitment to allow for stakeholder participation in all areas of the program (Ansell 2014).

Fome Zero operated in parallel to existing transfer programs, "seemingly ignoring" their existence (Tavares 2005, 8). During a speech three months into his term, Lula once more criticized Cardoso's (now technically his own) programs as a distraction from the much-needed "structural reforms" needed for Brazilians to be able to escape poverty (Azevedo 2017). Nevertheless, although Lula de-emphasized the CCTs, he did not attempt to scrap them as by then they had developed their own constituencies (Melo 2007, 49–50; Melo 2008, 180).

Lula's ambitious initiative was widely criticized from the get-go. As Tomazini (2019, 35) puts it, "An acid rain of criticism from the media, academics and Congress fell daily on the heads of Fome Zero's team and the Lula government." Critiques were so widespread that in March 2003, a mere three months into the administration, Lula was summoned to defend the program before the PT's National Directorate (Cantanhêde 2003). For starters, critics challenged the program's most basic assumption—that hunger was the most urgent problem facing Brazil's poor (Tavares 2005, 8). As Rocha (2013, 81) notes, eradicating hunger was "an effective marketing slogan for a government that saw itself as focused on poverty relief" but this slogan did not reflect Brazil's reality. In fact, by the 2000s obesity was a bigger problem than hunger with poor Brazilians more likely to be overweight than rich ones (IBGE 2004; Arends-Kuenning 2009, 209).

In a clear act of insubordination, Buarque, who Lula appointed education minister and was thus in charge of Bolsa Escola Federal, openly criticized his boss's flagship policy. In a television interview less than two months into the administration, Buarque said his ministry's program could, if expanded and made more generous, lift more people out of poverty at a lower cost than Fome Zero, all while improving school attendance. He estimated that Bolsa Escola Federal could be doubled in size with just 20% of Fome Zero's total budget (Cantanhêde 2003; Breve and Hashizume 2004; Folha de S. Paulo 2004b). Buarque remained critical of the administration's anti-poverty initiatives and was unceremoniously fired in January 2004.[18]

From the Senate, Suplicy (2004, 141) criticized the use of food stamps and in-kind benefits for being paternalistic and urged the administration to trust the poor to make their own decisions. He predicted that the poor would sell their benefits at below face value in exchange for what they really needed—cash. As Suplicy (2004, 141) put it:

The poor person needs more than to kill hunger. If it is getting cold, you need to buy a sweater or a blanket. If the roof or the door of your house is damaged, you must repair them. If a child has become ill, it is necessary to buy medicine urgently.

This view was also shared by World Bank economists advising the government (Patú 2013) and some civil society groups (Ansell 2015, 33–34).

At the other end of the spectrum, some activist groups criticized the program for not going far enough. They argued that social policy under Lula was too focused on cash transfers and food stamps and that Fome Zero's proposed municipal projects and structural reforms were moving too slowly. From their perspective "Zero Hunger merely 'gave a man a fish rather than teaching him to fish,' in other words, that it was guilty of the very assistencialismo its proponents had critiqued during the 1990s" (Ansell 2014, 34).

Fome Zero proved too complex and less effective at relieving poverty than Cardoso's more modest programs. Structural reforms never got off the ground. Crop purchases and milk distribution were very limited and land reform was too controversial to be seriously considered. At the local level, there were so many different policies "implemented by so many agencies (government at all levels, NGOs, multilateral development agencies, etc.) that they were impossible to keep track of, let alone evaluate" (Ansell 2014, 33). Projects were expensive and difficult to coordinate and the government lacked the resources to enact them in every community that demanded them.

Cartão Alimentação and existing cash transfers offered clear advantages over the more ambitious policies: they were substantially cheaper (as much as 25%), relieved poverty immediately, and posed little risk of failure (Ansell 2014, 118). Because of this, Fome Zero ended up being synonymous with Cartão. Yet even this seemingly simple program was heavily criticized for using political criteria to select beneficiaries, for the exclusion of eligible families, and for its duplication of benefits. Even Graziano, its architect, admitted to targeting errors of up to 30% (Hall 2006, 696). Cartão's coverage peaked at roughly half a million beneficiaries, a fraction of Bolsa Escola Federal's size (CEPAL 2018).

3.2.2 The Birth of Bolsa Família

Fome Zero's quick and resounding failure forced Lula to change course 10 months into his administration and finally endorse CCTs. Lula merged Cardoso's programs with Cartão—the only functional part of his flagship initiative—to create a single unified CCT.[19] The new program, Bolsa Família, would ultimately define Lula's legacy.

Contrary to Lula's revisionist and self-congratulatory recollection of events presented in this chapter's introduction, Bolsa Família's creation was not a case where Lula, given his personal understanding of Brazilian poverty and political instincts, challenged "most experts and international organizations" (Tepperman 2017, 34). In fact, Lula's long-held antipathy toward CCTs placed him outside the Brazilian and Latin American social policy mainstream. All of the components of Bolsa Família already existed—they only needed to be assembled and improved.

Not even the idea of unifying existing CCTs was new. Near the end of the Cardoso administration, Social Assistance Minister Wanda Engel floated the idea with her boss (Cariello 2012). Unification as a means of reducing inefficiencies and overlap was also mentioned in *A Agenda Perdida* (The Lost Agenda), a set of policy proposals prepared by prominent liberal economists in the run-up to the 2002 elections.[20] Furthermore, during Bolsa Família's launch, Lula credited Marconi Perillo, the PSDB governor of the state of Goiás, who, during a meeting in August 2003, had urged him to unify existing programs and award benefits through a single magnetic card as he had done in his state (Safatle, Borges, and Oliveira 2016, 249; Azevedo 2017).[21]

Aware of Fome Zero's unviability, Finance Minister Antonio Palocci, a moderate who, as mayor of Ribeirão Preto, a midsized city in São Paulo state, had enacted a CCT, suggested to Lula that he refocus his social policy on CCTs, but on a larger scale than had been tried before.[22] Central to Palocci's plan was the expansion and improvement of another Cardoso initiative—the Cadastro Único registry. According to an official who participated in discussions over what became Bolsa Família, Lula's responded by stating that "if there's anything good in the drawer, let's open the drawer, give it another name and we go ahead" (Safatle, Borges, and Oliveira 2016, 247–48).

Multilateral banks also worked hard to convince Lula of the benefits of cash transfers over hunger relief and food distribution (Patú 2013). In

March 2003, as Fome Zero's problems were becoming increasingly apparent, World Bank president James Wolfensohn and former Inter-American Development Bank president Enrique Iglesias organized a private meeting between Lula and Santiago Levy, the architect behind Mexico's Progresa. Levy reportedly convinced Lula that CCTs were the best way forward (Lindert et al. 2007, 13–14; Reid 2007, 234; Lustig 2011, 12; Morais 2017, 126). In the words of Kathy Lindert, a human development specialist at the World Bank who has written extensively on CCTs and Bolsa Família:

> Actually, the World Bank should take the credit for the introduction of Bolsa Familia (in Brazil). Lula initially wanted to get rid of CCTs and introduce food stamps. We organized for a secret visit from Santiago Levy to persuade him of the merits of CCTs. Levy literally flew in over the weekend, and then flew back out; no one even knew he was in the country. (cited in Brearley 2011, 110)

Following the meeting, Lula requested a cash transfer proposal. Technocrats from the Social Assistance Ministry and economists from Brazil's Institute of Applied Economic Research, with technical assistance from the World Bank and other donors, set out to design such a program. As Fome Zero's failure became more obvious, Lula distanced himself from Graziano and looked outside the PT, embracing instead the ideas of Ricardo Paes de Barros, a University of Chicago–trained liberal economist and one of the authors of the previously dismissed *A Agenda Perdida* (Tavares 2005; Cariello 2012).[23]

This new direction met with resistance both from within the PT and from those in charge of existing programs. Lula's decision to create a unified CCT reignited the Brazilian left's long-standing debate over the merits of targeting versus universalism (Cariello 2012). Far-left *petistas* continued to deride transfer policies as "paternalist and demanding" and little more than "handouts" (Hunter 2010, 155). Ministers and social policy bureaucrats worried that the new program would reduce their power. Seeing the most ambitious parts of their agenda scrapped in favor of Cartão, Fome Zero's team was particularly demoralized by its loss of standing (Morais 2017, 128; Tomazini 2019, 35).

Despite his long-standing advocacy of cash transfers, Buarque complained that Bolsa Escola would be watered down if incorporated into a larger program centered on relieving poverty rather than increasing human capital. He also decried the symbolism of the program's name change (replacing *Escola* with *Família*) and the decision to transfer its administration from the Education Ministry to the newly created "super ministry" of Social Development and the Fight against Hunger (MDS). In his words, "it's one thing for the mother to receive money when you tell her that it's so her son will study, it's another when you tell her that she receives it because they are poor" (YouTube Tony Show 2016).

Despite these complaints, those with the final say, Lula and Palocci, had made up their minds (cited in Cariello 2012; see also Patú 2013). Bolsa Família launched provisionally in October 2003 under the control of the MDS. Lula signed a law making the program permanent in January 2004. As a face-saving measure, the administration would continue to refer to Bolsa Família as the flagship program of a broader Fome Zero agenda. But in reality, as soon as the former was enacted, the latter ceased to exist (Freire 2004).

3.2.3 The Evolution of Bolsa Família

The abandonment of Fome Zero did not mean a full-blown embrace of Cardoso's CCTs. Rather, Lula and later Rousseff made cash transfers their own, using them as a platform for moving Brazil closer to having a universal income floor, albeit within the confines of a CCT. While not the radical break with existing policy that Lula originally promised, Bolsa Família still proved groundbreaking. Those enrolled in existing programs were quickly incorporated into the new program, new beneficiaries were enrolled as coverage expanded dramatically, and stipends became more generous. The result was a more universal program that comes close to offering a guaranteed income floor for all Brazilians in economic need. The Brazilian case offers clear evidence that government ideology still shapes the design of social policy.

Coverage numbers tell only part of the story. The Brazilian left reformulated the CCTs it inherited in accordance with its programmatic goals and in response to its long-standing critiques of means-tested programs. In a clear step in the direction of providing an income floor for all, Bolsa Família included an unconditional basic benefit of R$50 for families in extreme poverty, regardless of whether they had children. Coverage was then extended to 16 and 17 year olds in 2008. Rousseff continued to broaden the program's target population. As part of the Brasil Sem Miséria (Brazil Without Misery) initiative launched in 2011, the government increased the maximum number of beneficiaries per household from three to five and began actively seeking out families that remained outside the program.[24] The following year, Rousseff introduced a supplemental subsidy, determined on a case-by-case basis, for families that remained in extreme poverty despite receiving cash transfers.

Bolsa Família was also more generous than its predecessors. Benefits at launch were roughly equal to those received by a family simultaneously enrolled in Bolsa Escola Federal, Bolsa Alimentação, and Cartão. In practice, this represented a major increase since the average poor family had been enrolled in only 1.8 of Bolsa Família's predecessors (Suplicy 2007, 2). Furthermore, as previously noted, stipend levels increased steadily starting in mid-2007, first compensating for inflation and later increasing in real terms (see fig. 3–2).

Thus, Bolsa Família was qualitatively different from its predecessors. Its focus was a product of the left's programmatic orientation and affinity toward universal programs. As Cotta (2009, 283–84) notes, particularly during the program's early years, "It was believed that it would be the first step towards the implementation of a minimum income program in the country, once adequate fiscal and political conditions were in place."[25] Or, as Pereira (2015, 1689) further notes, "Influenced by the idea of a basic or minimum income, the government chose to err on the side of inclusion" (see also Tomazini 2019, 37). Public statements by Lula and other officials presented transfers as a universal right available to all those who needed them and a tool that would allow the poor to make effective their constitutional rights to education and healthcare (Britto 2008, 188; Sugiyama and Hunter 2013, 44; Morais 2017, 164).

Targeting and conditionality took a backseat to expanding coverage and relieving poverty. As Arends-Kuenning (2009, 2015) notes bluntly, "The policy emphasis of social welfare programs was shifted from improving human capital to providing income transfers." Targeting was "not considered a priority element of the program, but rather a necessary mechanism to implement it under budgetary constraints" (Britto 2008, 188). Conditionality enforcement was even less of a priority. In fact, prior to September 2006 there was no compliance monitoring whatsoever (Soares 2012, 9). Like other advocates of basic income schemes, the government operated from the premise that all parents *wanted* to send their children to school but some were *unable* to do so because of poverty. By boosting incomes,

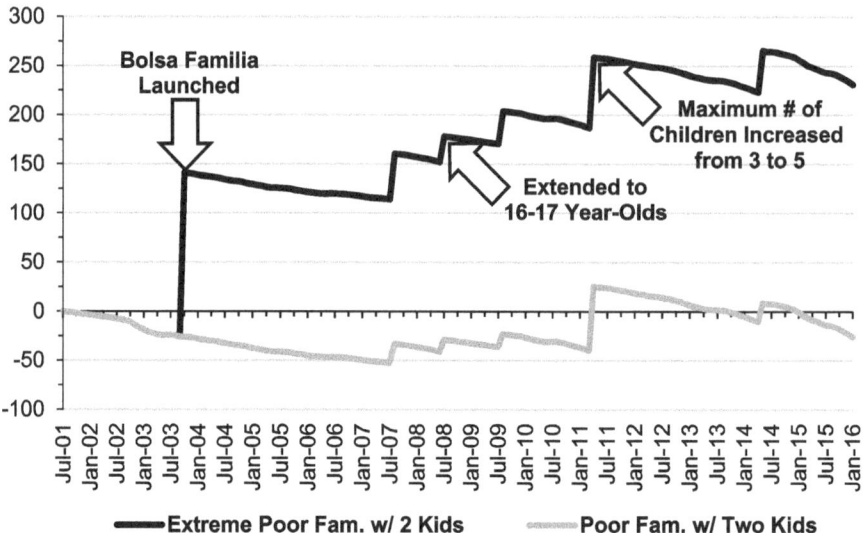

Figure 3-2. Inflation Adjusted Value of CCT Stipends (July 2001 = 100)
Notes: Assumes (1) a family has two school-aged children under 15 and (2) the two children were enrolled in Bolsa Escola Federal in July 2001. Cartão Alimentação is not counted as it was not an education-linked CCT.
Sources: IBGE (2018) and Hellman (2015).

Bolsa Família was to ensure that parents would comply with the program's conditions willingly and without the need for punitive (and expensive) enforcement.[26]

3.2.4 Backlash against Bolsa Família

Brazil's media and public did not share this permissive attitude toward conditionality. In July 2004, with municipal elections approaching, several media outlets began reporting on the absence of enforcement (Kamel 2004; Schwartzman 2005, 4; Lindert and Vicensini 2010). The reports sparked a wave of newspaper exposés that revealed further irregularities including duplication of benefits and instances in which benefits were awarded to local politicians, municipal employees, and their families (Lindert and Vicensini 2010, 40). Criticism reached a fever pitch when, on October 14, 2004, two weeks before the municipal runoff election, the popular television show *Fantástico* broadcast a report alleging that middle-class families in three cities benefited from the program while a poor girl remained excluded (Schwarzman 2005, 4; Tepperman 2017, 37–38). In the week following the report, MDS's Bolsa Família hotline received 1,946 complaints from across the country (Lindert and Vicensini 2010, 49).

Lula was caught off guard as "critics from the right and the left united to accuse the government of turning a truly innovative program into a paternalistic and old-fashioned version of social assistance" (Britto and Soares 2011, 6). The PSBD (2004) criticized Lula for transforming Cardoso's policies into populist *assistencialismo* designed to buy off the poor. Buarque, who by then had left the PT and become a critic of Lula, argued that lax conditionality enforcement transformed a previously progressive program into something more akin to the traditional "conservative governing strategy" of vote buying, a "nationalized form of *coronelismo*" (cited in Cotta 2009, 246–47).[27]

In response, Bolsa Família underwent a major managerial change that resulted in enforcement becoming a greater priority (Britto and Soares 2011, 6). In January 2005, Lula personally presided over the launch of an oversight strategy aimed at detecting and remedying fraud (Lindert and Vicensini 2010, 50; Tepperman 2017, 37–39). Enforcement gradually improved and by 2007 surpassed levels seen during the Cardoso administration (Lindert et al. 2007).

The administration's response to these scandals sought a compromise between unconditional transfers and a strict approach that immediately expels vulnerable noncompliers from the program. Since 2006, conditionality has been actively monitored but enforced in a permissive manner. In contrast to the more punitive approach used in countries such as Mexico, noncompliance is interpreted as a "red flag"—a sign that a family faces an additional vulnerability that municipal social workers should seek to resolve. Initial instances of noncompliance are met with warnings. Subsequent violations lead to temporary suspensions of benefits. Only after five violations can a family be expelled from the program (Hellmann 2015, 18–20). In practice, it remains quite difficult to lose Bolsa Família benefits for noncompliance.

The reforms contributed to the program's popularity and political sustainability, demonstrating that, at least with regard to anti-poverty programs, "'what works technically' (targeting accuracy, fraud and error controls, monitoring of conditionalities, and proven impacts), largely aligns with 'what works politically' (with increased political support and votes)" (Lindert and Vincensini 2010, 6). Maintaining this balance remains crucial to Bolsa Família's long-term legitimacy. Despite finding strong public support for the program, surveys also find that over 80% of Brazilians worry that nonpoor households benefit from the program (Oliveira de Castro et al. 2009) and reveal strikingly little support for an unconditional basic income scheme (Waltenberg 2013).

3.3 Conclusion

Asked in 2007 what Lula had done well as president, 43% of respondents to a nationwide survey cited "Bolsa Família" as their first answer (cited in Morais 2017, 146).[28] It is ironic that Lula, who for more than a decade resisted and was at times openly hostile to cash transfers, now counts Bolsa Família as his greatest achievement. In fact, despite repeatedly rejecting and criticizing CCT proposals, Lula is today seen as their global ambassador (Boultinghouse 2015, 13). The spectacular failure of Fome Zero at the start of his administration forced Lula to reconsider and ultimately embrace the policy he once derided as "Bolsa Esmola." But he went beyond merely continuing or even just expanding the policies he inherited. Lula used Cardoso's CCTs, which were modeled on Buarque's human-capital-focused program, to create a more ambitious program more closely resembling Suplicy's basic income proposal. Contrary to what Lula and much of the PT originally believed, CCTs could significantly reduce Brazil's stubbornly high levels of poverty and inequality and, in the process, advance the left's ultimate goal of constructing social democracy, defined as the existence of near-universal, rights-based social policies accessible independently of labor status (Thomé 2013).

Bolsa Família allowed Lula to keep his inauguration-day promise to pay the country's "historical debt to the poor." At the end of his second term in 2010, Lula handed Rousseff the reins of a Brazil in which the share of people unable "to eat breakfast, lunch and dinner" had dropped to its lowest level in history. Poverty and extreme poverty during Lula's last year were, respectively, 13% and 23% lower than they would have been in the program's absence (Soares, Ribas, and Osório 2010). While eye-catching, changes in poverty head counts severely understate the program's effects. Those who escaped poverty through Bolsa Família constitute a minority of total beneficiaries. These numbers pale in comparison with the tens of millions of households who, though still poor after Bolsa Família, saw the severity of their poverty reduced (Thomé 2013; Bither-Terry 2014). The program's contributions to the incomes of Brazil's neediest were responsible for as much as one-fifth of the historic decline in inequality that occurred during the Lula years (Soares et al. 2009; Soares, Ribas, and Osório 2010; Hoffman 2013).

Politically, Bolsa Família paid off handsomely for Lula and later Rousseff. In a clear example of retrospective economic voting, beneficiaries rewarded PT presidential candidates at the ballot box (Hunter and Power 2007; Zucco 2013). In the process, PT's core base of support changed from urban middle-class voters in the more developed Southeast to poor voters in the rural Northeast, the country's poorest region (Zucco 2008). This new constituency was instrumental in allowing Lula and Rousseff to easily win the 2006 and 2010 presidential elections. During tougher economic times in 2014, Bolsa Família may very well have made the difference that allowed Rousseff to win her extremely close reelection race (Brasil 2014; Zucco 2015). Notably, these political gains occurred in the absence of the clientelism and outright vote-buying that have traditionally marred Brazilian elections, particularly in rural areas (Fried 2012; Sugiyama and Hunter 2013).

There continues to be significant debate within left-wing policy circles over whether Bolsa Família constitutes a building block toward the construction of a universal basic income or rather a stumbling block that relieves poverty just enough to defuse political mobilization in favor of more ambitious policies. Although Suplicy himself has been very supportive of Bolsa Família and sees it as a first step toward enacting an income floor for all Brazilians (Morais 2007, 142; Tomazini 2019, 37), more maximalist left-wing economists remain critical of the program. Influential economist Lena Lavinas (2013b, 44) goes so far as to call the program "the antithesis of a citizens' income" in that it is neither universal nor a right (see also Britto and Soares 2011; Lavinas 2013a, 38). Transfers remain far below the minimum wage and there appears to be no intention to raise them to that level. As it stands, the program's eligibility thresholds punish poor families that succeed in clawing their way out of poverty.[29]

I agree with Soares (2012, 2) that, in practice, the differences between Bolsa Família and a basic income are "minor" and "what matters is that poor people are getting money." In reaching almost the entirety of the country's poor, Bolsa Família does, in fact, ensure that all Brazilians (including those without children) have a guaranteed minimum standard of living.

Thomé (2013) calls this "smart universalism"—basically everyone who needs the program can receive it without the high cost of providing benefits to those who do not need them. Lavinas's concerns over conditionality have more merit today than they did when the program was first launched but, in practice, it remains quite difficult to be kicked out of the program for failing to comply with conditionalities. Bolsa Família comes very close to providing a guaranteed basic income, albeit within the confines of a CCT program.

Whether Bolsa Família advances or obstructs the creation of a true basic income is a moot point as there is little support among Brazilians for an unconditional social policy (Waltenberg 2013). In fact, as demonstrated by the scandals stemming from the nonenforcement of conditionality, the requirement that beneficiaries attend school and receive medical checkups helps explain Bolsa Família's strong public support. The scandals damaged the program's reputation and forced the Lula administration into damage control mode. The resulting compromise—a nonpunitive approach to enforcement—strikes a balance between caring for the poor and allaying taxpayer concerns.

More broadly, the Brazilian case demonstrates the existence of two distinct models of CCTs—a more targeted and conditional approach concerned primarily with improving human capital advocated by Buarque and implemented by Cardoso and a more universalistic and less punitive approach more concerned with poverty reduction and the creation of an income floor for all citizens advocated by Suplicy and implemented by Lula. The latter addresses many of the left's original concerns about CCTs and exemplifies a more expansive vision of social policy more attuned to the long-term goal of decommodifying labor.

The next chapter will contrast these two approaches to CCTs in greater detail by comparing Bolsa Família with Mexico's pioneering Progresa/Oportunidades program.

CHAPTER 4

Human Capital vs. Basic Income

Models of Cash Transfers in Mexico and Brazil

Under the watch of center-left President Luiz Inácio Lula" da Silva (2003–10), Brazil's modest Bolsa Escola and Bolsa Alimentação were transformed into the significantly more ambitious Bolsa Família. The differences were qualitative as well as quantitative. Yes, Bolsa Família covers a far larger share of Brazil's population—more than one in four Brazilians every year since 2009—than its predecessors, but, more importantly, it also became more generous, less punitive in its enforcement of conditionality and, as critics including Cristovam Buarque himself have noted (Cotta 2009, 246–47), less focused on keeping children in school. Under Lula and his handpicked successor Dilma Rousseff (2011–16), conditional cash transfer programs moved closer to providing Brazilian families with an income floor similar (but by no means identical) to the one Eduardo Suplicy advocated for throughout his political career.

Bolsa Família gradually evolved into something quite different from Buarque's proposals and Mexico's Progresa/Oportunidades, Latin America's first national-level CCT.[1] As Cotta (2009, 293) aptly puts it, the two programs "are like identical twins, equal in appearance but distinct in personality and spirit."[2] Enacted and implemented by successive right-wing presidents, Mexico's program prioritizes long-run human capital accumulation over immediate poverty reduction. It uses precise rules to narrowly target beneficiaries with the intent of ensuring that only the truly needy receive aid. Conditionality is strictly enforced to ensure that beneficiaries keep up their end of the deal. And stipends increase with each successive grade to counteract the fact that the opportunity cost of remaining in school rather than entering the workforce increases as students get older.

Critics of CCTs can rightfully claim that overly narrow targeting runs the risk of excluding eligible families. Strict conditionality enforcement threatens to exclude the poorest of the poor, who are the most likely to have difficulty attending school and receiving medical checkups in the first place (Tutu 2006; Rodríguez-Castelán 2017). Differentiated stipends, while less objectionable from a poverty reduction standpoint, do represent a move away from the goal of ensuring that every person is guaranteed the same income floor. Implicitly mindful of these critiques, Brazil's left transformed the CCTs it inherited into a program that emphasizes poverty reduction over human capital accumulation. Compared to Progresa/Oportunidades, Bolsa Família has broader and less precise targeting and much more lenient conditionality enforcement. Although 16 and 17 year olds do receive a more generous stipend, the program pays the same stipend to all other beneficiaries.

Thus, while Mexico's right and Brazil's left agree that CCTs are a vital tool to relieve poverty and enhance the poor's human capital, they differ in the weighting they assign to each of those goals. This chapter argues that there exist two distinct types of CCTs in Latin America that differ in the extent to which they prioritize those twin goals: "human capital" and "basic income" CCTs. In Mexico, center-right President Ernesto Zedillo (1994–2000) of the long-ruling Institutional Revolutionary Party (PRI) enacted the first national-level human capital CCT, which was then continued and expanded under successive administrations from the right-wing National Action Party (PAN). In Brazil, the center-left under Lula and later Rousseff expanded and transformed centrist President Fernando Henrique Cardoso's (1995–2003) programs to create the first basic income CCT.

The chapter also explores the intellectual origins of these two contrasting models and the role of political ideology in determining the choice of model. The human capital model embraced by Mexico's right was, at its essence, a neoliberal response to the persistence of extreme poverty in the aftermath of market reform. Developed by a team of technocrats led by Santiago Levy, a US-trained Mexican economist associated with the World Bank, Progresa/Oportunidades envisioned cash transfers as a means of incentivizing the extreme poor to invest in their children's education and health. The resulting program's ultimate goal was to ensure that beneficiary children acquired the tools needed to succeed in the labor market as adults. In sharp contrast, the basic income movement that influenced the Brazilian left's version of CCTs envisioned cash transfers as a means of guaranteeing an income floor for every person. Such a policy would advance the left's ultimate goal of decommodifying workers (i.e., disconnecting their well-being from the market).

However, as the previous chapter demonstrated, electorates appear unwilling to support even relatively small transfers to poor children if they perceive that the government is not enforcing conditionality. Given this reality, there is unlikely to be support for the kind of universal, no-string-attached, living-wage income transfers envisioned by the left's most ambitious basic income advocates. Thus, the Brazilian left was forced to accept CCTs. Yet, as Bolsa Família shows, CCT design can be tweaked to closely resemble a basic income program. That cash transfers first entered Latin America's political agenda as part of the neoliberal policy toolkit did not mean that they had to be used to advance neoliberal policy goals (Ferguson 2010).

4.1 Human Capital Theory

As detailed in the previous chapter, Buarque saw cash transfers primarily as a tool to keep children from poor families in school and out of the workforce. By the mid-1980s, Buarque (1999) was arguing that, as "producers of human capital," poor parents be compensated for the income they forgo when their children attend school rather than work. Rather than couch his policy, as Suplicy did, in the language of rights and freedoms, Buarque spoke of incentives and opportunity costs. In this regard, Buarque's views on cash transfers had more in common with those of Levy and Zedillo than with those of Suplicy and Lula.

Whereas Suplicy and Lula emphasized the immediate effects of cash transfers—relieving poverty by boosting incomes and, ideally, eradicating it by providing an income floor for all citizens—Buarque and Levy emphasized the long-term potential of conditionality to prevent poverty by incentivizing families to invest in their children's human capital. For Buarque and Levy, CCTs were innovative, not because they effectively target the poor and relieve poverty but, because, by boosting incomes, they gave parents a chance to prevent their children from being poor as adults. Cash transfers are not, as basic income advocates argue, a means of "emancipating us from the despotism of the market" (Van Parijs and Vanderborght 2017, 109). Rather, they are a tool to ensure that those who are born poor will acquire skills valued by the market that will allow them to "work their way out of poverty" (Levy 1991, 85).

In making a case for what became Mexico's pioneering CCT, Levy (1991) went beyond Buarque's education-centric definition of human capital. Levy's evolving proposal (1991, 2006; see also Levy and Rodríguez 2004) emphasized the complex interactions between food intake, nutrition, health, education, and poverty. Specifically, Levy made a case for incorporating healthcare and nutritional components into Mexico's CCT in addition to the educational conditionality present in Buarque's proposal and eventual local-level program. Citing a broad social science literature, Levy explains that, as a result of their parents' lower incomes and levels of education, poor children are less likely to receive regular medical care and thus more prone to contracting preventable diseases. Similarly, with regard to nutrition, very poor households rely heavily on cheap, high-calorie foods with low nutritional value (Levy 1991, 49). Nutritional deficiencies during the first years of life increase both vulnerability to diseases and the likelihood of cognitive underdevelopment. Poor health and nutrition may permanently impair school and work performance, increasing the likelihood of poverty during adulthood (Levy and Rodriguez 2004, 198).

Furthermore, low-income women are more likely than their nonpoor counterparts to lack information about and access to birth control. As a result, they tend to have higher birth rates and have children at a younger age, leading to families with higher dependency ratios—fewer workers for each nonworker.[3] This forces families to divide their already low incomes between more individuals, making them less able to get by without additional income from working children (Levy and Rodriguez 2004, 224). Inability to invest in their children's education is indicative of a broader problem. Low incomes prevent poor families from making investments and taking risks that could significantly improve their situation, such as planting new crops, purchasing productivity-enhancing tools, or migrating to more prosperous parts of the country.

This "vicious cycle," Levy argued, could be overcome by boosting the poor's purchasing power through a single program that incentivized simultaneous improvements in nutrition, health, and education. Higher incomes allow families to keep their children in school longer, consume more and better foods, and attend regular medical checkups. Better-fed children do better in school, which, in turn, improves their long-term economic prospects. In addition to improving overall health outcomes, more frequent visits to the doctor increase women and girls' usage of birth control, leading to smaller families that can invest more in each child. Addressing all of these interconnected issues requires a single cross-cutting cash transfer program. Like Buarque, Levy was adamant about the importance of conditioning benefits on good behavior and strictly enforcing those conditions. In Levy's (2006, 135–36) words:

> Participation must be systematically enforced.... If enforcement of conditions weakens, the program runs the real risk of becoming just a mechanism for effecting pure income transfers to the poor: today's consumption is enhanced, but tomorrow's potential is wasted.

4.1.1 A Neoliberal Initiative

In contrast to Brazil, where both Buarque and Suplicy initially struggled to convince first Cardoso and later Lula of the merits of CCTs, President Zedillo, himself a technocrat with a doctorate in economics from Yale, was both open to cash transfers and a proponent of human capital theory (Valencia and Aguirre 1998, 76). Zedillo (2009) insulated social policy technocrats from politics and granted them full autonomy to design, implement, and evaluate what came to be known as the Education, Health and Nutrition Program (Progresa, To Progress). From his perch as undersecretary of finance for expenditures, Levy, a Boston University–trained economist, worked closely with José Gómez de León, a Harvard-trained demographer and general secretary of the National Population Council (CONAPO), to design Latin America's first national-level CCT.[4]

Progresa was part of a broader transformation in Mexican social policy that began with the 1988 election of Carlos Salinas de Gortari (1988–94). In the context of the 1980s debt crisis and subsequent market reforms, Mexican governments sought to create a safety net for the millions who fell into poverty while simultaneously reducing the size of the state. Anti-poverty policy under Salinas centered around the National Solidarity Program (PRONASOL), a social investment fund that provided communities with resources for infrastructure projects. Inaugurated in December 1988 to great fanfare, PRONASOL came to be widely criticized for being both ineffective and clientelistic (Dresser 1994; Molinar and Weldon 1994; Bruhn 1996; Dion 2000; Díaz-Cayeros, Estévez, and Magaloni 2016).

Levy first presented the ideas that evolved into Progresa in a 1991 World Bank research paper. In line with evolving neoliberal thinking on poverty, he accepted that growth alone would be insufficient to adequately tackle extreme poverty, which was concentrated in rural areas (Levy 1991, 30). Traditionally, Mexican governments sought to prevent hunger through food price subsidies, which were expensive and regressive, and direct food distribution, which was prone to corruption and had trouble reaching the most remote, and thus poorest, communities. On a more fundamental level, Levy (1991, 4–5) argued that fighting poverty indirectly through food policy was both inefficient and distorted economic incentives at a time when governments were working to impose market discipline. He proposed replacing generalized food policies with vouchers exclusively targeting rural families in extreme poverty. Interestingly, that proposal explicitly rejected using cash transfers for fear that they would disincentivize work and cause "welfare dependency" (Levy 1991, 52).

To promote human capital formation, the vouchers were to be conditional on children receiving regular medical checkups and parents attending classes on hygiene, birth control, and food preparation (Levy 1991, 85). Notably, at this time, benefits were not conceived as conditional on school attendance. Levy (1991, 64) was emphatic that the program's purpose was to induce behavioral changes and, as such, that its success should be assessed in terms of its "ability to lower infant mortality, reduce undernutrition, decrease fertility, reduce morbidity, and improve elementary health and hygiene behavior. . . . The program should have no other objectives" (Levy 1991, 64).

With his appointment to the Finance Ministry in December 1994, Levy got the chance to implement the proposal. The need for an effective antipoverty program further increased following the so-called Tequila Crisis, a severe balance of payments crisis inherited from the previous administration that sent the economy into a deep recession and pushed 16 million Mexicans into poverty. Like the debt crisis before it, the new crisis simultaneously increased the need for safety nets and constrained public finances. Sidestepping the Social Development Ministry (SEDESOL), Zedillo tasked two teams of technocrats with designing a replacement for PRONASOL (Garay 2016, 232). While Levy's team worked on turning his proposal into a reality, Gómez de León's team worked on a program targeted at mothers aimed at increasing children's access to education (Yaschine and Orozco 2010, 63; Garay 2016, 232).

There were immediate tensions between the technocrats and SEDESOL's policy specialists led by Social Development Minister Carlos Rojas, the "father of PRONASOL." The two sides fundamentally disagreed on the very purpose of anti-poverty policy and who it should target. Whereas the former wanted to focus exclusively on extreme poverty, the latter also worried about the moderately poor. As Valencia and Aguirre (1998, 70) explain, "Under one logic it was stressed that the poor must be guaranteed, as a constitutional right, a basic floor; under the other, [it was argued] that the extreme poor need to satisfy certain minimums to be qualified to participate in the market."

Tensions were further heightened because Levy, who had been critical of PRONASOL's subsidized credit component and arbitrary targeting, had final say over Rojas's budgets. The ministry's team considered it "heresy" that a "technocrat's" approach to fighting poverty would replace "one of the most ambitious anti-poverty programs" in the country's history (Valencia and Aguirre 1998, 76). In the words of a high-ranking SEDESOL official at the time, "the technocrats have no field experience and try to directly apply their 'desk theories' without having any experience with development programs" (cited in Valencia and Aguirre 1998, 76).

A pilot of Levy's proposal covering 31,000 households launched in three cities in the southeastern state of Campeche in October 1995 and was expanded to select rural communities in nine poor states in June 1996.[5] In lieu of subsidized milk and tortilla rations, participants received an electronic card exclusively for purchases of food at selected stores and tortilla shops.[6] Benefits were conditional on children attending regular medical checkups. Additionally, malnourished children, pregnant and lactating mothers, and children under five were given in-kind nutritional supplements.

Although beneficiaries overwhelmingly preferred vouchers to subsidized food (Levy and Rodriguez 2004, 243), lack of infrastructure limited the electronic card's usefulness in the most remote towns. As a result, vouchers were replaced with direct cash transfers (Hernández Franco 2008, 44; Cortés and Rubalcava 2012, 37). Scaling the program nationally required creating an objective targeting mechanism, a task Gómez de León spearheaded (Levy and Rodriguez 2004, 254; Lustig 2014, 109). And, most importantly, given education's central role in human capital formation, it was deemed necessary for benefits to also be conditional on school attendance (Levy and Rodriguez 2004, 243). With that, Levy and Gómez de León's proposals were merged into a single program covering education, health, and nutrition.

4.1.2 The Politics of CCT Adoption in Mexico

Zedillo officially requested congressional funding for Progresa during his 1996 report to Congress (Levy and Rodríguez 2004, 242). This proved controversial. First, given PRONASOL's reputation for clientelism, opposition legislators were skeptical about funding what they feared could become "Zedillo's PRONASOL" (Levy 2006, 108; De La O 2015, 75–76). Second, debate over cash transfers "took a very clear partisan turn, particularly with respect to the left-right cleavage" (Tomazini 2019, 38). The left-wing Party of the Democratic Revolution (PRD) criticized the proposal's narrow targeting, arguing instead for universal polices (Dion 2009, 76; Garay 2016, 244–45). The administration ultimately won over the right-wing PAN by guaranteeing that the program would not be disproportionally targeted toward PRI strongholds and would be rigorously evaluated, both of which the technocrats had intended to do all along. The PRD, however, remained opposed (De La O 2015, 78; Garay 2016, 233–34).

Mindful of PRONASOL's wretched reputation, "to prevent legislators and public opinion from associating the new scheme with electoral calculations and clientelism" (Garay 2016, 233), Zedillo waited to launch the program until August 1997, after the midterm legislative elections in which his party lost its majority in the lower house. Coverage increased rapidly from 300,000 families in nearly 6,000 rural communities across 12 states at launch to nearly 2.5 million families in 53,000 rural localities across all 31 states by the end of Zedillo's term (Levy 2006, 26). The program's success represented a definitive victory for the technocrats. Citing the ministry's neglect of moderate poverty and criticizing Levy by name, Enrique del Val, the SEDESOL official in charge of the infrastructure development programs that the technocrats had so roundly criticized, resigned in May 1998. Days later, Esteban Moctezuma, a Zedillo ally, replaced Carlos Rojas as minister (Valencia and Aguirre 1998, 82).

In line with Zedillo's promise to PAN legislators and its designers' technocratic worldview, Progresa began being evaluated almost immediately after its launch. The program's team worked closely with the International Food Policy Research Institute, a Washington-based policy research organization, and independent researchers to facilitate the evaluation of practically all aspects of the program. Resource limitations required a gradual rollout of the program. Participating communities were selected randomly, making it possible to conduct experimental studies contrasting beneficiaries and nonbeneficiaries both before and after the program (Levy and Rodríguez 2004, 307). The results were overwhelmingly positive, confirming that the program was cost-effective and well targeted. It reduced poverty, inequality, and child labor, as well as increased school attendance, family planning, and both the quantity and quality of food consumption (Levy and Rodríguez 2004, 354–55).

In demanding evaluations, PAN legislators likely saved Progresa from being scrapped after the 2000 elections, which saw PAN's Vicente Fox (2000–2006) break the PRI's 70-year stranglehold on the presidency. There were "strong rumors" in early 2000 that incoming Social Development Minister Josefina Vázquez Mota would replace Progresa with a "charity-based poverty alleviation program" (Lustig 2014, 105). It is widely acknowledged that the positive results of the International Food Policy Research Institute's independent evaluations convinced Fox and Vázquez Mota to not only continue the program but also to extend it to cover the three final years of high school (Levy 2006, 113–14; Behrman 2010, 1476).[7] In March 2002, Progresa was renamed Oportunidades (Opportunities) and expanded to urban areas. Coverage doubled during Fox's term to more than 5 million families in 90,000 localities across the entire country (Yaschine and Orozoco 2010, 68).

Given its ideological orientation, the PRD never fully embraced targeted anti-poverty programs. As Garay (2016, 244–45) explains, "the PRD had different preferences with respect to income support" than parties to the right and "contested the use of conditionality and advocated for broader transfers." Tellingly, the party failed to offer alternative anti-poverty policies when in power. Successive PRD mayors of Mexico City ignored the issue, focusing instead on universal healthcare and pension programs (Yanes 2013; Luccisano and Macdonald 2014; Garay 2016, 244–45). Given the program's success and popularity and the PRD's perceived hostility toward it, the party's presidential candidates—Cuauhtémoc Cárdenas in 2000 (González Rodríguez 2000) and Andrés Manuel López Obrador in 2006 and 2012 (Nieto and Gómez 2012)—went out of their way to assure voters that they would continue the program if elected.

4.2 The Basic Income Movement

Keeping children in school was of secondary concern for Suplicy. In fact, his original cash transfer proposal did not even target children. Although he has been a strong supporter of Brazil's CCTs from the start, Suplicy always saw them as stepping-stones toward something more ambitious—a legal entitlement guaranteeing all Brazilians the right to a basic standard of living, regardless of income, family composition, or labor market status.[8] Thus, while advocating for the same policy tool, Suplicy and Buarque, let alone the technocrats behind Mexico's CCT, fundamentally disagreed on that tool's ultimate purpose.

Suplicy is part of a long line of scholars and philosophers dating back to the 18th century who have advocated for a universal basic income (UBI). Whereas Buarque and the Mexicans saw cash transfers as a tool to equip children with the skills needed to succeed in the labor market as adults, Suplicy and members of the basic income movement saw them as a way of disconnecting people's fate from the vagaries of the market. In other words, UBI advocates envision cash transfers as tool to *decommodify* beneficiaries. Or, as Philippe Van Parijs (2013, 174), perhaps the world's foremost authority on UBI, puts it:

> An unconditional basic income is . . . about the power to say no to the dictates of a boss, a bureaucrat, or a spouse. And it is about the power to say yes to activities that are poorly paid or not paid at all, but are nonetheless attractive either in themselves or because of the training and the contacts they provide. The expectation is that spreading more evenly this bargaining power, the power to say yes and to say no, will not only make our societies more equal, but also systematically improve the quality of work—and thereby the quality of life—through the very operation of the capitalist labor market. . . . Unconditional basic income arguably constitutes a capitalist road to Marx's realm of freedom, to a world free of drudgery.

UBI policies have three defining characteristics (Van Parijs and Vanderborght 2017, 8). First, they target individuals, rather than households. Thus, for example, housewives are entitled to their own benefit independent of their husbands.[9] Second, they are universal as opposed to targeted toward particular groups (e.g., workers, the elderly, or disabled people) and do not select beneficiaries via a means test (e.g., the poor). Finally, they are obligation-free, meaning that benefits are not conditional on particular behavior, such as sending children to school or working a certain number of hours a month.

Proponents cite several advantages of UBI relative to traditional policies targeting the poor. Most notably, UBI eliminates the dependency/unemployment trap: the tendency of means-tested programs to disincentivize work. In a textbook case of perverse incentives, earnings from a better job or working more hours may be partially or even completely offset by the loss of government benefits. Unless the new job pays very well, fear of losing benefits may lead beneficiaries to remain on the dole indefinitely. In Latin America and other developing regions, beneficiaries may, to retain benefits, choose lower-paying jobs in the informal sector over higher-paying ones in the formal sector. Because informal-sector firms tend to be smaller and have lower productivity than formal ones, this behavior, although rational at the individual level, is pernicious for the economy as a whole (Levy 2008). UBI avoids this problem altogether by eliminating the trade-off between earnings and benefits.

UBI also resolves many problems affecting traditional anti-poverty programs. For starters, everyone is enrolled automatically. It can take weeks, even months, to enroll beneficiaries in a CCT. In the meantime, families with an out-of-work breadwinner or facing an emergency must endure hardship. Further, means-testing is inevitably imperfect. Even in the best-designed programs, some eligible individuals will be excluded while some who are not eligible will slip through the cracks. Universality makes this problem moot. In addition, conditionality tends to be regressive because the poorest and most vulnerable tend to have the most difficulty complying (Tutu 2006; Rodríguez-Castelán 2017). Governments also stand to save on administrative expenses from monitoring eligibility and enforcing conditionality. Universality and unconditionality, respectively, spare beneficiaries the stigma associated with means-tested programs (Soss 1999; Mettler 2002) and the intrusiveness and potential humiliation of conditionality enforcement (Van Parijs and Vanderborght 2017, 7).[10]

Furthermore, universal programs could be expected to be more generous and politically sustainable than targeted ones (Gelbach and Pritchett 2002). Programs whose benefits are restricted to politically weak groups such as the poor are highly vulnerable to budget cuts and even cancellation. Universality ensures a broad coalition in support of a program's continued survival and expansion (McGuire 2013).

These advantages, however, are likely to be more than offset by UBI's hefty price tag. For example, Van Parijs and Vanderborght's (2017, 11) proposal for advanced industrialized countries, which they describe as between "modest" and "generous," is predicted to cost 25% of a country's GDP.[11] As a point of reference, the average Latin American CCT in 2015 cost just 0.35% of GDP (Cecchini and Atuesta 2017; see table 1–2). Naturally, the proposal could be modified to reduce its cost, but doing so would involve either providing less generous benefits, possibly to the point of no longer "liberating" workers from the market, or reducing coverage, which brings back the dependency trap and targeting problems. As Luke Martinelli, another prominent UBI researcher, puts it, "an affordable UBI is inadequate, and an adequate UBI is unaffordable" (cited in Zamora 2017).

4.2.1 A Left-Wing Policy?

Basic income holds the promise of bringing about the left's ultimate goal: the decommodification of workers. Although advocates of UBI run the gamut from Friedrich Hayek ([1944] 1994) and Milton Friedman ([1962] 2002) on the right to John Kenneth Galbraith ([1966] 1986) and Yannis Varoufakis (2016) on the left, it has been the left that has most actively worked to turn this idea into a reality at the national level.[12] The two most significant efforts to enact a national UBI were spearheaded by the British Labour Party during the interwar period and by American economists linked to the Democratic Party in the 1960s and 1970s. While its popularity has ebbed and flowed over time, UBI has increased in prominence in recent years in light of rising inequality and concerns over automation-related job losses in rich countries. Once more, the left is leading the charge (Stern 2016; Van Parijs 2018).

In response to a spike in poverty following World War I, members of the British Labour Party led the first serious attempt to put basic income on the political agenda. Advocating for the "moral right to subsistence," Dennis and Mabel Milner proposed a universal "state bonus" of about 20% of GDP in 1918 (Van Parijs and Vanderborght 2017, 79). The proposal, however, was ultimately rejected at the Labour Party's 1920 congress. Labour-affiliated intellectuals, most notably George D. H. Cole, who first coined the term "basic income," and Nobel prize-winning economist James Meade, continued advocating for the policy (Van Parijs and Vanderborght 2017, 80–81). Talk of UBI ceased following the 1942 publication of the Beveridge Report, which set the direction the British welfare state has followed to this day (Van Parijs and Vanderborght 2017, 81).

The American left seriously considered UBI during the late 1960s and early 1970s. With the intent of reducing chronic poverty, particularly among blacks, economics Nobel laureate James Tobin began advocating for a universal household income tax credit or "demogrant" in 1965. Two years later, civil rights leader Martin Luther King Jr. wrote in support of a guaranteed income. The following year, Tobin, Galbraith, Paul Samuelson, and more than a thousand economists signed a petition calling on Congress to enact income guarantees. Amid this climate, a commission created by President Lyndon Johnson (1963–69), a Democrat, proposed replacing welfare policies with annual cash transfers at a cost of 15% of GDP (Van Parijs and Vanderborght 2017, 90). The policy was shelved after the Republican Richard Nixon (1969–74) won the presidency in 1968. Tobin and Galbraith later drafted a more ambitious proposal providing $1,000 a year to every American that served as a centerpiece of Democratic Senator George McGovern's 1972 presidential campaign (Van Parijs and Vanderborght 2017, 91). McGovern ultimately withdrew the plan amid criticism both from within his party and from Nixon.[13] By the middle of the decade UBI had fallen out of fashion.

Left-wing politicians have retaken the mantle of UBI in recent years. Members of the Swiss Socialist Party were among the leading supporters of an unsuccessful 2016 referendum on enacting UBI in that country (Van Parijs 2018). Benoit Hamon, the French Socialist Party's 2017 presidential candidate, campaigned on UBI. Democrat Hilary Clinton admitted that she seriously considered proposing UBI during the 2016 US presidential campaign, but desisted because she "couldn't make the numbers work" (Clinton 2017, 239). Businessman Andrew Yang proposed a universal income policy as the centerpiece of his campaign to be the Democratic nominee in the 2020 US election (Yang 2018).

This is not to say that there is consensus behind UBI on the left. Critics on the left consider it too expensive and inefficient (Wilson 2018) and therefore politically unworkable (Hassel 2018; Rothstein 2018). On a more philosophical level, UBI is not entirely compatible with the left's goals. The left finds capitalism problematic because it forces workers to sell their labor to survive and enables capitalists to appropriate gains from a product without contributing their labor to its production. There is consensus on the first point: the left supports policies that shield workers from the market and increases their leverage in negotiations over the sale of their labor. UBI is one such tool. The second point is more controversial. In providing an obligation-free livelihood, UBI allows beneficiaries (much like capitalists!) to appropriate gains from other people's labor. This "laborist" objection is particularly strong among labor unions and orthodox communist parties (Van Parijs and Vanderborght 2017).[14]

Thinkers on the right have also advocated for UBI. For the right, however, UBI is attractive mainly as a replacement for existing programs and thus a way to shrink government. Libertarians such as Friedman ([1962] 2002) and, more recently, Charles Murray (2006) have proposed replacing all existing social programs (not just anti-poverty programs) with a single universal policy. Doing so, they argue, would be both cheaper and more effective at combating poverty than what they consider to be a myriad of poorly targeted, paternalist, and incentive-distorting programs.[15]

4.2.2 Latin America's Left Settles for CCTs

Strong advocates of UBI have a "tendency to frame the move to universalism in 'big bang' or 'all or nothing terms,'" ruling out "the possibility of tailoring social protection measures to local needs at a pace permitted by local resources" (Kabeer 2014, 351). Yet it is worth noting that the two most significant attempts at enacting UBI, both carried out by the left, failed to get off the ground. And it remains to be seen whether the basic income movement's current incarnation will succeed.

Basic income faces two large, perhaps insurmountable, obstacles: the cost of covering everyone and the public legitimacy of handing out money with no strings attached. With regard to Latin America, the simple truth is that, although the region's population overwhelmingly believes that the causes of poverty are beyond poor people's control and strongly supports government redistribution (Lindert, Skoufias, and Shapiro 2006, 60; Gaviria 2007), there is very little support for universal or unconditional cash transfers, or both, to able-bodied working-age adults. This opposition is confirmed by survey research on Brazil and the region as a whole (Waltenberg 2013) and in case studies from across the region (Lo Vuolo 2013a). Moreover, as the case of Brazil detailed in the previous chapter showed, targeting errors and lax conditionality enforcement can spark public backlash.

Cheaper and more politically palatable, CCTs offer a viable alternative to UBI in Latin America. For better or worse, the region's elites and citizens believe that cash transfers should be limited to "deserving beneficiaries"—children who are poor through no fault of their own and are seen as taking steps to prevent becoming poor adults by attending school (Lo Vuolo 2013b,

263). The following observation on Brazil by Melo (2008, 167) is particularly telling:

> At the beginning of the decade [1990s], many political actors had regarded Suplicy's crusade as an oddity. His charismatic individual style made it appear a Utopian project without any chances of being implemented. But after the link with education was established, policymakers and politicians turned their attention to the issue.

The good news is that embracing CCTs need not imply a complete betrayal of UBI's principles. With regard to targeting, in their commitment to universality, UBI advocates confuse equality of transfers with equality of outcomes (Hoddinott 2007; Devereux 2016). UBI seeks to make effective a right to a basic level of income security. Universal cash payments are not the right in question, they are merely an instrument for making that right effective. As Devereux (2016, 170) argues, "Income security can be guaranteed by giving money to people who need it—it is illogical and wasteful for the state to give a living allowance to every person in the country." This is particularly true for cash-strapped developing countries. Furthermore, empirical evidence confirms that targeted programs transfer more funds to the poor than nontargeted ones (Coady, Grosh, and Hoddinott 2004; Hanna and Olken 2018).

Nor is CCT conditionality as "punitive" as sometimes portrayed. Conditionalities attached to CCTs are unlikely to be stigmatizing because what they require is behavior that all citizens are expected to comply with regardless of income level. This differs sharply from workfare programs, which require beneficiaries to do jobs that nonbeneficiaries would not do and might find demeaning (Pérez-Muñoz 2017, 452).[16] Politically, conditionality is beneficial because it increases program legitimacy (Gaarder 2012; Pritchett 2012). In that sense, conditionality is valuable beyond any actual improvement in human capital it produces inasmuch as it helps counteract the widely, if wrongly (Banerjee et al. 2017), held view that aiding the poor makes them lazy and helps fund their vices. Program advocates can credibly claim that a conditional transfer, rather than a handout, is a helping hand that allows beneficiaries to invest in themselves. Taxpayers will, in turn, be more likely to see those beneficiaries as "deserving poor" (Prichett 2012).

Most importantly, the differences between CCTs and UBI are not black and white (Gaarder 2012). Rather than stark, contrasting choices, these two models of cash transfers constitute ideal types along a continuum. As the evolution of Brazil's Bolsa Família detailed in the previous chapter showed, CCTs are not one-size-fits-all and can be tailored to more or less closely resemble UBI, albeit within limits. The following section and the next chapter demonstrate that governments have substantial flexibility with regard to targeting, conditionality enforcement, and other aspects of design.

In line with this reasoning, while there continue to be maximalists who see CCTs as a betrayal of UBI's mission (Lavinas 2013b; Lo Vuolo 2013b), many leading advocates of UBI have (begrudgingly) accepted CCTs as a second-best and (hopefully) temporary measure. Some, like Suplicy (2007) and Standing (2008), optimistically argue that CCTs have furthered their cause by demonstrating that cash, previously dismissed, is the most effective means of relieving poverty. Experience with CCTs, they argue, will increase awareness of the problems of targeting and conditionality, paving the way for UBIs.[17] Less optimistic, Van Parijs and Vanderborght (2017, 161–62) pragmatically accept that, because a large share of economic activity in developing countries is informal and therefore untaxed, UBI cannot be established there any time soon.

4.3 Conditional Cash Transfer Models

Lula and the PT's social policy team responded to the failure of the ambitious Fome Zero by transforming Cardoso's "neoliberal" anti-poverty programs into something better attuned to the left's universalistic aspirations and Suplicy's vision of a Brazilian UBI, albeit within the confines of a CCT. Bolsa Família constitutes a more expansive and universalistic type of CCT than Mexico's human capital-focused Progresa/Oportunidades. Thus, there exist at least two distinct CCT models in Latin America.[18]

The differences between these two programs reflect the inherent tension between the twin goals of reducing poverty in the short term and increasing human capital over the long run (Soares, Ribas, and Osório 2010). On the one hand, adopting a more draconian approach to conditionality enforcement makes sense when building human capital is the main priority. A growing and methodologically diverse literature analyzing cases from across Latin America (Schady and Araujo 2008; Brauw and Hoddinott

2011; Paiva et al. 2016) and Africa (Baird, McIntosh, and Özler 2011; Akresh, de Walque, and Kazianga 2012; Robertson et al. 2013) provides robust evidence that conditional transfers are more effective at improving human capital outcomes than unconditional ones.[19] Notably, evidence from Mexico finds that conditionality has a particularly strong effect on the likelihood that elementary school students will continue on to lower secondary school (Brauw and Hoddinott 2011). Further, a meta-analysis by Baird et al. (2014) reveals that, among CCTs, those with stricter conditionality enforcement tend to have larger effects on enrollment and attendance than more permissive ones.

On the other hand, because noncompliance tends to be higher among vulnerable groups, revoking the benefits of noncompliers is counterproductive if reducing poverty is the main priority. This is confirmed by research on Mexico's Progresa/Oportunidades, whose strict conditionality enforcement disproportionately expels the poorest (Alvarez, Devoto, and Winters 2008; González-Flores, Heracleous, and Winters 2012).[20] Experimental research contrasting the effects of conditional and unconditional transfers on adolescent girls in Malawi further highlights this issue (Baird, McIntosh, and Özler 2011). Compared to girls receiving unconditional transfers, those receiving conditional transfers were simultaneously less likely to drop out of school but also, paradoxically, more likely to get married or become pregnant, or both. The latter occurred because noncompliance pushed the most at-risk girls out of the CCT scheme. This made them more likely to drop out of school and thus they were more vulnerable to teen pregnancy and marriage.

CCTs can be tailored to prioritize one objective over the other. Programs can vary not only with regard to conditionality enforcement (weak vs. strong), a dimension highlighted by Cecchini and Martínez (2012), but also in terms of their target populations and approaches to targeting (broad vs. narrow), as well as the formula used for assigning stipend amounts (uniform for all beneficiaries vs. differentiated depending on risk of exiting the school system) (see table 1-1). Thus, CCTs can be designed to prioritize poverty reduction—"basic income CCTs"—or human capital accumulation—"human capital CCTs."

What determines the choice of model? Rodríguez-Castelán (2017, 5) deduces that unconditional transfers will be preferred over conditional ones "if a government has a sufficiently high degree of poverty aversion, that is, if beyond the poverty headcount, it cares about how poor the poor are or how far away from the poverty line the poorest among the poor are living and, thus, about the distributional effects of CCTs on these indicators." It is safe to assume that left-wing governments will be more likely to exhibit "a high degree of poverty aversion" and will thus exhibit a stronger preference for unconditional transfers than their centrist and right-wing counterparts. Yet, as discussed in the previous section and chapter, unconditional transfers are not politically feasible in Latin America at this time. Left-wing governments have had to settle for CCTs. But, as Bolsa Família shows, CCTs can be tailored to emphasize poverty reduction over human capital accumulation.

4.3.1 Contrasting Mexican and Brazilian CCTs

It is thus no coincidence that Brazil, a country where the left dominated politics for three consecutive presidential terms, and Mexico, where the left until very recently was unable to win the presidency, would develop CCTs that differ significantly in the extent to which they prioritize human capital formation and poverty reduction. Progresa/Oportunidades is the product of strong policy consensus behind boosting human capital. Bolsa Família represents a compromise between those seeking to establish a UBI and an electorate that is unsupportive of unconditional social policy. It could thus be described as a "minimum income program with conditionalities" (Cotta 2009, 283).

These differing motivations manifest themselves in terms of targeting, conditionality, and stipend structure (see table 4–1). Tellingly, although both are national in scope, Mexico's program is limited to areas "where there is access and good capability to provide healthcare and education services" (Dávila Lárraga 2016, 8). Thus, some of the most remote and poorest parts of the country are "doubly excluded"—excluded from basic services as well as from poverty relief (Hevia 2011, 343; Yanes 2013, 68–71). With regard to targeting, whereas Mexico's program prioritizes minimizing errors of inclusion, Brazil's is more focused on minimizing errors of exclusion. Whereas Mexico selects beneficiaries using a stringent proxy means test based on observable household characteristics, Brazil relies on self-reported incomes (Lindert et al. 2007; Soares, Ribas, and Osório 2010), a feature that the World Bank has criticized (Briere and Lindert 2005, 13). As a result, "Oportunidades has more efficient targeting than Bolsa Família, but at the price of the program covering fewer poor households" (Soares,

Table 4–1. Contrasting Mexican and Brazilian CCTs (circa 2015)

	Progresa/Oportunidades	Bolsa Escola/Família
Adopted	1997	2001
Initiating President's Ideology	Center-Right	Center
% of Existence under Left-Wing Government	0%	87%
Coverage (2015)[1]	24.11%	27.71%
Coverage—Poverty (2014)[2]	−3.39 percentage points	+9.60 percentage points
Cost as % GDP (2015)[1]	0.42%	0.47%
Program Design[3]		
Geographic Scope	National (in locations with access to healthcare and education services)	National
Target Population	Infants and young children School-aged children	Infants and young children School-aged children Adults in extreme poverty without children
Targeting Mechanism	Proxy means test	Self-reported income
Conditionalities	School attendance (grades 3–12) Health visits (all household members) Participate in health and nutrition workshops (parents and 15 and older)	School attendance (ages 6–17) Health visits (children 0–7 and pregnant/lactating mothers)
Strictness of Conditionality[4]	Monitored and penalties enforced for noncompliance	Monitored but enforcement only after repeated noncompliance
Stipend Structure	Variable by grade and sex One-time bonus for high school completion before age 22	Uniform, except for ages 16–17 (receive larger stipend)
Payment Schedule	10 months/year (school stipends) Year-round (nutrition stipends)	Year-round

Notes: [1.] As a percentage of the country's population (CEPAL 2018); [2.] A positive sign means coverage exceeds the number of poor people living in the country. A negative sign means the opposite. Poverty is measured as the percentage of the population living on less than $4.00 a day in 2014 measured in 2005 dollars at purchasing power parity (SEDLAC 2018). As the most recent poverty data for Mexico at the time of writing was from 2014, I present data for that year. It should be noted that poverty in Brazil increased +two percentage points during 2015, reducing its result to +7.60 percentage points; 3. With the exception of assessment of strictness of conditionality, all data on program design come from Dávila Lárraga (2016) for Mexico and Hellman (2015) for Brazil; [4.] Lindert (2014). For more details, see table 4–3.

Ribas, and Osório 2010, 177). By 2009, Bolsa Família had more beneficiaries than Brazil had poor people (defined as living on $4.00 a day).[21] This remained the case until at least 2015, when coverage surpassed the share of the population living in poverty by 7 percentages points. In contrast, coverage in Mexico has remained 3 to 4 percentage points lower than the share of the population living in poverty (see fig. 4–1).

Table 4–2 compares conditionality enforcement across the two pro-

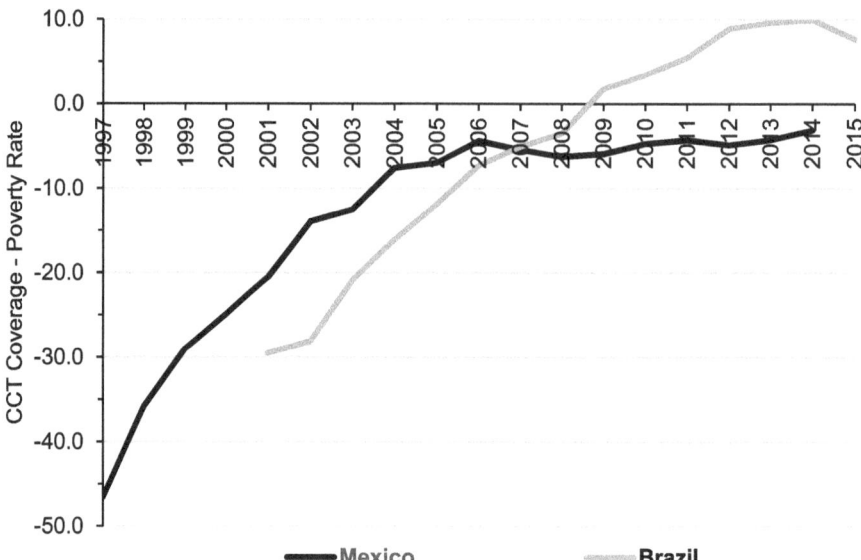

Figure 4-1. Mexico and Brazil: CCT Coverage as a Percent of Population Minus Poverty Rate (>$4.00/day) (1997–2015)
Sources: Coverage defined as number of CCT beneficiaries as a share of a country's population as compiled by the Non-contributory Social Protection Programmes Database (CEPAL 2018).
Poverty is measured as the share of a country's population living on $4.00 or less a day in 2005 dollars at purchasing power parity as estimated by the Socio-Economic Database for Latin America and the Caribbean (SEDLAC 2018).

grams. Mexico follows a stricter, more punitive, approach. Whereas in Brazil initial noncompliance merely leads to a warning, in Mexico it leads to the loss of that month's benefits. In Brazil, a second violation within six months of a warning leads only to a one-month delay in benefits. It is only after a third violation that benefits are lost. Progresa/Oportunidades expels beneficiaries for the remainder of the school year if they violate conditionality during three months or accumulate 12 unexcused absences (Dávila Lárraga 2016, 33). In practice, it is quite difficult to be entirely expelled from Bolsa Família. As Soares (2012, 327) notes, "Noncompliance with co-responsibilities is a sign that a family faces an additional vulnerability. A social worker should verify the reasons for the family failing to uphold the co-responsibilities and also help it to overcome these difficulties."

The programs also differ with regard to stipends. Tellingly, whereas new

CCT beneficiaries in Mexico are required to comply with conditionalities for a month before receiving their first stipend, Brazilian beneficiaries receive their first payment upon enrollment (Bastagli 2008, 99). Furthermore, in contrast to Bolsa Família, which operates year-round, Progresa/Oportunidades education stipends are paid only during the 10-month school year.[22] Because the opportunity costs associated with choosing school over work increase as students become older, Mexico's stipends increase with each grade starting in third grade.[23] And, because girls have

Table 4–2. Mexican vs. Brazilian CCT: Penalties for Noncompliance

	Progresa/Oportunidades	Bolsa Familia
Condition	May not have more than four unjustified absences in a month or more than 12 in a school year.	Must maintain 85% monthly attendance if under 15 or 75% if 16–17 years old.
First Violation	**Suspension:** does not receive that month's benefit.	**Warning:** no consequences. Receives benefit without financial repercussion. Warning is valid for six months. If after those six months the family has a new episode of noncompliance, a new warning is issued.
Second Violation	**Suspension:** does not receive that month's benefit.	**Blockage:** benefit blocked for 30 days, after which family receives the accumulated benefit (previous and current month).
Third Violation	**Termination:** does not receive that month's benefit. Excluded from the program for the remainder of the school year.	**First Suspension**: benefit suspended for 60 days. After the 60-day period, the family receives current month benefit but without any accumulation
Fourth Violation	N/A	**Second Suspension**: If the family continues to fail to comply a second time during the six months following the last suspension, benefits are again suspended for 60 days. After the 60-day period, the family receives the current month's benefit but without any accumulation.
Fifth Violation	N/A	**Termination**: Benefit can only be canceled if family is in second suspension phase; if there has been monitoring by social assistance services, and if the conditions of noncompliance continued for longer than a 12-month period.

Sources: Dávila Lárraga (2016, 33–34); Hellman (2015, 18–19); and Lindert et al. (2007, 60).

historically received less schooling than boys, they receive larger stipends beginning in seventh grade. Furthermore, given its emphasis on human capital, Progresa/Oportunidades pays a one-time stipend to beneficiaries who graduate from high school by age 22. In line with its roots in the basic income movement, Bolsa Família pays all households living in extreme poverty an unconditional base stipend regardless of whether they have children. The CCT component provides a flat stipend for each child under 15. Breaking with this mold, in 2008 the program began providing a more generous stipend for 16 and 17 year olds. Beyond this, the program includes a supplemental subsidy determined on a case-by-case basis for families that remain in extreme poverty after receiving benefits.

Finally, the two programs differ in the extent to which they prioritize rigorous evaluation. As Morais (2017, 151) notes, "Most evaluations of Bolsa Família have been done on a small scale and quietly, whereas Oportunidades/Progresa set up an evaluation unit since its beginning and has made its evaluations internationally available" (see also Sugiyama 2012b, 181). The Mexican government has worked closely with researchers to evaluate all aspects of the program's operation and particularly its effects on human capital. In contrast, there is relatively little research on Bolsa Família's effects on education (Morais 2017, 137). This also reflects their differing priorities. If cash transfers are envisioned as tools to boost human capital, it is necessary to prove that they in fact improve enrollment, attendance, and other relevant indicators. If transfers are envisioned as a right owed to all citizens, there is little need to evaluate their effectiveness. The transfers are justified on moral grounds.

4.4 Conclusion

Contrasting the intellectual history and design of the region's largest and best-known anti-poverty programs, this chapter has demonstrated that not all CCTs are created equal. Policymakers have significant flexibility with regard to CCT design and can tailor programs to more heavily prioritize either human capital accumulation or poverty reduction. In Mexico, a group of neoliberal technocrats supported by a president who shared their vision created Progresa/Oportunidades, a highly targeted program with strict conditionality enforcement and variable stipends. In Brazil, policymakers influenced by the basic income movement transformed the CCTs they inherited into Bolsa Família, a program with broader targeting, permissive conditionality enforcement, and (mostly) uniform stipends.

What explains the choice of CCT model? Granted, as shown in chapter 2 and earlier research (Díaz-Cayeros and Magaloni 2009; Sugiyama 2011), there is no direct link between ideology and likelihood of CCT adoption. Yet the expansion in coverage and transformation in design of Bolsa Família under center-left leaders detailed in the previous chapter and the design differences presented in this chapter between Brazil's CCT and that of Mexico, where the left had not been in power, suggest that ideology may in fact influence CCT design. The Mexican right enacted a human capital CCT. The Brazilian left reformed the program it inherited in a basic income direction. It is quite likely that Bolsa Família would more closely resemble a UBI had the left not met with political and popular backlash against lax conditionality enforcement.

Relying on cross-national data, the next chapter systematically tests whether CCTs operated by left-wing governments cover more people than those operated by centrist and right-wing governments and whether presidential ideology influences program design.

PART 2

Ideology and the Diffusion of CCTs

CHAPTER 5

The Effect of Presidential Ideology on CCT Scope and Design

A Quantitative Test

Chapter 3 told the story of how Lula, while slow to embrace conditional cash transfer programs, combined and dramatically expanded the programs inherited from his centrist predecessor. The previous chapter demonstrated that the region's most iconic anti-poverty programs, Mexico's Progresa/Oportunidades and Brazil's Bolsa Família, represent two distinct models of CCT programs and their differences are, in turn, attributable to ideological differences between the presidents who governed those countries and, ultimately, controlled the programs. Thus, Mexico's right-wing presidents enacted and expanded a human capital CCT, a program featuring narrow means-tested targeting of beneficiaries and strict enforcement of program conditionality centered on building human capital. In contrast, Brazil's left transformed the upstart Bolsa Escola into Bolsa Família, a basic income CCT. Compared with its Mexican counterpart, Brazil's program is more universal in scope and substantially less punitive in enforcement of the program conditions. For the Brazilian left building human capital over the long term took a back seat to short-term poverty reduction.

But how generalizable are the Mexican and Brazilian experiences to the rest of the region? This chapter addresses this question through a series of quantitative tests. The first set of tests assesses whether CCTs operated by left-wing governments have a broader scope than those operated by centrist and right-wing governments. This is done through time-series cross-sectional regressions of the determinants of various measures of CCT coverage and spending across 18 Latin American countries over a 20-year period. Further regressions assess whether left-wing governments increase CCT coverage in response to poverty and inequality and whether nonleft governments increase coverage in response to weak educational attainment and high levels of child labor. Regressions, however, constitute only a rough test of the book's argument, which is about overall program *design* and not just program *scope* or *coverage*. The final part of the chapter analyzes the design of the 10 CCTs adopted following the Brazilian left's "invention" of the basic income model. Programs are assessed in terms of the scope of the target population, strictness of conditionality enforcement, and stipend structure.

The three analyses confirm that presidential ideology does indeed shape CCT design across the region. The regressions find that in countries governed by the left CCTs come 1.29–1.51 percentage points closer to covering the entirety of a country's poor population than in countries governed by the center or right. Similarly, CCTs in countries governed by the left tend to cover an additional 1.30–1.61% of a country's population compared to those operated by nonleft presidents. Furthermore, left-wing presidents proved more responsive to a country's levels of poverty and inequality than their nonleft counterparts. The greater the share of a country's population living in poverty and the more unequal its income distribution, the larger the effect on CCT coverage of having a left-wing president. Furthermore, the analysis of program design confirms that CCTs enacted and operated by centrist and right-wing presidents tend to closely resemble Mexico's Progresa/Oportunidades and the human capital model. Programs enacted and operated by the left resemble the basic income model. In fact, countries where the left enacted a CCT from scratch and where the entirety of a program's existence has taken place under a left-wing president, namely Argentina, Bolivia, and Uruguay, operate programs that come closer to the basic income model than even Brazil's ambitious Bolsa Família.

Taken together these tests provide strong evidence supporting this book's central claim: there exist two distinct models of CCTs in Latin America and the choice of model is determined by presidential ideology. The following section begins the analysis by discussing cross-national differences in CCT coverage levels.

5.1 Testing for Determinants of CCT Scope

To test whether CCTs operated by left-wing presidents are broader in scope than those operated by right-wing and centrist presidents, this section estimates a series of time-series cross-sectional regressions on the determinants of various measures of CCT coverage as well as the amount governments spend on CCTs each year. The analysis covers 1996, the year before the launch of Mexico's pioneering program, through 2015, the last year for which data was available.

5.1.1 Hypotheses and Measurement

Dependent variables. The main measure of CCT scope tested is the difference between the share of a country's population enrolled in a CCT and the share of that country's population living in poverty (measured as having income of less than $4.00 a day) during a given year.[1] Poverty data comes from the Socio-Economic Database for Latin America and the Caribbean (SEDLAC 2018). CCT data come from and the Economic Commission for Latin America and the Caribbean's (CEPAL) Non-contributory Social Protection Programmes Database (CEPAL 2018).

Assuming that the left aspires to establish a basic income guarantee, it would be expected to offer coverage levels that come close to or even exceed the share of the population living in poverty. Focusing on human capital rather than poverty relief, let alone on creating an income floor, nonleft governments would, at most, be expected to limit coverage to the poor and, possibly, only to specific segments of the population with particularly severe human capital deficiencies.

The second measure is simply the share of a country's population enrolled in a CCT during a given year. Although a less precise measure of the underlying concept studied in this book than the prior variable, coverage is more straightforward and thus allows for a more intuitive presentation of the findings.

CCT coverage varies substantially by both country and year. With regard to the former, average coverage levels during the period of study range from zero in Venezuela to about 18% of the population in Brazil and Mexico (see fig. 5–1).[2] The unweighted average of the share of national populations benefiting from CCTs grew steadily from the launch of the first national-level program in 1997 until 2011, when it peaked at an average of 13.2%. It then declined slightly during each of the following four years to 11.7% in 2015 (see fig. 5–2).

As robustness checks, scope is also measured in terms of year-on-year change in the percentage of a country's population covered by CCTs and

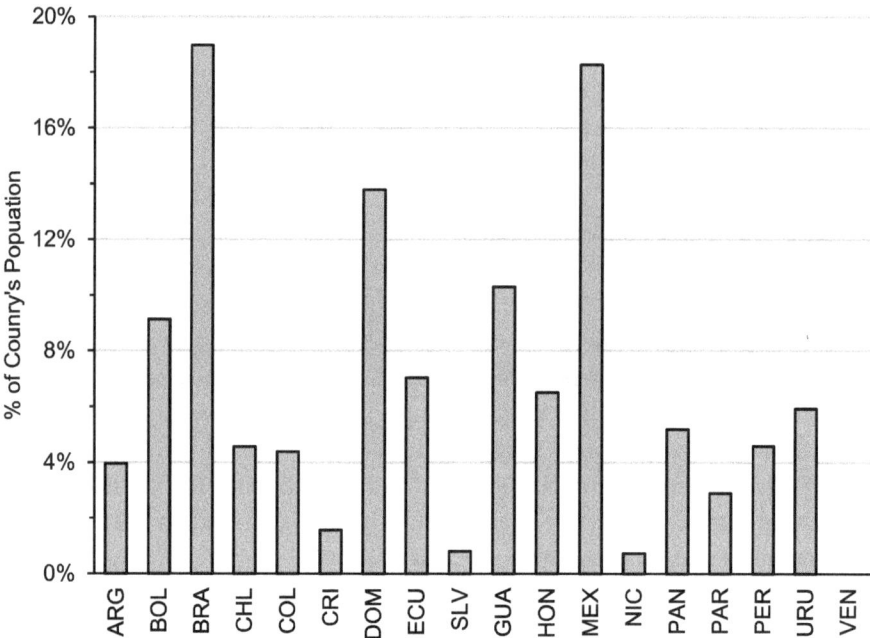

Figure 5-1. Average CCT Coverage in 18 Countries (1996–2015)
Source: Own calculations based on Non-contributory Social Protection Programmes Database (CEPAL 2018).

spending on CCTs as a percentage of GDP, both of which are reported by CEPAL (2018).

Key explanatory variable. Presidential ideology is measured dichotomously (left versus nonleft) based on assessments by country experts compiled in the Dataset on Political Ideology of Presidents and Parties in Latin America (Murillo, Oliveros, and Vaishnav 2010).[3] Some models disaggregate the dichotomous measure of ideology, replacing it with an index of presidential ideology ranging from right (1) to left (5).

Left-leaning presidents were in power during 32.5% of the country-years analyzed (123 of 378). A simple comparison of means reveals a substantial difference in average levels of the two dependent variables under left-wing and nonleft presidents. Coverage as a share of the population averaged 9.33% under the left compared to 5.14% under the center and right. This difference is even larger when excluding Venezuela (10.8%), where the left-wing Chavista regime controlled the presidency during most

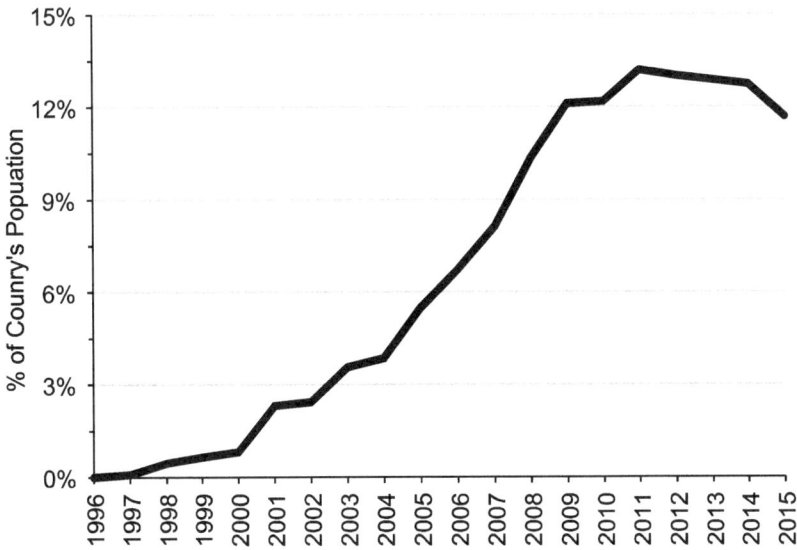

Figure 5-2. Unweighted Average of CCT Coverage for 18 Countries (1996–2015)
Source: Own calculations based on Non-contributory Social Protection Programmes Database (CEPAL 2018).

of the period of study but never adopted a CCT. A similar pattern is present when subtracting the poverty rate from coverage. That figure ranges from -33.93 percentage points under nonleft governments to -22.23 percentage points under left ones (see fig. 5–3).

Based on the arguments presented in previous chapters, the following can be expected:

> **H1a:** *Countries with left-wing presidents will have CCT coverage levels that come closer to or even exceed the share of the population living in poverty relative to countries with centrist or right-wing presidents.*
> **H1b:** *CCTs controlled by left-wing presidents will cover a larger share of a country's population than those in countries with centrist or right-wing presidents.*
> **H1c:** *Countries with left-wing presidents will increase CCT coverage at a faster rate than those with centrist or right-wing presidents.*
> **H1d:** *Countries with left-wing presidents will spend more on CCTs than countries with centrist or right-wing presidents.*

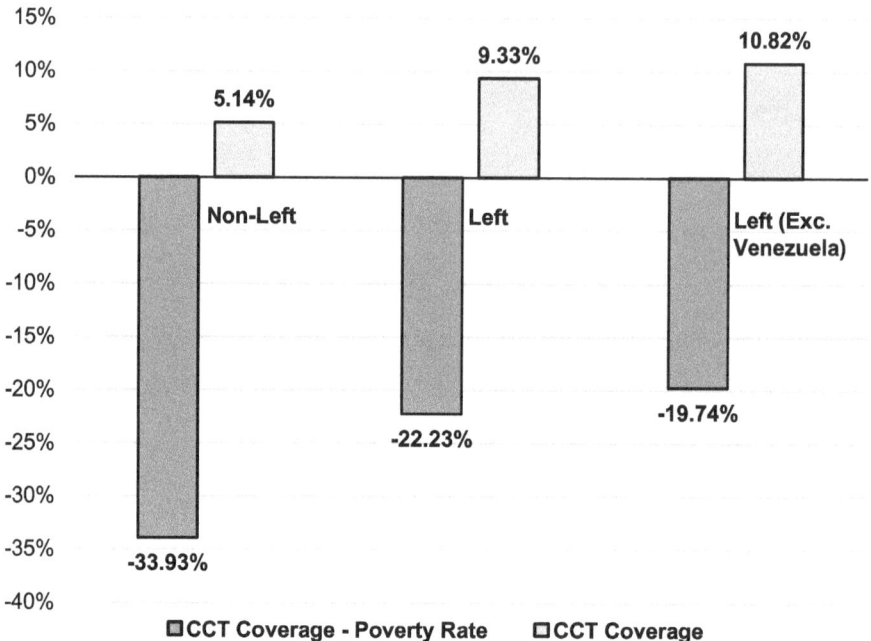

Figure 5-3. Unweighted Average of the Main Dependent Variables by Presidential Ideology (1996–2015)
Source: Own calculations based on SEDLAC (2018) and CEPAL (2018).

Other Explanatory Variables

Objective need for CCTs. CCTs serve two, at times contradictory, objectives: reducing poverty over the short run and increasing human capital over the long run. The models will test to what extent CCT scope is explained by those policy objectives.

Poverty reduction motive. The objective need for programs to address poverty is measured in terms of both level of poverty, measured as the share of a country's population living in poverty (defined as having an income of less than $4.00 a day), and the level of income inequality, measured in terms of the Gini coefficient. The poverty data was compiled by SEDLAC (2018).[4] The inequality data comes from the Standardized World Income Inequality Database (Solt 2016).

Human capital motive. Given that CCTs seek to address deficiencies in human capital, coverage should be higher in countries with low levels of educational attainment and where a substantial share of the school-age population tends to prematurely exit the education system. Education attainment is measured as the average years of schooling among 15–24 year olds as reported in the Education Attainment Dataset (Barro and Lee 2013). Child labor is measured as the share of 5–14 year olds in the workforce as compiled by the United Nations Children's Fund (UNICEF 2018).

Political variables. CCTs select beneficiaries through transparent, rules-based criteria. Such rules do not, however, eliminate the possibility that the electorate will, in an act of retrospective voting, reward politicians who expand CCTs. There is, after all, robust evidence from across the region that CCT beneficiaries disproportionately support incumbent governments (Layton and Smith 2015; Manacorda, Miguel, and Vigorito 2011; De La O 2013; Zucco 2013) even when those governments merely inherited their programs (Díaz-Cayeros, Estevez, and Magaloni 2009; Zucco 2013) and may even tip the balance in particularly close presidential races (Díaz-Cayeros, Estevez, and Magaloni 2009; Zucco 2015). Thus, it can be expected that presidents will expand the scope of CCTs prior to an election. This temptation is captured though a dichotomous variable identifying whether a presidential election was held during a given year.

However, the ability of presidents to increase coverage for political gain will be constrained by the existence of strong checks on their authority, most notably the presence of divided government and the existence of a large number of veto players (Tsebelis 2002). Following De La O (2015), constraints on the executive are measured using an index derived from the Database of Political Institutions (Scartascini, Cruz, and Keefer 2018).[5]

Presidents could also be tempted to expand CCT coverage as a means of diffusing political tensions, such as protests. This is captured through a count variable tallying up the total number of major antigovernment demonstrations and riots in a country during a given year.[6] This data was compiled by the Cross-National Time-Series data archive (Banks 2011).

International context. Previous chapters and prior studies, both qualitative (Lana and Evans 2004; Ancelovici and Jenson 2013) and quantitative (Sugiyama 2011; Brooks 2015; Osorio Gonnet 2018, chap. 4), have shown that, in enacting and expanding CCTs, Latin American presidents were emulating their neighbors. Diffusion is incorporated into the models through a measure of the share of countries in Latin America (excluding the one in question) with CCTs. This measure ranges from a value of zero for Mexico during the first years of its pioneering program to a value of 94%

for Nicaragua and Venezuela during 2008–15, when every other country in the sample had a CCT.

Additional controls. CCTs may substitute for other human capital investment programs. To account for this, models control for human capital spending (education plus healthcare) as a share of GDP as reported by CEPAL (2018). Regardless of political conditions, CCT coverage in a country is likely to be influenced by the size of the school-age population, which is incorporated into the models as the percentage of a country's population under 15 as reported in the World Bank's (2020) World Development Indicators. In addition, CCT expansion, like all policy objectives, may be constrained by lack of resources. Financial constraints are operationalized as the government's total tax intake as a percentage of GDP as compiled by the Organization of Economic Development and Cooperation (2018) and the country's external debt, also as a percent of GDP. Additionally, the models control for GDP per capita and annual GDP growth rate. These last three measures were obtained from the World Development Indicators (World Bank 2020).

5.1.2 Estimation Technique

The statistical technique used to estimate the models merits discussion. The models are estimated using ordinary least squares with panel-corrected standard errors , incorporate country-fixed effects, and correct for first-order auto-regression (Beck and Katz 1995). Panel-corrected standard errors help mitigate many of the problems inherent to regression analyses involving several countries over time. Time-series cross-sectional data are problematic in that they tend to be both cross-sectionally correlated and heteroskedastic. With regard to the former, CCT expansion is an example of policy diffusion, and, as such, coverage in one country is likely influenced by coverage in another. On the latter, errors have different variances across units and these variances tend to be correlated with the size of the unit studied (i.e., error terms for countries with high coverage levels tend to be larger than those for countries with lower coverage levels).

Country-fixed effects are used to control for country-specific characteristics that are not adequately captured by the model's explanatory variables. This is necessary because these types of data may conceal unit and period effects—coverage may be influenced by conditions unique to a particular country or reflect causal heterogeneity across time and space, or both. In other words, the factors that explain the dependent variable may not be the same across all countries in the sample or during the entirety of the period of study, or both. Fixed effects minimize these risks as well as the risk of omitting an explanatory variable that significantly affects CCT scope.

Correcting for first-order auto-regression helps address the problems stemming from the "stickiness" of coverage levels—coverage during a given year is largely determined by coverage during the previous year, meaning that the vast majority of beneficiaries during a given year were also beneficiaries during the previous one.

As an additional check of the robustness of the results, some models estimate year-fixed effects. Furthermore, to reduce the likelihood of endogeneity, all of the independent variables, with the exception of presidential ideology, election year, and checks and balances, are lagged by one year.

5.1.3 Results

Before proceeding to the full models, the analysis begins by estimating the effects of having a left-wing president on CCT coverage minus the poverty rate while only controlling for fixed effects. The goal in doing this is to demonstrate that the effect of having a left-wing president does not depend on the inclusion or exclusion of any particular explanatory variable. The results presented in table 5-1 confirm that having a left-wing president has a positive and statistically significant effect on the dependent variable. This is true for models with country-fixed effects (model 1-1), year-fixed effects (model 1-2), and for both types of fixed effects simultaneously (model 1-3).

Table 5-1. Preliminary Time-Series Cross-Section Analysis of CCT Coverage (as % of Population) Minus Poverty Rate (1996–2015)

	(1–1)	(1–2)	(1–3)
Left President	3.570***	2.793**	4.201***
	(1.052)	(1.048)	(1.108)
Constant	−17.988***	−28.708***	−15.428***
	(3.812)	(2.602)	(3.353)
Observations	331	331	331
R-squared	0.506	0.426	0.742
Country-Fixed Effects	YES	NO	YES
Year-Fixed Effects	NO	YES	YES

Standard errors in parenthesis.
+p <=0.1 *p <=0.5; ** p <=0.01; *** <=0.001 in two-tailed test.

The models incorporating the full range of explanatory variables are presented in table 5-2. In line with expectations, these models find that left-wing presidents increase coverage to levels closer to covering the entirety of the poor population. Moving from a nonleft to a left-wing president is associated with an increase in the dependent variable of between 1.29 (model 2-5) and 1.73 percentage points (model 2-4) depending on the model specification. The results hold when the dichotomous measure of ideology is replaced with the five-point index (models 2-7 and 2-8), implying that the farther left a president is, the closer a country's CCT will come to covering or even surpassing the entirety of the poor population. Moving from a far-right (1) to a far-left president (5) would be associated with an increase in the dependent variable between 2.86 (model 2-8) and 3.10 (model 2-7) percentage points. However, although presidential ideology's effect is robust to all specifications tested that control for country-fixed effects, it fails to achieve statistical significance in one of the models that controls for year-fixed effects (model 2-6).

The two poverty reduction motive variables—poverty rate and income inequality—have robust and statistically significant *negative* effects.[7] Thus, the higher the poverty rate and the more unequal a country, the less likely CCT coverage is to extend to the entirety of the poor population. The results for the human capital motive variables—average years of schooling and child labor—are mixed. In most models, the more schooling a country's population has on average, the closer coverage comes to reaching all of a country's poor. Child labor does not achieve statistical significance in any of the models tested. Similarly, none of the political variables—whether there is an election during a given year, the level of checks and balances on the executive, or the number of protests—achieve significance in any of the models.

With regard to the control variables, human capital spending does not have a statistically significant effect on the outcome studied (models 2-1 and 2-2). Since the inclusion of this variable significantly reduces the sample of cases (from 331 to 284), it is excluded from subsequent models. The share of the population under 15 and GDP per capita have consistent statistically significant negative and positive effects, respectively. There is some evidence that financial constraints limit CCT scope. Levels of debt and tax collection have the expected signs but their statistical significance is not robust. GDP growth does not affect this measure of CCT scope.

Discussion now turns to table 5-3, which presents the result for CCT coverage and other measures of scope. Countries governed by the left con-

Table 5-2. Time-Series Cross-Section Analysis of CCT Coverage (as % of Population) Minus Poverty Rate (1996–2015)

	(2-1)	(2-2)	(2-3)	(2-4)	(2-5)	(2-6)	(2-7)	(2-8)
Left President?	1.549**	1.639*	1.507**	1.728*	1.294**	1.350	—	—
	(0.511)	(0.799)	(0.500)	(0.795)	(0.492)	(0.888)		
Pres. Ideology Index	—	—	—	—	—	—	0.620**	0.571**
							(0.217)	(0.206)
Poverty Rate	−0.906**	—	−0.955***	—	−0.953***	—	−0.951***	−0.952***
	(0.059)		(0.056)		(0.052)		(0.055)	(0.051)
Gini Coefficient	—	−1.628***	—	−1.554***	—	−0.591*	—	—
		(0.313)		(0.359)		(0.280)		
Avg. Years of Schooling	0.917*	—	1.018**	—	1.002*	—	0.963*	0.927+
	(0.380)		(0.392)		(0.499)		(0.396)	(0.504)
Child Labor	—	0.066	—	0.085	—	0.161	—	—
		(0.123)		(0.123)		(0.108)		
Diffusion	2.846*	0.667	3.374*	1.401	—	—	3.512*	—
	(1.442)	(1.789)	(1.438)	(1.974)			(1.425)	
President Election Year?	−0.317	−0.454	−0.133	−0.168	−0.105	−0.107	−0.148	−0.118
	(0.229)	(0.348)	(0.214)	(0.320)	(0.223)	(0.347)	(0.221)	(0.226)
Checks and Balances	−0.404+	−0.636+	−0.117	−0.199	−0.117	−0.142	−0.140	−0.133
	(0.237)	(0.354)	(0.212)	(0.336)	(0.224)	(0.377)	(0.208)	(0.217)
Protests	−0.091	−0.125	−0.077	−0.092	−0.015	−0.020	−0.089	−0.027
	(0.059)	(0.077)	(0.059)	(0.079)	(0.073)	(0.105)	(0.062)	(0.075)
Human Capital Spending	−0.685+	−0.062	—	—	—	—	—	—
	(0.378)	(0.526)						
% of Pop. under 15	−0.768**	−1.428***	−0.649**	−1.586***	0.442*	−1.459***	−0.670**	0.445*
	(0.263)	(0.432)	(0.239)	(0.371)	(0.217)	(0.357)	(0.241)	(0.217)
Taxes to GDP	0.536***	0.739**	0.256*	0.396+	0.212+	0.194	0.250+	0.216+
	(0.145)	(0.225)	(0.128)	(0.219)	(0.124)	(0.166)	(0.130)	(0.125)
Debt to GDP	0.002	−0.086***	0.008	−0.054**	−0.017	−0.084***	0.008	−0.017
	(0.014)	(0.020)	(0.011)	(0.017)	(0.012)	(0.020)	(0.012)	(0.013)
GDP Growth	−0.027	0.029	0.018	0.038	−0.010	0.059	0.018	−0.007
	(0.032)	(0.057)	(0.032)	(0.055)	(0.036)	(0.076)	(0.032)	(0.036)
GDP per Capita	0.427*	1.109***	0.461*	1.392***	0.130	1.402***	0.463*	0.123
	(0.168)	(0.212)	(0.182)	(0.227)	(0.246)	(0.330)	(0.184)	(0.251)
Constant	11.730	77.442***	13.041	82.669***	−15.245	38.647**	12.953	−15.737
	(10.713)	(20.535)	(9.428)	(21.385)	(10.055)	(12.135)	(9.591)	(9.887)
Observations	284	284	331	331	331	331	331	331
R-squared	0.890	0.839	0.894	0.807	0.832	0.715	0.895	0.832
Country-Fixed Effects	YES	YES	YES	YES	NO	NO	YES	NO
Year-Fixed Effects	NO	NO	NO	NO	YES	YES	NO	YES

Standard errors in parenthesis. +p <=0.1 *p <=0.5; ** p <=0.01; *** <=0.001 in two-tailed test.

Table 5-3. Time-Series Cross-Section Analysis of CCT Scope (1996–2015)

Dependent Variable	(3-1) CCT Coverage (% Pop.)	(3-2) CCT Coverage (% Pop.)	(3-3) Annual Δ in CCT Coverage	(3-4) CCT Spending (% GDP)	(3-5) CCT Coverage (% Pop.)	(3-6) CCT Coverage (% Pop.)	(3-7) CCT Coverage (% Pop.)	(3-8) CCT Coverage (% Pop.)
Left President?	1.612**	1.296*	1.299**	0.065***	-1.564+	-28.129**	—	—
	(0.494)	(0.590)	(0.502)	(0.016)	(0.915)	(7.118)		
Nonleft President	—	—	—	—	—	—	-4.996	1.725+
							(3.947)	(0.939)
Poverty Rate	0.059	—	—	0.017	0.017	—	0.041	—
	(0.053)			(0.059)	(0.059)		(0.057)	
Gini Coefficient	—	0.504*	0.357**	-0.004	—	-0.569*	—	-0.242
		(0.214)	(0.128)	(0.006)		(0.244)		(0.216)
Left*Poverty	—	—	—	—	0.085**	—	—	—
					(0.028)			
Left*Gini	—	—	—	—	—	0.622***	—	—
						(0.153)		
Avg. Years of Schooling	1.116***	—	—	—	0.904*	—	0.668	—
	(0.334)				(0.410)		(0.505)	
Child Labor	—	-0.024	0.044	-0.007***	—	-0.021	—	0.078
		(0.074)	(0.047)	(0.002)		(0.083)		(0.086)
Nonleft*Schooling	—	—	—	—	—	—	0.411	—
							(0.446)	
Nonleft*Child Labor	—	—	—	—	—	—	—	-0.244***
								(0.067)
President Election Year?	-0.108	-0.083	-0.107	0.012+	2.616**	2.339*	2.630**	2.532*
	(0.205)	(0.200)	(0.277)	(0.007)	(0.887)	(1.061)	(0.883)	(1.034)
Checks and Balances	-0.116	-0.074	-0.304+	-0.000	0.036	0.093	0.022	0.097
	(0.211)	(0.221)	(0.158)	(0.006)	(0.231)	(0.236)	(0.227)	(0.226)
Checks*Election Year	—	—	—	—	-0.734**	-0.666*	-0.747**	-0.730*
					(0.246)	(0.290)	(0.245)	(0.286)
Constant	22.211**	-21.551	-19.261*	0.344	11.975	45.256**	17.145+	32.271*
	(8.281)	(13.605)	(9.155)	(0.382)	(10.013)	(16.124)	(9.572)	(14.891)
Observations	331	357	339	377	331	357	331	357
R-squared	0.273	0.151	0.122	0.402		0.429	0.383	0.417
Country-Fixed Effects	YES	NO	YES	YES	YES	YES	YES	YES
Year-Fixed Effects	NO	YES	NO	NO	NO	NO	NO	NO

Standard errors in parenthesis. +p <=0.1 *p <=0.5; ** p <=0.01; *** <=0.001 in two-tailed test. For brevity the table excludes coefficient estimates and standard errors for diffusion, protests, population under 15, tax take, debt, GDP growth, and GDP per capita.

sistently have higher coverage as a share of their populations (models 3–1 and 3–2), expand coverage at a faster rate (model 3–3), and spend more on their programs (model 3–4). The effect of ideology holds when the dichotomous measure of ideology is replaced with the five-point index (not shown).

Moving from a nonleft to a left-wing president is associated with an increase in CCT coverage of between 1.30 (model 3–2) and 1.61% of a country's population (model 3–1). Although this may appear small at first glance, its magnitude is substantively larger when presented in terms of the number of people affected. To put it in perspective, the models estimated that, had Mexico had a left-wing president in 2005, an additional 1.41–1.75 million people would have been enrolled in Progresa/Oportunidades. Conversely, had the left not controlled Brazil's presidency that year, an estimated 2.42–3.01 million fewer people would have been enrolled in Bolsa Família. Even in Uruguay, the least populous country in the sample, having a left-wing government is estimated to have extended coverage to an additional 43,000–54,000 people in 2005. Table 5–4 provides estimates for all of the countries in the sample.

Discussion now turns to the results of the individual models. Model 3–1

Table 5–4. Estimated Effect of Having a Left-Wing President on CCT Coverage by Country

Country	Total Population in 2005 (in Millions)	Lower-Bound Estimate (1.29%)	Upper-Bound Estimate (1.61%.)
Argentina	39.15	507,326	631,025
Bolivia	9.13	118,265	147,102
Brazil	186.92	2,422,449	3,013,108
Chile	16.15	209,266	260,291
Colombia	43.29	560,982	697,764
Costa Rica	4.25	55,052	68,475
Dominican Republic	9.24	119,719	148,910
Ecuador	13.74	178,009	221,412
El Salvador	6.03	78,135	97,187
Guatemala	13.10	169,725	211,108
Honduras	7.37	95,560	118,860
Mexico	108.47	1,405,800	1,748,572
Nicaragua	5.38	69,716	86,715
Panama	3.33	43,163	53,687
Paraguay	5.80	75,110	93,423
Peru	27.61	357,831	445,080
Uruguay	3.33	43,100	53,609
Venezuela	26.78	347,123	431,761

Source: Own calculations based on table 5–3 and population data from World Bank (2018).

finds that left-wing presidents are associated with an additional 1.61 percentage points of coverage. The results for the human capital motive are significant but in the opposite direction to what was predicted: average school attainment has a positive and significant effect. Thus, paradoxically, CCT coverage tends to be higher in the countries that least need policies designed to keep children in school. Each additional year in average schooling is estimated to increase coverage by 1.12 percentage points. As an example, moving from the average level of schooling reported by Guatemala, the sample's worst performer (5.10 years), to that of Chile, its best performer (10.03 years), would increase CCT coverage by 5.52 percentage points, about half the region's average level of coverage in 2015.

There is no evidence, however, that the poverty reduction motive or the political context influence coverage levels. Neither the poverty rate, the strength of checks on the government, whether elections are held in a given year, nor the intensity of public protests affect coverage levels.

Model 3–2 replaces poverty with inequality, years of schooling with child labor, and controls for year rather than country-fixed effects. Left-wing presidents are associated with an additional 1.30 percentage points of coverage. The Gini coefficient has a positive and statistically significant effect, meaning more unequal countries tend to cover a larger share of their populations. As an example, moving from the average level inequality reported in Uruguay, the sample's most egalitarian country (0.4074), to that of Colombia, the most unequal (0.5153), would increase CCT coverage by 5.43 percentage points, slightly less than that half the regional average in 2015. With regard to the human capital motive, child labor is negatively signed but fails to achieve statistical significance. The results for the remaining variables are similar to those of model 3–1.

The next two models analyze the effect of having a left-wing president on alternative measures of program scope. In line with De La O (2015, 103), CCT coverage in countries with left-wing presidents increases at a faster rate, with an estimated 1.30% more of a country's population than under centrist and right-wing presidents (model 3–3). This represents more than twice the average rate of annual growth in coverage reported in the sample (0.63% of the population). Countries governed by left-wing presidents tend to spend an additional 0.07% of GDP on CCTs than those with nonleft presidents (model 3–4). This result is substantively significant, amounting to about two-thirds of the region's average level of CCT spending in 2005 (0.10% of GDP) or slightly more than a quarter of average spending in 2015 (0.26% of GDP).

5.2 Do the Left and Nonleft Have Different Priorities?

The models discussed above confirm that left-wing governments provide greater CCT coverage, expand coverage at a faster rate, and spend more on these types of programs. Based on the experiences of pioneering CCTs in Mexico and Brazil, the previous chapter argued that left and nonleft politicians are attracted to CCTs for different reasons. Whereas center-left Brazilian president Lula da Silva and his Workers' Party saw Bolsa Família primarily as a means of reducing poverty, center-right Mexican president Ernesto Zedillo (1994–2000) and the team of technocrats behind Progresa/Oportunidades saw their program primarily as a tool for boosting human capital.

To test the generalizability of these claims, multiplicative terms are added to the previous models with the aim of capturing the interaction between presidential ideology and the variables measuring the objective need for CCTs, namely poverty, inequality, school attainment, and child labor. Based on the Mexican and Brazilian experiences it can be expected that

> **H2:** *Left-wing presidents will increase CCT coverage in response to severe poverty and inequality.*
> **H3:** *Nonleft presidents will increase coverage in response to low school attainment and high levels of child labor.*

The results are presented in the final four models of table 5–3. Most notably and consistent with the predictions on the left's vision of CCTs, the models reveal that CCT coverage under left-wing presidents increases in line with both the poverty rate (model 3–5) and level of income inequality (model 3–6). In contrast, there is no support for predictions regarding the drivers of CCT coverage among nonleft governments. In fact, and against expectations, coverage under nonleft presidents actually *declines* in line with the share of children in the workforce (model 3–8). There is no evidence of an interaction between levels of schooling and presidential ideology (model 3–7).

Properly assessing the direction and magnitude of interaction terms requires going beyond discussing coefficients and p-values by plotting their estimated consequences and respective confidence intervals (Brambor, Roberts Clark, and Golder 2006). Based on model 3–5, figure 5–4 visually captures how the poverty rate affects CCT coverage under left-wing presi-

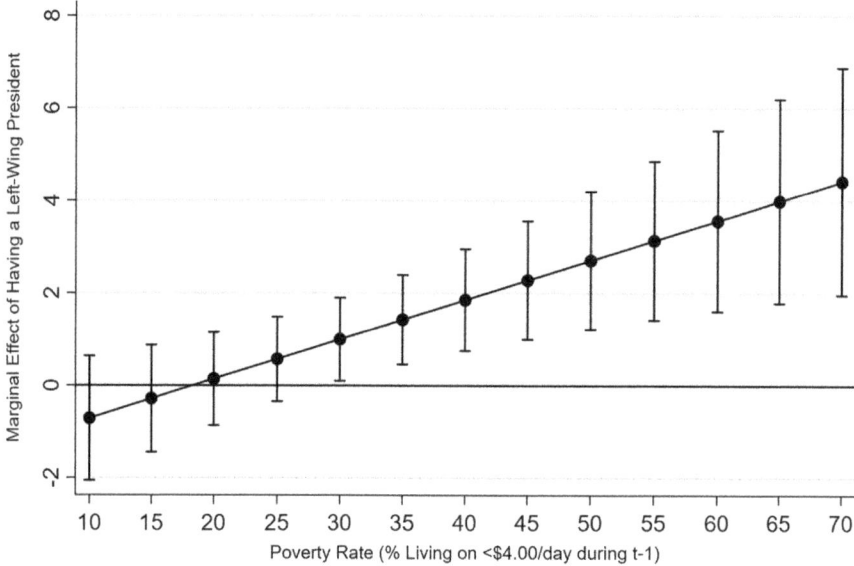

Figure 5-4. Marginal Effect of Having a Left-Wing President on CCT Coverage at Different Poverty Levels
Source: Table 5-3, Model 3–5.

dents. The previously discussed effect is statistically different from zero only at poverty levels above 29%, a level well below the sample average (37.39%). In practice, this means that, under a left-wing presidency, a one-standard-deviation increase in the poverty rate (15.79 percentage points) is associated with an increase in CCT coverage of approximately 1.35 percentage points. Put another way, if a country's poverty rate were to increase from the regional average to the average level reported by Honduras (61.25%), the region's worst performer, having a left-wing president would be expected to increase coverage by 2.04 percentage points.

Figure 5–5 captures how income inequality affects CCT coverage under left-wing presidents (model 3–6). The effect is statistically different from zero at Gini coefficient levels above 0.472, just above the sample average (0.471). This means that, under a left-wing president, a one-standard-deviation increase in the Gini coefficient (0.386) would be associated with an increase in CCT coverage of approximately 2.40 percentage points. Put another way, if a country's Gini coefficient increased from 0.475 to the average level reported by Colombia (0.515), the region's worst performer, hav-

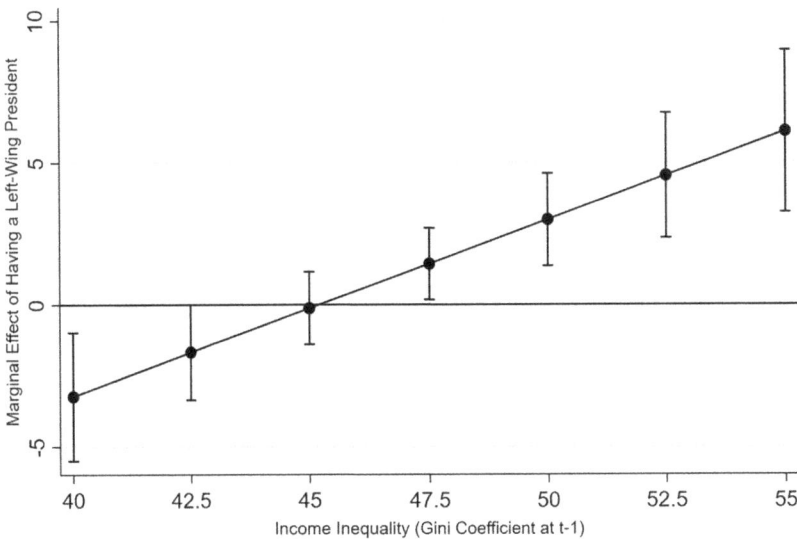

Figure 5-5. Marginal Effect of Having a Left-Wing President on CCT Coverage at Different Inequality Levels
Source: Table 5-3, Model 3-6.

ing a left-wing president would be expected to increase coverage by 2.49 percentage points.

Finally, figure 5-6 captures how the level of child labor affects CCT coverage under centrist and right-wing presidents (model 3-8). The effect is statistically different from zero at levels of child labor above 11.9%, slightly above the sample average (11.73%). This means that, under a nonleft presidency, a one-standard-deviation increase in child labor (7.78 percentage points) would be associated with a decline in CCT coverage of approximately 1.90 percentage points. Put another way, if a country's level of child labor were to increase from 11.9% to the average level reported by Guatemala (28.09), the region's worst performer, coverage would be expected to decrease by 3.98 percentage points under a centrist or right-wing president.

Additionally, these models incorporate a multiplicative term capturing the interaction between the strength of checks and balances and whether a presidential election was held during a given year. Echoing earlier research by De La O (2015, chap. 5), governments subject to strong checks and bal-

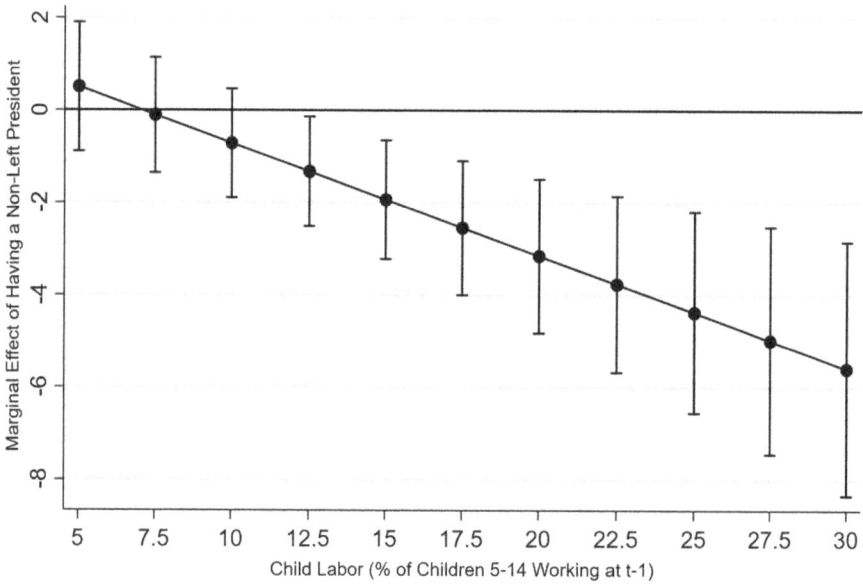

Figure 5-6. Marginal Effect of Having a Nonleft-Wing President on CCT Coverage at Different Child Labor Levels
Source: Table 5-3, Model 3-8.

ances find it difficult to increase coverage during election years. Beyond this, the estimates for the remaining variables do not vary significantly from those reported in the baseline models.

5.3 Beyond Coverage: Ideology and Models of CCTs

The previous sections provide robust evidence that CCTs operated by left-wing presidents have a broader scope than those operated by their centrist and right-wing counterparts. Coverage levels, however, represent, at best, a rough proxy for the claims made in the previous chapter, namely that there exist two distinct types of CCTs that differ in their approaches to targeting (broad vs. narrow), conditionality enforcement (weak vs. strong), and in the formula used for assigning stipend amounts (uniform for all beneficiaries vs. differentiated depending on risk of exiting the school system), and that the choice of said model is determined by presidential ideology. This section tests whether CCTs enacted or managed by left-wing presidents, or both, resemble Brazil's program and the basic income model and whether those enacted or managed by nonleft presidents, or both, resemble Mexico's program and the human capital model.

Based on the ideology of the presidents in power at the time a CCT was enacted, table 5-5 makes the following predictions regarding the design the 10 CCTs adopted after Brazil's "invention" of the basic income model:[8]

To assess these hypotheses, I compile an index measuring the extent to which these 10 programs resemble an ideal human capital or basic income CCT. Programs are assessed with regard to their target population (do they target the entire country and students in every grade?), income target (how restrictive are eligibility requirements?), stipend structure (do stipends vary depending on the year of schooling or other criteria?), and strictness of conditionality enforcement. More detailed information on how CCTs were coded is available in the appendix. For ease of interpretation, the index is scaled as a percentage ranging from 0 for an ideal human capital CCT to 100 for an ideal basic income CCT. The results for 2013, the last year for which data was available, are presented in table 5-6.

The index quantifies the substantive differences between the Mexican (33%) and Brazilian (62%) programs. Taking these pioneering CCTs as benchmarks, programs with scores of 40 or lower are designated as human capital CCTs while those with scores of 60 or higher are designated as basic income CCTs.

Using this criteria, seven of the 10 programs adopted following the launch of Bolsa Família correctly match the predictions made above. That is, four of the five programs launched by the left meet the criteria for basic income, while three of the five launched by nonleft presidents qualify as

Table 5-5. Predicted CCT Type of Post–Bolsa Família Programs

Country	Year CCT Adoption	President Ideology When CCT Adopted	Predicted Type
El Salvador	2005	Right	Human Capital
Dominican Republic	2005	Center	Human Capital
Paraguay	2005	Center-Right	Human Capital
Peru	2005	Center-Right	Human Capital
Costa Rica	2007	Center	Human Capital
Uruguay	2005	Center-Left	Basic Income
Panama	2006	Center-Left	Basic Income
Bolivia	2006	Left	Basic Income
Guatemala	2008	Center-Left	Basic Income
Argentina	2009	Center-Left	Basic Income

Table 5–6. Ideology and CCT Design

Country	Ideology at Adoption[1]	% Left Gov.[1]	Coverage (2013)[2]	CCT Design Index (2013)					Total (as %)	Meets Prediction?
				Target Pop[2]	Income Target[2]	Stipend[2]	Enforcement[3]	Total		
Template Programs										
Mexico	CR	0%	24%	1.00	0.33	0.00	0.00	1.33	33%	NA
Brazil	C	79%	27%	1.00	0.33	0.80	0.33	2.46	62%	NA
Post–Bolsa Família Programs										
El Salvador	R	50%	6%	0.50	0.00	0.00	0.00	0.50	13%	✓★
Dominican Rep.	C	0%	25%	1.00	0.33	0.00	0.33	1.66	42%	✓★
Paraguay	CR	44%	5%	0.50	0.00	1.00	0.33	1.83	46%	✗★
Peru	CR	22%	9%	0.50	0.00	0.80	0.00	1.30	33%	✓★
Costa Rica	C	0%	4%	0.50	0.33	0.00	0.00	0.83	21%	✓★
Uruguay	CL	100%	16%	1.00	0.66	1.00	0.66	3.32	83%	✓★
Panama	CL	50%	8%	1.00	0.00	1.00	0.00	2.00	50%	✗★
Bolivia	L	100%	19%	1.00	1.00	1.00	0.66	3.66	92%	✓★
Guatemala	CL	50%	27%	0.50	0.33	1.00	0.66	2.49	62%	✓★
Argentina	CL	100%	8%	1.00	0.66	1.00	0.66	3.32	83%	✓★
Average										
Left-Initiated CCT			16%	0.90	0.53	1.00	0.53	2.96	74%	✓★
Nonleft-Initiated CCT			10%	0.60	0.13	0.36	0.13	1.22	31%	✓★
Left Dominated Presidency			14%	1.00	0.77	1.00	0.66	3.43	86%	✓★
Presidency Was Split			12%	0.63	0.08	0.75	0.25	1.71	43%	✓★
Nonleft-Dominated Presidency			7%	0.50	0.17	0.40	0.00	1.07	32%	✓★

Notes: CCTs scoring 60% or higher are coded as "Basic Income." Programs scoring 40% or lower are coded as "Human Capital." For detailed coding methodology, see appendix.

Sources: [1] Dataset on Political Ideology of Presidents and Parties in Latin America (Murillo, Oliveros, and Vaishnav 2010); Political Ideology of Presidents and Parties in Latin America (Murillo, Oliveros, and Vaishnav 2010); [2] Non-contributory Social Protection Programmes Database (CEPAL 2018); [3] Lindert (2014).

human capital. Furthermore, one case, the Dominican Republic, whose program was initiated by a centrist, received a score of 42%, slightly above the human-capital threshold. The bottom of the table, which contrasts the average design scores of different country groupings, provides further support for the argument. Programs initiated by left presidents had an average score of 74%—well above Brazil's score. Programs initiated by the nonleft had an average score of 31%, similar to Mexico's score.

Given the Brazilian experience, where an incoming left-wing administration transformed the CCT it had inherited in the basic income direction over more than a decade in power, it may make more sense to compare programs in terms of the extent to which the left has dominated politics during a program's lifetime. Comparing average scores based on this criteria, countries where the left has been in power since a CCT was adopted, namely Argentina, Bolivia, and Uruguay, have an average score of 86%—well beyond Brazil's score. In contrast, countries where the left was in power during a quarter or less of the program's existence, namely Costa Rica, Dominican Republic, and Peru, have an average score of 32%, practically the same as Mexico.

Figure 5–7 presents a graphical representation of this relationship. The majority of cases cluster in three locations. Countries where the left was largely out of power emphasized human capital and cluster in the bottom-left corner of the graph (Mexico, Costa Rica, and Peru). The Dominican Republic, where the left was not in power during the period of study, is also located in this part of the graph, but, as noted above, its program misses the cut-off point for a human capital CCT (42%). Countries where the left has dominated politics emphasized poverty reduction and cluster at the opposite end of the graph (Brazil, Argentina, Bolivia, and Uruguay). The latter three, however, come much closer to meeting the basic income ideal than Brazil's Bolsa Família.

Two countries where the left controlled the presidency for about half the period had programs that scored in between both models (Panama and Paraguay). These are located near the center of the graph. Guatemala is located very close to those cases. Although its lifetime was equally divided between left and right, the program, which was enacted by center-left President Alvaro Colom (2008–12), just barely qualifies as basic income (62%). The most notable outlier is El Salvador, whose program comes the closest of any program analyzed to the human capital ideal despite being controlled for half of its lifetime by presidents from the Farabundo Martí Front for

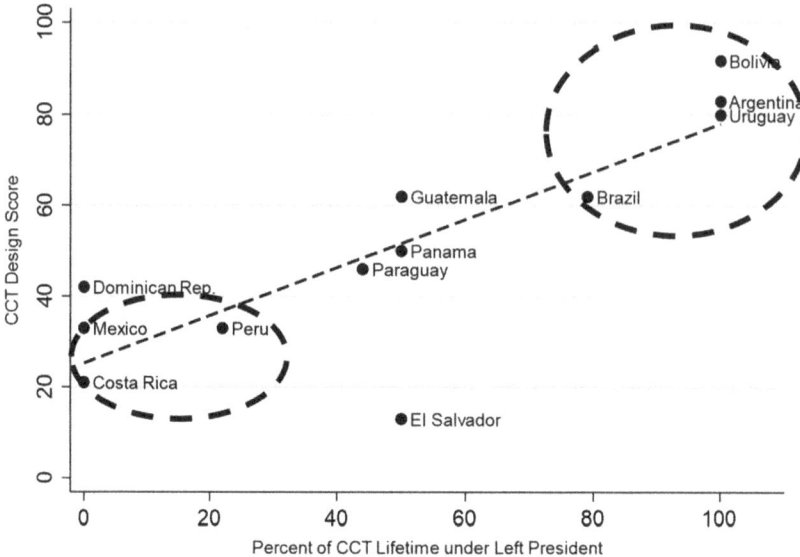

Figure 5-7. Influence of Left Government on CCT Designs
Source: Table 5-6.

National Liberation (FMLN), a left-wing party with roots as a revolutionary guerrilla movement. That program, it should be noted, was enacted by right-wing president Antonio Saca (2004–09).

Thus, there is evidence suggesting that both CCTs initiated by the left and CCTs in countries where the left dominated politics tend to have a basic income design. In fact, the latter come substantially closer to providing a universal income floor than the Brazilian program that influenced them. In contrast, both CCTs initiated by nonleft governments and CCTs in countries where the left has been weak tended to follow the Mexican example in developing human capital programs.

5.4 Conclusions

This chapter has demonstrated that presidential ideology influences the scope and design of CCT programs. CCTs operated by left-wing presidents tend to cover more people than those operated by centrist and right-wing governments. Beyond coverage, left-wing governments have tended to follow Brazil in enacting CCTs with broad target populations, permissive conditionality enforcement, and the same flat stipend for all beneficiaries. The opposite is true of CCTs operated by centrist and right-wing governments.

In short, presidential ideology greatly influences the design of CCTs. Earlier chapters detailed the left's initial skepticism (if not outright hostility) toward CCTs. Given this initial opposition, the left turn might well have put a brake on their diffusion. It was not until Lula begrudgingly embraced CCTs following the failure of Fome Zero and transformed Bolsa Escola into the more universalistic Bolsa Família that left-wing politicians across the region fully embraced CCTs. Thus, the spread of CCTs in countries governed by the left during the second half of the 2000s was contingent on Lula adapting the programs he inherited in a basic income direction and creating a new model of CCT that appealed to the left. Once on board with CCTs, left-wing governments across the region followed the Brazilian example in enacting larger, more generous, and less punitive basic income CCTs.

The next two chapters seek to further flesh out ideology's role in the diffusion, adoption, and design of CCTs through in-depth case studies of a human capital CCT in Costa Rica and two basic income CCTs in Argentina and Bolivia.

5.5 Appendix

Coding Rules for CCT Design Index

1) **Target Population**: 1 if program covers all years of basic education and the entire country, 0.5 if it only meets one of the prior criteria, 0 if it only covers certain years of education and parts of the country.
2) **Income Target:** 1 if program is universal, 0.66 if it targets the economically vulnerable and poor, 0.33 if it targets the poor, 0 if it targets only the extreme poor.
3) **Stipend Structure:** 1 if uniform across all beneficiaries, 0.8 if uniform except for one category, 0 variable depending on year of schooling.
4) **Conditionality Enforcement:** 1 if unconditional, 0.66 if conditionality is announced but not enforced, 0.33 if conditionality is monitored but enforced only after repeated noncompliance, 0 if strictly enforced.

5) **Total:** sum of the components, ranges from 0 (Human Capital CCT) to 4 (Basic Income CCT).
6) **Total (as %):** rescales Total as percentage. Programs with scores of 60% or higher are considered basic income CCTs. Programs with scores of 40% or below are considered human capital CCTs.

CHAPTER 6

Diffusion Revisited

Presidential Ideology and the Two-Track Diffusion of CCTs

Echoing earlier cross-national quantitative analyses on the topic (Sugiyama 2011; Brooks 2015), chapter 2 confirmed that the widespread adoption of conditional cash transfer programs in Latin America during the 2000s was a case of policy diffusion. Specifically, as the share of countries in the region with CCTs increased, countries without programs became more likely to adopt their own. That analysis also confirmed that ideology did not influence the likelihood of *adoption*—left-wing governments were just as likely as centrist and right-wing ones to adopt CCTs. Qualitative evidence from across the region, however, painted a more nuanced picture, demonstrating that left-wing politicians were *initially skeptical* if not *outright opposed* to CCTs. Yet many left-wing governments did ultimately adopt CCTs. *Why and how did the left come to embrace these programs?*

The previous chapter demonstrated that a strong relationship exists between presidential ideology and the design of CCT programs in Latin America. Not only do countries governed by the left tend to have higher levels of CCT coverage and spend more on their programs, the programs enacted and operated by left-wing governments tend to more closely resemble Brazil's basic income model than Mexico's human capital model. Conversely, countries governed by the right tend to have lower levels of CCT coverage and spend less on their programs, and the programs enacted and operated by right-wing governments tend to more closely resemble Mexico's human capital model. *What explains this correlation?*

The first half of the chapter clarifies the relationship between presidential ideology, CCT design, and policy diffusion. It argues that diffusion occurred along two distinct tracks, the choice of which was determined by ideology. While the World Bank and Inter-American Development Bank

(IDB) were busy promoting and, in specific instances, even imposing the human capital model, Brazil, under the leadership of charismatic center-left President Luiz Inácio Lula da Silva (2003–10), actively promoted its basic income model. Whereas centrist and right-wing governments saw the former mainly as a tool for boosting human capital, left-wing governments gravitated toward the latter, envisioning it primarily as a tool to address poverty and a stepping-stone toward enacting a universal income floor. Thus, whereas the adoption of human capital CCTs by centrist and right-wing governments was an example of vertical diffusion (international institution to country), the left's adoption of basic income programs was an example of horizontal (country to country) diffusion.

The second half of the chapter outlines why CCT programs adopted by Costa Rica, Bolivia, and Argentina during the second half of the 2010s are ideal cases for studying the political process connecting presidential ideology and diffusion to CCT adoption and design. Those case studies are presented in the next chapter.

6.1 Conditional Diffusion: The Role of Ideology

Understanding of policy diffusion has increased significantly over the last 15 years. Whereas early work on clustering of policies across time and space was largely limited to confirming or rejecting the existence of diffusion, more recent work traces the pathways through which diffusion occurs. Simmons and Elkins (2004) distinguish between two broad types of mechanisms: altered payoffs and learning. In the former, adoption by a first country puts a second country at a material or reputational disadvantage. This mechanism was not relevant to CCT adoption. Unlike, say, tax or investment policies aimed at creating a more attractive business climate, a country's adoption of an anti-poverty program does not exert pressure on neighboring governments to follow suit.[1] There is, however, significant evidence of diffusion via learning (Hunter 2021, 108). Learning can occur through three distinct channels: success, communication, and reference groups (Simmons and Elkins 2004). International financial institutions (IFIs), most notably the World Bank and IDB, and a vibrant epistemic community (Haas 1992) of scholars and policymakers *communicated* the *potential* and *early successes* of CCTs through hundreds of reports and at dozens of conferences (Osorio Gonnet 2018, chap. 5). With regard to *reference groups*, the attractiveness of CCTs was enhanced by the fact that they were a home-grown Latin American innovation pioneered by Mexico and Brazil, the region's two largest and most influential countries (Handa and Davis 2006, 514; Hanlon, Barrientos, and Hulme 2010, 19–20).

Ideological copartisans constitute another key reference group. Diffusion occurs because, rather than create unique policies tailored to their jurisdictions, policymakers often make decisions by analogy (Walker 1969). Given their cognitive limitations and biases, policymakers process outside information selectively, paying particular attention to policies believed compatible with their own worldviews. A growing body of work has found that diffusion is conditional on ideology (Grossback et al. 2004; Martin 2010; Butler et al. 2017; Butler and Pereira 2018). Simply put, faced with uncertainty over the consequences of a new policy, left-wing policymakers will be more attracted to policies previously adopted by other left-wing governments and skeptical of policies associated with right-wing governments and vice versa. The ideology of early adopters is particularly important when a new policy cannot be easily identified as "liberal or conservative" (Grossback et al. 2004, 526). This was the case with CCTs, which, although highly progressive and thus potentially attractive to the left, were also targeted, conditional, and endorsed by neoliberal technocrats and IFIs, which made the left wary of them. Furthermore, politicians from different parties may draw different lessons from the same policy (Gilardi 2010). Whereas right-wing governments may have been attracted to CCTs because they are relatively cheap and equip beneficiaries with skills that will allow them to lift themselves up by their bootstraps, left-wing governments may be attracted to them because they reach the poorest members of society and help make effective their right to education.

CCTs were always an easy choice for centrist and right-wing politicians. They were ideologically receptive to innovations coming from Mexico's right-wing governments and open to receiving technical assistance and financing from the World Bank and IDB. Conversely, for those same reasons, the left's knee-jerk reaction was to oppose CCTs. This view began changing after Lula begrudgingly embraced CCTs following the failure of his more ambitious Fome Zero program (see chapter 3). Given Lula's impeccable left-wing credentials, his endorsement went a long way toward removing the stench of neoliberalism that had originally plagued CCTs. *It also did not hurt that, in addition to being effective, Bolsa Família was wildly popular and contrib-*

uted to Lula's 2006 reelection (Hunter and Power 2007; Zucco 2008, 2013; Zucco and Power 2013).

Yet, as also detailed in chapter 3, Lula's contribution went beyond simply endorsing CCTs and rebranding them as social democratic. He transformed the policies he inherited from his centrist predecessor in a way that addressed many of the left's initial misgivings. *Bolsa Família demonstrated to left-wing politicians across the region that, despite originally being conceived as targeted and punitive, CCTs could be adapted to advance the left's programmatic goal of providing an income floor for a large segment of the population.* In other words, the Brazilian basic income model better matched the left's worldview and was thus a more attractive import for left-wing governments than Mexico's human capital model.

6.2 Two-Track Diffusion

The discussion of CCT diffusion presented above focused on their importation—*why did governments adopt them and why did the initially skeptical left come to embrace them?* This section focuses on their exportation—*who promoted and facilitated the adoption of CCTs?* Diffusion proceeded along two distinct tracks. Whereas the World Bank and IDB primarily promoted the Mexican human capital model, Brazil's own government promoted the basic income model with Lula himself acting as its global ambassador. This is not to say that IFIs opposed basic income CCTs or that they would not fund such programs. Yet, when advising governments, the banks advocated for programs resembling Mexico's. In the words of a senior Brazilian policy analyst:

> My impression is that the World Bank and the IDB, they never liked Bolsa Família that much. So Brazil was never the big example that they wanted to disseminate in Latin America. Whenever they have [an event] they invite the Mexicans or the Chileans! (cited in Peck and Theodore 2015, 111)

The huge disparity in the number of references to each program on the banks' websites lends credence to this claim (see fig. 6–1).

Citing interviews with policymakers, Morais (2017, 151) attributes the banks' preference for the Mexican over the Brazilian approach to the former's strict focus on building human capital and the greater availability and

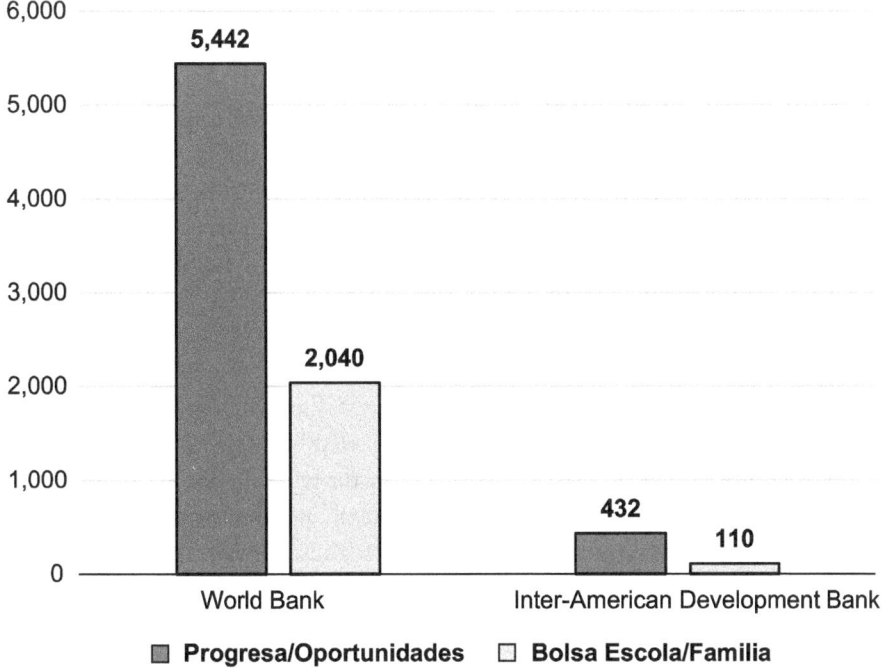

Figure 6-1. Number of Entries on International Financial Institution Websites for Brazilian and Mexican CCTs (Up to 2010)
Source: Morais de Sá e Silva (2017, 151).

sophistication of evaluations of its effectiveness. Greater reliance on foreign funding and the fact that most Mexican policymakers had studied at American universities, which was less common among their Brazilian counterparts, further strengthened the connections between IFIs and Progresa/Oportunidades.[2]

Whereas diffusion of Mexico's human capital model occurred "vertically" (from international institutions to countries), the diffusion of Brazil's basic income program occurred "horizontally" (country to country) with the Brazilian government directly promoting its program. Human capital models were promoted by IFIs, which, in addition to technical expertise, had money to lend and, particularly during tough economic times, possessed significant leverage over would-be adopters. In contrast, Brazil, though large and influential, remains a developing country. Even though the country actively promoted its model and provided technical assistance to interested countries, it did not dictate program design, let alone provide funding.

Vertical diffusion ensured that human capital programs tended to be very similar to one another—IFIs had a clear vision of CCTs that was replicated across different countries. The basic income CCTs that resulted from horizontal diffusion, in contrast, featured much more variation in terms of program design and greater adaptation to local conditions. The CCT design scores for 2013 presented in table 5–6 support these claims. The four human capital CCTs, all of which were enacted by centrist or right-wing presidents, had scores ranging from 33% for Mexico and Peru to 13% for El Salvador, a difference of 20 percentage points. In contrast, the design scores of the five basic income CCTs, four of which were enacted by left-wing governments and another (Brazil's) had been operated by the left for a decade at the time of measurement, ranged from 62% for Brazil and Guatemala to 92% for Bolivia, a difference of 30 percentage points. Thus, whereas the diffusion of human capital CCTs was a case of what Weyland (2006, 17) calls model diffusion—the policies adopted followed a "neat, concrete, well-defined blueprint, largely replicating the original model"—the spread of basic income CCTs was an example of principle diffusion—the "basic thrust" of policies was the same "but specific design features and institutional characteristics differ."

6.2.1 IFIs and the Vertical Diffusion of Human Capital CCTs

The Mexican human capital model has since its inception been closely associated with the World Bank. After all, Santiago Levy (1991) first detailed the ideas that evolved into Progresa in a World Bank working paper. The bank also provided significant technical assistance during the program's design process (Levy 2006, 114).[3] Thus, the Progresa team and IFIs were of one mind over how to tackle Mexico's social challenges. Or, as Iliana Yaschine (1999, 58), formerly the program's evaluation director, puts it, there was a "confluence of ideology between the actors dictating the international trend [IFIs] and the technocratic political elite that has ruled Mexico."

The World Bank and IDB began promoting the program almost immediately after its launch. In sharp contrast with the Brazilian experience, the Mexican government did not directly promote its star program (Boltvinik 2012, 13). When Mexican technocrats promoted CCTs abroad or consulted with interested governments, they did so on behalf of IFIs (Boltvinik 2012, 19). The most notable case of this occurred in March 2003, when World Bank president James Wolfensohn and former IDB president Enrique Iglesias organized a private meeting at which Levy reportedly convinced Lula that CCTs, not hunger relief policies, were the best way forward (Lindert et al. 2007, 13–14; Reid 2007, 234; Lustig 2011, 12; Morais 2017, 126). Lula, however, went on to transform Brazil's CCTs into something different from what Levy and the bank had in mind.

IFIs were directly responsible for putting CCTs on the agenda in many of the early adopter countries. The IDB was central to the adoption of CCTs in Honduras and Nicaragua. Working alongside the International Food Policy Research Institute, the organization that conducted Progresa's highly influential evaluation, the IDB designed and provided the lion's share of the initial funding for both countries' programs (Moore 2010). In fact, the Honduran policymakers administering the Programa de Asignación Familiar 2 (Family Allowance Program, Phase 2) CCT first learned "how the program would work" in meetings with representatives from those institutions (Moore 2010, 108).[4] Nicaragua's Red de Protection Social (Social Protection Network) was essentially a copy of Progresa, all the way down to requiring mothers and adolescents to attend seminars on hygiene, birth control, and food preparation (Moore 2010, 118).

In Colombia and Ecuador, two countries hit by severe banking crises during 1998–99, IFIs leveraged their power as lenders of last resort to promote CCTs. Colombian officials agreed to strengthen social safety nets as part of an International Monetary Fund bailout. CCTs were not included in the "long laundry list of ideas" Colombian social policy experts subsequently presented to the World Bank and IDB (Brearley 2011, 157–58).[5] As Luis Alfonso Hoyos, director of social policy during the early years of the country's Familias en Acción (Families in Action) CCT, put it: "*Familias* was initially suggested and funded by World Bank and IBD: it was pushed on us!" (cited in Brearley 2011, 157). The banks sent Colombian social policy officials on study trips to Mexico and Brazil and the rest is history (Brearley 2011, 158).[6]

Similarly, the banks proposed that Ecuador adopt a CCT to mitigate the social consequences of its economic crisis. The country's first experience with cash transfers was Bono Solidario (Solidary Bonus), an unconditional cash transfer for poor heads of households, the elderly, and disabled people adopted in 1998 to compensate for cuts in fuel and electricity subsidies

(Osorio Gonnet 2018, 209). CCTs entered the political agenda the following year as part of debt negotiations with the World Bank. Citing improper targeting and lack of conditionality, bank officials rejected center-right President Jamil Mahuad's (1998–2000) request to fund Bono Solidario and instead earmarked funding for a means-tested CCT linked to education (Lana and Evans 2004, 204–5).

The World Bank and IDB instead hired Cristovam Buarque and his NGO Missão Criança (Children's Mission) to help the country import Brasilia's human-capital-oriented Bolsa-Escola CCT (Lana and Evans 2004, 205; Osorio Gonnet 2018, 222). Simply put, "the Ecuadorian government had little autonomy in choosing where to search for lessons" (Lana and Evans 2004, 206). Though local officials were enthusiastic, IFI conditionality was the main driver of CCT adoption (Lana and Evans 2004, 206), or, as policymakers involved put it, "the negotiation was not very horizontal and highly influenced by the loans" (cited in Osorio Gonnet 2018, 219). The result, following some setbacks, was the Beca Escolar (School Scholarship), a small CCT adopted in 2002 that, with further IFI loans and assistance, evolved into Bono de Desarollo Humano (Human Development Bonus) the following year.[7] Overall, Osorio Gonnet (2018, 219) describes the adoption of CCTs in Ecuador as an example of diffusion via "moderate coercion" and, to a lesser extent, emulation of foreign models.

During the second half of the decade, with the region's economies booming and knowledge of CCTs now widespread, governments began taking the lead in enacting CCTs, with IFIs, when involved, acting as secondary partners. It is worth noting, however, that IFIs were consulted by the governments of El Salvador and Costa Rica, which went on to enact the two programs that most closely resemble the human capital ideal type (Martínez Franzoni and Voorend 2011; see fig. 5–7). Thus, at a time when Bolsa Família was available as an alternative model, the banks continued advocating for human capital CCTs and centrist and right-wing governments continued enacting them. In sharp contrast, at around the same time, left-wing governments excluded IFIs from the design and funding of the three CCTs that most closely resemble the basic income CCT ideal type, those of Argentina, Bolivia, and Uruguay (see fig. 5–7).

6.2.2 Brazil and the Horizontal Diffusion of Basic Income CCTs

Lula's conversion and the subsequent transformation of Bolsa Família helped to weaken the association between CCTs and neoliberalism (Hevia 2011,

331), paving the way for other left-leaning leaders to pursue their own more expansive and less punitive programs. The Brazilian experience demonstrated to the previously skeptical left that, despite being conceived as targeted and residualistic, CCTs could be adapted to advance the decommodifying goal of providing an income floor for a large segment of the population. It also did not hurt that CCTs were effective, affordable, and popular.

As expected of diffusionary processes, there was a lag in learning: Lula began creating his basic income CCT in late 2003, while other basic income CCTs begun appearing in countries governed by the left starting in 2005. The left's embrace of CCTs following the emergence of Bolsa Família can be understood as a case of policy learning under bounded rationality (Weyland 2006). In line with the availability heuristic, left-leaning presidents paid disproportionate attention to Brazil's striking, geographically proximate model associated with a respected leftist statesman. Left-leaning governments extrapolated lessons from the Brazilian case, which were interpreted as applicable to their countries, an example of the representativeness heuristic. In line with the anchoring heuristic, although peripheral elements of the model were adapted to local needs, the left's programs remained loyal to the basic income model's emphasis on short-term poverty reduction, broad coverage, and permissive (if any) conditionality enforcement.

The new model's merits were publicized in no small part by Lula himself. The Lula administration dramatically increased diplomatic contact with Brazil's Latin American neighbors as well as with other developing regions, mostly notably sub-Saharan Africa (Costa Leite, Suyama, and Pomeroy 2013; Bry 2017; Costa Leite, Pomeroy, and Suyama 2017).[8] Charismatic, popular, and widely respected, Lula made Bolsa Família a central plank of this ambitious foreign policy (Faria 2012; Boultinghouse 2015).[9] As Boultinghouse (2015, 12) puts it, "From its inception, Lula defined the Bolsa Família as a national narrative, directly tethering its domestic success to the international clout Brazil was set to gain." In fact, Lula began touting the program as a Brazilian export during its October 2003 launch:

> Here in Brazil, we have to be sure that if we do it here and achieve the success that I imagine we can have, I have no doubt that we can contribute so that other countries in the world can stop hunger in their countries. (Folha de S. Paulo 2003)

Lula eagerly promised technical cooperation on social policy to foreign governments during his frequent travels abroad and when foreign leaders visited Brasilia (Morais 2017, 149–50). Brazilian spending on development cooperation in Latin America and Africa increased more than fivefold under Lula (Costa Leite 2015, 1447). The Social Development Ministry (MDS) created a department charged with promoting Bolsa Família and addressing queries from foreign governments and international institutions. During the program's first decade, MDS hosted delegations from 21 countries and established cooperation agreements with most Latin American countries (Carvalho 2013, 401). During 2011–14, MDS received 345 delegations, half from Latin America and a third from Africa (UNDP 2016, 20).

Outside of Latin America, the Brazilian model proved more attractive to sub-Saharan African governments and European development aid agencies than Progresa/Oportunidades. In 2006, the United Kingdom's Department for International Development launched the Africa-Brazil Cooperation Program on Social Development, which funded study tours of Brazil for representatives from six sub-Saharan African countries and made it possible for MDS to assist in the design of Ghana's cash transfer program.[10] In 2014, MDS along with several international organizations including the World Bank launched the Brazil Learning Initiative for a World without Poverty, an online resource charged with documenting and disseminating lessons and best practices derived from Brazilian social policy.[11]

Two factors—foreign donor priorities and state capacity—explain Africa's preference for basic income CCTs. With regard to the former, funding for African programs came primarily from institutions adhering to a "rights-based approach to development," namely national donor agencies like the UK's Department for International Development and international organizations focused on operationalizing human rights such as the United Nations Children's Fund (UNICEF) (Gaarder 2012, 131). The World Bank, in contrast, was less active in promoting cash transfers in Africa than it had been in Latin America (Gaarder 2012, 131; Morais 2017, 30–39). But where the World Bank was involved, governments tended to adopt conditional programs (Simpson 2018). With regard to state capacity, the very factors that made Progresa/Oportunidades the favorite among IFI technocrats made it difficult to export to the poorest countries. Precise targeting and rigorous conditionality enforcement require a strong bureaucracy and are expensive to implement. The more permissive Brazilian model proved easier to adapt to the poorest countries (Ancelovici and Jenson 2013).

Bolsa Família's influence in Africa leads Ancelovici and Jenson (2013) to argue that it, and not Progresa/Oportunidades, now constitutes the "standard model" for anti-poverty programs in the Global South. In their (2013, 309) words:

> Brazilian policy analysts quietly let drop the notion of "conditionality," which had initially aligned CCTs with neoliberals' emphasis on "making families more responsible" as well as strengthening markets. Instead, their attention turned to whom to target and how to target. Thus, a CCT became very similar to a CT [cash transfer].

6.3 Presidential Ideology's Effect on CCT Adoption and Design

The quantitative analyses conducted in the previous chapter identified strong correlations between presidential ideology and various measures of CCT scope as well as the choice of CCT model. Such analyses, while useful at providing an overall picture of *what* occurred across the region, do not explain *how* presidential ideology and CCT design are related. Missing are the causal mechanisms—the political processes, motivations, and actions of political actors and the complex sequencing of events—that link presidential ideology with CCT design choices (Hedström and Swedberg 1996). Quantitative methods are poorly equipped to achieve these tasks.

The next chapter uses in-depth qualitative case studies to trace the connections between ideology and the adoption and design of three CCTs adopted in the second half of the 2000s: Costa Rica's Avancemos, Bolivia's Bono Juancito Pinto, and Argentina's Asignación Universal por Hijo. This is not to say that government ideology was the immediate or sole cause behind the adoption of those programs. To be clear, this book does not claim that government ideology determines the timing of adoption. It does argue, however, that once a president decides to adopt a CCT, ideology determines its design.

The cases are based on face-to-face interviews with politicians, social policy technocrats, and independent policy analysts conducted during field research in those countries during 2012–13. Adopting a mixed-methods approach takes advantage of the differences between quantitative and qualitative research, using each approach's strengths to compensate for the other's weaknesses (Lieberman 2005; Seawright 2016).

6.3.1 Case Selection

The cases selected are ideal for testing this book's arguments for three reasons (see table 6–1). First, they vary with regard to the main variable of interest—presidential ideology. Additionally, the programs were adopted at around the same time, between 2006 (Bolivia) and 2009 (Argentina).[12] Finally, the cases offer a fairly representative sample of countries from across Latin America.

As noted, the purpose of the case studies is to flesh out the connection between the dependent and independent variables of the previous chapter's quantitative analyses. When that is the goal, Lieberman (2005) recommends selecting "on-the-line" cases (or "on-liers")—cases that are representative of a quantitative model's findings (see also Seawright and Gerring 2008). For these types of studies, Seawright (2016, chap. 4) further recom-

Table 6–1. Country Cases (circa 2012–2013)

	Costa Rica	Bolivia	Argentina
Political Variables			
Initiating President	Oscar Arias	Evo Morales	Cristina Fernández de Kirchner
Initiator's Ideology[1]	Center	Left	Center-Left
% of History under Left[2]	0%	100%	100%
CCT Details			
Program Name	Avancemos	Bono Juancito Pinto	Asignación Universal por Hijo
Year of Adoption	2006 (Pilot) 2007 (Nationwide)	2006	2009
Coverage (% Pop.)[3]	3.63%	18.14%	8.15%
Coverage—Poverty[4]	–8.65 percentage points	–9.11 percentage points	–2.44 percentage points
Cost (% GDP)[3]	0.19%	0.18%	0.47%
Target Population	Low-Income Secondary School Students	Public School Students	Children (18 and under) of Informal/Unemployed Workers
Targeting Mechanism	Proxy Means Test	Public Schools	Parent Employment Status
Conditionality	Started Lax, Became Stricter	Nominally CCT, but Essentially No Enforcement	80% Unconditional, 20% Conditional, Lax Enforcement
Stipend Structure	Variable by Grade	Uniform	Uniform

Notes: The observations are from 2013 or thereabouts because the field research for the case studies was carried out during 2012–13.

Sources: [1] Dataset on Political Ideology of Presidents and Parties in Latin America (Murillo, Oliveros, and Vaishnav 2010); [2] From the day the CCT launched until the start of 2013; [3] Non-contributory Social Protection Programmes Database (CEPAL 2018); [4] *Socio-Economic Database for Latin America and the Caribbean* (SEDLAC 2018).

mends selecting cases with extreme values on the main explanatory variable. Returning to figure 5–7, the three cases are located close to the line. In Costa Rica, a centrist president enacted a textbook human capital program closely resembling Mexico's Progresa/Oportunidades. In Bolivia and Argentina, by contrast, left-wing presidents enacted programs that resembled Brazil's basic income model. In fact, those left-initiated CCTs went further in the basic income direction than Brazil's Bolsa Família, which had its roots in earlier programs enacted by a centrist president. The three cases are also "extreme" in the sense that government ideology remained constant throughout the entirety of the period of study. Whereas Bolivia and Argentina had left-wing presidents during the entire period, Costa Rica was one of only a handful of Latin American countries that did not elect a left-wing president during the first decade of the 2000s.[13]

Cross-case comparison is further facilitated by the fact the decisions regarding the adoption and design of these programs occurred in the second half of the 2000s, well after Brazil had "invented" and started promoting the basic income model. Given my reliance on in-person interviews, focusing on newer programs offers practical advantages. Time is of the essence when attempting to reconstruct policy adoption processes. Actors involved form part of ad-hoc networks that disperse soon after a policy transfer occurs or fails (Evans and Davies 1999, 375; Lana and Evans 2004, 194). Studying recent programs maximizes the likelihood of identifying and locating the key policymakers involved and increases the reliability of the information obtained through interviews.

Selection of diverse cases is recommended when conducting qualitative research on policy diffusion. As Starke (2013, 569) notes, "Qualitative diffusion scholars cannot use Mill's methods of agreement and difference (also known as the 'most similar cases design') as these designs do not allow for interdependence of cases." Therefore, they should pick "cases that represent the universe of cases, at least approximately." The three countries studied come close to providing a representative sample of Latin American countries. Geographically, they span Latin America's three subregions: the Southern Cone (Argentina), the Andes (Bolivia), and Central America (Costa Rica). They also include one of the region's most prosperous countries (Argentina, second out of 18 in 2013), one whose income is close the regional average (Costa Rica, tenth), and one of the poorest (Bolivia, sixteenth).

The three cases run the gamut with regard to their welfare regimes

(Esping-Andersen 1990). Argentina is a regional pioneer that began its social policy expansion in the early twentieth century. Its welfare regime, under which most benefits have tended to be linked to employment status, most closely resembles Europe's conservative corporatist welfare regimes, with the caveat that workers in the informal sector have been excluded (Huber 1996, 159). Costa Rica was a late bloomer with regard to social policy, dramatically expanding social services during the second half of the twentieth century. The country possesses what has been described as the region's only "embryonic social democratic regime" in that most social services constitute universal rights unrelated to income or employment status (Huber 1996, 159). Bolivia, by contrast, has been a laggard by regional standards. To the extent that it is possible to speak of a welfare regime, it is "informal-familialist," meaning that government programs are limited in scope and exclude much of the population. In the absence of state involvement, families must step in to fill the vacuum (Martínez Franzoni 2008).

6.3.2 Overview of the Programs

As on-the-line cases, the programs closely match both CCT ideal types. Whereas the two basic income CCTs aim to cover most if not all children, Costa Rica's human capital CCT covers a more restrictive sample. Among the three countries, only Costa Rica selects beneficiaries using a rigorous proxy means test. In contrast, Argentina's program is open to all children whose parents are unemployed or employed in the informal sector. Together, this program and contributory child allowances ensure that all parents receive a benefit that partially offsets the cost of raising children. Bolivia's program is practically universal, targeting all public-school students. Costa Rica has universal enrollment at the elementary level but strikingly high rates of secondary school desertion (Román 2010, 37; Acosta el al. 2015, 18; Oviedo et al. 2015, 48). As a result, its program is restricted to secondary school students. In contrast, Argentina, which also has universal elementary school enrollment and where, on average, students complete more years of schooling than in Costa Rica (Barro and Lee 2013), opted to cover all children under 18, including those too young to attend school. Bolivia, which has more serious desertion problems at all levels, particularly in rural areas and among the indigenous, currently covers all grades, though it initially covered only up to fifth grade.[14]

The programs also differ with regard to stipend structure and conditionality enforcement. To compensate for the increasing opportunity cost of remaining in school and outside the labor force as the student grows older, Costa Rica followed Mexico in increasing the size of the stipend with each passing grade. Said stipends were rigorously determined based on surveys of how much minors could expect to make in the informal sector at different ages (Sauma 2013). In contrast, Argentina and Bolivia pay a flat stipend per student, regardless of grade or sex. Neither provided a technical justification for the stipend amounts.

With regard to conditionality, Costa Rica aspired to Mexican-style rigorous enforcement (Cecchini and Martínez 2011, 111). Enforcement was initially weak but improved significantly with the adoption of an electronic platform for monitoring attendance (La Nación 2012).[15] Argentina's program is semiconditional in that 80% of the stipend is unconditional while the remaining 20% can only be collected at the end of the school year by proving school attendance (Bertranou and Maurizio 2012). Even then, enforcement of these conditionalities has been lax (OEBA 2012). Although Bolivia's is technically conditioned on school attendance, conditionality is not enforced (OSPE-B 2011, 24).

6.4 Predictions/Hypotheses

The values of the dependent and independent variables are already known: the presidents of these countries adopted CCTs with designs that matched what would be expected given their ideological leanings. The purpose of the case studies presented in the next chapter is to detail the process connecting those variables and to test claims that cannot be easily quantified. Based on previous chapters and claims regarding two-track diffusion presented above, the case studies will assess the validity of the following hypotheses.

Ideology and Attitudes toward CCTs

> **H1a:** *Center and right-wing politicians will be early and enthusiastic supporters of CCTs.*
> **H1b:** *Left-wing politicians will initially be skeptical if not outright opposed to CCTs, particularly ones that are narrowly targeted, have strict conditionality, or are proposed by international financial institutions.*

Presidential Ideology and Reasons for Adopting CCTs

H2a: *When adopting a CCT, center and right-wing presidents will emphasize a program's potential effects on human capital more than its effects on poverty.*

H2b: *When adopting a CCT, left-wing presidents will emphasize a program's effects on poverty more than its effects on human capital. In particular, they will emphasize the program's role in building a universal safety net.*

Presidential Ideology and Two-Track Diffusion of CCTs

H3a: *When center and right-wing presidents commit to enacting CCTs, they will seek technical assistance and funding from the World Bank or the Inter-American Development Bank, or both.*

H3b: *When left-wing presidents commit to enacting CCTs, they will not seek assistance and funding from international financial institutions. They may, instead, receive direct assistance or encouragement from Brazil's government.*

6.5 Conclusion

This chapter argued that the diffusion of CCTS across the region proceeded along two distinct tracks. Ideology determined which foreign actors were seen as credible and which policies were perceived as worthy of emulating. The center and right were eager to copy Mexico's program and work with IFIs. The left was skeptical of the Mexican right's policies and IFIs but highly receptive to ideas emanating from Lula's Brazil.

The next chapter re-creates and compares the political processes that culminated in the adoption and shaped the design of a human capital CCT in Costa Rica and basic income CCTs in Bolivia and Argentina.

CHAPTER 7

Presidential Ideology's Effect on CCT Adoption and Design

The Cases of Costa Rica, Bolivia, and Argentina

The previous chapter argued that the correlation between presidential ideology and conditional cash transfer program design is explained by the tendency of politicians to emulate policies that had already been tried by those in their ideological peer group (Grossback, Nicholson-Crotty, and Peterson 2004; Martin 2010; Butler et al. 2017; Butler and Pereira 2018). Specifically, it was argued that left-wing leaders emulated the Brazilian left's basic income CCT while center and right-wing governments emulated the Mexican right's human capital program, which was actively promoted by the World Bank and the Inter-American Development Bank. This chapter tests these claims through in-depth qualitative case studies of the politics of CCT adoption and design of three CCT programs adopted during the second half of the 2000s: Costa Rica's Avancemos (Let's Advance), Bolivia's Bono Juancito Pinto (Juancito Pinto Bonus), and Argentina's Asignación Universal por Hijo (Universal Child Allowance).

The differing priorities of Costa Rica's human capital CCT and Argentina's and Bolivia's basic income CCTs are evident in the first sentences of the presidential decrees that gave them life—all three programs were launched via decree.[1] The decree enacting Costa Rica's Avancemos begins by stating the goals of "universalizing high quality secondary education" and increasing education spending (Presidencia de Costa Rica 2006). Poverty is first mentioned in the third article in reference to how education can reduce its severity. In contrast, the first paragraph of the decree enacting Bolivia's Bono Juancito Pinto (BJP) starts by referencing the "objective of eradicating extreme poverty and the exclusion of people, families and communities" (Presidencia de Bolivia 2006). Only in the second paragraph is there a mention of "programs and projects destined to strengthen, protect and develop human capabilities, primarily favoring the country's children." Similarly, the decree launching Argentina's Asignación Universal por Hijo (AUH) begins by referencing the government's responsibility to provide "policies that will improve the situation of children and adolescents facing economic vulnerability" (Presidencia de Argentina 2009). It is not until the seventh paragraph that education is mentioned and, even then, it is in the same sentence as the right to "obtain social security benefits." These differing objectives, themselves a function of presidential ideology, go a long way toward explaining variation in CCT coverage and spending levels.

The analysis begins with Costa Rica's Avancemos, the lone human capital case, and then covers the two basic income cases chronologically, first Bolivia's BJP and then Argentina's AUH. The chapter concludes by assessing how well the cases match the hypotheses presented at the end of the previous chapter.

7.1 Costa Rica: Centrist President Adopts a Human Capital CCT

Costa Rican president Oscar Arias (1986–90; 2006–10) explicitly campaigned in 2006 on what became Avancemos. Influenced by programs elsewhere in the region, Arias saw CCTs primarily as a tool for reducing the country's stubbornly high secondary school dropout rate. This was a deeply personal issue for Arias, who, as president in the 1980s in the midst of the deepest economic crisis in the country's history, witnessed a "lost generation" of young people drop out of school to support their families only to never return (interview, Oscar Arias). It is worth noting that CCTs were absent from the campaign platform of Ottón Solís of the center-left Citizens' Action Party, Arias's opponent in 2006.[2]

The country's CCT was initially envisioned not as an anti-poverty program or a social safety net, but rather as a means of incentivizing the accumulation of human capital (interviews with Manuel Barahona and Diego Víquez). Arias and his advisors saw cash transfers as a tool for addressing a very specific human capital deficiency—school desertion in grades 7–12, which causes the country to have lower education levels than would be expected given its GDP per capita, education spending, and otherwise exemplary human development indicators (Oviedo et al. 2015, 48). Given

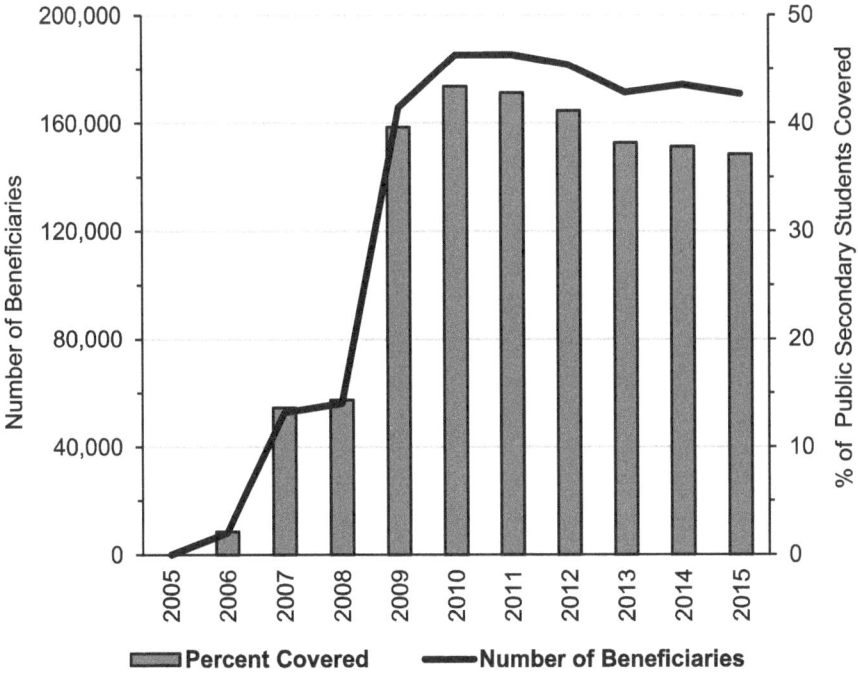

Figure 7-1. Avancemos: Evolution of Coverage (2005–2015)
Source: Non-contributory Social Protection Programmes Database (CEPAL 2018) and Programa Estado de la Nación (2017).

that the country had long possessed near-universal primary school (grades 1–6) completion rates, Arias and his team saw no need to further incentivize attendance at that level (interview, Diego Víquez).

Given its narrow mandate and target population, Avancemos is among the region's smallest CCT in terms of share of the population covered (Cecchini and Atuesta 2017, 25). Even so, since 2010 the program has covered roughly 40% of secondary school students (see fig. 7-1). Given its goal of fully compensating adolescents for foregone wages, Avancemos is one of the more generous programs in the region in terms of benefits per student (Cecchini and Atuesta 2017, 38). Tellingly, its cost as a share of GDP is similar to that of Bolivia's program, which covers between four and five times as many beneficiaries as a share of the population (Cecchini and Atuesta 2017, 34).

The resulting program closely resembled the human capital ideal type. At its inception, Avancemos targeted secondary school students living in moderate or extreme poverty as determined through a rigorous proxy means test measuring 56 socioeconomic, demographic, and geographic variables (Víquez 2010, 11). With the intent of fully compensating students for the opportunity cost of choosing school over work, stipends increased with each grade and were determined based on household surveys measuring the earnings of working minors at different ages (interviews with Manuel Barahona and Pablo Sauma; Sauma 2013). The program's architects also aspired to rigorous conditionality enforcement that would ensure students held up their end of the bargain—at least 80% attendance. However, coordination problems between the multiple institutions originally involved in the program complicated enforcement, which remained weak during the program's first years. It has since improved.

7.1.1 Socioeconomic Context

Costa Rica stands out among Latin American countries for coming the closest to having a social democratic welfare regime (Esping-Andersen 1990; Huber 1996). At the center is the National Health Service (Caja Costarricense del Seguro Social), which provides universal public healthcare with standardized benefits de-linked from employment status or contributions into the system. The country has also been a regional pioneer with regard to anti-poverty programs. The early 1970s saw the creation of the Mixed Institute for Social Assistance (IMAS), the main institution in charge of operating targeted anti-poverty programs, and the Social Development and Family Allowance Fund, a permanent and well-funded social assistance fund (Román 2012; Martínez Franzoni and Sánchez-Ancochea 2013).[3]

Despite these notable achievements, in 2006, when Arias first proposed Avancemos, roughly a third of 13–18 year olds had dropped out of the school system. Only about two in five 19–21 year olds had completed secondary school. That figure dropped to less than one in five among those in the bottom quintile (Trejos 2012, 17). This is surprisingly low given the country's high education spending (Jiménez 2014, 44) and strong human development (Sandbrook et al. 2007, chap. 4; Martínez Franzoni and Sánchez-Ancochea 2013, 2016).[4] Low education levels present a serious obstacle to the country's current development strategy centered on the attraction of high-tech foreign direct investment (Rodríguez-Clare 2001; Paus 2005).

As noted, Costa Rica's underperformance in secondary education dates back to the 1980s debt crisis (Jiménez 2014). This was truly a "lost decade"—real GDP per capita declined by 15% during the first half of the decade and did not return to precrisis levels until 1992. Real social spending per capita declined sharply and did not return to its precrisis peak until 2015 (Mata and Trejos 2018, 4). Most notably, the crisis halted the expansion of secondary education that started in the 1970s (interview, Pablo Sauma). Secondary school coverage declined sharply during 1980–85 as tens of thousands of teenagers left school prematurely and entered the workforce, dooming themselves to a lifetime of lower incomes. Coverage did not return to its 1980 level until the mid-1990s (Jiménez 2014, 13–14). Among the poorest quintile, the share of 19–21 year olds who had graduated did not surpass its 1980 level (16.3%) until well into the 2000s (Trejos 2012, 17). When all was said and done, the debt crisis had set Costa Rican education back two decades.

The country was significantly more successful at fighting poverty, which, after peaking at over 50% in 1982, returned to its precrisis levels of around 30% in 1987 (Sauma and Trejos 2014, 6). Improved growth and targeted anti-poverty programs brought poverty down to 20% in the mid-1990s. With the exception of a few years of very fast growth toward the end of the 2000s, poverty has remained stable at that level, give or take 1.5 percentage points (Sauma and Trejos 2014, 5). Starting with the first Arias administration (1986–90), each president launched his own flagship anti-poverty strategy funded through the Social Development and Family Allowance Fund. These strategies were centered on targeted programs that were dismantled by the following administration (Morales and Cubero 2005, 52).

Superémonos (Let's Overcome), the country's first CCT, was one such program. It was launched in 2000 to little fanfare by center-right President Miguel Angel Rodríguez (1998–2002). The program sought to reduce the dropout rate among poor 6–18 year olds by awarding their families 10,000 colones ($30 at the time) a month during the 10-month school year. The education conditionality was reportedly rigorously enforced with families being required to prove attendance twice during the school year (Duryea and Morrison 2004, 7). In sharp contrast to earlier anti-poverty programs, Superémonos was subject to an external evaluation (Trejos 2009, 24), which found that it reduced the dropout rate among beneficiaries by 5.0–8.7 percentage points during 2000–2001. Although the program appeared to increase the likelihood of advancing to the next grade at the end of the schoolyear, it had no effect on child labor (Duryea and Morrison 2004, 5). The program peaked at 12,000 beneficiaries before being canceled by centrist President Abel Pacheco (2002–6), who, despite being from the same party as Rodríguez, launched his own short-lived anti-poverty programs (Morales and Cubero 2005). Nevertheless, IMAS acquired experience operating a CCT (interview, Olga Sonia Vargas).

7.1.2 Adoption and Expansion

The Arias administration hit the ground running, publishing a decree announcing a pilot program on May 19, 2006, a mere 10 days after taking office. Avancemos was strictly a presidential initiative, enacted via decree without input from legislators or civil society (Martínez Franzoni and Voorend 2011, 288). When interviewed, Arias was blunt about why he chose to sidestep the legislature: "if we would have done it through a law we would still be discussing it" (interview, Oscar Arias).[5] A tight-knit group of technocrats overseen by Fernando Zumbado, the social development and housing minister, handled day-to-day operations. The pilot began paying stipends in July.

The quick rollout was possible because work on the program began in February, just days after Arias won the election (interview, Diego Víquez). The design process brought together politicians loyal to Arias and several of the country's top academic social policy experts. The academics were keenly aware of and influenced by CCTs already operating across the region, most notably Mexico's Progresa/Oportunidades (interviews with Manuel Barahona, Leonardo Garnier, Juan Diego Trejos, and Diego Víquez), but were also determined to create a program tailored to Costa Rica's unique conditions (Víquez 2010, 40; Martínez Franzoni and Voorend 2011, 288; Villalobos 2014, 2). IFI involvement was limited to the IDB funding a series of workshops with officials from Chile's Chile Solidario and Mexico's Oportunidades, including with Miguel Székely, who had directed the latter program's expansion to urban areas (interviews with Manuel Barahona and Pablo Sauma; Víquez 2010, 40). Officials from Oportunidades were encouraged to provide input on Avancemos but only after its design was practically complete (Martínez Franzoni and Voorend 2011, 288). The program was financed entirely out of the national budget with no IFI assistance. Regardless, the final result closely resembled Mexico's program.

The academics and politicians began clashing as soon as the program became a reality. The academics' vision, which involved a multiyear pilot program with a control group and carefully calibrated incentives, was incompatible with that of the politicians, who wanted quick results. The original pilot was to cover 3,500 13–17 year olds from 11 urban secondary schools selected by the United Nations Children's Fund (UNICEF). It was to generate experimental data that would serve as inputs with which to assess the program's impact and improve its design (interviews with Manuel Barahona and Pablo Sauma; Román 2010) as occurred in the much-publicized Mexican case.

Arias believed the pilot project was too small and demanded that it include at least 6,000 beneficiaries (interviews with Oscar Arias, José Antonio Li, and Juan Diego Trejos). Zumbado, who was crafting a public image as the "Minister of the Poor" (La Nación 2008a) and eventual successor to Arias, also pushed for a bigger program (interviews with Pablo Sauma, Carla Valverde, and Diego Víquez).[6] In end, the pilot included 10,000 beneficiaries and lasted only six months. The program rolled out nationwide in early 2007 with coverage reaching 50,000 by the end of the year. Plans for an experimental evaluation were quietly dropped as the staff's energy focused on rapidly expanding the program's scope (interview, Carla Valverde). In the rush to expand, conditionality enforcement was neglected (interview, Diego Víquez). Meanwhile, the government began spending heavily on advertising the program, including placing giant ads on the side of commuter trains (Avancemos 2009, 19).

The program's transformation from a small, selectively targeted, human capital intervention to the government's flagship anti-poverty program remains a sore issue for most of the academics (interviews with Manuel Barahona, Pablo Sauma, Carla Valderde, and Diego Víquez). As Víquez explained, "Arias needed two or three big accomplishments. We needed a full administration to measure the program's impact. Arias was not going to wait. The program lost its vision. It became a machine for giving away money."

This transition toward an anti-poverty program sped up as the economy slowed in 2008 and entered into recession in 2009. Extending Avancemos to 200,000 beneficiaries and a 150%-increase in non-contributory pensions were the central planks of the social policy portion of the Arias administration's Plan Escudo (Shield Plan) stimulus package (Villareal and Gómez 2010, 276). Arias was overly ambitious and ultimately had to scale down the expansion plans (Mata 2009). Still, by 2010 the program was reaching 185,000 beneficiaries or 43% of secondary school students. Arias defended the decision in light of the crisis:

We had to move faster. Without that, the crisis would have worsened poverty and desertion. The great thing is the crisis didn't affect them.... The crisis could have been devastating. The crisis under [President Rodrigo] Carazo (1978–82) created a lost generation. Avancemos was an essential shield. (interview, Oscar Arias)

7.1.3 Evolving Program Design

The rupture between the Arias administration and the academics only deepened as the program expanded in the aftermath of the global financial crisis. Arias and his centrist successor Laura Chinchilla (2010–14) steadily loosened the program's eligibility requirements, opening it to a larger share of the population. The now-estranged social policy experts resented the ad hoc manner in which the program, which, in their opinion, had been the best-designed CCT in the region, expanded into just another anti-poverty program (interviews with Manuel Barahona, Pablo Sauma, and Diego Víquez). Despite this expansion, Avancemos remains one of Costa Rica's most progressive social programs. Upwards of 70% of beneficiaries are from the bottom two quintiles (Oviedo et al. 2015, 118) and rural students are overrepresented (Meza-Cordero et al. 2015, 71).

Whereas the pilot covered only 13–17 year olds living in extreme and moderate poverty (scores of 1 and 2 on the proxy means test), the nationwide program expanded the target population to 12–21 year olds and to "at risk" nonpoor students (score of 3). In 2010, coverage was extended up to age 25 and, at the discretion of IMAS case workers, to certain students not deemed at risk (score 4). The Chinchilla administration loosened eligibility criteria once more in 2013, this time to include students who were retaking a grade for a second time—since the pilot beneficiaries had only been allowed to retake a grade once. These decisions allowed the program to improve coverage among the large share of secondary students—as much as 15%—who have failed at least one grade (Programa Estado de la Nación 2017, 190). Critics interpreted it as a watering down of the program human capital objectives.

Technical criteria also took a back seat to political expediency with regard to stipend amounts. Faced with tighter budgets because of the program's expansion and slowing economy, the Arias and Chinchilla administrations discarded the pilot program's provision requiring that stipends be adjusted for inflation every year (CGR 2012, 12). They opted for

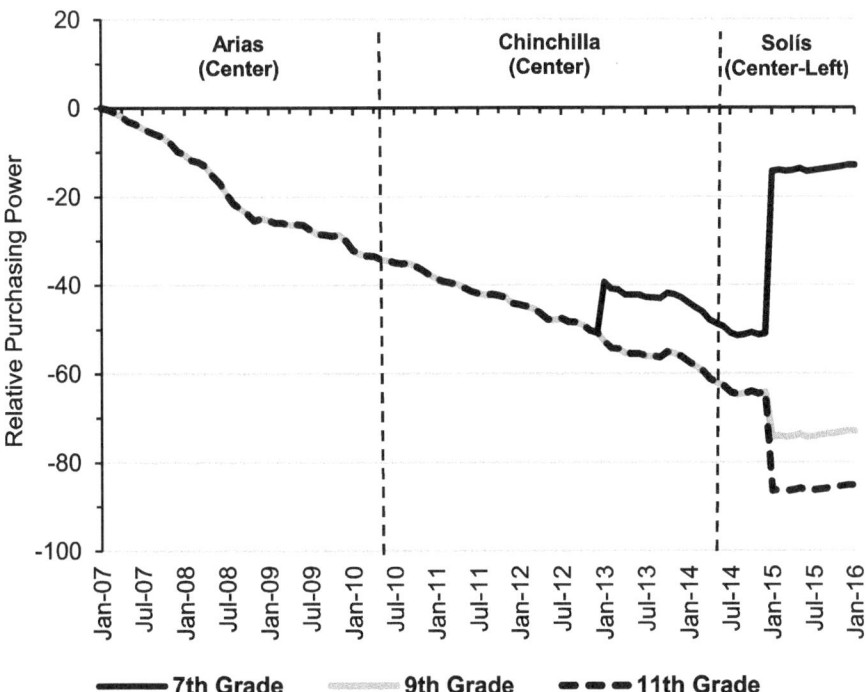

Figure 7-2. Avancemos: Stipend Purchasing Power by Grade Over Time (2007–2016)
Sources: Own calculations based in inflation data from the INEC (2020) and news reports.

increased coverage (poverty reduction) over compensating for the opportunity cost of remaining in school (human capital) (interviews with Juan Manuel Cordero and José Antonio Li). As Arias put it in an interview, "We got to all those who needed the program. We would have liked to adjust the amounts—the higher, the better. But we could not because of the crisis." By January 2013, when the stipend for (and only for) seventh grade increased by 13%, stipend purchasing power had decreased by close to 50% (see fig. 7-2).

Conditionalities also became less ambitious. In 2008, officials scrapped the program's health conditionality, which was never enforced. Though Costa Rica has universal healthcare, teenagers tend to underuse those services. Proponents hoped that conditionality would increase their use of preventative care (interview, Diego Víquez) and that, by informing dropouts about the program, clinics would stimulate reenrollment (interview,

Manuel Barahona). Bureaucratic infighting prevented this from happening. The autonomous National Health Service repeatedly questioned the plan's feasibility and dragged its feet until the government gave up (interviews with Rosibel Herrera, María José Morales, and Olga Sonia Vargas).[7]

Major administrative changes also shifted Avancemos's focus more toward poverty reduction. At its onset, the program was implemented jointly by IMAS and the Education Ministry's National Scholarship Fund, which awarded merit-based scholarships to low-income students.[8] Whereas the former had experience operating large anti-poverty programs and precisely targeting beneficiaries, the latter was present in every school in the country. As with the healthcare conditionality, coordination proved difficult (CGR 2008, 2012; Román 2010). Avancemos was ultimately folded into IMAS in 2009 and thus lost its eyes and ears in the schools (interview, María José Morales). Resistance from teachers, who complained about the additional work created by the conditionality and later resented "having to work for IMAS," further complicated conditionality enforcement (interviews with María José Morales and Olga Sonia Vargas).

Thus, neither targeting nor conditionality enforcement lived up to the original plan. This led to the publication of a string of critical news reports (La Nación 2008b, 2008c, 2009, 2011) as well as a scathing report by the Comptroller's Office (CGR 2008). IMAS responded by taking steps to prevent ineligible people from receiving benefits and improve conditionality enforcement (La Nación 2010). In 2012, it launched a new information technology platform to monitor enrollment and attendance that greatly improved conditionality enforcement (La Nación 2012; Hernández Romero 2016, 16–17). Principals could now update school rosters in real time, making it easier to identify dropouts, particularly those who quit midyear (interview, Rosibel Herrera).

Having analyzed the politics of Costa Rica's human capital CCTs, the next section looks at the case of Bolivia's basic income CCT.

7.2 Bolivia: Left-Wing President Adopts Basic Income CCT

Named after a 12-year-old Bolivian boy believed to have sacrificed his life fending off Chilean troops during the War of the Pacific (1879–83), Bono Juancito Pinto is Bolivia's flagship CCT.[9] The program, which was adopted in October 2006 by left-wing President Evo Morales (2006–19), is the Latin

American CCT that comes the closest to the basic income ideal type. It has the broadest scope of any program in the region—by 2014 it covered essentially all public-school students or about one in five Bolivians—and is, in practice, unconditional (OSPE-B 2011, 24).

Like other left-wing leaders, Morales was a late convert to CCTs. Such programs were absent from his 2002 and 2005 presidential campaign platforms (McGuire 2013, 9). The omission from the latter is noteworthy given how popular CCTs had become in Latin America by that time and the fact that right-wing Bolivian politicians had, for several years, proposed such programs at the national level and even successfully enacted one at the local level in El Alto, a mostly indigenous city on the outskirts of La Paz, the country's capital (McGuire 2013, 9–10). Given his ideology, Morales was deeply skeptical of targeted programs. In fact, during his first months in office, he rejected a Planning Ministry proposal for a nationwide targeted CCT with variable stipends for each grade because it was not universal (interviews with Werner Hernani-Limarino, Erick Meave, and Ernesto Yáñez). In enacting a universal program, Morales went against the advice of the World Bank (2006, 34–35).

The adoption of BJP as well as the adoption of Bono Juana Azurduy (Juan Azurduy Bonus), a universal CCT aimed at promoting healthcare usage among expectant mothers and infants, and the expansion of Renta Dignidad (Dignity Income), a universal non-contributory pension program, was made possible by Morales's much-publicized nationalization of the country's hydrocarbon resources in May 2006.[10] Morales justified universalism on the grounds that the natural resource wealth being nationalized belonged to *all* Bolivians and, as such, should be spent on everyone and not just the neediest (Medinaceli and Mokrani 2010; Durana 2012, 63). In Morales's own words when announcing the program, "The only thing Evo Morales has done as president is to return the money of the people, back to the people, through Bono Juancito Pinto" (cited in Durana 2012, 63).

The program aims to guarantee an income floor to all families with children enrolled in public schools. Human capital is of secondary concern. At its inception, the program only covered students up to fifth grade, but eligibility expanded steadily and all grades were covered by 2014 (see fig. 7–3). While the program nominally requires beneficiaries to attend school 80% of the time, there is no evidence of conditionality enforcement, straining its classification as a CCT program. All students receive the same yearly stipend—200 bolivianos ($25 at launch)—in cash personally delivered to each

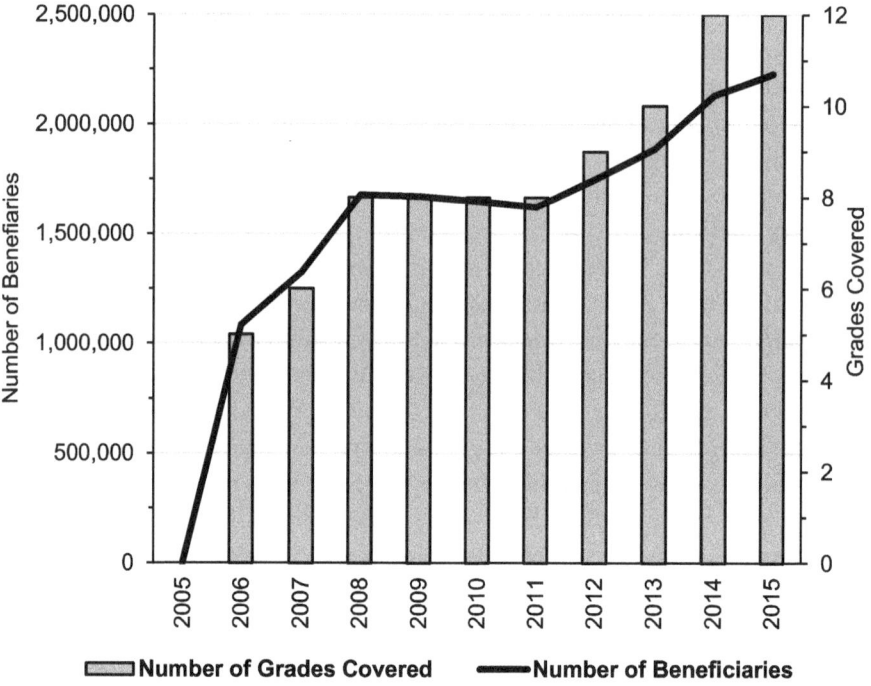

Figure 7-3. Bono Juancito Pinto: Evolution of Coverage (2006-2015)
Source: Non-contributory Social Protection Programmes Database (CEPAL 2018).

school by members of the armed forces or, sometimes, by Morales himself. That amount was determined politically and is not based on any technical criteria (Medinaceli and Mokrani 2010, 249). Although universalism makes sense given Bolivia's high poverty and low state capacity, the country's significant educational disparities—male-female, urban-rural, and mestizo-indigenous—may justify targeting and variable stipends.

7.2.1 Socioeconomic Context

In addition to being one of the poorest countries in the hemisphere, Bolivia has historically been one of its most unequal and among the worst performers in terms of poverty reduction and economic growth. This set into motion a negative policy feedback loop: high inequality hindered both poverty reduction during economic expansions and economic growth during recessions (Gray Molina and Yáñez 2010, 1). Education, through a combination of low overall achievement levels and relatively high wages for graduates, was the single most important driver of inequality during the decade preceding Morales's election (Gray Molina and Yáñez 2010, 19). Faced with this context, beginning in the early 2000s, politicians of the center-right—not the left—began proposing education-linked cash transfer programs at the local and national levels (McGuire 2013, 11).

Given its low level of economic development, Bolivia is one of a handful of countries in the region where net primary enrollment remains below 90%. Net enrollment in secondary school is significantly lower at about 75% (Fiszbein and Stanton 2018, 12). Aggregate enrollment figures, however, tell only part of the story. There are significant, albeit declining, disparities in educational attainment by sex, ethnicity, and geographic area (Gray Molina and Yáñez 2010, 12; Zambrana 2010).[11] Furthermore, a high proportion of students, particularly among those of indigenous descent or living in the countryside, or both, enter school at an older age than suggested. In 2006, 39% of children 6–8 were not enrolled in school and 45% of children 9–11 were enrolled in a grade lower than the one corresponding to their age (Canelas and Niño Zarazúa 2018, 8). Late enrollment leads to a higher dropout rate later on. Older students are more valuable in the labor market and thus face a stronger incentive to drop out and begin working full time. A cash benefit starting in first grade was seen as a way of incentivizing parents to enroll their children at the suggested age.

Bolivia's high rates of child labor further justified adopting a CCT. Though the number has since dropped significantly (U.S. Department of Labor 2017), in 2002 nearly a quarter of children 7–14 were engaged in labor activities (U.S. Department of Labor 2006, 99). In the countryside, child labor in agriculture is "embedded into normative aspects and tradition, whereby it is considered as part of children's instruction and skill development" (Canelas and Niño Zarazúa 2018, 7). However, given the short length of school days and the school term—Bolivia has the lowest number of yearly classroom hours in South America (Marco Navarro 2012, 13)—child labor may not necessarily substitute for school attendance (Canelas and Niño Zarazúa 2018, 3).

The country's high poverty rate further justified adopting a CCT. When Morales assumed the presidency in 2006, three in five Bolivians were poor, two-thirds of which lived in extreme poverty. Those figures reached 75% and 60%, respectively, in rural areas (Ramos Menar et al. 2017, 173) and were even higher among children under 12 and the indigenous (Castellani and Zenteno 2015, 4). Furthermore, poverty rates had been essentially stagnant for a decade (Ramos Menar et al. 2017, 173).

Bolivia's first targeted anti-poverty program was the Emergency Social Fund, which was enacted in 1986 to ameliorate the negative consequences of the country's shock-therapy-style stabilization (Newman, Jorgensen, and Pradhan 1991; Graham 1992). The program provided communities and nongovernmental organizations with funding for labor-intensive infrastructure projects that employed local residents. It was widely criticized for failing to reach the poorest and was plagued by allegations that the selection of beneficiaries was politicized.

The country's first attempt to fight poverty through cash transfers was Bono Solidario (Solidarity Bonus, Bonosol), a universal non-contributory pension adopted in 1997. Though universal, the program's roots were unabashedly neoliberal. It was enacted as part of the partial privatization of state-owned enterprises during the first administration of center-right President Gonzalo Sánchez de Lozada (1993–97; 2002–3). The dividends from the privatized assets were distributed to all Bolivians over 65 in the form of an annual payment. The World Bank and IDB opposed the decision to forego means testing (McGuire 2013, 27).[12] In October 2007, Morales increased the program's stipends by a third, reduced the eligibility age to 60, and renamed it Renta Dignidad (Dignity Payment). It was the region's first universal non-contributory pension program (Müller 2009; Arza 2017).

During his successful 2002 presidential campaign, Sánchez de Lozada promised to complement Bonosol with two CCTs targeting particularly vulnerable groups. Bono Educación (Education Bonus) was to increase primary school attendance among low-income girls, while Bono Salud (Health Bonus) would promote healthcare usage among low-income children under five (MNR 2002, 77, 79–80). However, in October 2003, Sánchez de Lozada was forced to resign before the programs could be enacted as a result of the so-called Gas War, massive protests against his government's plans to export Bolivian gas through Chilean ports that resulted in 59 deaths.

Although education-linked cash transfers failed to materialize at the national level, they were successfully implemented at the local level in El Alto. In September 2003, the city's center-right mayor Luis Paredes launched Bono Esperanza (Hope Bonus), which paid every first grader in the city four installments of 50 Bolivianos (about $6.50 at the time). The program was then expanded to other grades.[13] Its popularity prompted former president Jorge "Tuto" Quiroga (2001–2), Morales's centrist opponent in 2005, to promise a targeted national Bono Esperanza conditioned on school attendance and on receiving medical checkups (Agencia Noticias Fides 2005; Caracol Radio 2005; McGuire 2013, 10).[14]

7.2.2 Adoption and Expansion

The only president to be elected by an outright majority since Bolivia democratized in 1982, Morales came into office in January 2006 with a strong mandate to enact a new constitution refounding Bolivia as a plurinational state, nationalize the country's gas reserves, and redistribute income toward the poor (Madrid 2011, 239). Yet the instruments he would use to carry out that redistribution remained unclear. The right had put cash transfers on agenda, while the left was, at best, ambivalent. Ultimately, as in Brazil under Lula, an initially reluctant left-wing president came to embrace, expand, and reinterpret CCTs in a more universal and less conditional direction (see chapter 3). Morales and his Movement toward Socialism (MAS) were slow to endorse cash transfers linked to education, but when they did, they transformed them into something more akin to a universal income floor.

But before Morales could implement his vision, he needed fresh resources. On Labor Day 2006, he signed a decree declaring state ownership of the country's gas reserves and authorizing the military and workers from the revitalized state-owned energy company Bolivian Fiscal Petroleum Deposits (YPFB) to seize control of gas wells operated by foreign firms. Under the new rules, private energy firms would continue to extract gas but would have to sell it to YPFB, which would handle all distribution and commercialization. As a result, the Bolivian state came to accrue more than 80% of the industry's profits (Fundación Jubileo 2012, 25). Fortuitously, nationalization coincided with a China-fueled spike in global commodity prices. As a result of nationalization and higher prices, the government's intake from taxes and royalties rose from 28% of GDP in 2004 to 45% in 2010 (De León Naveiro 2011, 58). Bolivia's fiscal situation further improved with the culmination of various debt forgiveness schemes, which reduced the government's debt obligations by more than half, from about 84% of GDP in 2003 to 31% in 2008 (Cali and Jemio 2010, 21).

Morales launched BJP in October 2006 via presidential decree. Neither legislators nor representatives of civil society were consulted, let alone involved in the program's design.[15] As Orlando Murillo, formerly head of analysis at the Education Ministry, explained, "The decision [to adopt BJP] came from the president and the cabinet. The reasoning was that it had to be done and we had to do it. A small team was built. It was a matter of executing it." The first payments were made five weeks later. BJP remains highly centralized within the executive. The program's budget is decided on an annual basis by the president and the finance minister (interview, Erick Meave). Legislators, particularly those from the opposition, remain shut out from discussions regarding the program (interview, Marcelo Antezana). More than a decade after its launch, BJP continues to operate via decree and there appear to be no plans to enshrine it in law. The legislature's oversight of BJP is further hampered by the fact that a large share, and, in some years the entirety, of its budget is paid by YPFB and other autonomous state-owned enterprises (Aguilar Pacajes 2014, 7–8; Eju! 2018).[16]

Sources interviewed noted that, although social policymaking in Bolivia has always been controlled by presidents, policymaking under Morales is more centralized than under his predecessors (interviews with Erick Meave and Ernesto Yáñez). Whereas in the past agencies such as the Planning Ministry played an active role in designing policies, under Morales the social policy bureaucracy's role has been limited to implementing the presidency's decisions. Interviewed shortly after Morales announced the extension of BJP to ninth graders, Erick Meave, an economist at the Planning Ministry's Social Policy Division, noted that "the decision to expand comes from the president. The president does not consult, he simply does. The decree got to us the day before the cabinet discussed it."

The decision to forgo means testing and make the program available to all public-school students can be attributed to three factors: presidential ideology, path dependence, and practical considerations. First, as demonstrated in chapter 2, left-wing leaders across the region, Morales among them, were skeptical of CCTs for their use of targeting and association with international financial institutions. A long-time critic of IFIs, Morales never embraced the targeted CCTs proposed by his opponents and rejected similar proposals from Planning Ministry technocrats (McGuire 2013, 9; interviews with Werner Hernani-Limarino, Erick Meave, and Ernesto Yáñez) and the World Bank (2006, 34–35).

Path dependence also played a role. Reliance on funding from the nationalization of hydrocarbons, which Morales himself had repeatedly said belonged to *all* Bolivians, and the precedent set by Bonosol created the expectation that the new programs would be universal. Dyer (2012, 3) goes so far as to argue that universalism was part of a broader strategy aimed at consolidating support among the diverse anti-neoliberal coalition that had brought Morales to power. Universal programs funded by hydrocarbon rents were central to his plan to refound Bolivia as a pluri-ethnic socialist state and create a shared sense of national identity capable of overcoming the country's regional cleavages and weak nationalism.

There were also practical reasons for going with a simpler, universal program. The Bolivian state's authority manifests itself unevenly across the country, conjuring up images of a "Swiss cheese state" (UNDP 2007). BJP's heterodox design was an attempt to adapt CCTs to a low-capability state. There were legitimate doubts regarding how well the Bolivian government would have been able to pull off a "state-of-the-art" CCT with precise means testing and strict conditionality enforcement. Furthermore, given the country's high poverty levels, a CCT with a reasonably high exclusion threshold would have likely covered much of the student population. Under such conditions, the administrative costs of means testing cease to be cost effective (interview, Verónica Paz Arauco; McGuire 2013).

Given the state's weakness and the limited reach of the country's financial system, BJP is paid only once a year in cash and delivered personally to schools by the military. Experts consulted praised the military's role, noting that it remains the only public institution capable of reaching every corner of the country at a low cost (interviews with Erick Meave and Ernesto Yáñez). The absence of means testing and reliance on the armed forces have kept BJP's administrative costs below 4% (interview, Erick Meave), comparable to Mexico's CCT, among the region's best run (Caldés, Coady, and Maluccio 2006, 834). In addition, Dyer (2012) argues that using the military yields the added political benefit of giving them a stake in MAS's political project. As the fourth president is as many years, Morales had a strong incentive to get on the military's good side.[17] Anecdotal evidence suggests officers are proud of their involvement (Dyer 2012, 58).

BJP's lack of conditionality enforcement, however, stretches the definition of CCT. There is no data on conditionality enforcement and all experts consulted agreed that the attendance requirement is not enforced (interviews with Werner Hernani-Limarino, Orlando Murillo, and Verónica Paz Arauco). The closest measure of conditionality enforcement comes from a survey of 3,666 students, which showed that 99.2% received the stipend (OSPE-B 2011, 24). Lack of proper documentation was the main reason cited in the handful of cases of nonpayment.[18] Tellingly, only six students said they had been excluded for failing to meet the enrollment requirements.[19]

7.2.3 The Trade-offs of Universalism?

It is worth assessing the trade-offs of opting for universalism. Although BJP is not means tested, it is still progressive inasmuch as better-off families tend to have fewer children than poor ones and are more likely to send their children to private schools (McGuire 2013, 14). By virtue of its universalism, the program covers the vast majority of the country's poor. In 2009, when up to ninth grade was covered, BJP reached 70.5% and 61.6% those in extreme and moderate poverty, respectively, as well as 37.9% of the nonpoor. Overall, just under half of recipients (47.5%) were poor (Paz Arauco et al. 2013, 339). That share, however, has likely declined as the program has expanded to grades in which poor children are less represented (interview, Werner Hernani-Limarino). Regionally, BJP holds the distinction of having both the highest coverage relative to eligible population but also below average spending levels relative to GDP (Cecchini and Atuesta 2017, 25, 34). These figures suggest that a targeted but more generous program would have a larger impact on poverty and inequality, albeit at a higher administrative cost.

The steady decline in the purchasing power of BJP's already quite small stipends presents a more serious problem than the absence of targeting. Stipend amounts have remained unchanged since the program's adoption and, by December 2015, their purchasing power had declined by nearly three-quarters (see fig. 7-4). The relative decline in BJP's generosity has more to do with political priorities than with its universalism. The Morales administration has chosen to spend roughly five times more on Renta Dignidad than on BJP and Bono Juana Azurduy combined, which cover two and a half times more people. At the launch, the former paid beneficiaries 150 bolivianos *per month*—three-quarters of what BJP recipients received in *a year*. Furthermore, the government has sought to adjust Renta Dignidad's stipends to keep up with inflation—increasing them by 25% in May 2013 and adding a thirteenth month of benefits (*aguinaldo*) in August 2014.[20] Ironically, Bolivia's non-contributory social programs suffer from the same pathology that has traditionally afflicted the region's social policy—relatively generous benefits for retirees (some as young as 60) and underinvestment in the next generation's human capital.

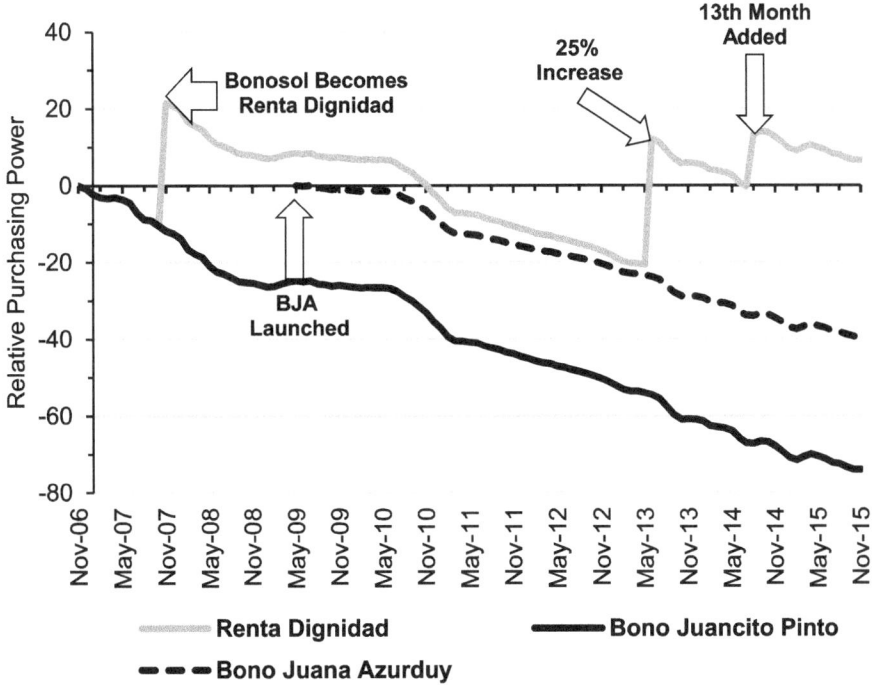

Figure 7-4. Bolivian Cash Transfer Programs: Stipend Purchasing Power (2006–2015)
Source: Own calculations based in inflation data from the BCB (2020) and news reports.

Having analyzed at the politics of a basic income CCT in Bolivia, the next section looks at Argentina's basic income CCT.

7.3 Argentina: Left-Wing President Adopts Basic Income CCT

Described as "the most important social right created since the return to democracy in 1983" (Etchemendy and Garay 2011, 296), Argentina's Asignación Universal por Hijo differs from most other programs in the region in that it is both a CCT and an attempt to universalize the country's longstanding system of child allowances for formal-sector workers. Thus, AUH represents a concerted effort by the center-left administration of Cristina Fernández de Kirchner (2007–15) to ensure that all families with children possess a minimum level of income.[21] In that regard, AUH seeks to break with Latin America's "bifurcated" approach to social policy characterized by permanent and, in some cases, quite generous benefits for formal-sector workers and modest, often ad hoc, social assistance for labor market outsiders.

Like Bolivia's Morales and other left-wing leaders across the region, Fernández was the last major political actor in her country to join the consensus in favor of CCTs. At the local level, the Buenos Aires city government launched the Ciudadanía Porteña (Porteña Citizenship) CCT in 2005.[22] During the 2007-9 legislature, opposition legislators from across the ideological spectrum proposed cash transfer bills that languished in the absence of government support (Repetto, Díaz-Langou, and Marazzi 2009). Domestic political challenges, namely a recession in the aftermath of the 2008-9 global financial crisis and a sharp drop in the government's popularity (Catterberg and Palanza 2012, 22), ultimately convinced Fernández to launch AUH in October 2009. In using a CCT to universalize family allowances, Argentina emulated its neighbor Uruguay, which under the center-left government of Tabaré Vázquez (2005-10; 2015-20) universalized its family allowances a year earlier via its Asignaciones Familiares CCT program (see Straschnoy 2011). IFIs were not involved in the program's design or initial funding (interview, Ezequiel Lo Valvo).

By 2014, the program, which covers up to five children per household, covered 3.6 million children, or about half of all Argentine public-school students (see fig. 7-5). Taken together, AUH and contributive family allowances cover more than 90% of poor and middle-class children (UNICEF et al. 2017, 24), significantly advancing the goal of guaranteeing an income floor for all Argentine families with children.[23] Despite its unique design as an extension of existing child allowances, AUH meets all the criteria for a basic income CCT. The program is not explicitly means tested, covers all grades, pays all beneficiaries the same flat stipend regardless of risk of dropping out of school, and has lax conditionality enforcement. Rather than target beneficiaries based on income, AUH is open to children under 18 whose parents are unemployed or work in the informal economy. AUH's emphasis on poverty reduction rather than boosting human capital is further evidenced by the decision to cover children too young to attend school. In line with its basic income classification, the program is "semiconditional" in that 80% of the monthly stipend is unconditional with the remainder conditioned on school attendance (Bertranou and Maurizio 2012).

AUH was subsequently complemented in 2011 with Asignación por

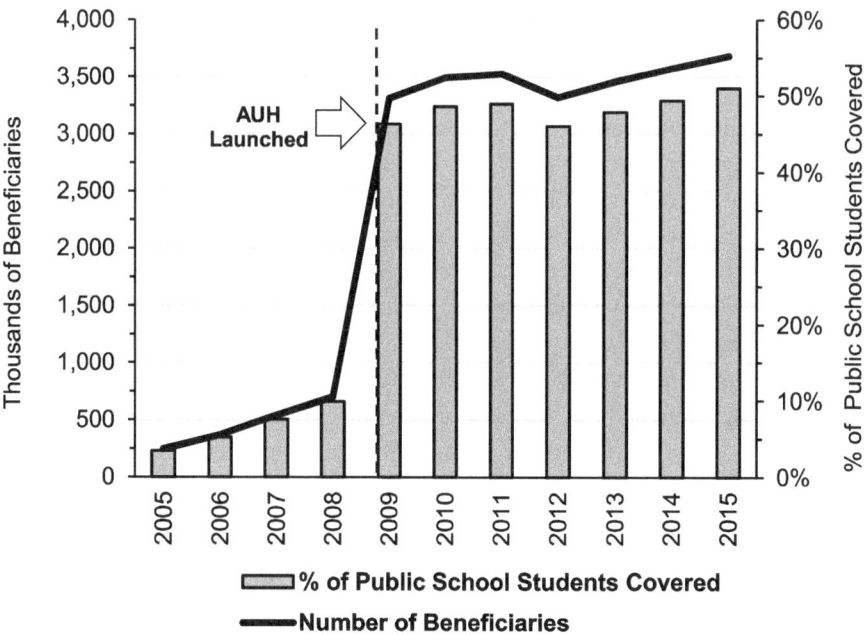

Figure 7-5. Argentine Cash Transfer Programs: Evolution of Coverage (2005–2015)
Sources: Repetto and Díaz-Langou (2010, 6) up to 2008 and Non-contributory Social Protection Programmes Database (CEPAL 2018) up to 2015.

Embarazo (Pregnancy Allowance), which awards stipends to new and expectant mothers conditional on prenatal care, and in 2014 with Progresar (Let's Make Progress), which awards 18–24 year olds stipends to finish high school or enroll in technical education. Like AUH, both programs target the unemployed and informal-sector workers and are semiconditional.

7.3.1 Socioeconomic Context

Permanent and widespread poverty is a recent phenomenon in Argentina (Levitsky and Murillo 2008, 153; Fenwick 2015, 119). Historically highly urbanized and industrialized, the country was a welfare pioneer, having laid the foundations for a comprehensive social security system based on contributory pensions and health insurance in the 1920s (Mesa-Lago 1990, xv). This system became practically universal during the first term of President Juan Domingo Perón (1946–55; 1973–74), the populist founder of the Justicialist Party, an ideologically flexible labor-based political movement best known as Peronism.

From the 1940s through the 1970s, low levels of unemployment and informality and high union membership kept poverty relief largely off the political agenda. This changed in the aftermath of the 1980s debt crisis and subsequent structural adjustment reforms that downsized the public sector and dismantled import substitution industrialization policies (Arcidiáno 2016, 97; Fenwick 2016, 119). As Fenwick (2016, 122) notes, "High poverty rates and unemployment only began to gain visibility in Argentina during [center-right] President [Carlos] Menem's first term (1989–1995)" (see also Levitsky and Murillo 2008, 153). Despite being a Peronist, Menem wholeheartedly embraced the Washington Consensus and turned Argentina into the "poster child" for neoliberalism. With unemployment and informality on the rise, the share of Argentines outside the social security system grew, threatening the Peronists' status as the party of the working class (Fenwick 2016, 124). Poverty was initially diagnosed as a temporary malady rather than a structural feature of the Argentine economy. Menem responded in 1996 with Plan Trabajar (Work Plan), the country's first large-scale anti-poverty program. A workfare program conditional on contributing labor to community projects, Plan Trabajar at its peak covered 20% of the country's poor. In contrast to AUH and other CCTs in the region, benefits were awarded in a highly clientelistic manner (Lodola 2005; Weitz-Shapiro 2006; Giraudy 2007).

The worrying poverty and unemployment trends further deepened during the country's 1999–2002 economic crisis, which culminated in a financial and political crisis at the end of 2001.[24] To put it in perspective, Argentina's economy shrank by more than 20% during that period (World Bank 2005, 1). A quarter of the population was unemployed and half of those who kept their jobs suffered wage cuts (Agis, Cañete, and Panigo 2010, 13). Massive protests against the government (*cacerolazos*) became a regular occurrence and ultimately forced Menem's successor, Fernando de la Rúa (1999–2001), a centrist from the Alliance for Work, Justice and Education (La Alianza) coalition, to resign.[25] In the span of 12 days, the presidency changed hands three times before Congress appointed Senator Eduardo Duhalde (2002–3), a centrist Peronist and the runner-up in the 1999 presidential election, to finish de la Rúa's term.[26]

Duhalde is remembered for ending the peso's parity to the dollar (*convertibilidad*) and launching Programa Jefes y Jefas de Hogar Desempleados

(Unemployed Heads of Households Program), a massive workfare program that was crucial to restoring social peace (Golbert 2004; Fenwick 2016, 129).[27] Jefes paid unemployed heads of households a 150-peso monthly stipend—$50 at launch or about half the cost of a basic basket of goods and 20% of the poverty line (Golbert and Giacometti 2008, 33)—in exchange for 20 hours of community labor and conditional on their children attending school. At its peak in mid-2002, Jefes reached roughly 20% of households (Golbert and Giacometti 2008, 29), 90% of which were below the poverty line (Galasso and Ravallion 2004).

Néstor Kirchner (2003–7), a center-left Peronist, was elected president in April 2003 and assumed office the following month. As the economy recovered in 2003 and, because of the sharp increase in commodity prices, boomed after 2005, the majority of Jefes beneficiaries "graduated" into formal-sector jobs. Yet poverty did not disappear, raising questions over how to address long-term poverty. Jefes, which was designed as a short-term emergency program, was ill-suited for this purpose. Enrollment was only open during April-May 2002 and never reopened, thus excluding 80% of eligible adults (Galasso and Ravallion 2004, 372). Further, its stipend was never adjusted for inflation. The program's flat per-household stipend limited its effect on large families, which tend to be disproportionately poor, particularly after inflation took off in late 2004. There was also substantial leakage of benefits: one-third of participants, primarily married women, were not in fact "unemployed heads of households" (Galasso and Ravallion 2004, 395–96; Golbert and Giacometti 2008). The program had also developed a bad reputation (*mala fama*) (Fenwick 2016, 146) for the widespread use of clientelism in selecting beneficiaries (Galasso and Ravallion 2004; Golbert 2004; Giovagnoli 2005; Giraudy 2007).

With regard to education, Argentina's main problem is secondary school completion. In 2008, the year before AUH's launch, net attendance was essentially universal (above 97%) for children of both primary (6–11) and lower-secondary (12–14) school age, but dropped significantly (to about 83%) among those of upper-secondary age (15–17) (Edo, Marchionni, and Garganta 2017, 6).[28] The latter figure dropped to 74% among students from the poorest 20% of households, compared to 93% among those in the richest 40% (Edo, Marchionni, and Garganta 2017, 7). Furthermore, that same year, only 30% of 17–18 year olds had graduated. That figure was closer to 20% for students from the bottom 40% of households (Marchionni and Edo 2017, 300).

Tenth grade constitutes the system's main bottleneck. A full quarter (26%) of students who enrolled in that grade in 2007 ultimately exited the school system. An additional 11% failed and had to repeat the grade while 10% passed but went on to fail eleventh grade (Argentinos por la Educación 2019, 8). With each grade failure, the student becomes one year older and more likely to choose the labor market over education at the cost of much-lower lifetime earnings. Argentina had a significant need for a CCT that could persuade low-income teenagers to stay in school.

7.3.2 Argentina Debates Basic Income and Human Capital

By the mid-1990s and particularly after the country's economic meltdown, it had become clear that high unemployment and informality were the new normal. This new class of labor-market outsiders, which in the mid-1990s outnumbered formal-sector workers (Lo Vuolo 1995, 131), found itself excluded from the country's contributory social security system. In response, Argentina played host to a lively debate between supporters of basic income and human capital cash transfer programs.

In a pioneering work, economists Rubén Lo Vuolo and Alberto Barbeito (1995) proposed that these problems be tackled through an unconditional basic income guarantee for all Argentines, starting with the universalization of child allowances. The proposal gained particular salience during the depths of the economic crisis. In December 2001, 2.7 million Argentines voted in an informal referendum on child allowance universalization organized by the National Front Against Poverty, a coalition spearheaded by the Argentine Workers' Central Union, a major labor union, and organizations representing unemployed workers (*piqueteros*) (Arcidiácono et al. 2012, 156; Rossi 2013, 145). However, de la Rúa resigned before the National Front Against Poverty could present the results.

In the meantime, social policy technocrats from the center-right Menem administration were, with assistance from the IDB, developing what would have been one of the region's first human capital CCTs—Ingreso para el Desarrollo Humano (Income for Human Development, IDH). In a book chapter detailing the program, Irene Novacovsky and Claudia Sobrón (1999, 232) of the Social Development Ministry described the proposal as "a bet on the development of human capital." The authors made a point to distinguish their program from both existing workfare programs and Lo Vuolo and Barbeito's basic income proposal (Novacovsky and Sobrón 1999, 230).

As would be expected from a program designed by a center-right administration with support from IFIs, IDH met all the criteria for a human capital CCT. A proxy means test would be used to narrowly target the poor and prioritize those in extreme poverty. Benefits were to be conditional on a detailed list of educational and health benchmarks that would vary by age and be rigorously enforced (Novacovsky and Sobrón 1999, 234). Stipends were to vary based on the estimated opportunity cost of remaining in school and the regional cost of living. In line with its human capital motivation, the program would pay additional bonuses for passing grades, particularly the ninth grade, the last before upper-secondary school (Novacovsky and Sobrón 1999, 231). The program was to be subject to rigorous evaluation, beginning with a pilot funded by IFIs (Novacovsky and Sobrón 1999, 238).

Neither basic income nor IDH were implemented in the immediate aftermath of the crisis. Duhalde doubled down on workfare by launching Jefes y Jefas. Néstor Kirchner inherited the program, which at the end of 2003 still covered 1.8 million households (Repetto and Díaz-Langou 2010, 6). Kirchner and his team were not fond of Jefes, which was associated with Duhalde, who was still seen as a formidable political rival (Fenwick 2016, 133), or of the CCTs that had started being adopted across Latin America. As left-leaning Peronists, they firmly believed that poverty should be tackled through the creation of formal employment (interviews with Laura Golbert and Pablo Vinocur; Arcidiácono 2016, 103). Opposition to CCTs was strongest from Alicia Kirchner, Néstor's sister and social development minister during most of the Kirchner administration and the entirety of Fernández's tenure. Alicia repeatedly derided CCTs as "neoliberal," "impositions from IFIs," or "pre-packaged programs" (*programas enlatados*) not suited for Argentina's reality (Kirchner 2010; interviews with Eduardo Amadeo, Leonardo Gasparini, and Pablo Vinocur).

Kirchner at first tried to have Jefes fade away as beneficiaries "graduated" and inflation, which, starting in late 2004 reached double digit annual rates, ate away at remainers' stipends. However, in October 2004, he signed a decree ordering the transfer of remaining beneficiaries to two new successor programs. Those deemed to have favorable employment prospects would move to Seguro de Capacitación y Empleo (Training and Employment Insurance), which would provide training and a stipend. Those with less favorable prospects (primarily single mothers without a secondary school education) were to be transferred to Programa Familias por la Inclusión Social (Families for Social Inclusion Program), a new, partially IDB-funded (Jaime and Sabate 2013) CCT modeled on IDH (Arcidiácono 2007; Campos, Faur, and Pautassi 2007, 14; Cruces and Gasparini 2008, 7; Zaga Szenker 2009, 12; Straschnoy 2015, 132; Trujillo and Retamozo 2019, 96).[29] Familias was envisioned as a strict human capital CCT with conditionality verification every three months (Campos, Faur, and Pautassi 2007, 16; Fenwick 2016, 150). The actual program was much less ambitious than the original IDH plan (Novacovsky and Sobrón 1999). Stipends were not differentiated by grade and there were no academic achievement bonuses. Conditionality enforcement never got off the ground. Conditionalities were only verified once during 2005 before being dropped altogether in 2006 (interviews cited in Fenwick 2016, 139).

Familias never came close to replacing Jefes. In 2009, shortly before AUH replaced both, 700,000 were enrolled in Familias while 550,000 remained in Jefes (Repetto and Díaz-Langou 2010, 6).[30] The program's launch was repeatedly delayed and it was not available in much of the country during its first years (Campos, Faur, and Pautassi 2007, 30). Fenwick (2016, chap. 5) attributes this to lack of buy-in from municipal governments, which are politically and financially beholden to state governors. The governors, in turn, did not support Familias, which, unlike Jefes, was highly centralized and thus could not be manipulated for political gain. Although this may have been true, Familias and other anti-poverty programs were simply not a priority for Kirchner or, initially, Fernández, as Levitsky and Murillo (2008, 28) explain:

> Though widely considered left-of-center, the [Néstor] Kirchner government neglected social policies aimed at combating poverty. Indeed, despite unprecedented fiscal health, the government did not invest heavily in either conditional cash transfers to the poor, or health and education programs for them. . . . Consequently, although unemployment and poverty rates declined sharply under Kirchner, these declines were rooted almost entirely in economic growth. In fact, levels of poverty and inequality remained higher in 2007 than they were during the mid-1990s.

This antipathy toward anti-poverty programs did not extend to other areas of social policy. Starting in 2004, Kirchner gradually doubled the share of the population covered by pensions to near universal levels (Golbert 2010, 152; Etchemendy and Garay 2011, 295). Minimum wages and pensions increased steadily under both Kirchner and Fernández (Golbert 2010, 150). And, in November 2008, Fernández renationalized the country's pension system, which Menem had privatized (Ewig and Kay 2011; Arza 2012).

7.3.3 Adoption and Evolution

This neglect of anti-poverty policy ended suddenly and dramatically once the global financial crisis hit Argentina. By the end of 2009, the economy was in recession, less than 20% of Argentines thought the country was headed in the right direction, and two-thirds disapproved of the government (Catterberg and Palanza 2012, 22). Fernández's declining popularity contributed to her faction of Peronism losing its legislative majority during the June 2009 midterm elections. Faced with growing social unrest, some of it demanding the adoption of a child allowance for labor-market outsiders (Garay 2016, 213), the same Fernández administration that had found it impossible to shut down Jefes and extend Familias to the entirety of the country's poor (Fenwick 2016) was able, in just a matter of weeks, to design and launch one of the region's most ambitious anti-poverty programs. Thus, as was the case in Brazil and Mexico, the adoption of Argentina's flagship anti-poverty CCT was a response to worsening economic circumstances and increasing political competition (see chapter 2).

The otherwise fragmented opposition was united on the need for a large-scale cash transfer program targeting children. As discussed above, the need for such a policy had been discussed since the late 1990s. More recently, the creation of an income floor for children had been the central plank of the presidential campaign of Elisa Carrió, the runner-up in the 2007 elections. Six cash transfer bills were being discussed in Congress prior to the 2009 midterms (Repetto, Díaz-Langou, and Marazzi 2009).

The recession and the midterm loss forced Fernández to finally accept that informal labor was a permanent feature of Argentina's economy and that a safety net targeting those families was both necessary and politically advantageous (interviews with Emilia Roca, Rafael Rofman, and Pablo Vinocur).[31] However, rather than seek a cross-party agreement with legislators, the administration opted to "surprise" the opposition (Repetto and Potenza 2011, 31) and "beat it to the punch" (*ganarle la mano*) (Kantor 2012, 12) and thus claim full credit for the new program (interviews with Fabio Bertanou, Laura Golbert, and Fabián Repetto). AUH was announced via decree on October 29, 2009, and the first payments were made December 1 (Misiones Online 2009)—the day the legislators elected in the midterm were sworn in.

The renationalization of the country's pension system the previous year provided Fernández with the resources necessary to sidestep Congress. The nationalization transferred the private pension system's substantial assets—estimated at $23 billion plus $4.5 billion in yearly contributions (Economist 2008)—to the National Social Security Administration, the agency placed in charge of AUH. This marked the key difference between the AUH decree and bills in Congress, which were premised on politically contentious tax reforms (Barbeito and Lo Vuolo 2009; Repetto, Díaz-Langou, and Marazzi 2009).

The political process that culminated in the adoption of AUH was a closed-door, top-down affair with neither Congress nor civil society playing a role.[32] As the World Bank's Rafael Rofman (interview) explained: "It was not a transparent process. The president decided. It was implemented. This is how things are decided in Argentina." Rubén Lo Vuolo (interview), one of the original proponents of a universal basic income in Argentina, further added: "It was a government decision. There were no actors at the table. The decision group was very closed. It has even been said that the labor minister found out afterward." Even within the National Social Security Administration, only "two or three people at the political level" knew about the program. The technical team learned about it 45 days before the first payment (interview, Ezequiel Lo Valvo).

Impressively, the program covered 3.3 million children at the launch—nearly five times as many as Familias at its peak. This can be attributed to the technical expertise of the National Social Security Administration, which is widely regarded as an island of competence and professionalism within Argentina's politicized bureaucracy (interviews with Leonardo Gasparini and Rafael Rofman). Although AUH does not explicitly target based on income, because unemployed and informal workers tend to be poor, the program is, in practice, highly progressive. In 2012, 43.2% of primary-school beneficiaries were from households in the bottom quarter of the income distribution and 72.9% were from the bottom half. Among secondary-school beneficiaries those figures drop to 37.8% and 65.3%, respectively (Salvia, Musante, and Mendoza Jaramillo 2013, 14).

Nonetheless, nearly a decade after the program's launch, an estimated 1.2 million children (9%) receive no child allowances (UNICEF et al. 2017, 24). This gap in coverage is explained by delays in the registration of births in rural areas and among indigenous communities as well as by teenagers, particularly 16–17 year olds that have dropped out of the school system (Bustos, Giglio, and Villafane 2012, 29; UNICEF et al. 2017, 47). The government's persistent inability to locate and register these children has been attributed to the National Social Security Administration's institutional culture. The agency's expertise is in operating a massive nationwide payments system, not in combating poverty. It lacks the social workers and local knowledge necessary to track down and sign up the poorest families in the remotest parts of the country (interview, Rafael Rofman). Politics has also likely played a role. Niedzwiecki (2018) finds that AUH coverage is lower in provinces with opposition governors. Her case studies reveal that, since the program's benefits are easily attributable to the federal government, opposition governors see the program as a political threat and may obstruct its implementation.

As in Bolivia, conditionality enforcement remains lax. A 2012 survey revealed that only 2% of primary and 10% of secondary school principals were aware of at least one student whose stipend had been revoked (OEBA 2012). In practice, a child can collect the unconditional 80% for a full two years without ever stepping foot in a school before being purged from the program's rolls (UNICEF et al. 2017, 45–46).[33] The remaining 20%, however, can only be collected at the end of the school year upon certifying school enrollment (not attendance) and having received a medical examination.[34]

AUH stands out compared to Avancemos and BJP in that its stipends have been regularly adjusted to compensate for and at times even surpass Argentina's high inflation (see fig. 7–6).[35] It should, however, be noted that three of the adjustments occurred in the months prior to an upcoming election. The adjustment before the 2013 legislative elections was particularly large (35%). In July 2015, shortly before leaving office, Fernández signed a law mandating that stipends be adjusted for inflation twice a year. More controversially, the law also mandated higher stipends for beneficiaries in the country's southernmost provinces to compensate for their higher living costs. These provinces, which include the Kirchners' home province of Santa Cruz, are among the country's most developed and are significantly better off than the traditionally poor northeast and northwest provinces (Abrevaya 2015).[36]

7.4 Conclusions

With an emphasis on the role of government ideology and policy diffusion, this chapter reconstructed the political processes that culminated in the

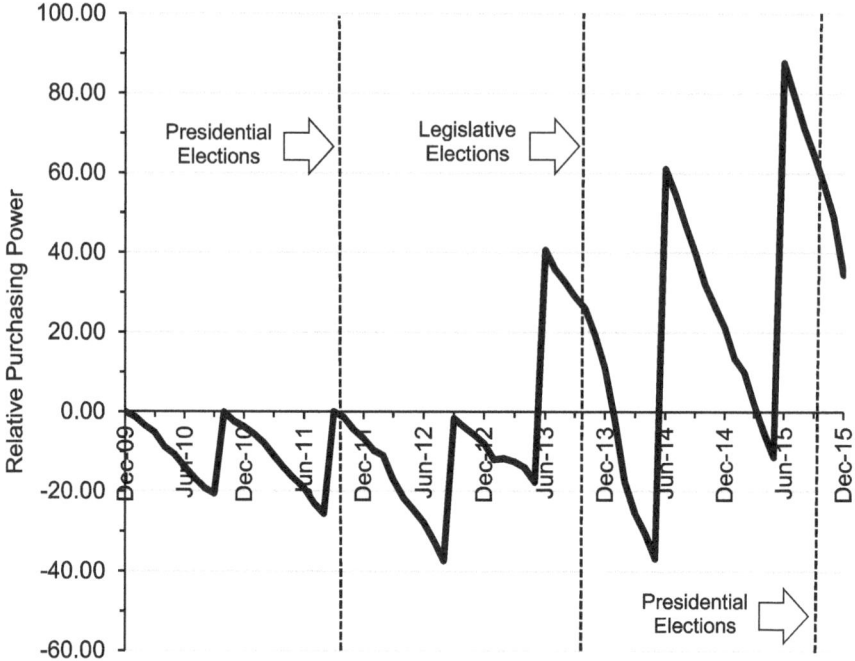

Figure 7-6. Asignación Universal por Hijo: Stipend Purchasing Power (2009–2015)
Source: Own calculations based in independent inflation data compiled by Cavallo and Bertolotto (2016) and news reports.

adoption and influenced the design of CCTs adopted by the governments of Costa Rica, Bolivia, and Argentina. The following paragraphs evaluate to what extent the case studies provide evidence in support of the hypotheses presented at the end of the previous chapter.

Attitudes toward CCTs. There is strong support for both hypotheses regarding ideology and attitudes toward CCTs. In all three countries, center-right politicians put CCTs on the political agenda. In Costa Rica, Rodríguez enacted the country's first, albeit short-lived, CCT. In Bolivia, Sánchez de Lozada and later Quiroga campaigned on national CCTs. Paredes, the center-right mayor of El Alto, enacted that country's first CCT at the local level. In Argentina, academics and social movements started discussions regarding cash transfers, but it was the Menem administration that devised IDH, which served as the basis for Familias, the country's first CCT.

Left politicians were initially skeptical, if not outright opposed, to CCTs in all three countries. In Costa Rica, Solís, Arias's center-left opponent in 2006, did not campaign on CCTs. In Bolivia, Morales did not propose a CCT during any of his campaigns, even though they had been proposed at the national level by his right-wing opponents and enacted in El Alto. Despite significantly expanding pensions and other forms of social policy, Kirchner and, initially, Fernández underinvested in poverty relief. Ironically, at the same time as they openly criticized "prepackaged," IFI-supported social programs such as CCTs, they operated the IDB-funded Familias. Yet Familias was never a priority for either administration and remained modest in size. That program represented an (unsuccessful) attempt to replace Jefes, which was associated with Duhalde, a potential rival.

Reasons for adopting CCTs. There is also strong support for the hypotheses regarding the role of ideology in justifying CCT adoption. The left and non-left's differing priorities are confirmed by the decrees that launched the programs, presidential rhetoric, and the adoption of complementary programs. Arias saw Avancemos as a tool for addressing a specific human capital deficiency—low secondary school enrollment and graduation rates—for which he felt partially responsible. He assembled a team of technocrats to design a program that came close to the human capital CCT ideal type. However, political imperatives and, ultimately, the global financial crisis led him to broaden the program's target population and de-emphasize conditionality enforcement.

In adopting their respective programs, both Morales and Fernández emphasized poverty reduction and building a universal safety net. Morales rejected a targeted proposal early on in his administration and maintained that, since BJP was funded through revenues from nationalized resources, it should be universal. As noted above, Kirchner and, initially, Fernández did not emphasize Familias, which was narrowly targeted and supposed to have strict conditionality. In adopting AUH, Fernández explicitly sought to universalize family allowances. Her timing—during the middle of the financial crisis—further evidences her motivations. The program was launched to counteract rising poverty and unemployment. Furthermore, both left-wing leaders later complemented their flagship CCTs with programs extending the income floor to new and expectant mothers. Fernández later created a CCT for 18–24 year olds.

Two-track diffusion of CCTs. While there is strong evidence that center and right-wing governments worked alongside IFIs, particularly the IDB, to enact human capital CCTs, there is, counter to expectations, little direct evidence of Brazilian officials promoting the basic income model. The IDB played a role, albeit a small one, in designing Avancemos. It is telling that the Avancemos team opted to consult with Mexican rather than Brazilian officials. The IDB helped fund the design of Argentina's IDH under Menem and later funded the operation of Familias. IFIs did not take part in the funding or design of AUH or BJP.

The field research did not provide a "smoking gun" in the form of direct evidence of high-level Brazilian involvement in the design of AUH and BJP. There is, however, evidence of bilateral cooperation between Brazil and Bolivia at the bureaucratic level (Carvalho de Lorenzo 2013, 401). Sources interviewed noted that AUH was inspired by another left-wing neighbor's basic income CCT, that of Uruguay, which also universalized family allowances (interview, Rafael Rofman; Straschnoy 2011). This program was directly influenced by Bolsa Família and Brazil's efforts to combat hunger (La Nación 2005) and benefited from Brazilian technical cooperation (Presidencia Uruguay 2005; Carvalho de Lorenzo 2013, 401). More generally, left-wing leaders were very much aware of Brazil's basic income CCT and were, via regional summits and bilateral diplomatic visits, in constant contact with Lula, who saw himself as the program's global ambassador. Similarly, in 2006 Eduardo Suplicy wrote letters to left-wing presidents including Morales and Fernández urging them to take steps toward enacting a universal basic income in their countries by emulating Bolsa Família and offering to personally assist them in this process (Suplicy 2006, 56–57). What is known is that, having a choice between two CCT models, Morales and Fernández chose to enact programs that more closely resembled Brazil's basic income CCT than Mexico's human capital CCT. While by no means direct evidence, these facts do constitute circumstantial evidence of a second "left" track of diffusion.

The book's final chapter will tie together the findings from the last six chapters, briefly assess how recent shifts in presidential ideology have affected the design of CCTs studied in earlier chapters, and conclude by analyzing the next set of social policy challenges facing the region's countries.

PART 3

Ideology and the Future of CCTs

CHAPTER 8

Conclusion

The Future of CCTs

Ironically, many of the left-wing leaders who came to power across Latin America during the 2000s after campaigning on promises of expanding social policy and redistributing income to the poor initially opposed the homegrown Latin American invention that became "the world's favorite new anti-poverty device" and "as close as you can come to a magic bullet in development" (Nancy Birdsall, cited in Dugger 2004). That invention, the conditional cash transfer program, promised to simultaneously address the region's high levels of poverty and low levels of educational attainment.

Many on the left, most notably Brazilian center-left President "Lula" da Silva (2003–10), who later became the leader most closely associated with CCTs, initially saw highly targeted programs with strict conditionality enforcement such as Mexico's pioneering Progresa/Oportunidades and the direct predecessors of Bolsa Família as little more than charity, an *esmola*, directed toward the poor. Such programs were a distraction from the left's programmatic mission of enacting comprehensive and universal welfare states.

Despite these initial misgivings, the left ultimately embraced CCTs, but it did so on its own terms. Left-wing presidents remade CCTs in accordance with their programmatic goals. The programs they enacted and reformed were more expansive, less punitive, and more attuned to the left's universalistic aspirations. Thus, there came to be two models of CCTs: a "human capital" model associated with the center and right, emphasizing narrow, means-tested targeting of beneficiaries and strict conditionality enforcement, and a more universalistic "basic income" model associated with the left, with broader target populations and more permissive conditionality.

This chapter begins by briefly summarizing the book's main findings and contributions to existing knowledge on the politics of CCTs and on the relationship between ideology and social policy under globalization. This is followed by a section revisiting the CCT programs of four of the countries studied over the course of the book—Costa Rica, Argentina, Mexico, and Brazil—that have in recent years experienced shifts in government ideology. The chapter and book conclude by discussing the pending agenda for Latin American social policy now that CCTs have become ubiquitous. Overall, CCTs have been successful at achieving their short-term goals of reducing poverty and increasing schooling. There are, however, serious questions regarding their long-term effectiveness, specifically their ability to help beneficiaries break the intergenerational cycle of poverty. Achieving this goal will require significant improvements in the quality of education. This, in turn, will require enacting complex, uncertain, and politically difficult long-term reforms that will challenge powerful vested interests, most notably teachers' unions.

8.1 Main Findings

This book demonstrates that government ideology continues to shape the scope, generosity, and degree of universalism of social policy in the region, despite the supposed constraints imposed by globalization.

Chapter 2 revisited earlier quantitative tests of the determinants of CCT adoption (Díaz-Cayeros and Magaloni 2009; Sugiyama 2011; Brooks 2015) and then reinterpreted them in light of qualitative evidence. Echoing prior research, an event history analysis covering 18 countries confirmed that the widespread adoption of CCTs in the region was a case of policy diffusion—as more countries adopted these programs, countries without programs became more likely to adopt their own. It was also confirmed that left-wing presidents were no more likely to *adopt* CCTs than their center or right-wing counterparts. Yet a deeper analysis of the political process behind CCT adoption in six countries revealed, counterintuitively, that these policies tended to be *proposed* by the right and center and were initially *opposed* by the left. While out of power, the left opposed national-level programs in Mexico and Brazil. The left-wing presidents that ultimately adopted CCTs in Argentina and Bolivia did so in response to proposals from the right. Left-leaning presidents in Nicaragua and Venezuela actually dismantled existing programs upon taking office. The left's objections were threefold: programmatic opposition to narrow targeting and concern that CCTs would detract from the construction of universal policies, worries that CCTs would be used clientelistically, and the association of CCTs with right-wing governments and international financial institutions.

The evolution of CCTs in Brazil under Lula marked the turning point in the left's stance. Chapter 3 details how Lula, a widely respected left-wing statesman, was, like other left-wing politicians, initially critical of CCTs. He rejected a CCT proposal in the early 1990s, criticized his country's early CCTs on the campaign trail in the early 2000s, and de-emphasized those programs during his first year as president in 2003. Yet Lula ultimately embraced CCTs following the failure of his own, more ambitious flagship anti-poverty strategy. But Lula did more than continue the CCTs he inherited. Influenced by proponents of a universal basic income, most notably fellow leftist Eduardo Suplicy, Lula and later Dilma Rousseff (2011–16), his handpicked successor, gradually expanded and transformed Brazil's CCTs in line with the left's universalistic aspirations. The resulting program made CCTs palatable, indeed desirable, to other leftist governments. *It also did not hurt that this program was incredibly popular and played an important role in ensuring Lula's reelection in 2006* (Hunter and Power 2007; Zucco 2008, 2013).

As a result, there came to exist two distinct models of CCTs in Latin America. Chapter 4 describes these two models and traces their distinct intellectual histories. Human capital CCTs, exemplified by Mexico's CCT under right-wing presidents, feature narrow targeting and prioritize human capital accumulation through strict enforcement of school attendance and other conditionalities. Basic income CCTs, exemplified by Brazil's Bolsa Família, prioritize poverty reduction through broader targeting and a more lenient approach to conditionality. These differences reflect the inherent tension between reducing poverty and increasing human capital. Because conditionality works as intended, strict enforcement makes sense as a strategy to promote school attendance and thus human capital accumulation. However, because noncompliance is higher among the most vulnerable, revoking the benefits of noncompliers is counterproductive to the goal of reducing poverty.

The two models stemmed from distinct intellectual traditions that simultaneously yet independently concluded that direct cash transfers were the most effective tool for accomplishing their policy objectives. The human capital model is, at its essence, a neoliberal response to the persistence of extreme poverty in the aftermath of market reform. Developed by Santiago Levy and a team of technocrats linked to IFIs, this model envisioned transfers as a means of incentivizing parents to invest in their children's education and health. In contrast, Suplicy and the basic income movement that influenced the Brazilian left's version of CCTs envisioned cash transfers as a means of guaranteeing an income floor for every person, starting with children.

Chapter 5 tested whether the association between ideology and CCT design found in Mexico and Brazil extended to the rest of the region. As a first approximation, a regression analysis of the determinants of CCT scope in 18 countries over two decades found that CCT *coverage* and *spending* were higher in countries with left-wing presidents. Furthermore, coverage in countries governed by the left increased in line with both poverty and inequality. Moving beyond coverage, an analysis of the design of the 10 CCTs adopted after Bolsa Família's launch confirmed that CCTs enacted and operated by center and right-wing governments tended to have narrower target populations, stricter conditionality enforcement, and variable stipends aimed at compensating for the higher opportunity cost older students face in choosing school over work. By contrast, CCTs enacted and operated by the left tended to have broader target populations, less punitive conditionality enforcement, and paid the same flat stipend to all beneficiaries.

Returning to the issue of policy diffusion, the last two empirical chapters traced how government ideology influenced CCT design. Based on evidence from across the region, chapter 6 demonstrated that diffusion occurred along two distinct tracks. While IFIs were busy promoting the human capital model, Lula's Brazil actively promoted its basic income model. Whereas centrist and right-wing governments tended, often with IFI funding and technical assistance, to adopt human capital programs, left-wing governments gravitated toward basic income ones. Thus, whereas the adoption of human capital CCTs by centrist and right-wing governments was an example of vertical diffusion (international institution to country), the left's adoption of basic income programs was an example of horizontal diffusion (country to country).

Through in-depth case studies based on field research, chapter 7 traced the political processes behind the adoption and design of CCTs in three countries. In Costa Rica, President Oscar Arias (1986–90; 2006–10), a centrist, openly campaigned on enacting a CCT to reduce the country's secondary school dropout rate. With some assistance from the Inter-American Development Bank, Arias enacted a program similar to Mexico's but exclusively targeting low-income secondary-school students. In contrast, Bolivia's Evo Morales (2006–19) and Argentina's Cristina Fernández de Kirchner (2007–15), both left wing, were originally skeptical of CCTs proposed by right-wing rivals. When they finally adopted programs, those decisions were framed in terms of reducing poverty. Those programs, which had no IFI input or funding, went further in the basic income direction than even Brazil's pioneering program.

8.1.1 Main Contributions

Summing up, this book finds that ideology continues to determine the design and scope of social policy in contemporary Latin America. Left-wing governments enacted more expansive and universalistic CCTs than their centrist and right-wing counterparts. This finding addresses a major gap in the recent literature on the politics of social policy in the region. Past research has produced substantial evidence that left-wing governments are more likely to expand social policy and that, as a result, they have reduced poverty and inequality more than their centrist or right-wing counterparts (Birdsall, Lustig, and McLeod 2012; Huber and Stephens 2012). Surprisingly, however, no relationship was found between presidential ideology and the adoption of CCTs (Díaz-Cayeros and Magaloni 2009; Sugiyama 2011), the most progressive policy available to Latin American governments (Goñi, López, and Servén 2008, 20; Lindert, Skoufias, and Shapiro 2006, 71). Marshalling quantitative and qualitative evidence from across the region, this book shows that, after overcoming its initial skepticism, the left enacted CCTs that covered more people, were less punitive, and thus came closer to constituting a universal income floor.

This book has clarified the relationship between the left turn and the diffusion of CCTs, two of the most important developments in Latin American politics during the 2000s. This relationship was not straightforward or mechanical. As a result of their deeply held commitment to universalism and distaste for narrow targeting, Latin America's left was initially hesitant to embrace what turned out to be the most effective policy in its arsenal. Given this initial opposition, the left turn might well have stopped CCT diffusion, as it did in Venezuela and Nicaragua. The spread of CCTs in countries governed by the left during the second half of the 2000s was contingent on Lula adapting the programs he inherited in a basic income direction. Lula demonstrated that CCTs could advance the left's agenda. Left-wing leaders elsewhere in the region followed Lula in adopting basic income CCTs.

The diffusion of CCTs, and the basic income model in particular, offers strong evidence against the race to the bottom thesis. It would be a mistake to argue (as the Latin American left initially did) that the diffusion of CCTs constitutes an example of convergence toward a "neoliberal bottom," inasmuch as it involves the spread of means-tested, targeted programs. CCTs are rules-based entitlements that *extended* social policy to those who most needed it and had traditionally been excluded from the region's "narrow but deep" welfare policies (Haggard and Kaufman 2008). In sharp contrast with the previous wave of social policy diffusion in the region during the 1990s, which retrenched social policy (Huber 1996; Madrid 2003; Weyland 2006; Brooks 2009), this most recent wave has increased the state's role in social policy.

By demonstrating that diffusion of CCTs was mediated by government ideology, this book warns against making excessively sharp distinctions between domestic and international drivers of policy change. Yes, the spread of CCTs was an example of policy diffusion: it advanced in the classic S-shaped pattern and within a few years there came to be geographical clustering and commonality among diversity (Weyland 2006, 18–19). But diffusion occurred along two tracks, the choice of which was determined by ideology. Presidential ideology shaped which foreign actors were deemed credible and which policies were seen as worth emulating. With support from IFIs, the center and right eagerly emulated Mexico's program. The left was skeptical of the Mexican right's policies and IFIs but highly receptive to ideas emanating from Lula's Brazil. Thus, both international influences and domestic politics mattered. Future comparative politics research should take a page from recent work in American politics in considering ideology's role in policy diffusion (Grossback et al. 2004; Martin 2010; Butler et al. 2017; Butler and Pereira 2018).

8.2 Revisiting the Cases: Effects of Recent Ideological Shifts

The previous chapters demonstrated that left and nonleft presidents had different preferences regarding CCT design. In Brazil, successive left-wing governments transformed the programs they inherited into the region's first basic income CCT. In Argentina and Bolivia, left-wing presidents who enacted their own programs from scratch went further in the basic income direction than even Brazil. In contrast, nonleft governments in Mexico and later Costa Rica enacted and maintained human capital CCTs. This leaves two questions unanswered. *Do other left-wing leaders who inherit human capital CCTs follow the Brazilian example in reforming them in a basic income direction? And, conversely, do centrist and right-wing presidents who inherit basic income CCTs reform them in a human capital direction?* Recent changes in government ideology in four of the five countries discussed in detail in this book offer an opportunity to tackle these questions.

As Latin America's economies deteriorated following the end of the global commodity boom, voters across the region began voting out incumbent parties, leading to 180-degree shifts in government ideology.[1] In April 2014, Costa Ricans elected their first left-wing leader, Luis Guillermo Solís (2014–18) of the center-left Citizens' Action Party (PAC).[2] The following November, Argentines elected Mauricio Macri (2015–19) of the center-right Republican Proposal, thus ending 12 years of center-left Kirchner presidencies. Facing impeachment proceedings amid what turned out to be the longest and deepest recession in Brazilian history (Biller and Shinohara 2017), center-left President Rousseff was replaced in May 2016 by her vice-president, Michel Temer (2016–18), a center-right politician from the Movement for Brazilian Democracy, ending 13 years of center-left Workers' Party governments.

In 2018, amid mounting frustration over weak economic performance, large-scale corruption scandals, and rampant crime and violence, voters in the region's two most populous countries elected populist leaders who promised major political transformations.[3] In July, Mexicans overwhelmingly elected left-wing populist Andrés Manuel López Obrador (2018–present) of the National Regeneration Movement (MORENA), marking the first time since the transition to democracy in 2000 that the country has been governed by the left. And, in October, Brazilians elected Jair Bolsonaro (2019–present), a far-right populist former army captain.[4]

Brief and, in the cases of Mexico and Brazil under Bolsonaro, preliminary overviews of the evolution of CCTs in the four countries discussed above largely support this book's arguments. Following in the footsteps of Brazil's Lula, Costa Rica's left-wing governments reformed the human capital CCT they inherited in a basic income direction. In Mexico, AMLO, as López Obrador is commonly known, replaced Progresa/Oportunidades, the prototypical human capital CCT, with a series of broadly targeted unconditional transfers.

In contrast, right-wing governments in Argentina and Brazil did not reform the basic income programs they inherited in the human capital direction. However, both governments, and Brazil's in particular, gradually retrenched cash transfers, primarily via policy drift (Hacker 2004; Niedzwiecki and Pribble 2017). In neither country did coverage keep up with big expansions in the poor population. It should, however, be noted that both countries faced deep economic crises that slashed the resources available to fight poverty precisely when they were most needed.[5] Further research would be required to fully disentangle the effects of ideology and economic crises.

Finally, and more concerning, there is evidence that Mexico's and Brazil's populist leaders utilized cash transfer policy clientelistically during their first year in office. These were still new administrations at the time of writing and therefore any conclusions about their behavior are preliminary. However, this is a deeply worrying trend, particularly given the outsized influence these countries played in the diffusion of CCTs across Latin America and the world.

Costa Rica. Since 2014, the country has been governed by two consecutive center-left administrations, those of Solís and Carlos Alvarado (2018–present). As in Brazil under the PT, left-wing governments have reformed the country's Avancemos human capital CCT in a basic income direction. Solís moved to equalize the program's stipends. More recently, Alvarado extended CCT coverage to low-income primary school students.

PAC governments made Avancemos stipends more uniform across grades. In 2015, the number of stipend categories was collapsed from six to two (one for grades 7–9, another for grades 10–12). Stipends were increased for grades 7–8 and cut for the remaining grades. Whereas seventh grade stipends increased to 91% of their initial 2007 purchasing power, stipends for grades nine and 11, respectively, retained just 54% and 47% of their original purchasing power. Whereas grade 12 stipends were originally more than three times larger than grade seven ones, that difference shrunk to just 1.5 times (see fig. 7–2).[6] Alvarado, then Solís's human development minister, justified the decision in terms of both human capital and poverty reduction. With regard to the former, Alvarado noted that desertion (leaving school) peaks during the transitions from primary to secondary education (grades six to seven) and from lower to upper secondary school (grade nine to 10). It was thus unnecessary to increase stipends with each grade. With regard to reducing poverty, he promised that the stipend cuts would free up resources to seek out and enroll additional beneficiaries (Repretel Costa Rica 2014). True to his word, by the end of 2019, Avancemos covered 203,000 students—9.7% more than during the years following the global financial crisis (IMAS 2020, 9).

As president, Alvarado moved to further expand CCTs and transform them into a right. In late 2018, the Costa Rican congress approved a government-drafted law making Avancemos permanent (rather than dependent on presidential decrees) and mandating that it receive at least 8% of the anti-poverty budget (IMAS 2018).[7] In June 2019, the Education Ministry's primary-school scholarships were replaced with Crecemos (Let's Grow), a new CCT operated by the Mixed Institute for Social Assistance, the institution in charge of Avancemos (IMAS 2019).[8] By the end of 2019, Crecemos covered 210,000 children (IMAS 2020, 9). Taken together, the two CCTs covered 8.3% of the country's population. Thus, six years after the left assumed power, coverage was at peak levels, stipend amounts were closer to uniform, and CCTs had been extended to all grades.

Argentina. Although the center-right Macri administration did not conduct major reforms to the design of the country's Asignación Universal por Hijo (AUH) basic income CCT, the program did undergo significant retrenchment. The program's eligible population and total number of beneficiaries increased slightly under Macri. However, this expansion did not keep pace with rising poverty levels. Purchasing power also declined significantly, particularly following changes to the rules for updating stipends (Sacco et al. 2019). Furthermore, Progresar, a program introduced in the final years of the Fernández administration that provided stipends for unemployed and out-of-school 18–24 year olds to finish school or enroll in technical education, was largely dismantled (Letcher and Strada 2019).

Given AUH's popularity, one full year before the election, Macri promised to maintain the program, which he described as one of his predecessor's few successes (La Nación 2014). During a presidential debate in late 2015, he even promised to extend coverage to the children of so-called *monotributistas*, self-employed workers subject to a simplified tax regime (Tarricone 2018). During Macri's first month in office, AUH beneficiaries received a Christmas bonus, a practice that was continued during the remainder of the administration.[9] True to his word, in April 2016, Macri signed a decree extending eligibility to the children of monotributistas. By the end of his term, 462,000 were enrolled in the AUH, representing 11.0% of beneficiaries. Later reforms simplified the eligibility requirements for temporary workers and scrapped rules excluding beneficiaries of provincial and municipal programs from AUH (Obarrio 2016).

However, tough economic times—the economy shrank during three of the administration's four years and inflation averaged 41.6% a year—forced Macri to pursue retrenchment via stealth. Following successful midterm elections in October 2017, the administration pushed through a pension reform aimed at reducing the fiscal deficit and making the pension system more financially sustainable.[10] Specifically, the reform altered the rules for indexing to inflation various government benefits including AUH. The highly controversial reform, which passed amid violent protests thanks to a last-minute deal between Macri and opposition governors (Cué 2017), steadily eroded the purchasing power of AUH stipends over the remainder of the administration (Lechter and Strada 2017; Slipczuk 2017; Quiroga and Juncos Castillo 2020; ODS-CTA-A 2019). Overall, the real value of stipends declined by roughly 12% between the end of Macri's first and last year.[11] The government, however, did attempt to partially offset this decline through several ad hoc bonus payments during 2018 and 2019.[12]

Overall, by the time Macri stepped down, 4.12 million children benefited from AUH, an increase of 12.5%. However, this increase did not keep pace with rising poverty. The share of the population living in poverty and extreme poverty, respectively, increased by 24.6% (about 3.7 million) and 61.0% (about 1.7 million) during Macri's term.[13] Under such circumstances, a moderate increase in coverage could be construed as retrenchment and a move away from the goal of ensuring a basic income for all those who need it.

Beyond AUH, Macri largely dismantled Progresar, which was envisioned as a "bridge" connecting AUH beneficiaries with the labor market and higher and technical education (Letcher and Strada 2019, 9). In early 2018, the administration transformed the program from a benefit available to all low-income young adults to a merit-based academic scholarship. This significantly reduced the number and altered socioeconomic profile of beneficiaries with critics alleging that the academic requirements disproportionately hurt the very type of student the program was originally intended to help. Overall, under Macri, the number of beneficiaries declined 42% (Letcher and Strada 2019, 2) while the real value of transfers declined between 46% and 62% depending on the type of benefit (Letcher and Strada 2019, 4).

Brazil. As in Argentina, the right turn in Brazilian politics following Rousseff's controversial impeachment did not lead to major changes to the design of the country's Bolsa Família basic income CCT. Retrenchment under the right was more explicit in Brazil than in Argentina, however. Upon taking office in May 2016, Temer launched Operação Pente Fino (Operation Fine-Tooth Comb), an aggressive monitoring of the program's rolls aimed at weeding out families with higher incomes and outdated or incomplete personal information (Cortes da Costa 2019). This policy continued under Bolsonaro. Worryingly, Bolsonaro's government has been credibly accused of using the program to discriminate against the country's Northeast, the PT's heartland and the part of the country where he fared worst during his campaign for the presidency and polled worst during his first year in office (Ribeiro 2019).

Osmar Terra, who oversaw Bolsa Família during most of the Temer administration and the first 13 months of the Bolsonaro administration, was the architect of Pente Fino.[14] Upon his initial appointment, Terra criticized the program's reliance of self-reported incomes (Matos 2016) and estimated that at least 10% of beneficiaries were underreporting their incomes and should be expelled (Mariz 2016). In November 2016, Terra announced the blockage of 654,000 accounts (4.7% of beneficiaries) and the outright cancellation of a further 469,000 (3.3%) (MDSA 2016). Several large purges occurred during the remainder of the Temer presidency (Prengaman, DiLorenzo, and Trielli 2017; Madeiro 2017; Peduzzi 2018; Sakamoto 2018).

Overall, average monthly account blockages and cancellations during the Temer administration were, respectively, 34.5% and 33.8% higher than during the Rousseff administration's final two and a half years.[15] Terra openly presented the cuts as part of the administration's broader austerity policies, which were centered on a December 2016 constitutional amendment freezing public spending in real terms for 20 years. Responding to opposition legislators concerned about the cuts, Terra went so far as to state that "in practice, the major tax reform taking place in the country is being carried out by the Ministry of Social Development" (MC 2017).

In contrast to other right-wing politicians discussed in this book, Bolsonaro had a long history, dating back to at least 2010, of openly criticizing

Bolsa Família. Bolsonaro's attacks revolved around three claims: that it made beneficiaries idle, that they remained on the program indefinitely, and that the PT used it to buy votes, particularly in the Northeast (Grillo and Prado 2018). As late as August 2017, when he was already expected to run for president, Bolsonaro commented that "to be a candidate for president, you have to say that you will expand Bolsa Família. Then, vote for another candidate. I will not engage in demagogy and please anyone to seek a vote" (Toledo 2017).

However, by August 2018 Bolsonaro was saying that Bolsa Família had to be continued for "humanitarian reasons" and claiming that reports of his opposition to the program were "fake news" (Fortuna 2019). Even so, he maintained that 30% of beneficiaries were committing fraud by underreporting their incomes (Fernandes 2018). The transformation was complete following his first place showing in the first round of the presidential election in October.[16] The day after the vote, Bolsonaro uploaded a video directed at Northeastern voters announcing his plan to enact a Christmas bonus—a thirteenth payment in December. Bolsonaro won the second round by a comfortable margin.[17]

At an event commemorating his first 100 days in office in March 2019, Bolsonaro officially announced the bonus. Said payment would be in lieu of an adjustment to program stipends (Brant 2019). Beneficiaries would still come out ahead as the extra payment, which amounted to an 8.3% increase, was more than twice the rate of inflation since the previous adjustment. However, the administration did not budget the expansion's cost. Terra instead maintained that the ongoing fight against fraud would save enough money to cover the bonus (Pereira 2019).

Indeed, Pente Fino continued apace under Bolsonaro with an additional 972,000 families (6.9%) being removed from the program during the administration's first year. Regardless, the crackdown did not generate nearly enough savings. At least five times during 2019, Terra requested additional funds but was rebuffed by the economic team (Resende 2020c).

In the absence of fresh funds, Terra further retrenched the program. Going well beyond Pente Fino, the administration drastically reduced the number of families admitted into the program each month from an average of 250,000 during January–May to just 5,400 a month during June–October (Menna Barreto 2019; Zylberkan 2020). This resulted in a waiting list to join the program that, by the end of 2019, extended to 1.5 million families or 3.5 million individuals (Valfré and Fernandes 2020). Similarly, readmission requests from beneficiaries that had previously "graduated" from or been kicked out of the program dropped by 75% in 2019 compared to the previous year and none were incorporated between June and October (Madeiro 2020a). Ultimately, the additional funds for the bonus were secured by delaying the approval of new pension applications (Resende 2020a). Retrenchment was set to continue in 2020. The administration's original budget called for an 8% cut in spending, did not foresee the incorporation of any additional beneficiaries, and did not set aside funds for a bonus payment (Menna Barretto 2019).

Overall, despite the absence of explicit reforms to its design, Bolsa Família under the right has, in practice, moved in the human capital direction with regard to targeting. Between April 2017, well into the Pente Fino era, and February 2020, families living in extreme poverty increased as a share of total beneficiaries from 77.1% to 83.1%. Similarly, the share of poor families declined from 17.5% to 12.5%. Pente Fino marked a shift in concern to errors of inclusion relative to the concern over errors of exclusion of the PT era.

Bolsa Família's evolution under the right offers an example of the politics of welfare retrenchment (Pierson 1996) via policy drift (Hacker 2004). Despite repeated claims by the right that the program's rolls were inflated, total coverage at the end of Bolsonaro's first year was only 5.19% lower than when Rousseff was forced to step down (1.39 versus 1.32 million). However, despite two adjustments under Temer, stipend purchasing power in 2020 was 18.8% lower than in 2014.[18] Furthermore, given Brazil's recent economic context, keeping the program's size constant, let alone shrinking it slightly, constitutes retrenchment and a move away from the goal of ensuring a basic income for all those who need it. The share of Brazilians living in extreme poverty increased by 67.1% (3.6 million) from 2014 to 2018. Poverty increased by 31.8% (6.5 million) during that period (FGV Social 2020).

Worryingly, Bolsa Família's management took a discretionary turn during Bolsonaro's first year with admission and expulsions being used to discriminate against the politically hostile Northeast. An investigation published by the daily newspaper *Folha de S. Paulo* in February 2020 revealed that the cuts and delays during the second half of 2019 disproportionally affected the poorest parts of the country. Between January and May, an average of 26 families from the country's 200 poorest municipalities were incorporated each month. Between June and October, however, only one family was incorporated in 37 of those municipalities and none were incorporated in another 64 (Resende 2020b). This despite the fact that an average of 5,400 families nationwide per month were incorporated into the program during that period.[19]

Continuing this pattern, the daily *O Estado de. S. Paulo* revealed the following month that the government discriminated against the Northeast once admissions resumed at a normal pace in January 2020. Of the 100,000 families incorporated that month, only 3,035 (3%) were from nine northeastern states representing 27% of Brazil's population. At 22%, those states had twice the poverty rate as the country as a whole. Furthermore, northeasterners represented 36% of program's wait list at the time. The much more prosperous South and Southeast, which overwhelmingly backed Bolsonaro in 2018, received 75% of the new spots (Tomazelli 2020). This sparked immediate backlash from both the PT (Rodrigues 2020) and northeastern legislators including former Senate president Renan Calheiros of the Movement for Brazilian Democracy, who described these events as a "criminal migration" of benefits away from the Northeast and requested an investigation (Senado Noticias 2020).

Despite the backlash, this behavior continued. Just two months later, as the severity of the COVID-19 pandemic was becoming evident, the Northeast was again disproportionally targeted in a routine sweep of the program. Northeasterners made up 61.1% of the 158,000 families expelled in March (Madeiro 2020b). In response, the governors of seven Northeastern states sued the government. The Supreme Federal Court promptly ordered that the cuts be reversed. By then, however, the cuts had already been reversed as part of a massive expansion of cash payments aimed at mitigating the pandemic's economic effects (Onofre 2020).

Mexico. As in Costa Rica, the left turn in Mexican politics following AMLO's election has shifted policy in the basic income direction. However, as in Brazil, the election of a populist raised concerns over clientelistic use of cash transfers.

Citing the failure of Progresa/Oportunidades to eradicate poverty over its two decades of existence, AMLO, in one of his first acts as president, replaced his country's iconic and internationally lauded human capital CCT with a series of broadly targeted unconditional cash transfers. Although these reforms represent moves in the basic income direction, they resulted in a reduction in benefits for most CCT beneficiaries, particularly mothers with multiple children under 15 and students in upper secondary school (grades 10–12). That these changes were enacted in a rushed manner without evidence-based justifications has raised doubts about their potential effectiveness (Masse and Olvera 2019, 25; Rivera 2019). More worrying still, the opaque manner in which beneficiaries are selected for these new programs has raised serious concerns about potential clientelism (Casar 2019; Hernández Estrada 2019; Sánchez Talanquer 2020).

AMLO had long been skeptical of targeted and conditional programs, having opted for universal programs as mayor of Mexico City from 2000 to 2005 (Luccisano and Macdonald 2014). He later claimed, without evidence, that Oportunidades was used to buy votes and blamed it for his razor-thin loss in the 2006 presidential election (Méndez and Becerril 2006).[20] AMLO's widely known dislike of the program was such that he and his team went out of their way in both 2012 (Nieto and Gómez R. 2012) and 2018 (Olmos 2018) to assure voters that the popular program would continue were he elected. After the election, while still promising to continue the program (Galván 2018), AMLO laid the groundwork for its replacement by claiming, again without evidence and counter to credible studies (Beltrán and Castro Cornejo 2015), that the program's rolls were inflated by as much as 50% with as many as 3.5 million "ghost" beneficiaries (Guerrero 2019).

AMLO replaced Progresa/Oportunidades with the unconditional Becas para el Bienestar Benito Juárez (Benito Juárez Well-Being Scholarships), informally known as Becas AMLO (AMLO Scholarships).[21] Low-income parents with children under 15 became eligible for a single flat bimonthly stipend, regardless of number of children. During the program's first year, when it was still partially working off its predecessor's operating rules, the transfers were limited to families in extreme poverty (DOF 2019a). However, in 2020 they were extended to those in poverty (DOF 2019b). All students enrolled in a public upper secondary school (grades 10–12, generally ages 15–18), regardless of income, became eligible for their own bimonthly stipend, separate from the under-15 scholarship. In line with the basic income model, both types of scholarships pay the same flat stipend, regardless of grade or sex.

Leticia Animas, the administration's scholarship coordinator, justified these decisions based on basic income arguments. She argued that conditionality, particularly the requirement that mothers take children for medical checkups and attend nutrition classes, constituted an undue "burden." Animas also cited anecdotal claims that mothers were required to pay clinics bribes to have their health conditionality paperwork validated.[22] She also criticized targeting, claiming that having some neighbors receive benefits while others were excluded caused "tears in the social fabric of communities" (Hernández Alcanzar 2019; see also Russell 2019). In line with this rights-based perspective, in March 2020, the government secured the approval of a constitutional amendment that enshrines the right of students at all levels of education, with priority given those in poverty, to scholarships that allow them exercise their right to education. More importantly, the amendment prohibits governments from reducing the real value of benefits (La Verdad 2020).

In line with the left's more expansive ambitions, the scholarships were complemented by cash transfers for young adults. Jóvenes Construyendo el Futuro (Youths Building the Future) provides unemployed and out-of-school 18–29 year olds with one-year paid apprenticeships.[23] Jóvenes Escribiendo el Futuro (Youths Writing the Future) provides college scholarships to students who are indigenous, afro-descendant, low-income, or from particularly violent areas. At launch, these programs were, respectively, 4.5 and three times more generous than scholarships for school-age children. This has raised concerns about the financial sustainability and the overall progressivity of AMLO's social policy agenda.[24]

In broad strokes, AMLO has increased the share of students eligible to receive cash transfers. The new programs represent a potential boon for those previously excluded, namely upper secondary students not in extreme poverty, moderately poor parents with children under 15, and young adults. This, combined with the extension of non-contributory pension benefits to all people over 68 and indigenous peoples over 65, represents a step in the direction of guaranteeing an income floor for all Mexicans.[25]

However, this has come at the cost of a reduction in the overall level of benefits received by most CCT beneficiaries. The reduction is particularly notable for families in extreme poverty with multiple children under 15, which must now get by on just one stipend. The new bimonthly stipend is higher than the total amount previously paid for each child enrolled in primary school (grades 1–6), but lower than the amount paid for each child in grades seven and above. There is no scenario under which a family with two or more children would receive more money than it did under the previous program. The declines were largest for the higher grades with males and females in grade 12 seeing declines of 39% and 45%, respectively.[26]

Overall, as in Bolivia (see chapter 7), the move toward universality has come at the expense of progressivity, raising doubts about AMLO's promise of *primero los pobres* (the poor first) (Jaramillo Molina 2019, 154). The new policies prioritize upper secondary (as well as postsecondary) at the expense of basic education (Martínez Vargas 2020). Universal stipends for upper secondary students have come at the cost of forcing poor families with multiple young children to make do with less. Only 34% of Mexican upper secondary students come from the bottom half of the income distribution and only 17% come from rural areas (Jaramillo Molina 2019, 154). Furthermore, the extension of stipends to *all* upper secondary students came at the cost of cutting the stipends for upper secondary students in extreme poverty.

As in Brazil, populism brought increasing discretion to cash transfer policy. With regard to execution, the decision to completely reject the social policy infrastructure inherited from past administrations and the slapdash manner in which the new programs were designed practically ensured that the transition would be rife with problems. Throughout 2019, there were reports of poor families formerly enrolled in Progresa/Oportunidades who were, for reasons that were never explained, excluded from the new programs (Vega 2019; Gutiérrez 2020). Well into 2020, there continued to be widespread and frequent payment delays (Agencia EFE 2019; Milenio 2019; Un1ón Jalisco 2019; Gutiérrez 2020; Sánchez Jiménez 2020).

Concerns about the possibility that AMLO's programs could be used clientelistically stem from the manner in which their beneficiary rolls were compiled. In August 2018, nearly four months before AMLO was sworn in, some 18,000 volunteers, mainly from his MORENA party, began traversing the country to conduct a "Well-Being Census" of the population's social policy needs and sign up beneficiaries for the incoming administration's programs. The process was notoriously opaque. It was never properly explained why the process was necessary—Mexico already possessed comprehensive social policy registries—or why these unqualified so-called Servants of the Nation—not Mexico's well-regarded National Institute of Statistics and Geography—were charged with conducting the "census" (Associated Press 2019; Hernández Estrada 2019). It was also unclear who paid the servants' salaries and operation costs (Casar 2019). What is known, however, is that nearly all of them were later hired by the administration without competing in public hiring processes (Associated Press 2019).

It was not until May 2020, more than a year and a half after the process began, that the administration, under pressure from the media and civil society, finally made public the census's opaque methodology and results.

An analysis by Núñez González and Guzmán Martínez (2020) reveals that, in all, the servants interviewed 32.5 million people, far short of the estimated 52.4 million Mexicans living in poverty in 2018, let alone the 73.3 million in the previous administration's social policy registries. No information was provided on what share of beneficiaries of existing programs were confirmed eligible for AMLO's programs, how many of them were deemed ineligible and lost their benefits, or how many previously excluded people were enrolled. In Núñez González and Guzmán Martínez's (2020) words, "without any kind of transparent information on the matter, all there is are doubts about the real purpose of the Well-Being Census." In fact, it was not until December 2019, almost a year after the programs launched, that the administration complied with Mexican law by publishing the beneficiary rolls (Aristegui Noticias 2019).

Simply put, for all the talk of rights and the basic income discourse, the census was a public relations exercise designed to link the new programs directly to AMLO and brand the new president, in Casar's (2019) words, as "the great benefactor" (see also Rivera 2019). In violation of Mexican law, the servants wore clothing with AMLO's name and likeness while conducting the census. They also frequently told would-be beneficiaries that they had come "on the part of the president of the republic *licensiado* Andrés Manuel López Obrador to provide support for your family" (Associated Press 2019). In December 2019, in response to a complaint by opposition legislators, the Federal Judicial Branch's Electoral Tribunal ruled that 36 servants had illegally used public resources to promote AMLO's name and likeness. The servants were also found to have flagrantly defied an August ruling by the National Electoral Institute ordering them to immediately cease promoting AMLO (INE 2019). However, neither AMLO nor top social policy officials were found liable for these crimes (TEPJF 2019). Furthermore, due to the lack of requisite legislation, the servants themselves could not be punished either, let alone fired (Lindero 2020).

8.3 The Limits of CCTs

Despite differing preferences regarding CCT design and scope, Latin American politicians of all stripes accept the need for these programs. Thus, CCTs have become a permanent feature of Latin American social policy and politics more broadly. They are widely heralded as effective, low-cost tools that simultaneously relieve poverty and increase education levels. Yet the limits to their ability to achieve these twin goals have become increasingly apparent in recent years.

At first glance, CCTs appear to have reached a saturation point. After expanding dramatically during the second half of the 2000s, coverage and investment stabilized after 2010 (see figs. 1–1 and 5–2). The total number of beneficiaries in 2013 was equal to 89.5% of the region's poor and 250.9% of its extreme poor (Robles, Rubio, and Stampini 2019, O90). These numbers, however, obscure significant targeting problems. The expansion was accompanied by a substantial increase in leakage to nonpoor households (Stampini and Tornarolli 2012; Robles, Rubio, and Stampini 2019). Thus, in 2013 an estimated 40.4% of CCT beneficiaries were not poor (Robles, Rubio, and Stampini 2019, O87).[27] At the same time, an estimated 49.5% of extremely poor and 62.7% of poor households with children still lacked coverage (Robles, Rubio, and Stampini 2019, O90).

Absent a significant acceleration in economic growth, further progress on poverty and inequality will require some combination of better targeting, increased coverage, and more generous stipends, all of which involve politically difficult trade-offs. Extending coverage to the excluded poor would require aggressive (and costly) efforts to track down eligible households, particularly in remote rural areas, as well as better adapting enrollment rules to the needs of urban families with precarious incomes, which tend to cycle in and out of poverty (Robles, Rubio, and Stampini 2019). Funding for this could be freed up by adopting a more proactive approach to "graduating" nonpoor households. However, revoking the benefits of tens of millions would be politically unpopular. Furthermore, a large share of nonpoor beneficiaries remain vulnerable to falling into poverty, particularly during tough economic times.

Further expansion of CCTs would be difficult. Political backlash against CCTs has so far been avoided because their adoption and expansion has not come at the expense of existing entitlements for labor market insiders (Holland and Schneider 2017; Hunter 2021). Funding for further coverage expansions could be secured by "redistributing" funds from traditional contributory social insurance to CCTs or by raising additional revenues. The former would pit the interests of the poor against those of the better-organized middle class. Raising additional revenues would be more difficult still. Obtaining fresh revenues would likely require raising income and property taxes, which are low in most of the region (Mahon, Bergman, and Arnson 2015). This, however, would generate resistance from the rich.

If funding obstacles could be overcome, further decreases in poverty could also be achieved by increasing stipends. However, as Holland and Schneider (2017, 994) note, "If non-contributory benefits become more generous, more workers will choose informal employment (and the coverage of universal and non-contributory programs) to the costly contributions and low expected benefits from formal employment." This would have pernicious effects on the overall health of Latin American economies (see Levy 2008).

8.3.1 CCTs Are Not an Education Policy

CCTs are responsible for improvements in school enrollment, attendance, and grade completion, as well as for reductions in dropout rates (Baird et al. 2014; García and Saavedra 2017; Bastagli et al. 2019). They are also associated with reductions in both the prevalence (likelihood of working) and intensity (number of hours worked) of child labor (de Hoop and Rosati 2014; Bastagli et al. 2019). In that sense, CCTs appear to be resoundingly successful.

Yet the few studies that have tested the most innovative and potentially transformative feature of CCTs—the expectation that more schooling will translate into more and better human capital, which in turn will lead to better employment opportunities and a ticket out of poverty—have tended to produce disappointing results. The handful of studies of long-term effects conducted describe their findings as "inconclusive" (Molina-Millan et al. 2016, 25) or, at best, "modest" (Araújo, Bosch, and Schady 2017, 16). In particular, the two studies on the long-term effects of Mexico's Progresa/Oportunidades have yielded mixed results. Yaschine (2015) finds that 18–24 year olds who received CCT benefits continuously for 10 years did not, on average, have higher-quality jobs than comparable young adults who were enrolled in the program for less time or not at all. Long-term beneficiaries were, despite their much higher educational attainment, just as likely as their parents to work in agriculture and manual labor. A more recent (and encouraging) long-term study by Kugler and Rojas (2018) finds that those who received 17 years of CCT benefits were 36.6 percentage points more likely to be employed, 6.6 percentage points more likely to have a permanent contract, and 2.3 percentage points more likely to receive non-wage benefits than comparable individuals who never joined the program. Furthermore, long-term beneficiaries, on average, worked nine hours more per week and earned five pesos (26 cents) more an hour than nonenrollees. This is evidence of upward mobility, but far from conclusive proof of a break in the intergenerational cycle of poverty.

With its strict enforcement of school attendance and additional healthcare and nutritional conditionalities, Progresa/Oportunidades should represent an "easy case" for the long-term benefits of CCTs. That evaluations of this program's long-term results are inconclusive raises doubts about the long-term effectiveness of other, less human capital-oriented, programs. Yaschine (2015) attributes the limited upward mobility of Mexican CCT beneficiaries to low-quality education, a problem that afflicts the entire region. Thus, the path to unleashing the full promise of CCTs runs through the political minefield that is education reform.

8.3.2 The State of Education in Latin America

CCTs are premised on the naïve assumption that students will receive education that equips them with skills that employers demand. Thus, the ability of CCTs to achieve their long-term objectives will depend on the quality of a country's education system. And, although there is significant variation both across and within the region's countries, it is fair to say that basic education in Latin America is of low quality (Bruns and Luque 2015; Fiszbein and Stanton 2018).

In the broadest sense, education policy has two main components: access and quality. Latin America has made tremendous progress with regard to the former, in no small part thanks to CCTs. By 2017, net enrollment in primary school had reached 93%, just 3 percentage points lower than in industrialized countries.[28] At 77%, net enrollment at the secondary level was 20 points higher than at the turn of the century and 10 points higher than the average for middle-income countries, though still significantly behind rich countries (Fiszbein and Stanton 2018, 7).

Yet, as economist Lant Pritchett (2013) famously remarked, "*schooling ain't learning.*" While crucial, increasing enrollment and completion rates does not ensure that students will acquire the skills needed to get ahead. International and regional assessment exams consistently show that a large share of Latin American students fail to meet basic learning benchmarks

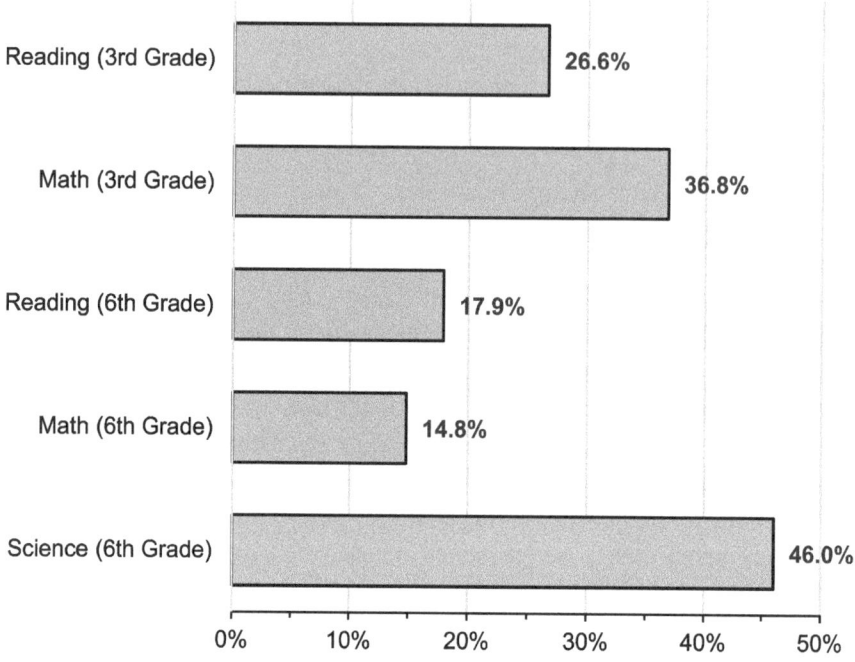

Figure 8-1. Share of Students Scoring "Low" on 2013 TERCE Exam (By Grade and Subject)
Sources: UNESCO (2016); Fiszbein and Stanton (2018, 15).

and underperform relative to their peers in comparable countries. Nor is it simply a matter of throwing more money at the problem. Education spending in the region as a share of GDP increased by 3 percentage points on average over the last 25 years with every country increasing spending by at least 1.5% of GDP (Busso et al. 2017, 59). In fact, more than half of the countries in Latin America and the Caribbean (17 of 29) currently spend more on education relative to GDP than the average for rich countries (4.8%) (Fiszbein and Stanton 2018, 27).

At the primary level, a third (36.8%) and a quarter (26.6%) of third graders scored one or below (out of four) in math and reading, respectively, in the United Nations Educational, Scientific and Cultural Organization's (UNESCO) Third Comparative Regional and Explicative Exam (TERCE) (see fig. 8-1). On the positive side, by sixth grade those figures improved to 14.8% and 17.9%, respectively. However, nearly half (46%) of sixth graders scored at one or below in science (Fiszbein and Stanton 2018, 15). Only

13.7% of sixth graders scored a four in reading and the shares for math and science were half that level (UNESCO 2016, 13).

Results are no better at the secondary level. The 10 Latin American countries participating in the Organization for Economic Cooperation and Development's (OECD) 2015 Programme for International Student Assessment (PISA) exam scored below what would be expected given their per capita income levels and ranked in the bottom 40% of the 72 participating countries (see fig. 8–2). The 50–75-point gap between the average science score for OECD countries (493) and those of the region's top performers—Chile (447), Uruguay (435), and Costa Rica (420)—amounts to two years of schooling. That gap rises to three years for Colombia and Mexico (416), Brazil (401), and Peru (397). Dominicans (332), the worst PISA performers, lagged behind OECD students by a full five years—practically the entire length of secondary school (Bos et al. 2016, 3). And the share of students exiting the school system before age 15 (when students take PISA) is significantly higher in Latin America than in rich countries. Further, based on TERCE, it can be assumed that secondary education systems in countries that did not participate in PISA are in even worse shape than those of participating countries (Bruns and Luque 2015, 4).

Low teacher quality constitutes a "binding constraint" on education in the region (Bruns and Luque 2015, 2), and thus on the ability of CCTs to fully deliver on their potential. After all, "the effectiveness of individual teachers is the single most important school-level determinant of student learning outcomes" (Bruns, Macdonald, and Schneider 2019, 28). In general, Latin American teachers show a "weak mastery of academic content" and fail to incorporate best practices in teaching (Bruns and Luque 2015, 2). Put succinctly, "virtually all countries in the region appear trapped in a low-level equilibrium of low standards for entry into teaching, low-quality candidates and undifferentiated salaries, low professionalism in the classroom, and poor education results" (Bruns and Luque 2015, 11).

Increased investment in education and policies aimed at increasing coverage, CCTs chief among them, are keeping more students in school for longer. Yet low education quality is preventing those students from acquiring the skills that will allow them to break the intergenerational cycle of poverty. Improving education quality should therefore be the region's top social policy priority. Yet, unlike successful efforts to expand coverage, reforms to improve quality are politically difficult.

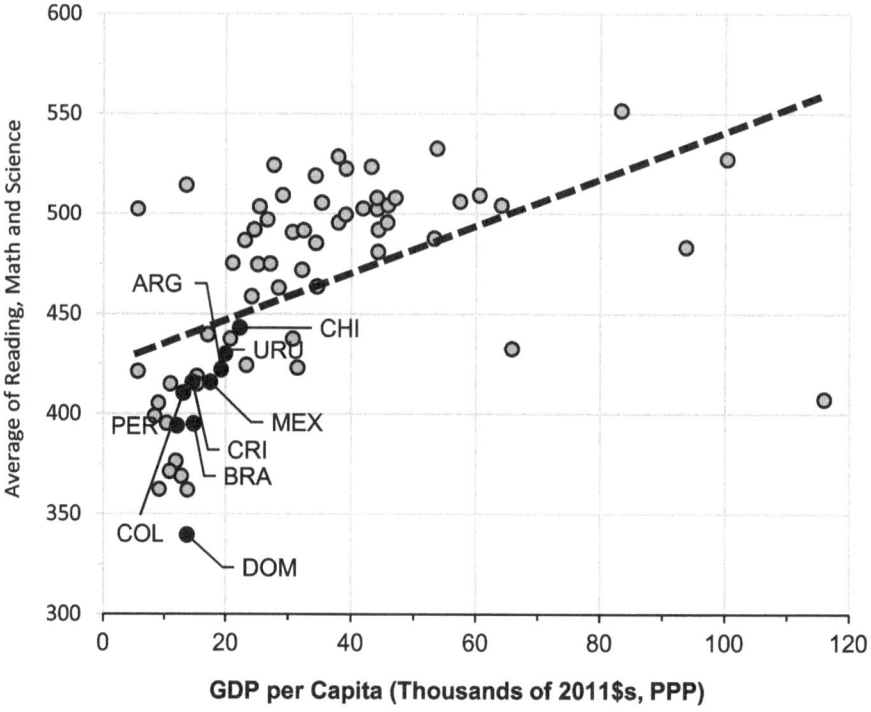

Figure 8-2. PISA Score (Average of Reading, Math and Science) and Income per Capita (2015)
Sources: OECD (2016) and World Bank (2018).

8.3.3 The Difficult Politics of Education Quality

Quality of education is a more powerful determinant of economic development and inclusive growth than education coverage or spending (Hanushek and Woessmann 2007; Hanushek 2009). However, the politics of access are much easier than those of quality. Access reforms produce many winners and few losers. Parents benefit from closer schools, teachers get jobs, and unions gain new members and increased political clout (Corrales 1999; Grindle 2004; Stein et al. 2006, chap. 10; Bruns, Macdonald, and Schneider 2019). Crucially, the effects of access reforms are immediate and visible and thus easily attributable to the government in office. The main challenge, which Latin America has so far been able to overcome (Busso et al. 2017, 59), is paying for the expansion.

Quality reforms, on the other hand, are the definition of contentious politics. Reforms demanding better performance and greater accountability from teachers directly threaten entrenched vested interests. Teachers are generally organized into powerful labor unions capable of challenging government reforms in the streets, sometimes violently. Yet given their weight—in 2012 teachers represented 4% of the region's workforce and 20% of its technical and professional workers (Bruns and Luque 2015, 1)—unions often do not even need to engage in collective action to co-opt or veto threatening reforms. Some unions are closely linked to particular political parties, while others, most notably Mexico's National Union of Education Workers, "rent" their members' votes to the parties that will most benefit members (Murillo 1999; Chambers-Ju 2020).

The political benefits for reformist politicians are highly uncertain. The costs of reform are front-loaded. Reformers can expect difficult, drawn-out negotiations with unions that may culminate in disruptive, long-term strikes. By keeping children out of school, protests and strikes can paralyze an entire country, placing tremendous pressure on governments to water down or even abandon reforms. The benefits, however, are back-loaded. Improvements in student learning and employability occur over the long term and are thus unlikely to be attributed to the politicians that expended political capital to make them happen (Nelson 2007; Bruns, Macdonald, and Schneider 2019).

Nor can reformers expect much help from civil society. Whereas unions have an incentive to do everything in their power to stop reforms they oppose, supporters seldom constitute a countervailing coalition (Stein et al. 2005, chap. 10). As a case in point, "parents' organizations, business groups, or pro-education civic alliances were conspicuously absent" from the cases analyzed in Grindle's (2004, 198) seminal review of education reforms in the region during the 1990s. Building proreform coalitions is made all the more difficult by the high and growing share of students—one in five in 2013 (Elacqua, Iribarren, and Santos 2018, 8)—enrolled in private education, itself a consequence of low education quality. The growing exodus of middle-class families weakens a crucial source of pressure to improve public schools.

Furthermore, there are no internationally proven and easy to emulate blueprints for improving quality comparable to CCTs for increasing attendance and enrollment. The lack of certainty over "what works" makes reforms harder to sell to the public (Nelson 2007). Implementation is opaque. Reform success is ultimately determined by teachers in classrooms across the country, a world away from education ministries in capital cities. Student learning and teacher performance are difficult to measure. And, therefore, "it is difficult to reward teachers who effectively implement reforms and to sanction those who resist" (Bruns, Macdonald, and Schneider 2019, 28).

Finally, given the long-term nature of reforms, there is always a possibility that the next government will water down or even roll back hard-fought reforms to win over the unions. This is precisely what happened in Rio de Janeiro, Brazil during the 2000s (Bruns, Macdonald, and Schneider 2019, 29) and, more recently in AMLO's Mexico (Economist 2019).

8.4 The Future of CCTs

Despite their shortcomings, CCTs have marked a revolution in social policy that has changed the lives of tens of millions of Latin Americans for the better. Today there exists a broad consensus across the ideological spectrum in favor of CCTs. But it was not always that way. The great irony is that, through seemingly neoliberal social policies that they originally opposed, left-wing presidents moved further toward their goal of constructing social democracy, defined as near-universal, rights-based social policies accessible independently of labor status, than they ever could have through the region's traditional social policies. Kicking and screaming, the left learned to love CCTs and later used them as a jumping off point for moving, albeit modestly, in the direction of achieving its ultimate goal of emancipating labor from the market.

The left's reluctant acceptance and subsequent transformation of CCTs constitutes an example of policy learning. Brazil's left overcame a malady that has consistently plagued policymaking in Latin America, what Hirschman (1981, 155) called *fracasomania*: "the insistence on the part of each new set of policymakers to decry as utter failure everything that had been done before; consequently . . . one had to start from scratch over and over again." In line with *fracasomania*, the first instinct of Lula and other left-leaning leaders was to reject the social policies they inherited from market reformers and start anew. The facts on the ground forced Lula to reconsider and place a bet on CCTs. Lula and later Rousseff tweaked the design of the CCTs they inherited to better achieve their programmatic goals. Bolsa Família then served as an example that influenced other left-wing leaders who enacted their own basic income CCTs.

What AMLO has done to Progresa/Oportunidades is therefore deeply troubling. In a textbook case of *fracasomania*, rather than, as Lula did, adapt the successful program he inherited to better match his programmatic preferences, AMLO opted to completely dismantle it. With little warning or justification and counter to campaign promises, he replaced a tried and tested, albeit imperfect, program with a series of opaque and improvised programs. He also discarded painstakingly compiled social registries that contained valuable information on the Mexican population's needs, opting instead to rely on the results of the unsystematic and seemingly politicized "Well-Being Census."

The clientelistic turn that Progresa/Oportunidades and Bolsa Família have taken under populist presidents threatens to undo the quiet revolution Latin American social policy has undergone over the past two decades. Those pioneering programs marked pathbreaking developments in the social policies of their respective counties and of Latin America as a whole. Despite their differing designs and counter to the many attacks AMLO and Bolsonaro hurled at them over the years, the two programs stood out for having clear eligibility criteria and transparent rules that in turn limited governments' ability to manipulate them for political gain (De La O 2015). Bolsonaro's seeming use of Bolsa Família to reward politically supportive regions and punish the PT-backing Northeast represents a major step backward in the region's much-heralded shift away from the bad old days of clientelism and discretionary spending toward a new era of programmatic policies and rules-based entitlements. AMLO's so-called census sent a clear message that cash transfers would, from now on, be benefits bestowed upon the population by the president, not an entitlement provided by the Mexican state.

As this book has shown, the story of CCTs is one of diffusion from Mexico and Brazil to the rest of the region. It is therefore deeply worrying that the gold standards in both human capital and basic income CCTs are in danger of degenerating into two more in the long line of clientelistic antipoverty initiatives that used to come and go with each new presidential administration. Hopefully, the concerning actions discussed above will be mere blips in the history of CCTs.

Although Mexico's recent experience is a reminder that the temptation of *fracasomania* persists, one can hope that, rather than seeking to reinvent the wheel for the sake of having a program to call their own, current and future governments, regardless of ideology, will follow the Brazilian left's example in continuing to build and improve upon successful programs they inherit. Ideally, governments will also prove willing to build the political and social coalitions and expend the political capital necessary to enact urgently needed reforms to improve education quality. Only then will CCTs and, more importantly, the region's low-income students have a real chance of achieving their full potential.

NOTES

Chapter 1

1. Technically, Bangladesh launched a nationwide CCT—Female Secondary School Stipend Project—in 1994, but this program covered only girls of secondary school age (Schurmann 2009). In late 1996, Brazil launched its first federal CCT, Programa de Erradicação do Trabalho Infantil (Program for Eradication of Child Labor, PETI), but it only targeted areas where children were most at risk of working in dangerous activities (see chapter 3). Throughout this book, the Mexican CCT will be referred to as Progresa/Oportunidades. The name Progresa was an acronym for *Progr*ama de *E*ducación, Salud y *A*limentación (Education, Health and Nutrition Program). It was renamed to Oportunidades in 2002 following a change in ruling party. It was renamed yet again, this time to Prospera (To Prosper) in 2012 following another change in the party in government. Despite the name changes, the program remained largely unchanged until it was replaced with unconditional transfers by left-wing President Andrés Manuel López-Obrador (2018–present) in early 2019 (see chapter 8).

2. This listing excludes in-kind transfers conditional on school attendance, unconditional cash transfer programs, and cash transfer programs conditional on actions other than school enrollment. Including the latter two, there are cash transfer programs in approximately 70 countries.

3. For a dissenting view on industrialized countries, see Korpi and Palme (2003) and Allan and Scruggs (2004).

4. This occurs because contributory programs are seldom financially self-sufficient. They are partly funded through taxes, which everyone, including the poor and informal-sector workers, pay. This regressiveness is compounded by the region's heavy reliance on consumption taxes, which disproportionately hurt the poor, who consume most (if not all) of their incomes, and the relative underdevelopment of income and property taxes, which fall primarily on the rich.

5. Diego Sanches Corrêa challenges this widely held view, arguing that, although it makes sense for CCT beneficiaries to reward incumbents, nonbeneficiaries, who pay for these programs but receive nothing in return, should be expected to punish incumbents. Thus, the effect of CCTs on support for incumbents should be indeterminate. At the macro level, Corrêa (2015) finds that CCT coverage does

not affect the extent to which an incumbent overperforms in a given election relative to the prior election's incumbent. At the individual level, Corrêa and Cheibub (2016) find nonbeneficiaries become more likely to vote against incumbents, even if they had previously supported said incumbent. For another dissenting view on the political effects of CCTs, see Bohn (2011).

6. During Mexico's 2006 elections, Felipe Calderón (2006–12) of the incumbent right-wing National Action Party (PAN) defeated Andrés Manuel López Obrador of the left-wing Democratic Revolution Party (PRD) by 243,000 votes or 0.6% of votes cast. Although the outgoing PAN administration of Vicente Fox (2000–2006) did not launch the CCT, it did expand it to urban areas. During the second round of Brazil's 2014 elections, President Dilma Rousseff (2011–16) defeated Aécio Neves of the centrist Brazilian Social Democracy Party (PSDB) by 3.5 million votes or 3.28% of votes cast.

7. Violeta Barrios de Chamorro (1990–97), a center-right politician from the 14-party National Opposition Union (UNO) coalition defeated sitting president Daniel Ortega (1985–90; 2007–present) of the left-wing Sandinista Front for National Liberation by 14 percentage points (54.74% to 40.82%) or nearly 200,000 votes. Ortega originally came to power "via bullets" in 1979 as part of an insurgent movement that unseated the long-standing Somoza dynasty.

8. Turning the argument on its head, Remmer (2012) attributes the left's rise to improving external economic conditions, which relaxed the constraints on policy choice, enhanced the credibility of anti-status-quo politicians and created opportunities for redistributive policies. At the macro level, she finds that the odds of electing a leftist-populist president increased alongside improvements in the terms of trade. At the individual level, support for leftist-populist presidents was positively associated with satisfaction with the state of the economy. Relatedly, Murillo, Oliveros, and Vaishnav (2011) find that a reduction in economic constraints, namely a larger current account surplus and the absence of an agreement with the International Monetary Fund, increases the likelihood that a president will move to the left.

9. There has been considerable debate over to how to categorize the governments of the left turn. Castañeda (2006) divides the left into social democratic and populist variants. Given the normative implications of this typology (i.e., the claim that there is a "good" and a "bad" left), Weyland (2010) opts for moderate and contestatory, respectively. Levitsky and Roberts (2011) categorize the left in terms of level of institutionalization (established party versus new political movement) and locus of political authority (dispersed versus concentrated). Scholars have also sought to explain why the left became radicalized in some countries but moderated in others. Explanations proposed include access to natural resource rents (Weyland 2009), degree of party system institutionalization (Flores-Macias 2010), whether traditional left-leaning or labor-backed parties were responsible for implementing market reforms (Madrid 2010), and extent of electoral mandate (Biglaiser 2016), among others.

10. There has been considerable debate over how to classify Argentina's Néstor Kirchner (2003–7) and his wife and successor Cristina Fernández de Kirchner

(2007–15). Castañeda's (2006) influential typology classified Néstor as part of the populist left. Later typologies tended to place the Kirchners somewhere between the two poles (Madrid, Hunter, and Weyland 2010, 143; Flores-Macias 2012, 32). This book follows the Dataset on Political Ideology of Presidents and Parties in Latin America (Murillo, Olivero, and Vaishnav 2010) in labeling them center-left.

11. Huber and Stephens (2012) find no effect of left political strength (an index measuring strength at both the presidential and legislative levels) on social spending during 1970–2007. McLeod and Lustig (2011) do find a positive effect for the years 1988–2008.

12. The differences between the two lefts are much clearer with regard to their effects on quality and even survival of democracy with Weyland (2013, 19) going so far as describe the radical left as the first "sustained, coordinated threat" to democratic consolidation in the region in decades. This is surprising given that the right (with military backing) has been responsible for the vast majority of democratic breakdowns in the region. The most notable case of democratic decay under the radical left has been Venezuela, where, over the course of the presidencies of Chávez and his anointed successor Nicolás Maduro (2013–present), democracy was gradually undermined from within to the point of collapse. More modest declines in democratic quality occurred in Bolivia and Ecuador. The latter's democracy has since registered significant improvements under Lenin Moreno (2017–2021), Correa's handpicked successor. Originally seen merely as a placeholder for Correa, Moreno has worked to depoliticize the justice system and enacted a constitutional reform that dashed his mentor's hopes of returning to power and achieving permanent reelection (Torre 2018).

13. Scores are based on Coppedge (1997) and its extensions, including Huber, Mustillo, and Stephens (2008), Murillo and Martinez-Gallardo (2007), and Weisehomeier and Benoit (2007), as well as consultations with country experts.

Chapter 2

1. For an analysis of the determinants of adoption of non-contributory pensions in Latin America, see Carnes and Mares (2014).

2. De La O (2015, chap. 4) finds that countries with divided governments are more likely to enact CCTs with rules that limit administrative discretion over the selection of beneficiaries and that possess rigorous program evaluations.

3. Focusing on program design, Garay (2016) finds that Argentina and Brazil, both of which exhibited high levels of social mobilization, adopted income support programs (a broader category that includes CCTs as well as non-contributory pensions) that target a broader population and feature more generous benefit levels and greater citizen participation than those in Mexico and Chile, which had comparatively lower levels of civil society mobilization.

4. De La O (2015, 67) acknowledges that the idea of transferring money to poor households was spread through diffusion but argues that a program's design depended on domestic factors. This book shares this view.

5. Decades before, International Labour Organization–inspired social security reforms diffused across the region (Collier and Messick 1975).

6. Osorio Gonnet (2018) provides a comprehensive listing of conferences, seminars, and workshops held in Latin America during this period. In addition to the aforementioned institutions, these types of events were also sponsored by the United Nations Economic Commission for Latin America and the Caribbean (CEPAL), the Food and Agriculture Organization (FAO), and the United Nations Development Programme (UNDP).

7. For example, that Cuba remained a dictatorship does not negate the existence of a diffusionary wave of democratization across Latin America during the 1980s (Gleditsch and Ward 2008; Mainwaring and Pérez-Liñán 2013). Nor does Brazil's failure to emulate Chile's private pension system (Mesa-Lago 2008, 29) discredit research defining as diffusion the model's adoption across Latin America and Eastern Europe (Brooks 2009; Madrid 2003; Weyland 2006).

8. The dataset covers only the years 1976–2008. Coding for the years 2009–15 was conducted based on prior dataset entries as well as news reports by Reuters and *Latin America Weekly Report*.

9. No distinction is made between whether a peer is also a contiguous neighbor. Given that the drivers behind diffusion are the presence of shared political, economic, and cultural ties, and constant interaction, Latin American countries should be as likely to emulate noncontiguous peers as geographic neighbors.

10. Measured in 2005 dollars at purchasing power parity. Few Latin American countries publish internationally comparable poverty data on a yearly basis. As a result, and given that poverty levels and income distribution change little over a given year, missing observations were estimated using linear interpolation in order to make the data compatible with the time-series, cross-sectional research design.

11. Banks (2011) defines demonstrations as "any peaceful public gathering of at least 100 people for the primary purpose of displaying or voicing their opposition to government policies or authority, excluding demonstrations of a distinctly antiforeign nature." Riots are defined as "any violent demonstration or clash of more than 100 citizens involving the use of physical force."

12. There is growing evidence pointing to reduced crime as an unintended benefit of CCTs. Higher CCT coverage at the neighborhood and state level is, respectively, associated with less crime in São Paulo, Brazil (Chioda, De Mello, and Soares 2016) and lower homicide rates across Brazilian and Mexican states (Lance 2014). Similarly, Camacho and Mejía (2013) find that thefts in Bogotá, Colombia declined during the days following CCT payments.

13. Following Carter and Signorino (2010), time dependence is modeled though a cubic polynomial approximation, that is, variables accounting for time (t), time squared (t^2), and time cubed (t^3). Failure to account for temporal dependence in this manner would likely produce overly optimistic assessments of statistical significance and incorrect standard errors. Robust (Huber-White) errors with clustering by country are estimated to account for likely heteroskedasticity.

14. Models including poverty rate and Gini coefficient as well as years of school-

ing and child labor tested positive for multicollinearity. As a result, the decision was made to include only one from each pair of variables in the models.

15. The time variables do not exactly match calendar years. The time variables for Costa Rica and Nicaragua restart on the years following the elimination of their CCTs. In all other cases year 1 is 1995, year 2 is 1996, and so on.

16. Given the reduced sample size it was necessary to remove one control variable. Thus, the model eliminated consumption taxes. Excluding other variables has no substantive effect on the variables of interest.

17. In fact, the World Bank, which was negotiating with Mexico at the time (Levy and Rodríguez 2004, 257), protested being excluded from the program's development and funding (Dion 2010, 204).

18. Sánchez de Lozada resigned in the aftermath of the Gas War, violent protests over potential natural gas exports via Chile's ports that resulted in an estimated 59 deaths. Upon resigning, Sánchez went into exile in the United States. The Morales government unsuccessfully sought his extradition.

Chapter 3

1. Lula shares this title with President Getúlio Vargas (1930–45 and 1951–54) (Hunter 2014).

2. The PT's control of the presidency ended in 2016 following Rousseff's impeachment. Rousseff was removed for manipulating budget numbers in the context of a severe economic crisis and the massive Lava Jato (car wash) corruption scandal. Rousseff has not been directly implicated in the scandal. Much has been written on Bolsa Família's political effects, particularly in relation to the 2006 elections. See also Soares and Terron (2008); Licio, Rennó, and de O; (2009); Canêdo-Pinheiro (2015). For a dissenting view, see Bohn (2011). For a response to Bohn, see Zucco and Power (2013). The general consensus is that beneficiaries rewarded presidential candidates from the incumbent party, but are less willing to reward the incumbent party's legislative candidates.

3. One such expert was Cristovam Buarque, whose nonprofit Missão Criança helped design Ecuador's Bono Solidario based on Brasilia's CCT (see chapter 6).

4. During the 1970s, Brazil's military government enacted the pioneering Renda Mensal Vitalicia (Lifetime Monthly Income), the region's first non-contributory pension, which benefited the rural elderly poor and the disabled. While ahead of its time, the program's small size and meager benefits prevented it from obtaining much international recognition. The program was expanded in the aftermath of the 1988 constitution and renamed Benefício de Prestação Continuada (Continuous Cash Benefit). For more information, see Rocha (2013, chap. 1).

5. Itamar Franco (1992–94) replaced Collor, who was impeached on corruption charges in December 1992.

6. For a critical take on the spread of subnational CCTs, see Rocha (2013, chap. 2).

7. Political competition may have also prompted PT mayors to adopt CCTs.

Coêlho (2012b) and Melo (2007) find that the intensity of interparty political competition within a municipality was a key determinant of adoption. Sugiyama (2008), however, finds no support for this claim.

8. The first generation of PT mayors, elected in 1988, remained loyal to party orthodoxy. Of the 36 mayors elected that year, one-third left office before their terms ended. Of the remaining 24 municipalities, only 12 elected a PT mayor in 1992 (see Couto 2003; Macaulay and Burton 2003).

9. To avoid a runoff election, a mayoral candidate must win at least 50% of the vote.

10. PGRM was scheduled to begin in 1998 but implementation was postponed until 1999 as a result of the gubernatorial and presidential elections and pressure from mayors from communities excluded from the program (Coêlho 2012a, 69).

11. Magalhães Teixeira died of liver cancer in September 1996.

12. Buarque did criticize the program for starting off too big and launching before conditionality enforcement had been perfected. He criticized the fact that school attendance under Bolsa Escola Federal was verified quarterly rather than monthly (as in Brasilia's program) (O Estado de S. Paulo 2001c).

13. In fact, in 1996, prior to the launch of Mexico's CCT, the Mexican government sent a delegation to Brazil to learn from several municipal Bolsa Escola programs (Lindert et al. 2007, 12).

14. Despite receiving an electoral boost from the new CCTs (Zucco 2013), Serra lost the October 2002 runoff by more than 20 percentage points.

15. The government asked supermarket chains and large multinationals including Ford and Unilever to contribute to Fome Zero's corporate social responsibility component (Hall 2006, 695; 2008, 804).

16. The Citizenship Institute was renamed the Lula Institute in 2011.

17. Graziano initially announced that Cartão beneficiaries would be required to submit receipts to the government proving benefits were spent on food (Rocha 2013, 89–90; Ansell 2014, 33–34). Given the enormous amount of work this would have entailed, the requirement was never implemented.

18. Buarque was fired over the phone while vacationing in Portugal (Folha de S. Paulo 2004a). He left the PT and unsuccessfully challenged Lula during the 2006 elections, winning less than 3% of the vote.

19. Beyond Bolsa Escola Federal and Bolsa Alimentação, the Cardoso administration also operated Bolsa Renda, which provided temporary assistance to drought victims, and Auxilio Gas, which provided subsidized cooking gas.

20. Prominent PT economists derided the proposal. Guido Mantega, who went on to serve as finance minister, called it *agenda fajuta* (fake or low-quality agenda). Social policy advisor Maria da Conceição Tavares blasted the proposal for its endorsement of social policy targeting and emphasis on fiscal responsibility (Patú 2013).

21. See also YouTube JSerra2010 (2010).

22. Palocci was accused within the PT of being a "neoliberal" (Newsweek Staff 2005; Guimarães 2015).

23. Graziano was reduced to a presidential advisor before being tapped to head the Latin America and Caribbean office of the United Nations Food and Agricultural Association in 2006. He was named head of the agency in 2011.

24. More than a CCT, Brasil sem Miséria aimed to serve as an umbrella social investment strategy for the eradication of extreme poverty. At its core, it sought to connect beneficiaries with a wide range of government-provided services that would allow them to overcome extreme poverty (see Fenwick 2017).

25. On January 8, 2004, one day before signing Bolsa Família into law (no. 10,836), Lula also signed into law a heavily modified version of Suplicy's basic income proposal (no. 10,835). The law called for the gradual implementation of a universal basic income "at the discretion of the Executive branch, giving priority to the neediest segments of the population" while "taking into consideration the country's level of development and budget possibilities." While on the books, this law has not been implemented (Britto and Soares 2011; Lavinas 2013b).

26. Conditionality enforcement was also complicated by teachers' reluctance to report noncompliance for fear that families would lose their benefits (Bastagli 2008, 144; Pereira 2015, 1689).

27. *Coronelismo* (rule by colonels) is a Brazilian term describing patron-client relationships in the countryside. A *coronel* is a local elite who, in exchange for political obedience, uses his economic resources for the benefit of the common people in his area.

28. Focus groups in Northeast Brazil carried out by Hunter and Sugiyama (2014, 835) support this finding.

29. The informal-sector jobs available to the poor tend to be precarious and intermittent. A job may allow a family to escape poverty and thus leave Bolsa Família. The precariousness of these types of jobs, however, creates the possibility that such a family could find itself without a job or transfer income.

Chapter 4

1. This is not to say that Bolsa Escola Federal was directly influenced by Mexico's CCT. Officials in the Cardoso administration claim not to have been influenced by Mexico's program and the subsequent diffusion of its approach to CCTs to other countries in the region (Sugiyama 2012a, 42). Overall, there is little evidence of "cross-fertilization" among Brazil's and Mexico's first CCT experiences (Morais 2017, 10).

2. Approaching CCT design from a different perspective, De La O (2015, 8) stresses the similarities between both programs, most notably the fact that they both have clear operational rules designed to prevent executives from manipulating them for political gain.

3. Giving birth at a younger age is associated with higher infant mortality, which is, in turn, associated with higher birth rates.

4. Zedillo, Levy, and Gómez de León met in the 1970s while working for the Bank of Mexico's research department (Lustig 2014, 113). The Finance Ministry's

Evelyne Rodríguez and CONAPO's Daniel Hernández, who succeeded Gómez de León as Progresa's national coordinator, were also crucial to the program's development (Berhman 2010, 1474). Technically, Niños en Solidaridad (Children in Solidarity), part of PRONASOL, was the first Mexican program to award families benefits conditional on school attendance. However, the program was small and did not select beneficiaries using objective criteria (Garay 2016, 233–34).

5. The pilot was called Nutrition, Health and Education Program (PASE). The states covered were Chiapas, Guanajuato, Guerrero, Hidalgo, México, Michoacán, Oaxaca, Puebla, and Veracruz (Cortés and Rubalcava 2012, 38).

6. Critics referred to this as the *pobremático*, a play on the words *pobre* (poor) and *cajero automático* (automatic teller machine).

7. Equally important was fear of political backlash from CCT beneficiaries. Shortly after the election, Carlos Flores, social policy coordinator for Fox, noted that "we can't take the benefit away from 2 million 300 thousand families on December first (inauguration day)" (Herrera 2000).

8. As noted in the previous chapter, while a law establishing said right was enacted in 2004, it was never executed and there are no plans to do so.

9. Proponents of UBI disagree on whether children should be included. Proposals restricted to adults tend to be complemented with child-benefit schemes (Van Parijs and Vanderborght 2017, 9).

10. Focus group research on Bolsa Família beneficiaries finds the opposite. Beneficiaries report the program fosters a sense of belonging and efficacy (Hunter and Sugiyama 2014).

11. This amounts to monthly stipends of $1,163 in the United States or $180 in Brazil.

12. It should be noted that the Alaska Permanent Fund, the longest-running example of a fully functioning UBI, was enacted by Jay Hammond, a Republican governor. The program has in recent years transferred about $2,000 a year on average to each of Alaska's 650,000 residents. The policy has reduced poverty and inequality (Goldsmith 2002) without affecting employment (Jones and Marinescu 2018). It is worth noting, however, that transfers are funded by the state's oil wealth rather than by taxation.

13. Ironically, McGovern's plan was not dramatically different from Nixon's unsuccessful negative income tax proposal. While universal, Nixon's proposal had a work requirement (Van Parijs and Vanderborght 2017, 90–93; Heller 2018).

14. Van der Veen and Van Parijs (2006) respond to this argument by noting that UBI offers a means of getting to communism (i.e., "for each according to his abilities, to each according to his needs") while skipping socialism (i.e., "to each according to his labor").

15. This view was not shared by Friedrich Hayek, the father of neoliberalism. Hayek argued that "the security of a minimum income" for all constitutes "an indispensable condition of real liberty" (cited in Van Parijs and Vanderborght 2017, 86).

16. Under this logic, requiring beneficiary mothers to attend classes that they otherwise would not attend, as required by Progresa/Oportunidades, could be stig-

matizing and therefore illegitimate. Not all CCTs have these components and those that do could eliminate them or make them voluntary (Pérez-Muñoz 2017, 456).

17. Lo Vuolo (2013b, 261–62) disagrees, arguing that the success of CCTs has further increased the legitimacy of targeted and conditional programs.

18. Chile followed its own path. Chile Solidario, the country's flagship antipoverty program until 2012, was a comprehensive social assistance program with a CCT component. It has not been emulated.

19. Robertson et al. (2013) find that, while positive, the difference in attendance between conditional and unconditional transfers among 6–12 year olds is small. The difference among 13–17 year olds is much larger.

20. Both papers also find that the burden of conditionality makes wealthier beneficiaries more likely to drop out of the program.

21. Measured in 2005 dollars at purchasing power parity as estimated by SEDLAC (2018).

22. Students receive stipends in five bimonthly installments between September and June. Nutritional stipends are paid year-round.

23. Benefits for first and second graders are only available to students from communities with fewer than 2,500 inhabitants.

Chapter 5

1. Estimated in 2005 dollars at purchasing power parity as estimated by SEDLAC (2018).

2. These rough averages consider the years prior to the enactment of CCTs, which are counted as having a coverage rate of 0%. Brazil enacted a national-level CCT later than Mexico (2001 compared to 1997). As a result, average coverage in Brazil during the period is similar to that of Mexico even though Brazil surpassed Mexico during the final years of the period of study.

3. The dataset only covers the years 1976–2008. Coding for the years 2009–15 was conducted based on prior dataset entries as well as news reports by Reuters and *Latin America Weekly Report*.

4. Measured in 2005 dollars at purchasing power parity. Few Latin American countries publish internationally comparable poverty data on a yearly basis. As a result, and given that poverty levels and income distribution change little over a given year, missing observations were estimated using linear interpolation in order to make the data compatible with the time-series, cross-sectional research design.

5. Developed by Beck et al. (2001), the index considers both the existence of divided control of legislative chamber(s) and the number of veto players. A case receives the index's maximum score (7) when the executive is competitively elected, if the opposition controls the legislature(s), and when the number of parties allied with the president's party have an ideological orientation closer to that of the main opposition party (see Cruz et al. 2016, 20–21; De La O 2015, 59).

6. Banks (2011) defines demonstrations as "any peaceful public gathering of at least 100 people for the primary purpose of displaying or voicing their opposition

to government policies or authority, excluding demonstrations of a distinctly antiforeign nature." Riots are defined as "any violent demonstration or clash of more than 100 citizens involving the use of physical force."

7. Models including poverty rate and Gini coefficient as well as years of schooling and child labor tested positive for multicollinearity. As a result, the decision was made to only include one from each pair of variables in the models.

8. Bolsa Família started in October 2003. Assuming it would take some time for the program to catch the attention of policymakers in other countries, the analysis looks at programs that were adopted in 2005 or later. This excludes Argentina's short-lived Plan Familias, which was adopted in 2004 (see chapter 7).

Chapter 6

1. Granted, it is possible that, upon learning about another country's social policies, civil society groups could mobilize to bring about diffusion. However, there is no evidence of this happening in Latin America with regard to CCTs.

2. Morais (2017, 151) was told that Bolsa Família, with its decentralized operation and reliance on self-reported incomes, was "'so Brazilian' that it was difficult to export." This claim is questionable given that Brazil's basic income model proved quite popular first among Latin American countries governed by the left and later among development aid agencies, which exported it to Africa.

3. Although the administration of Ernesto Zedillo (1994–2000) purposefully chose not seek financial support from IFIs during Progresa's early years (Dion 2010, 204; Levy and Rodríguez 2004, 257), the government of Vicente Fox (2000–2006) obtained a $1 billion loan from the IDB in 2002 to modernize the program and expand it to urban areas. This was the largest poverty loan awarded by the bank at the time (Levy 2006, 114).

4. The IDB also funded PRAF-1, which began in 1990. This was a food stamp program (not a cash transfer program) conditional on education. While more effective than direct food aid, the program was criticized for arbitrary and politically motivated targeting (Moore 2010, 106).

5. Citing Laura Rawlings, a social protection expert at the World Bank.

6. In Brazil, officials studied Brasilia's Bolsa Escola CCT, which was more focused on human capital than poverty reduction (see chapter 3).

7. Adoption of Beca Escolar faced two major setbacks. First, President Mahuad was forced to resign in January 2000 amid large-scale protests by indigenous groups and a subsequent military revolt. Second, the World Bank and IDB ultimately decided not to fund the program (Lana and Evans 2004, 205). Those institutions were later active in funding and shaping the transformation into Bono de Desarrollo Humano in 2003. By then Ecuador's economic situation had improved. This made it possible for the government to push back against some IFI suggestions, particularly with regard to conditionality enforcement (Osorio Gonnet 2018). It is also worth noting that, in line with this book's broader argument, the program underwent a dramatic increase in coverage and stipend generosity during the government of left-wing President Rafael Correa (2007–17).

8. Having spent 477 days or 16% of his eight years in power abroad and having visited 84 countries, Lula holds the distinction of being the Brazilian president who spent the most time abroad (Damé 2010).

9. In 2009, President Barak Obama (2009–17) jokingly called Lula "the most popular politician on earth" (Newsweek 2009).

10. Those countries were Ghana, Guinea-Bissau, Mozambique, Nigeria, South Africa, and Zambia. While Ghana's Livelihood Empowerment Against Poverty (LEAP) is conditional on paper, conditions were not enforced in practice (de Groot 2015).

11. Other participants include the International Policy Centre for Inclusive Growth of the United Nations Development Programme (UNDP) and Brazil's Institute for Applied Economic Research.

12. Argentina adopted a short-lived, small-scale CCT, Programa Familias (Families Program), in 2004. Although that program will be discussed, the focus of this chapter will be the much larger AUH, which replaced it in 2009.

13. Selecting cases knowing their outcomes in advance—a centrist government adopted a human capital CCT and left-wing governments adopted basic income CCTs—does not bias the results of the case studies. The purpose of the case studies is *not* to demonstrate that government ideology affects CCT design—that point was demonstrated in chapter 5—but rather to trace the mechanisms linking presidential ideology with CCT design choices.

14. Coverage was extended to grades six in 2007, eight in 2008, nine in 2012, 10 in 2013, and 12 in 2014.

15. The author personally observed the system at work (May 2013 in San José, Costa Rica).

Chapter 7

1. CCTs are enshrined in law in only five countries in the region—Argentina, Brazil, Chile, Costa Rica, and Uruguay. Argentina's program was enacted via a decree that modified existing legislation (Cecchini and Madariaga 2011, 161–65).

2. Solís served as planning minister during Arias's first term. He left Arias's National Liberation Party in protest of the party's embrace of neoliberalism.

3. The Social Development and Family Allowance Fund was the region's first social policy fund (Román 2012, 8). Starting with Bolivia in the 1980s (Graham 1992), most of the region's countries adopted these programs to ameliorate the social costs associated with structural adjustment (Siri 2000).

4. Budget allocation also helps explain the problems at the secondary level. Education spending is biased in favor of primary and tertiary with secondary receiving only 22% of the education budget. Both the share of public spending on secondary schooling and spending per secondary school student are low relative to the country's economic development (Oviedo et al. 2015, 113).

5. Costa Rica's legislature has experienced significant gridlock since the country's transition to a multiparty system in 2002. Borges (2014) attributes the paralysis to a combination of legislative fragmentation and polarization and the legislature's

preexisting rules of procedure, which allow legislators to easily block bills they oppose, even when those bills are supported by supermajorities.

6. As part of the effort to build this reputation, Zumbado famously spent a night in a shantytown in March 2007. His political aspirations were dashed in August 2008 after he was forced to resign for allegedly misusing a donation from Taiwan's government (Mata Blanco 2008). Zumbado was found guilty in January 2014, but ultimately absolved on appeal in May 2015 (Cambronero 2015).

7. Avancemos was also supposed to award graduating students a bonus that could be used for college tuition, language studies, or to start their own business. It was never implemented.

8. The National Scholarship Office provided merit-based scholarships to low-income students. However, unlike a CCT, the program had no fixed eligibility criteria and was therefore not an entitlement. Each school had its own council of teachers and parents charged with assigning benefits. This has resulted in pervasive accusations of favoritism and nepotism (interview, José Antonio Li). This was one of the reasons the National Scholarship Office was folded into IMAS in 2019.

9. The war pitted Chile against Bolivia and Peru. Chile won the war and with it control over significant stretches of resource-rich territory from both countries. The war cost Bolivia its Pacific coastline, which, to this day, remains a major source of tension between both countries.

10. Juana Azurduy de Padilla (1780–1862) was a female fighter during Bolivia's War of Independence, earning the rank of lieutenant colonel. In contrast to BJP, the World Bank was involved in BJA's design. However, Morales went against the bank's advice in making the program universal right off the bat (McGuire 2013, 18–19). The World Bank, which was supposed to cover half of the program's cost, ultimately walked away following disagreements over program evaluations (interview, Ernesto Yáñez).

11. Although the overall achievement gap between boys and girls is small and has been declining, this gap is particularly large among children whose parents received little to no education (Zambrana 2010, 15)

12. Declaring the program unsustainable, right-wing president Hugo Banzer (1971–78; 1997–2001) cancelled it in 1998 only to reinstate it six months later as the less-generous Bolivida. Sánchez de Lozada restored it to its previous name and value upon regaining the presidency (Müller 2009, 166).

13. Now that BJP covers every grade, Bono Esperanza focuses on children enrolled in kindergarten and disabled students (interview, Pablo Apaza).

14. Quiroga was Bolivia's vice-president in 1997 under Banzer. He assumed the presidency in August 2001 after Banzer resigned after being diagnosed with lung cancer.

15. The absence of civil society involvement in BJP's design is surprising given the close links between MAS and social movements. Social movements were heavily involved in securing the legislative passage of Renta Dignidad, which is enshrined in law (Carnes and Mares 2014; Anria and Niedzwiecki 2016).

16. BJA is paid out of the Central Bank's reserves.

17. Following Sánchez de Lozada's resignation, Vice-President Carlos Mesa (2003–5) assumed the presidency. Mesa resigned in June 2005 amid large-scale indigenous protests. Supreme Court chief justice Eduardo Rodríguez (2005–6) then assumed the presidency. Morales won the December 2005 elections and was sworn in one month later.

18. BJP prompted an increase in the share of births that were registered with the government. In 2005 only 56% of births were registered. By 2008 that figure had risen to 87% (Hunter and Brill 2016, 219).

19. The main problem with this survey is that children who left the school system were not interviewed.

20. Renta Dignidad was further increased in 2017 and 2019. BJP stipends have not increased.

21. For a justification for the Kirchners' designation as center-left, see note 10, chapter 1.

22. *Porteño/a* is a colloquial term used to refer to residents of the city of Buenos Aires.

23. High-income families with children receive an income tax deduction. The reasons why coverage is not universal are discussed in section 7.2.3.

24. For detailed analyses of the causes of the crisis, see Mussa (2002) and Blustein (2005).

25. Alianza was a coalition between the centrist Radical Civic Union, of which de la Rúa was a member, and the center-left Solidary Country Front (FREPASO).

26. De la Rúa resigned on December 22, 2001. Since his vice-president, Carlos Alberto Álvarez (1999–2000), had resigned a year prior, Congress appointed an interim president, Adolfo Rodríguez Saá (2001), the Peronist governor of San Luis Province. Citing lack of support from within his own party, Rodríguez Saá resigned one week later on December 30. Duhalde was appointed on January 2, 2002 after the presidents of both the Senate and Chamber of Deputies refused to assume the presidency. Duhalde ultimately decided to end his presidency early, causing presidential elections to take place six months ahead of schedule in April 2003.

27. During 1991–2002, the Argentine peso was pegged at one-to-one with the US dollar. The policy succeeded in taming the country's hyperinflation, but gradually eroded the economy's competitiveness, setting the stage for the country's 2001–2 economic meltdown.

28. Net enrollment rates measure the share of children enrolled in the appropriate grade for their age. This contrasts with gross enrollment, which is calculated by dividing the number of students enrolled in a specific level by the total number of children in that age group. It does not account for students who are either too young or too old for their proscribed grade and can thus exceed 100% (UIS 2017).

29. A version of IDH was implemented in 2002 in the aftermath of the economic crisis, technically making it Argentina's first CCT. However, the program was very small, covering only about 32,000 people (0.08% of the population) at its peak in 2004 and operating in just 62 mainly urban and indigenous municipalities (out of more than 2,000 total municipalities) (Virginia Tedeschi, coordinator of Plan

Familias, interviewed in Van Thienen 2015, 80). IDH's staff was charged with providing technical assistance and training to municipalities that were incorporated into Familias (Trujillo and Retamozo 2019, 96). During its brief existence, IDH came to be informally known as "familias" in some parts of the country, which led to its successor formally assuming that name (Virginia Tedeschi, coordinator of Plan Familias, interviewed in Van Thienen 2015, 80). Given IDH's small size and limited geographical scope, it is not considered a national-level CCT for the purposes of the quantitative analyses in chapters 2 and 5.

30. For a detailed account of why Jefes proved so hard to unwind, see Fenwick (2016, 136–37).

31. In targeting beneficiaries based on employment status rather than income, the program continues to reflect the Peronists' traditional focus on labor (Arcidiácono et al. 2012, 171).

32. De la O (2015, 93–95) argues that increased legislative oversight explains the noticeable reduction in discretion present in AUH relative to Jefes. This chapter's analysis contradicts her claim that legislators influenced the design of CCTs in Argentina.

33. Rolls are purged once a year. Although purges are supposed to take place in January, every year the deadline to turn in the paperwork and thus avoid expulsion is extended until March or April (Marchionni and Edo 2017, 276).

34. To obtain the conditional 20%, children six and under must certify that they are vaccinated and enrolled in a government public health program, which provides preventative care for mothers and children. Children 5–18 must demonstrate school enrollment. A major problem with withholding the 20% is that it loses much of its value to Argentina's high inflation (see fig. 7–4).

35. The Fernández administration manipulated the country's inflation data during 2007–15. In 2013, Argentina became the first country to be censured for misreporting GDP and prices by the International Monetary Fund (Economist 2016). Figure 7–6 relies on independently compiled data (Cavallo and Bertolotto 2016)

36. Though this resulted in differentiated stipend amounts, those differences were not justified based on the risk of exiting the school system as in the human capital CCT model. Rather, they were justified on the grounds of ensuring that all Argentine families with children possess the same minimum level of income. Accomplishing this requires compensating for differences in cost of living. Arguably, that constitutes an effort to build an income floor.

Chapter 8

1. After peaking during the second quarter of 2011, commodity prices declined slowly before plummeting during the first quarter of 2014. Excluding 2009, when, as a result of the global financial crisis, the region's economy shrank by 2%, Latin America grew by 5.2% a year on average from 2004 through 11. Regional growth decelerated sharply during 2012–14 before turning negative during both 2016 and 2017 (World Bank 2020).

2. Bolivia's Evo Morales did not escape this anti-incumbent backlash. He resigned the presidency and fled the country in November 2019 amid widespread public protests sparked by allegations of electoral fraud and subsequent pressure from the armed forces. Morales returned to the country in November 2020 following the election of Luis Arce (2020–present) of his Movement toward Socialism party.

3. Populism is defined as "a thin-centered ideology that considers society to be ultimately separated into two homogeneous and antagonistic groups, 'the pure people' versus 'the corrupt elite', and which argues that politics should be an expression of the volonté générale (general will) of the people" (Mudde 2004, 543). Under this definition, populists can be of the left as well as the right.

4. Bolsonaro represented the Social Liberal Party during the 2018 presidential campaign but left the party in November 2019.

5. In contrast, poverty had been stable in the other two countries. In 2019, after six years of left-wing governments, the share of Costa Ricans living in poverty remained largely unchanged while extreme poverty had declined by 10% (INEC 2019). Although the Mexican economy was slowing when AMLO was running for office, poverty had actually been declining (CONEVAL 2020; México, ¿Cómo Vamos? 2020).

6. Own calculations based on Avancemos stipend data and inflation data from INEC (2020).

7. More specifically, Avancemos is to receive at least 8% of the budget of the Social Development and Family Allowance Fund, the country's permanent and well-funded social assistance fund.

8. While the Education Ministry's scholarships targeted poor children and were conditional on enrollment, they were not a CCT. Scholarships were not an entitlement guaranteed to particular segments of the population and were instead awarded on a case-by-case basis by local scholarship committees. Students were required to reapply each year and the number of scholarships offered to each school varied from year to year (Villalobos 2016; Rodríguez Chaves 2017).

9. The bonus amount varied depending on the year.

10. Macri's center/center-right Cambiemos (Let's Change) coalition came in first, picking up 61 deputies and 12 senators.

11. Own calculations based on National Statistics and Census Institute (2020) inflation data. Credible government inflation data did not become available until December 2016.

12. Bonus payments were made in March and September 2018 and September and October 2019. These payments and the Christmas bonuses are not included in purchasing power calculations.

13. Own calculations based on National Statistics and Census Institute poverty data reported by Szafranko (2019).

14. Under the PT, Bolsa Família was under the purview of the Ministry of Social Development (MDS). Under Temer, it moved to a new Ministry of Social and Agricultural Development. Under Bolsonaro, it is under a new Ministry of Citizenship.

Terra was Temer's social and agrarian development minister from May 2016 until April 2018, when he stepped down to run for reelection as a legislator representing Rio Grande do Sul. He joined the Bolsonaro administration as citizenship minister in January 2019 and stepped down in February 2020.

15. Own calculations based on MC (2020). No data is available on blockages and cancellations prior to April 2014. The steady expansion Bolsa Família had been undergoing since its launch ended as a result of the 2015–16 recession. The Rousseff administration slowed admissions into the program, resulting in the emergence of a waiting list to enter the program. The Temer administration, through Pente Fino, expelled enough beneficiaries to clear the waiting list in 2018 (Zylberkan 2020).

16. Bolsonaro finished first but did not surpass the 50% threshold required to avoid a runoff.

17. Bolsonaro defeated PT's Fernando Haddad, who had served as Lula's education minister, by a margin of 55.1% to 44.9%. Bolsonaro lost in 11 of the country's 26 states, all of them in the Northeast. He lost Maranhão, Piauí, Bahia, and Ceará by a 70/30 margin and Rio Grande do Norte, Paraíba, Pernambuco, and Sergipe by a 60/40 margin.

18. Own calculations based on MC (2020). This, however, cannot be attributed entirely to the right. Purchasing power declined sharply under Rousseff, who, despite consumer prices increasing by 9.0% in 2015 alone, did not adjust benefits during her final two years.

19. Own calculations based on MC (2020).

20. Felipe Calderón of the incumbent center-right National Action Party (PAN) defeated AMLO in 2006 by just 243,000 votes, a mere 0.6% of votes cast. AMLO claimed fraud and refused to accept the results. Although Oportunidades likely swung the election in Calderón's favor (Diaz-Cayeros, Estevez, and Magaloni 2009), there is little evidence of vote buying (Beltrán and Castro Cornejo 2015).

21. Juárez (1858–72), Mexico's first president of indigenous descent, is AMLO's personal hero.

22. The only report of such claims in the media was published after the program closed and is based on testimonials from a promotional video for AMLO's social programs (Enciso L. 2019).

23. Construyendo has been plagued by anomalies (MCCI 2019).

24. Relatedly, 2019–20 was the first school year in two decades in which upper secondary enrollment dropped. Castañeda (2020) speculates that some students may have dropped out to claim the more generous apprenticeship stipend.

25. Although the new pension is more than twice as generous as its predecessor, its progressivity is questionable. Under President Enrique Peña Nieto (2012–18), non-contributory pensions were extended to all Mexicans over 65 without a contributory pension. To extend the basic pension to those who already had contributory pensions, AMLO raised the eligibility age for nonindigenous Mexicans without contributory pensions.

26. Own calculations based on Prospera (2018). The calculations do not include the yearly school supplies stipend.

27. Moderate and extreme poverty are calculated using national poverty lines.

28. Net enrollment rates measure the share of children enrolled in the appropriate grade for their age (UIS 2017).

REFERENCES

Abrevaya, Sebastián. 2015. "Un paso hacia la movilidad de la AUH." *Página/12*, July 2. https://www.pagina12.com.ar/diario/elpais/1-276187-2015-07-02.html

Achen, Christopher H. 2002. "Toward a New Political Methodology: Microfoundations and ART." *Annual Review of Political Science* 5 (1): 423–50. https://doi.org/10.1146/annurev.polisci.5.112801.080943

Acosta, Pablo, Rita Almeida, and Christine Lao Plena. 2015. "Central America Social Expenditures and Institutional Review: Costa Rica." 97416-CR. World Bank. http://documents.worldbank.org/curated/en/927631468011103545/Central-America-social-expenditures-and-institutional-review-Costa-Rica

Adato, Michelle, and John Hoddinott. 2010. "Conditional Cash Transfer Programs: A 'Magic Bullet'?" In *Conditional Cash Transfers in Latin America*, edited by Michelle Adato and John Hoddinott, 3–25. Baltimore: Johns Hopkins University Press.

Agencia EFE. 2019. "'Sí hay retrasos en programas.'" *El Siglo de Torreón*, May 13. https://www.elsiglodetorreon.com.mx/noticia/1575830.si-hay-retrasos-en-programas.html

Agencia Noticias Fides. 2005. "Tuto propone un plan para el 'borrón y cuenta nueva.'" *Agencia Noticias Fides*, October 10. http://www.noticiasfides.com/nacional/politica/tuto-propone-un-plan-para-el-borron-y-cuenta-nueva-43635

Agis, Emmanuel, Carlos Cañete, and Demian Panigo. 2010. "Asignación Universal por Hijo en Argentina." *Aulas y Andamios*, October.

Aguiar, Marcelo, and Carlos Henrique Araujo. 2002. *Bolsa-Escola: Educación para enfrentar la pobreza*. Brasilia: UNESCO.

Aguilar Pacajes, Hernán. 2014. "Evaluación del impacto del 'Bono Juancito Pinto' en Bolivia." *Revista de Análisis del BCB* 21 (2): 37–66.

Aith, Marcio. 2001. "Governo dos EUA diz que já não teme Lula presidente." *Folha de S. Paulo*, September 6. https://www1.folha.uol.com.br/fsp/brasil/fc0609200114.htm

Akresh, Richard, Damien de Walque, and Harounan Kazianga. 2012. "Alternative Cash Transfer Delivery Mechanisms: Impacts on Routine Preventative Health Clinic Visits in Burkina Faso." Policy Research Working Paper 5958. World Bank. http://documents.worldbank.org/curated/en/580251468020357878/Alte

rnative-cash-transfer-delivery-mechanisms-impacts-on-routine-preventative-health-clinic-visits-in-Burkina-Faso

Allan, James P., and Lyle Scruggs. 2004. "Political Partisanship and Welfare State Reform in Advanced Industrial Societies." *American Journal of Political Science* 48 (3): 496–512. https://doi.org/10.1111/j.0092-5853.2004.00083.x

Álvarez, Carola, Florencia Devoto, and Paul Winters. 2008. "Why Do Beneficiaries Leave the Safety Net in Mexico? A Study of the Effects of Conditionality on Dropouts." *World Development* 36 (4): 641–58. https://doi.org/10.1016/j.worlddev.2007.04.014

Ancelovici, Marcos, and Jane Jenson. 2013. "Standardization for Transnational Diffusion: The Case of Truth Commissions and Conditional Cash Transfers." *International Political Sociology* 7 (3): 294–312. https://doi.org/10.1111/ips.12024

Angell, Alan. 1995. "The Left in Latin America Since c. 1920." In *Cambridge History of Latin America Volume 6: 1930 to the Present, Part 2: Politics and Society*, edited by Leslie Bethel, 163-232. New York; Cambridge University Press.

Anria, Santiago, and Sara Niedzwiecki. 2016. "Social Movements and Social Policy: The Bolivian Renta Dignidad." *Studies in Comparative International Development* 51 (3): 308–27. https://doi.org/10.1007/s12116-015-9207-1

Ansell, Aaron. 2014. *Zero Hunger: Political Culture and Antipoverty Policy in Northeast Brazil*. Chapel Hill: University of North Carolina Press.

Ansell, Aaron. 2015. "Lula's Assault on Rural Patronage: Zero Hunger, Ethnic Mobilization and the Deployment of Pilgrimage." *Journal of Peasant Studies* 42 (6): 1263–82. https://doi.org/10.1080/03066150.2014.978297

Araujo, M. Caridad, Mariano Bosch, and Norbert Schady. 2016. "Can Cash Transfers Help Households Escape an Inter-Generational Poverty Trap?" Working Paper 22670. National Bureau of Economic Research. https://doi.org/10.3386/w22670

Arcidiácono, Pilar. 2007. "Programa Familias por la Inclusión Social: Brecha entre discurso y práctica." *Argentina: Asociación Argentina de Especialistas en Estudios del Trabajo*. https://www.aset.org.ar/congresos/8/pdf/05041.pdf

Arcidiácono, Pilar. 2016. "Transferencias de ingresos a los hogares en Argentina." *Revista de Ciencias Sociales* 151. Universidad de Costa Rica. https://doi.org/10.15517/rcs.v1i151.24972

Arcidiácono, Pilar, Verónica Carmona Barrenechea, Vilma Paura, and Mora Straschnoy. 2012. "La Asignación Universal por Hijo: ¿Una vía de transformación en la política social argentina?" In *Más derechos, menos marginaciones? Políticas sociales y bienestar en la Argentina*, edited by Laura C. Pautassi and Gustavo Gamallo, 149–79. Buenos Aires: Editorial Bibilios.

Arends-Kuenning, Mary. 2009. "A Report Card for Lula: Progress in Education." In *Brazil under Lula: Economy, Politics, and Society under the Worker-President*, edited by Joseph L. Love and Werner Baer, 205–20. Basingstoke, UK: Palgrave Macmillan.

Aristegui Noticias. 2019. "Inai transparenta padrones de ocho programas sociales de AMLO." December 5. https://aristeguinoticias.com/0512/mexico/inai-trans

parenta-padrones-de-ocho-programas-sociales-de-amlo/Argentinos por la Educación. 2019. "Mejoras perceptibles, aunque insuficientes, de la educación secundaria." https://cdn.uc.assets.prezly.com/45f28c71-3780-482f-b8f4-49bdbf acecdb/-/inline/no/argxeducinformesecundariaabril-2019.pdf

Arza, Camila. 2012. "The Politics of Counter-Reform in the Argentine Pension System: Actors, Political Discourse, and Policy Performance." *International Journal of Social Welfare* 21 (s1): S46–60. https://doi.org/10.1111/j.1468-2397.2012.00872.x

Arza, Camila. 2017. "The Expansion of Economic Protection for Older Adults in Latin America: Key Design Features of Non-Contributory Pensions." Working Paper 2017/29. Helsinki: UNU-WIDER. https://www.wider.unu.edu/sites/default/files/wp2017-29.pdf

Associated Press. 2020. "¿Gobierno de AMLO da uso político a programas sociales?" *El Siglo de Torreón*, January 19. https://www.elsiglodetorreon.com.mx/noticia/1664332.gobierno-de-amlo-da-uso-politico-a-programas-sociales.html

Avancemos, Secretaría Técnica del Programa. 2009. "Avancemos: Programa de transferencias monetarias condicionadas." Secretaría Técnica del Programa Avancemos. http://www.siteal.iipe.unesco.org/bdnp/235/avancemos-programa-transferencias-monetarias-condicionadas

Azevedo, Reinaldo. 2013. "Lula, o Bolsa Família, os detalhes de uma farsa e uma falha escandalosa da imprensa." *Veja.Com* (blog), October 30. http://veja.abril.com.br/blog/reinaldo/geral/lula-o-bolsa-familia-os-detalhes-de-uma-farsa-e-uma-falha-escandalosa-da-imprensa/

Azevedo, Reinaldo. 2017. "Reconstruindo a verdade—Lula admitiu no dia da criação do Bolsa Família: Foi idéia de um governador tucano! Mais: As políticas já existiam!" *Veja.com* (blog), February 21. https://veja.abril.com.br/blog/reinaldo/reconstruindo-a-verdade-8211-lula-admitiu-no-dia-da-criacao-do-bolsa-familia-foi-ideia-de-um-governador-tucano-mais-as-politicas-ja-existiam/

Baird, Sarah, Francisco H. G. Ferreira, Berk Özler, and Michael Woolcock. 2014. "Conditional, Unconditional and Everything in Between: A Systematic Review of the Effects of Cash Transfer Programmes on Schooling Outcomes." *Journal of Development Effectiveness* 6 (1): 1–43. https://doi.org/10.1080/19439342.2014.890362

Baird, Sarah, Craig McIntosh, and Berk Özler. 2011. "Cash or Condition? Evidence from a Cash Transfer Experiment." *Quarterly Journal of Economics* 126 (4): 1709–53. https://doi.org/10.1093/qje/qjr032

BCB (Banco Central de Bolivia). 2020. "Indicadores de Inflación." June 1. https://www.bcb.gob.bo/?q=indicadores_inflacion

Banerjee, Abhijit V., Rema Hanna, Gabriel E. Kreindler, and Benjamin A. Olken. 2017. "Debunking the Stereotype of the Lazy Welfare Recipient: Evidence from Cash Transfer Programs." *World Bank Research Observer* 32 (2): 155–84. https://doi.org/10.1093/wbro/lkx002

Banks, Arthur S. 2011. "Cross-National Time-Series Data Archive." https://www.cntsdata.com/

Barbeito, Alberto C., and Rubén M. Lo Vuolo. 2009. "Ingreso ciudadano para la niñez." Serie Documentos de Trabajo 70. CIEPP. http://www.ciepp.org.ar/index.php/documentosdetrabajo1/445-documentos-70.

Barchiesi, Franco. 2011. *Precarious Liberation: Workers, the State, and Contested Social Citizenship in Postapartheid South Africa*. Albany: SUNY Press.

Barrientos, Armando. 2004. "Latin America: Towards a Liberal-Informal Welfare Regime." In *Insecurity and Welfare Regimes in Asia, Africa and Latin America: Social Policy in Development Contexts*, edited by Ian Gough and Geof Wood, 121–68. New York: Cambridge University Press.

Barrientos, Armando. 2009. "Labour Markets and the (Hyphenated) Welfare Regime in Latin America." *Economy and Society* 38 (1): 87–108. https://doi.org/10.1080/03085140802560553

Barrientos, Armando. 2013. *Social Assistance in Developing Countries*. New York: Cambridge University Press.

Barrientos, Armando, and Claudio Santibañez. 2009. "Social Policy for Poverty Reduction in Lower-Income Countries in Latin America: Lessons and Challenges." *Social Policy & Administration* 43 (4): 409–24. https://doi.org/10.1111/j.1467-9515.2009.00671.x

Barro, Robert J., and Jong Wha Lee. 2013. "A New Data Set of Educational Attainment in the World, 1950–2010." *Journal of Development Economics* 104 (September): 184–98. https://doi.org/10.1016/j.jdeveco.2012.10.001

Bastagli, Francesca. 2008. "The Design, Implementation and Impact of Conditional Cash Transfers Targeted on the Poor: An Evaluation of Brazil's Bolsa Família." PhD diss., London School of Economics and Political Science. https://ethos.bl.uk/OrderDetails.do?uin=uk.bl.ethos.540368

Bastagli, Francesca, Jessica Hagen-Zanker, Luke Harman, Valentina Barca, Georgina Sturge, and Tanja Schmidt. 2019. "The Impact of Cash Transfers: A Review of the Evidence from Low- and Middle-Income Countries." *Journal of Social Policy* 48 (3): 569–94. https://doi.org/10.1017/S0047279418000715

Beck, Nathaniel, and Jonathan N. Katz. 1995. "What to Do (and Not to Do) with Time-Series Cross-Section Data." *American Political Science Review* 89 (3): 634–47. https://doi.org/10.2307/2082979

Beck, Nathaniel, Jonathan N. Katz, and Richard Tucker. 1998. "Taking Time Seriously: Time-Series-Cross-Section Analysis with a Binary Dependent Variable." *American Journal of Political Science* 42 (4): 1260–88. https://doi.org/10.2307/2991857

Beck, Thorsten, George Clarke, Alberto Groff, Philip Keefer, and Patrick Walsh. 2001. "New Tools in Comparative Political Economy: The Database of Political Institutions." *World Bank Economic Review* 15 (1): 165–76. https://doi.org//10.1093/wber/15.1.165

Behrman, Jere R. 2010. "The International Food Policy Research Institute (IFPRI) and the Mexican PROGRESA Anti-Poverty and Human Resource Investment Conditional Cash Transfer Program." *World Development* 38 (10): 1473–85. https://doi.org/10.1016/j.worlddev.2010.06.007

Beltrán, Ulises, and Rodrigo Castro Cornejo. 2015. "Clientelismo de gorra y camiseta." *Nexos*, October 1. https://www.nexos.com.mx/?p=26989

Bertranou, Fabio, and Roxana Maurizio. 2012. "Semi-Conditional Cash Transfers in the Form of Family Allowances for Children and Adolescents in the Informal Economy in Argentina." *International Social Security Review* 65 (1): 53–72. https://doi.org/10.1111/j.1468-246X.2011.01419.x

Biglaiser, Glen. 2016. "Mandate and the Market: Policy Outcomes under the Left in Latin America." *Comparative Politics* 48 (2): 185–204. https://doi.org/10.5129/001041516817037709

Biller, David, and Gabriel Shinohara. 2017. "Brazil's Lost Decade: The Invisible Costs of an Epic Recession." *Bloomberg Businessweek*, August 21. https://www.bloomberg.com/news/articles/2017-08-21/brazil-s-lost-decade-the-invisible-costs-of-an-epic-recession

Birdsall, Nancy, Nora Lustig, and Darryl McLeod. 2012. "Declining Inequality in Latin America: Some Economics, Some Politics." In *Routledge Handbook of Latin American Politics*, edited by Peter Kingstone and Deborah J. Yashar, 158–80. New York: Routledge.

Birdsall, Nancy, and Miguel Szekely. 2003. "Bootstraps Not Band-Aids: Poverty, Equity and Social Policy." Working Paper 24. Center for Global Development. https://www.cgdev.org/publication/bootstraps-not-band-aids-poverty-equity-and-social-policy-latin-america-working-paper-24

Birdsall, Nancy, and Augusto de la Torre. 2001. *Washington Contentious: Economic Policies for Social Equity in Latin America*. Washington, DC: Inter-American Dialogue.

Bither-Terry, Russell. 2014. "Reducing Poverty Intensity: What Alternative Poverty Measures Reveal about the Impact of Brazil's Bolsa Família." *Latin American Politics and Society* 56 (4): 143–58. https://doi.org/10.1111/j.1548-2456.2014.00252.x

Blustein, Paul. 2005. *And the Money Kept Rolling In (and Out): Wall Street, the IMF, and the Bankrupting of Argentina*. New York: PublicAffairs.

Bobbio, Norberto. 1996. *Left and Right: The Significance of a Political Distinction*. Translated by Allan Cameron. Chicago: University of Chicago Press.

Bohn, Simone R. 2011. "Social Policy and Vote in Brazil: Bolsa Família and the Shifts in Lula's Electoral Base." *Latin American Research Review* 46 (1): 54–79. https://doi.org/10.1353/lar.2011.0003

Boltvinik, Julio. 2012. "Mexico's Alleged Influence on Poverty Reduction Strategies in Latin America." *Estudios Críticos del Desarrollo* 2 (2): 13–40.

Bond, Patrick. 2014. "'Talk Left, Walk Right' in South African Social Policy: Tokenistic Extension of State Welfare versus Bottom-Up Commoning of Services." School of Development Studies, University of KwaZulu-Natal, February. http://ccs.ukzn.ac.za/files/Bond%20SA's%20tokenistic%20social%20policy.pdf

Borges, Fabián A. 2014. "Rules of Procedure as a Cause of Legislative Paralysis: The Case of Costa Rica, 2002–2012." *Latin American Politics and Society* 56 (4): 119–42. https://doi.org/10.1111/j.1548-2456.2014.00251.x

Borges, Fabían A. 2018. "Neoliberalism with a Human Face? Ideology and the Diffusion of Latin America's Conditional Cash Transfers." *Comparative Politics* 50 (2): 147–69. https://doi.org/10.5129/001041518822263647

Bos, María Soledad, Alison Elías, Emiliana Vegas, and Pablo Zoido. 2016. "Latin America and the Caribbean in PISA 2015: How Did the Region Perform?" Brief 1. Inter-American Development Bank. https://publications.iadb.org/en/publication/17197/latin-america-and-caribbean-pisa-2015-how-did-region-perform

Boultinghouse, Trent. 2015. "Brazilian Strategic Narrative and the Bolsa Família." IV Seminário Discente da Pós-Graduação, Universidade de São Paulo. http://143.107.26.205/documentos/seminariopos/BOULTINGHOUSEBrazilianStrategicNarrativeBolsaFam%C3%ADlia.pdf

Bourne, Richard. 2009. *Lula of Brazil: The Story So Far*. Berkeley: University of California Press.

Box-Steffensmeier, Janet M., and Bradford S. Jones. 2004. *Event History Modeling: A Guide for Social Scientists*. Cambridge: Cambridge University Press.

Brambor, Thomas, William Roberts Clark, and Matt Golder. 2006. "Understanding Interaction Models: Improving Empirical Analyses." *Political Analysis* 14 (1): 63–82. https://doi.org/10.1093/pan/mpi014

Brant, Danielle. 2019. "Bolsonaro segura reajuste anual para dar 13° salário no Bolsa Família." *Folha de S. Paulo*, April 9. https://www1.folha.uol.com.br/poder/2019/04/bolsonaro-segura-reajuste-anual-para-dar-13o-salario-no-bolsa-familia.shtml

Brasil, Felipe Moura. 2014. "Recordar é viver: 'José Dirceu me disse: Bolsa Família são mais de 40 milhões de votos', revelou ex-petista. Dilma foi mais votada onde há mais beneficiários do programa." *Veja.com* (blog), October 7. https://veja.abril.com.br/blog/felipe-moura-brasil/recordar-e-viver-8220-jose-dirceu-me-disse-bolsa-familia-sao-mais-de-40-milhoes-de-votos-8221-revelou-ex-petista-dilma-foi-mais-votada-onde-ha-mais-beneficiarios-do-programa/

Brauw, Alan de, and John Hoddinott. 2011. "Must Conditional Cash Transfer Programs Be Conditioned to Be Effective? The Impact of Conditioning Transfers on School Enrollment in Mexico." *Journal of Development Economics* 96 (2): 359–70. https://doi.org/10.1016/j.jdeveco.2010.08.014

Brearley, Emily. 2011. "The Politics of Poverty: The Political Economy of Social Protection in Latin America and the Rise of Conditional Cash Transfers." PhD diss., Johns Hopkins School of Advanced International Studies.

Breve, Nelson, and Maurício Hashizume. 2004. "Brazil, a Land of Nobles and Serfs." *Brazzil*, July 1. https://brazzil.com/15163-brazil-a-land-of-nobles-and-serfs/

Britto, Tatiana Feitosa de. 2008. "The Emergence and Popularity of Conditional Cash Transfers in Latin America." In *Social Protection for the Poor and Poorest: Concepts, Policies and Politics*, 181–93. Basingstoke, UK: Palgrave Macmillan.

Britto, Tatiana, and Fábio Veras Soares. 2011. "Bolsa Família and the Citizen's Basic Income: A Misstep?" Working Paper 77. International Policy Centre for Inclusive Growth. https://ideas.repec.org/p/ipc/wpaper/77.html

Brooks, Sarah M. 2009. *Social Protection and the Market in Latin America: The Transformation of Social Security Institutions*. New York: Cambridge University Press.
Brooks, Sarah M. 2015. "Social Protection for the Poorest: The Adoption of Antipoverty Cash Transfer Programs in the Global South." *Politics & Society* 43 (4): 551–82. https://doi.org/10.1177/0032329215602894
Bruhn, Kathleen. 1996. "Social Spending and Political Support: The 'Lessons' of the National Solidarity Program in Mexico." *Comparative Politics* 28 (2): 151–77. https://doi.org/10.2307/421979
Bruns, Barbara, and Javier Luque. 2015. *Great Teachers: How to Raise Student Learning in Latin America and the Caribbean*. Washington, DC: World Bank.
Bruns, Barbara, Isabel Harbaugh Macdonald, and Ben Ross Schneider. 2019. "The Politics of Quality Reforms and the Challenges for SDGs in Education." *World Development* 118: 27–38. https://doi.org/10.1016/j.worlddev.2019.02.008
Bry, Sandra H. 2017. "Brazil's Soft-Power Strategy: The Political Aspirations of South–South Development Cooperation." *Foreign Policy Analysis* 13 (2): 297–316. https://doi.org/10.1093/fpa/orw015
Buarque, Cristovam. 1999. *A segunda abolição: Um manifesto-proposta para a erradicação da pobreza no Brasil*. São Paulo: Paz e Terra.
Buarque, Cristovam. 2013. *Bolsa-Escola, History, Theory and Utopia*. Translated by Linda Jerome. Brasilia: Thesaurus Editora.
Busso, Matías, Julián Cristia, Diana Hincapié, Julián Messina, and Laura Ripani. 2017. *Learning Better: Public Policy for Skills Development*. Washington, DC: Inter-American Development Bank.
Bustos, Juan Martín, Georgina Giglio, and Soledad Villafañe. 2012. "Asignación Universal Por Hijo: Alcance e empacto por regiones del país." Serie Estudios 11. Ministerio de Trabajo de la República de Argentina.
Butler, Daniel M., and Miguel M. Pereira. 2018. "Trends: How Does Partisanship Influence Policy Diffusion?" *Political Research Quarterly* 71 (4): 801–12. https://doi.org/10.1177/1065912918796314
Butler, Daniel M., Craig Volden, Adam M. Dynes, and Boris Shor. 2017. "Ideology, Learning, and Policy Diffusion: Experimental Evidence." *American Journal of Political Science* 61 (1): 37–49. https://doi.org/10.1111/ajps.12213
Caldés, Natàlia, David Coady, and John A. Maluccio. 2006. "The Cost of Poverty Alleviation Transfer Programs: A Comparative Analysis of Three Programs in Latin America." *World Development* 34 (5): 818–37. https://doi.org/10.1016/j.worlddev.2005.10.003
Cali, Massimiliano, and Luis Carlos Jemio. 2010. "Bolivia: Case Study for the MDG Gap Task Force Report." Overseas Development Institute. https://www.odi.org/publications/5098-bolivia-case-study-mdg-gap-task-force-report
Camacho, Adriana, and Daniel Mejía. 2013. "The Externalities of Conditional Cash Transfer Programs on Crime: The Case of Familias en Acción in Bogotá." Latin American and Caribbean Economic Association, Mexico City. https://vox.lacea.org/?q=lacea2013/ccts_effects_on_crime

Câmara Neto, Alcino, and Matias Vernengo. 2007. "Lula's Social Policies: New Wine in Old Bottles?" In *Political Economy of Brazil: Recent Economic Performance*, edited by Philip Arestis and A. Saad-Filho, 73–93. Basingstoke, UK: Palgrave Macmillan.

Cambronero, Natasha. 2015. "Tribunal absuelve a exministro de vivienda Fernando Zumbado por pago extra a secretaria." *La Nación* (Costa Rica), March 20. https://www.nacion.com/el-pais/politica/tribunal-absuelve-a-exministro-de-vivienda-fernando-zumbado-por-pago-extra-a-secretaria/BNQQY62QHFC4LNKYT4WZBNRNAM/story/

Campos, Luis E., Eleonor Faur, and Laura C. Pautassi. 2007. "Programa Familias por la Inclusión Social: Entre el discurso de derechos y la práctica asistencial." Colección Investigación y Análisis 4. CELS. https://www.cels.org.ar/web/publicaciones/programa-familias-por-la-inclusion-social-entre-el-discurso-de-derechos-y-la-practica-asistencial/

Canêdo-Pinheiro, Mauricio. 2015. "Bolsa Família ou desempenho da economia? Determinantes da reeleição de Lula em 2006." *Economia Aplicada* 19 (1): 31–61. https://doi.org/10.1590/1413-8050/ea100264

Canelas, Carla, and Miguel Niño-Zarazúa. 2018. "Schooling and Labour Market Impacts of Bolivia's Bono Juancito Pinto." Working Paper 2018/36. United Nations University–WIDER. https://www.wider.unu.edu/publication/schooling-and-labour-market-impacts-bolivia%E2%80%99s-bono-juancito-pinto

Cantanhêde, Eliane. 2003. "Irritado com críticas, Lula cobra resultados de equipe." *Folha de S. Paulo*, March 17. https://www1.folha.uol.com.br/fsp/brasil/fc1703200302.htm

Caracol Radio. 2005. "Evo, Tuto y Samuel lanzan más ofertas por el voto sensato." *Caracol Radio*, September 12. http://www.caracol.com.co/nota_imp.aspx?id=228267

Cariello, Rafael. 2012. "O liberal contra a miséria." *Revista Piauí*, December 11. https://piaui.folha.uol.com.br/materia/o-liberal-contra-a-miseria/

Carnes, Matthew E. 2016. "Redefining Who's 'In' and Who's 'Out': Explaining Preferences for Redistribution in Bolivia." *Journal of Development Studies* 52 (11): 1647–64. https://doi.org/10.1080/00220388.2016.1156091

Carnes, Matthew E., and Isabela Mares. 2014. "Coalitional Realignment and the Adoption of Non-Contributory Social Insurance Programmes in Latin America." *Socio-Economic Review* 12 (4): 695–722. https://doi.org/10.1093/ser/mwt024

Carter, David B., and Curtis S. Signorino. 2010. "Back to the Future: Modeling Time Dependence in Binary Data." *Political Analysis* 18 (3): 271–92. https://doi.org/10.1093/pan/mpq013

Carvalho de Lorenzo, Marina. 2013. "Os desafios para difusão de experiência do Bolsa Família por meio da cooperação internacional." In *Programa Bolsa Família uma década de inclusão e cidadania*, edited by Tereza Campello and Marcelo Côrtes Neri, 397–415. Brasilia: Instituto de Pesquisa Econômica Aplicada.

Casar, María Amparo. 2019. "El Gran Benefactor." *Nexos*, March 1. https://www.nexos.com.mx/?p=41305

Castañeda, Jorge Andrés. 2020. "La política social de la ocurrencia." *El Heraldo de México*, July 16, sec. Opinión. https://heraldodemexico.com.mx/opinion/amlo-jovenes-construyendo-el-futuro-becas-educacion-basica-benito-juarez-jorge-andres-castaneda/

Castañeda, Jorge G. 1993. *Utopia Unarmed: The Latin American Left after the Cold War*. New York: Knopf.

Castañeda, Jorge G. 2006. "Latin America's Left Turn: There Is More Than One Pink Tide." *Foreign Affairs* 85 (3): 28–43.

Castellani, Francesca, and Jannet Zenteno. 2015. "Pobreza y movilidad social en Bolivia en la ultima década." Technical Note 889. Inter-American Development Bank. https://publications.iadb.org/es/publicacion/15490/pobreza-y-movilidad-social-en-bolivia-en-la-ultima-decada

Castiglioni, Rossana. 2005. *The Politics of Social Policy Change in Chile and Uruguay*. New York: Routledge.

Catterberg, Gabriela, and Valeria Palanza. 2012. "Argentina: Dispersión de la oposición y el auge de Cristina Fernández de Kirchner." *Revista de Ciencia Política* (Universidad Católica de Chile) 32 (1): 3–30. https://doi.org/10.4067/S0718-090X2012000100001

Cavallo, Alberto, and Manuel Bertolotto. 2016. "Filling the Gap in Argentina's Inflation Data." SSRN Scholarly Paper ID 2782104. Rochester: Social Science Research Network. https://papers.ssrn.com/abstract=2782104

Cecchini, Simone, and Bernardo Atuesta. 2017. "Conditional Cash Transfer Programmes in Latin America and the Caribbean: Coverage and Investment Trends." Serie Políticas Sociales 224. CEPAL. https://repositorio.cepal.org/handle/11362/42109

Cecchini, Simone, and Aldo Madariaga. 2011. *Conditional Cash Transfer Programmes: The Recent Experience in Latin America and the Caribbean*. Santiago, Chile: United Nations.

Cecchini, Simone, and Rodrigo Martínez. 2012. *Inclusive Social Protection in Latin America: A Comprehensive, Rights-Based Approach*. Santiago, Chile: United Nations.

CEPAL (United Nations Economic Commission for Latin America and the Caribbean). 2014. *Panorama Social de América Latina 2014*. Santiago, Chile: CEPAL.

CEPAL (United Nations Economic Commission for Latin America and the Caribbean). 2018. "Non-Contributory Social Protection Programmes in Latin America and the Caribbean Database." 2018. https://dds.cepal.org/bpsnc/cctCGR (Contraloría General de la República de Costa Rica). 2008. "Informe sobre el diseño y ejecución del programa de rransferencia monetaria condicionada denominado 'Avancemos.'" DFOE-SOC-17–2008. División de Fiscalización Operativa y Evaluativa, Área de Servicios Sociales. https://cgrfiles.cgr.go.cr/publico/docs . . . /SIGYD_D_2008017686.doc

CGR (Contraloría General de la República de Costa Rica). 2012. "Informe sobre la destión del programa de transferencia monetaria condicionada denominado 'Avancemos.'" DFOE-SOC-IF-10–2012. División de Fiscalización Operativa y

Evaluativa, Área de Servicios Sociales. https://cgrfiles.cgr.go.cr/publico/docs_cgr/2012/SIGYD_D_2012023427.pdf

Chambers-Ju, Christopher. 2020. "Adjustment Policies, Union Structures, and Strategies of Mobilization: Teacher Politics in Mexico and Argentina." *Comparative Politics* 53 (2): 185–207. https://doi.org/10.5129/001041521X15918883398085

Chávez Frías, Hugo. 2014. *Agenda Alternativa Bolivariana*. Caracas: Ediciones Correo del Orinoco.

Chioda, Laura, João M. P. De Mello, and Rodrigo Soares. 2016. "Spillovers from Conditional Cash Transfer Programs: Bolsa Família and Crime in Urban Brazil." *Economics of Education Review* 54: 306–20. https://doi.org/10.1016/j.econedurev.2015.04.005

Clinton, Hillary Rodham. 2017. *What Happened*. New York: Simon & Schuster.

Coady, David, Margaret Grosh, and John Hoddinott. 2004. "Targeting Outcomes Redux." *World Bank Research Observer* 19 (1): 61–85. https://doi.org/10.1093/wbro/lkhOI6

Coêlho, Denilson Bandeira. 2012a. "Brazil: Basic Income—A New Model of Innovation Diffusion." In *Basic Income Worldwide: Horizons of Reform*, edited by Matthew C. Murray and Carole Pateman, 59–80. Basingstoke, UK: Palgrave Macmillan.

Coêlho, Denilson Bandeira. 2012b. "Political Competition and the Diffusion of Conditional Cash Transfers in Brazil." *Brazilian Political Science Review* 6 (2): 56–87. https://doi.org/10.1590/S1981-38212012000200003

Collier, David, and Richard E. Messick. 1975. "Prerequisites versus Diffusion: Testing Alternative Explanations of Social Security Adoption." *American Political Science Review* 69 (4): 1299–1315. https://doi.org/10.2307/1955290

CONEVAL (Consejo Nacional de Evaluación de la Política de Desarrollo). 2020. "Pobreza en México." https://www.coneval.org.mx/Medicion/Paginas/PobrezaInicio.aspx

Coppedge, Michael J. 1997. "A Classification of Latin American Political Parties." Kellogg Institute Working Paper no. 244. November. Accessed July 24, 2020. https://kellogg.nd.edu/sites/default/files/old_files/documents/244_0.pdf

Cornia, Giovanni Andrea. 2010. "Income Distribution under Latin America's New Left Regimes." *Journal of Human Development and Capabilities* 11 (1): 85–114. https://doi.org/10.1080/19452820903481483

Cornia, Giovanni Andrea. 2014. "Recent Distributive Changes in Latin America: An Overview." In *Falling Inequality in Latin America: Policy Changes and Lessons*, edited by Giovanni Andrea Cornia, 1–22. New York: Oxford University Press.

Corrales, Javier. 1999. "The Politics of Education Reform: Bolstering the Supply and Demand; Overcoming Institutional Blocks." Education Reform and Management Series 22549. World Bank. http://documents.worldbank.org/curated/en/957741468740407109/The-politics-of-education-reform-bolstering-the-supply-and-demand-overcoming-institutional-blocks

Corrales, Javier, and Michael Penfold. 2015. *Dragon in the Tropics: Venezuela and the Legacy of Hugo Chávez*. 2nd ed. Washington, DC: Brookings Institution Press.

Corrêa, Diego Sanches. 2015. "Conditional Cash Transfer Programs, the Economy, and Presidential Elections in Latin America." *Latin American Research Review* 50 (2): 63–85. https://doi.org/10.1353/lar.2015.0020

Corrêa, Diego Sanches, and José Antonio Cheibub. 2016. "The Anti-Incumbent Effects of Conditional Cash Transfer Programs." *Latin American Politics and Society* 58 (1): 49–71. https://doi.org/10.1111/j.1548-2456.2016.00296.x

Cortes da Costa, Lucia. 2019. "A assistência social, previdência e transferência de renda em tempos de ajustes fiscais—de Temer a Bolsonaro." In *Brasil: Incertezas e Submissão?*, edited by Marcio Pochmann, 271–91. São Paulo: Fundação Perseu.

Cortés, Fernando, and Rosa María Rubalcava. 2012. "El Progresa como respuesta a la crisis de 1994." In *Pobreza, Transferencias Condicionadas y Sociedad*, edited by Mercedes González de la Rocha and Agustín Escobar Latapí, 27–50. Mexico City: Centro de Estudios Superiores en Antropología Social.

Costa Leite, Iara, Bianca Suyama, and Melissa Pomeroy. 2013. "Africa-Brazil Co-Operation in Social Protection: Drivers, Lessons and Shifts in the Engagement of the Brazilian Ministry of Social Development." Working Paper 2013/022. United Nations University--WIDER. https://www.wider.unu.edu/publication/africa-brazil-co-operation-social-protection

Costa Leite, Iara, Melissa Pomeroy, and Bianca Suyama. 2015. "Brazilian South–South Development Cooperation: The Case of the Ministry of Social Development in Africa." *Journal of International Development* 27 (8): 1446–61. https://doi.org/10.1002/jid.3191

Costa, Nilson do Rosário. 2009. "Social Protection in Brazil: Universalism and Targeting in the FHC and Lula Administrations." *Ciencia & Saude Coletiva* 14 (3): 693–706.

Cotta, Tereza Cristina Silva. 2009. "Visões de proteção social e transferência de renda condicionadas no Brasil e no México." PhD diss., Universidade de Brasília, Instituto de Ciências Sociais, Centro de Pesquisa e Pós-Graduação sobre as Américas. http://repositorio.unb.br/handle/10482/4408

Couto, Paulo Claudio Gonçalves. 2003. "The second time around: Marta Suplicy's PT administration in São Paulo." In *Radicals in Power: The Workers' Party and Experiments in Urban Democracy in Brazil*, edited by Gianpaolo Baiocchi, 79–90. New York: Zed Books.

Cruces, Guillermo, and Leonardo Gasparini. 2008. "Programas sociales en Argentina: alternativas para la ampliación de la cobertura." Documento de Trabajo 77. CEDLAS. http://sedici.unlp.edu.ar/handle/10915/3636

CTA (Central de Trabajadores de la Argentina—Autónoma). 2019. "Fuerte deterioro de la Asignación Universal Por Hijo y la Jubilación Mínima (A pesar de la aplicación de la Ley de Movilidad)." Buenos Aires: Observatorio del Derecho Social. http://ctanacional.org/dev/wp-content/uploads/2019/02/Asignacion_universal_por_hijo_y_la_jubilacion_minima-FEB2019.pdf

Cué, Carlos E. 2017. "Insultos, empujones y puñetazos en el congreso argentino por la reforma de las pensiones." *El País*, December 12. https://elpais.com/internacional/2017/12/12/argentina/1513117181_519785.html

Damé, Luiza. 2010. "Nos oito anos de governo, presidente Lula visitou 84 países." *O Globo*, December 24. https://oglobo.globo.com/politica/nos-oito-anos-de-governo-presidente-lula-visitou-84-paises-2905980

Daniel, Hernández Franco. 2008. *Historia de Oportunidades: Inicio y cambios del programa*. Edited by Fondo de Cultura Económica. Mexico City: Fondo de Cultura Económica.

Dávila Lárraga, Laura G. 2016. "How Does Prospera Work? Best Practices in the Implementation of Conditional Cash Transfer Programs in Latin America and the Caribbean." Social Protection and Health Division Technical Note 971. Inter-American Development Bank. https://publications.iadb.org/en/publication/17104/how-does-prospera-work-best-practices-implementation-conditional-cash-transfer

Debs, Alexandre, and Gretchen Helmke. 2010. "Inequality under Democracy: Explaining the Left Decade in Latin America." *Quarterly Journal of Political Science* 5 (3): 209–41. https://doi.org/10.1561/100.00009074

de Groot, Richard. 2015. "Ghana Leap Programme Increases Schooling Outcomes." Research Brief 4. Transfer Project. https://transfer.cpc.unc.edu/wp-content/uploads/2015/09/Ghana-LEAP-programme-increases-schooling-outcomes.pdf

de Hoop, Jacobus, and Furio C. Rosati. 2014. "Cash Transfers and Child Labor." *World Bank Research Observer* 29 (2): 202–34. https://doi.org/10.1093/wbro/lku003

de Janvry, Alain, Frederico Finan, Elisabeth Sadoulet, Donald Nelson, Kathy Lindert, Benedicte de la Briere, and Peter Lanjouw. 2005. "Brazil's Bolsa Escola Program: The Role of Local Governance in Decentralized Implementation." Social Policy Discussion Paper 90506. World Bank. http://documents.worldbank.org/curated/en/879681468336280805/Brazils-Bolsa-Escola-program-the-role-of-local-governance-in-decentralized-implementation

de la Brière, Bénédicte, and Kathy Lindert. 2005. "Reforming Brazil's Cadastro Único to Improve the Targeting of the Bolsa Família Program." 32757. Social Protection Discussion Paper Series. World Bank. https://documents.worldbank.org/en/publication/documents-reports/documentdetail

De La O, Ana L. 2013. "Do Conditional Cash Transfers Affect Electoral Behavior? Evidence from a Randomized Experiment in Mexico." *American Journal of Political Science* 57 (1): 1–14. https://doi.org/10.1111/j.1540-5907.2012.00617.x

De La O, Ana L. 2015. *Crafting Policies to End Poverty in Latin America: The Quiet Transformation*. New York: Cambridge University Press.

de la Torre, Carlos. 2018. "Latin America's Shifting Politics: Ecuador after Correa." *Journal of Democracy* 29 (4): 77–88. https://doi.org/10.1353/jod.2018.0064

de León Naveiro, Omar. 2011. "Bolivia: La construcción participativa del desarrollo." In *Nuevas estrategias económicas en América Latina: Los casos de Bolivia, Ecuador y Venezuela*, edited by José Déniz Espinós, de León Omar, and Antonio Palazuelos Manso, 11–80. Madrid: La Catarata.

Devereux, Stephen. 2016. "Is Targeting Ethical?" *Global Social Policy* 16 (2): 166–81. https://doi.org/10.1177/1468018116643849

Díaz-Cayeros, Alberto, Federico Estévez, and Beatriz Magaloni. 2009. "Welfare Benefits, Canvassing, and Campaign Handouts." In *Consolidating Mexico's Democracy: The 2006 Presidential Campaign in Comparative Perspective*, edited by Jorge I. Domínguez, Chappell H. Lawson, and Alejandro Moreno, 229–45. Baltimore: Johns Hopkins University Press.

Díaz-Cayeros, Alberto, Federico Estévez, and Beatriz Magaloni. 2016. *The Political Logic of Poverty Relief: Electoral Strategies and Social Policy in Mexico*. New York: Cambridge University Press.

Díaz-Cayeros, Alberto, and Beatriz Magaloni. 2009. "Aiding Latin America's Poor." *Journal of Democracy* 20 (4): 36–49. https://doi.org/10.1353/jod.0.0115

Dion, Michelle. 2000. "La Economía Política del Gasto Social: El Programa de Solidaridad de México, 1988–1994." *Estudios Sociológicos* 18 (53): 329–62.

Dion, Michelle. 2009. "Globalization, Democracy, and Mexican Welfare, 1988–2006." *Comparative Politics* 42 (1): 63–82.

Dion, Michelle. 2010. *Workers and Welfare: Comparative Institutional Change in Twentieth-Century Mexico*. Pittsburgh, PA: University of Pittsburgh Press.

DOF (Diario Oficial de la Nación). 2019a. "ACUERDO por el que se emiten las reglas de operación de PROSPERA Programa de Inclusión Social, para el ejercicio fiscal 2019." Secretaria de Desarrollo Social. https://www.gob.mx/cms/upl oads/attachment/file/442955/Reglas_de_Operacion_PROSPERA_2019.pdf

DOF (Diario Oficial de la Nación). 2019b. "ACUERDO por el que se emiten las reglas de operación del Programa de Becas de Educación Básica para el Bienestar Benito Juárez para el ejercicio discal 2020." Secretaría de Educación Pública. https://www.gob.mx/cms/uploads/attachment/file/522445/Reglas_operacion _S072_DOF_29_12_019.pdf

Dresser, Denise. 1994. "Bringing the Poor Back In: National Solidarity as a Strategy for Regime Legitimation." In *Transforming State-Society Relations in Mexico: The National Solidarity Strategy*, edited by Wayne Cornelius, Ann L. Craig, and Jonathan Fox, 143–65. La Jolla, CA: Center for U.S.-Mexican Studies.

Dugger, Celia W. 2004. "To Help Poor Be Pupils, Not Wage Earners, Brazil Pays Parents." *New York Times*, January 3. https://www.nytimes.com/2004/01/03/wo rld/to-help-poor-be-pupils-not-wage-earners-brazil-pays-parents.html

Durana, Alieza. 2012. "Morales' Bolivia: A New Paradigm in Egalitarian Governance." *Washington University International Review* 1: 56–75.

Duryea, Suzanne, and Andrew Morrison. 2004. "The Effect of Conditional Transfers on School Performance and Child Labor: Evidence from an Ex-Post Impact Evaluation in Costa Rica." Research Department Working Paper 504. Inter-American Development Bank. https://publications.iadb.org/en/publication/10 721/effect-conditional-transfers-school-performance-and-child-labor-eviden ce-ex-post

Dyer, Zachary Koenig. 2012. "Extracting Identity: Universal Social Policy in Post-Neoliberal Bolivia." Master's thesis, University of Texas, Austin. https://reposito ries.lib.utexas.edu/handle/2152/22513

Economist. 2003. "Three Square Meals a Day." *Economist*, February 20. https://www.economist.com/special-report/2003/02/20/three-square-meals-a-day

Economist. 2008. "Argentina: Harvesting Pensions." *Economist*, November 27. https://www.economist.com/the-americas/2008/11/27/harvesting-pensions

Economist. 2016. "Economic Data in Argentina: An Augean Stable." *Economist*, February 13. https://www.economist.com/the-americas/2016/02/13/an-augean-stable

Economist. 2019. "In Mexico, AMLO Seeks to Expel Merit from Schools." *Economist*, May 18. https://www.economist.com/the-americas/2019/05/18/in-mexico-amlo-seeks-to-expel-merit-from-schools

Edo, Maria, Mariana Marchionni, and Santiago Garganta. 2017. "Compulsory Education Laws or Incentives from CCT Programs? Explaining the Rise in Secondary School Attendance Rate in Argentina." *Education Policy Analysis Archives* 25 (76). https://doi.org/10.14507/epaa.25.2596

Eju! 2018. "Evo revela que el TGN dejó de financiar Bono Juancito Pinto y que el dinero ahora viene de las empresas públicas." *Eju!*, October 18. http://eju.tv/2018/10/evo-revela-que-el-tgn-dejo-de-financiar-el-bono-juancito-pinto-y-que-el-dinero-ahora-viene-de-las-empresas-publicas/

Elacqua, Gregory, Maria Luisa Iribarren, and Humberto Santos. 2018. "Private Schooling in Latin America: Trends and Public Policies." Education Division Social Sector Technical Note 01555. Inter-American Development Bank. https://doi.org/10.18235/0001394

Enciso L., Angélica. 2019. "Centros de salud quitaban a mujeres 80 pesos por la firma que pedía Prospera." *La Jornada*, May 29. https://www.jornada.com.mx/2019/05/29/sociedad/036n3soc?partner=rss

Esping-Andersen, Gøsta. 1985. *Politics against Markets: The Social Democratic Road to Power*. Princeton, NJ: Princeton University Press.

Esping-Andersen, Gøsta. 1990. *The Three Worlds of Welfare Capitalism*. Princeton, NJ: Princeton University Press.

Etchemendy, Sebastián, and Candelaria Garay. 2011. "Argentina: Left Populism in Comparative Perspective, 2003–2009." In *The Resurgence of the Latin American Left*, edited by Steven Levitsky and Kenneth M. Roberts, 283–305. Baltimore: Johns Hopkins University Press.

Evans, Mark, and Jonathan Davies. 1999. "Understanding Policy Transfer: A Multi-Level, Multi-Disciplinary Perspective." *Public Administration* 77 (2): 361–85. https://doi.org/10.1111/1467-9299.00158

Ewig, Christina, and Stephen J. Kay. 2011. "Postretrenchment Politics: Policy Feedback in Chile's Health and Pension Reforms." *Latin American Politics and Society* 53 (4): 67–99. https://doi.org/10.1111/j.1548-2456.2011.00134.x

Fajth, Gaspar, and Claudia Vinay. 2010. "Conditional Cash Transfers: A Global Perspective." MDG Insights 1. UNICEF. https://www.unicef.org/socialpolicy/files/Conditional_Cash_Transfers_A_Global_Perspective.pdf

Faria, Carlos Aurélio Pimenta de. 2012. "A difusão de políticas sociais como estratégia de inserção internacional: Brasil e Venezuela comparados." *Interseções* 14 (2): 335–71.

Fenwick, Tracy Beck. 2009. "Avoiding Governors: The Success of Bolsa Família." *Latin American Research Review* 44 (1): 102–31. https://doi.org/10.1353/lar.0.0073

Fenwick, Tracy Beck. 2015. *Avoiding Governors: Federalism, Democracy, and Poverty Alleviation in Brazil and Argentina*. Notre Dame, IN: University of Notre Dame Press.

Fenwick, Tracy Beck. 2017. "Presidents and Policy-Making: Has Brazil's CCT-Led Anti-Poverty Agenda Gone Far Enough?" *Policy Studies* 38 (3): 216–30. https://doi.org/10.1080/01442872.2017.1290230

Ferguson, James. 2010. "The Uses of Neoliberalism." *Antipode* 41 (s1): 166–84. https://doi.org/10.1111/j.1467-8330.2009.00721.x

Ferguson, James. 2015. *Give a Man a Fish: Reflections on the New Politics of Distribution*. Durham, NC: Duke University Press.

Fernandes, Talita. 2018. "Bolsonaro diz que há fraude em 30% do Bolsa Família." *Folha de S. Paulo*, October 8, sec. Poder. https://www1.folha.uol.com.br/poder/2018/10/bolsonaro-diz-que-ha-fraude-em-30-do-bolsa-familia.shtml

FGV Social. 2020. "FGV social comenta os cortes no Bolsa Família e o aumento da extrema pobreza no Brasil." Rio de Janeiro: Fundação Getúlio Vargas. https://cps.fgv.br/destaques/fgv-social-comenta-os-cortes-no-bolsa-familia-e-o-aumento-da-extrema-pobreza-no-brasil

Fiszbein, Ariel, and Sarah Stanton. 2018. "The Future of Education in Latin America and the Caribbean: Possibilities for United States Investment and Engagement." Inter-American Dialogue. https://www.thedialogue.org/wp-content/uploads/2018/06/USAID-Layout-6.12.2018-FINAL_PDF.pdf

Flores Hinojosa, Aylin Stephanie. 2017. "Resultados educacionales de una transferencia monetaria condicionada: Evaluación de impacto Bono Juancito Pinto Bolivia." Master's thesis, Universidad Alberto Hurtado and Georgetown University. http://repositorio.uahurtado.cl/80/handle/11242/8228

Flores-Macías, Gustavo A. 2010. "Statist vs. Pro-Market: Explaining Leftist Governments' Economic Policies in Latin America." *Comparative Politics* 42 (4): 413–33.

Flores-Macias, Gustavo A. 2012. *After Neoliberalism? The Left and Economic Reforms in Latin America*. New York: Oxford University Press.

Folha de S. Paulo. 2003. Leia a integra do discurso de Lula no lançamento do programa Bolsa-Família." *Folha de S. Paulo*, October 20. https://www1.folha.uol.com.br/folha/brasil/ult96u54596.shtml

Folha de S. Paulo. 2004a. "Cristovam Buarque é demitido por telefone." *Folha de S. Paulo*, January 23. https://www1.folha.uol.com.br/folha/brasil/ult96u57458.shtml

Folha de S. Paulo. 2004b. "Lula reclamava de críticas feitas Por Cristovam Buarque." *Folha de S. Paulo*, January 23. https://www1.folha.uol.com.br/folha/brasil/ult96u57439.shtml

Folha de S. Paulo. 2004c. "Leia a integra do discurso de Lula no lançamento do programa Bolsa-Família." *Folha de S. Paulo*, October 20. https://www1.folha.uol.com.br/folha/brasil/ult96u54596.shtml

Fortuna, Deborah. 2019. "Bolsonaro e o programa Bolsa Família: De crítico feroz a defensor." *Correio Braziliense*, April 11. https://www.correiobraziliense.com.br/app/noticia/politica/2019/04/11/interna_politica,748643/bolsonaro-e-o-bolsa-familia-de-critico-feroz-a-defensor.shtml

Freire, Sílvia. 2004. "Bolsa-Família desmobiliza ação do Fome Zero." *Folha de S. Paulo*, January 27. https://www1.folha.uol.com.br/fsp/brasil/fc0404200407.htm

Fried, Brian J. 2012. "Distributive Politics and Conditional Cash Transfers: The Case of Brazil's Bolsa Família." *World Development* 40 (6): 1042–53. https://doi.org/10.1016/j.worlddev.2011.09.022

Friedman, Milton. 2002. *Capitalism and Freedom: Fortieth Anniversary Edition*. Chicago: University of Chicago Press.

Fundación Jubileo. 2012. "Renta hidrocarburífera: Más allá de las regalías y del IDH." Serie Debate Público 24. Fundación Jubileo. https://jubileobolivia.com/publicaciones/Revistas-Especializadas/renta-hidrocarburifera-mas-alla-de-las-regalias-y-del-idh

Gaarder, Marie. 2012. "Conditional versus Unconditional Cash: A Commentary." *Journal of Development Effectiveness* 4 (1): 130–33. https://doi.org/10.1080/19439342.2012.658635

Galasso, Emanuela, and Martin Ravallion. 2004. "Social Protection in a Crisis: Argentina's Plan Jefes y Jefas." *World Bank Economic Review* 18 (3): 367–99. https://doi.org/10.1093/wber/lhhO44

Galbraith, John Kenneth. 1986. "The Starvation of the Cities." In *A View from the Stands: Of People, Politics, Military Power, and the Arts*. Boston: Houghton Mifflin.

Galván, Melissa. 2018. "No se cancelará Prospera ni ningún programa social: AMLO." *Expansión*, October 4. https://politica.expansion.mx/presidencia/2018/10/04/no-se-cancelara-ningun-programa-social-ni-prospera-amlo

Garay, Candelaria. 2016. *Social Policy Expansion in Latin America*. New York: Cambridge University Press.

García, Sandra, and Juan E. Saavedra. 2017. "Educational Impacts and Cost-Effectiveness of Conditional Cash Transfer Programs in Developing Countries: A Meta-Analysis." *Review of Educational Research* 87 (5): 921–65. https://doi.org/10.1016/j.jdeveco.2015.02.004

Garganta, Santiago, and Leonardo Gasparini. 2015. "The Impact of a Social Program on Labor Informality: The Case of AUH in Argentina." *Journal of Development Economics* 115: 99–110. https://doi.org/10.1016/j.jdeveco.2015.02.004

Garrett, Geoffrey. 2001. "Globalization and Government Spending around the World." *Studies in Comparative International Development* 35 (1): 3–29.

Gaviria, Alejandro. 2007. "Social Mobility and Preferences for Redistribution in Latin America." *Economía* 8 (1): 55–91. https://doi.org/10.1353/eco.2008.0003

Gelbach, Jonah B., and Lant Pritchett. 2002. "Is More for the Poor Less for the Poor? The Politics of Means-Tested Targeting." *B.E. Journal of Economic Analysis & Policy* 2 (1): 1–28.

Gilardi, Fabrizio. 2010. "Who Learns from What in Policy Diffusion Processes?" *American Journal of Political Science* 54 (3): 650–66. https://doi.org/10.1111/j.1540-5907.2010.00452.x

Giovagnoli, Paula. 2005. "Poverty Alleviation or Political Networking? A Combined Qul-Quant Analysis of the Implementation of Safety Nets in Post-Crisis Argentina." Development Studies Institute Working Paper 05–66. London School of Economics and Political Science. https://www.files.ethz.ch/isn/137893/WP66.pdf

Giraudy, Agustina. 2007. "The Distributive Politics of Emergency Employment Programs in Argentina (1993–2002)." *Latin American Research Review* 42 (2): 33–55. https://doi.org/10.1353/lar.2007.0021

Gleditsch, Kristian Skrede, and Michael D. Ward. 2008. "Diffusion and the Spread of Democratic Institutions." In *The Global Diffusion of Markets and Democracy*, edited by Beth A. Simmons, Frank Dobbin, and Geoffrey Garrett, 261–302. New York: Cambridge University Press.

Golbert, Laura. 2004. "¿Derecho a la inclusión o paz social? Plan Jefas y Jefes de Hogar Desocupados." Serie Políticas Sociales 84. CEPAL. https://repositorio.cepal.org//handle/11362/6071

Golbert, Laura. 2010. *De la sociedad de beneficencia a los derechos sociales*. Buenos Aires: Ministerio de Trabajo.

Golbert, Laura, and Claudia Giacometti. 2008. "Los programas de transferencia de ingresos condicionados: El caso argentino." Instituto Fernando Henrique Cardoso/Corporación de Estudios para Latinoamérica. http://www.plataformademocratica.org/PDF/Publicacao_222_em_06_05_2008_12_59_38.pdf

Goldsmith, Scott. 2002. "The Alaska Permanent Fund Dividend: An Experiment in Wealth Distribution." Geneva: Basic Income Europe Network Congress. http://www.basicincome.org/bien/pdf/2002Goldsmith.pdf

Goñi, Edwin, J. Humberto López, and Luis Servén. 2008. "Fiscal Redistribution and Income Inequality in Latin America." Policy Research Working Paper 4487. World Bank. http://documents.worldbank.org/curated/en/823571468263937903/Fiscal-redistribution-and-income-inequality-in-Latin-America

González Rodríguez, Sergio. 2000. "Cuauhtémoc Cárdenas." *Letras Libres*, June. https://www.letraslibres.com/mexico/cuauhtemoc-cardenas

González-Flores, Mario, Maria Heracleous, and Paul Winters. 2012. "Leaving the Safety Net: An Analysis of Dropouts in an Urban Conditional Cash Transfer Program." *World Development* 40 (12): 2505–21. https://doi.org/10.1016/j.worlddev.2012.05.020

Graham, Carol. 1992. "The Politics of Protecting the Poor during Adjustment: Bolivia's Emergency Social Fund." *World Development* 20 (9): 1233–51. https://doi.org/10.1016/0305-750X(92)90075-7

Graham, Carol, and Cheikh Kane. 1998. "Opportunistic Government or Sustaining Reform? Electoral Trends and Public-Expenditure Patterns in Peru, 1990–1995." *Latin American Research Review* 33 (1): 67–104.

Gray Molina, George, and Ernesto Yañéz. 2009. "The Dynamics of Inequality in the

Best and Worst of Times, Bolivia 1997–2007." Poverty Reduction Discussion Paper. UNDP. http://content-ext.undp.org/aplaws_publications/2726773/UNDP_Bolivia.pdf

Graziano da Silva, José, Mauro Eduardo Del Grossi, and Caio Galvão de França, eds. 2010. *Fome Zero—A experiência brasileira*. Brasilia: Ministério do Desenvolvimento Agrário. http://www.fao.org/family-farming-2014/resources/publication-detail/pt/item/206814/icode/

Grillo, Marco, and Thiago Prado. 2018. "Após criticar, Bolsonaro agora defende Bolsa Família." *O Globo*, June 7. https://oglobo.globo.com/brasil/apos-criticar-bolsonaro-agora-defende-bolsa-familia-22753361

Grimes, Marcia, and Lena Wängnerud. 2010. "Curbing Corruption through Social Welfare Reform? The Effects of Mexico's Conditional Cash Transfer Program on Good Government." *American Review of Public Administration* 40 (6): 671–90. https://doi.org/10.1177/0275074009359025

Grindle, Merilee S. 2004. *Despite the Odds: The Contentious Politics of Education Reform*. Princeton, NJ: Princeton University Press.

Grossback, Lawrence J., Sean Nicholson-Crotty, and David A. M. Peterson. 2004. "Ideology and Learning in Policy Diffusion." *American Politics Research* 32 (5): 521–45. https://doi.org/10.1177/1532673X04263801

Guerrero, Claudia. 2019. "Acusa AMLO inflación en Prospera." *Reforma*, April 25. https://www.reforma.com/aplicaciones/articulo/default.aspx?id=1662644&v=2

Guimarães, Bernardo. 2015. "Os 'neoliberais' infiltrados no primeiro governo Lula." *Instituto Mercado Popular*, September 18. http://mercadopopular.org/2015/09/neoliberais-infiltrados/

Gutiérrez, Gabriela. 2020. "Van 15 meses y el programa bienestar de AMLO aún no llega a las comunidades." *Cuestione*, February 25. https://cuestione.com/nacional/van-15-meses-y-el-programa-bienestar-de-amlo-aun-no-llega-a-las-comunidades/

Haas, Peter M. 1992. "Introduction: Epistemic Communities and International Policy Coordination." *International Organization* 46 (1): 1–35. https://doi.org/10.1017/S0020818300001442

Hacker, Jacob S. 2004. "Privatizing Risk without Privatizing the Welfare State: The Hidden Politics of Social Policy Retrenchment in the United States." *American Political Science Review* 98 (2): 243–60.

Haggard, Stephan, and Robert R. Kaufman. 2008. *Development, Democracy, and Welfare States: Latin America, East Asia, and Eastern Europe*. Princeton, NJ: Princeton University Press.

Hall, Anthony. 2006. "From Fome Zero to Bolsa Família: Social Policies and Poverty Alleviation under Lula." *Journal of Latin American Studies* 38 (4): 689–709. https://doi.org/10.1017/S0022216X0600157X

Hall, Anthony. 2008. "Brazil's Bolsa Família: A Double-Edged Sword?" *Development and Change* 39 (5): 799–822. https://doi.org/10.1111/j.1467-7660.2008.00506.x

Handa, Sudhanshu, and Benjamin Davis. 2006. "The Experience of Conditional Cash Transfers in Latin America and the Caribbean." *Development Policy Review* 24 (5): 513–36. https://doi.org/10.1111/j.1467-7679.2006.00345.x

Hanlon, Joseph, Armando Barrientos, and David Hulme. 2010. *Just Give Money to the Poor: The Development Revolution from the Global South*. Sterling, VA: Kumarian Press.

Hanna, Rema, and Benjamin A. Olken. 2018. "Universal Basic Incomes versus Targeted Transfers: Anti-Poverty Programs in Developing Countries." *Journal of Economic Perspectives* 32 (4): 201–26. https://doi.org/10.1257/jep.32.4.201

Hanushek, Eric A. 2009. "School Policy: Implications of Recent Research for Human Capital Investments in South Asia and Other Developing Countries." *Education Economics* 17 (3): 291–313. https://doi.org/10.1080/09645290903142585

Hanushek, Eric A., and Ludger Woessmann. 2007. "The Role of Education Quality for Economic Growth." Policy Research Working Paper 4122. World Bank. http://documents.worldbank.org/curated/en/260461468324885735/The-role-of-education-quality-for-economic-growth

Hassel, Anke. 2018. "Unconditional Basic Income Is a Dead End." In *Basic Income and the Left: A European Debate*, 67–72. London: Social Europe Edition.

Hawkins, Kirk A. 2010. *Venezuela's Chavismo and Populism in Comparative Perspective*. Cambridge: Cambridge University Press.

Hayek, F. A. 1994. *The Road to Serfdom: Fiftieth Anniversary Edition*. Chicago: University of Chicago Press.

Hedström, Peter, and Richard Swedberg. 1996. "Social Mechanisms." *Acta Sociologica* 39 (3): 281–308. https://doi.org/10.1177/000169939603900302

Heller, Nathan. 2018. "Who Really Stands to Win from Universal Basic Income." *New Yorker*, July 9.

Hellman, Aline Gazola. 2015. "How Does Bolsa Familia Work? Best Practices in the Implementation of Conditional Cash Transfer Programs in Latin America and the Caribbean." Social Protection and Health Division Technical Note IDB-TN-856. Inter-American Development Bank. https://publications.iadb.org/en/publication/17411/how-does-bolsa-familia-work-best-practices-implementation-conditional-cash

Hernández Alcanzar, Enrique. 2019. "Leticia Ánimas, coordinadora del programa de Becas para Bienestar Benito Juárez, nos habla acerca de la desmantelación del programa: Le quitan salud y alimentación, sólo se quedan becas." *Así El Weso*. XEW-AM. https://play.wradio.com.mx/audio/111RD380000000076374/

Hernández Estrada, Rafael. 2019. "Servidores de la Nación: La maquinaria electoral." *Nexos*, September 1. https://www.nexos.com.mx/?p=44276Hernández Franco, Daniel. 2008. *Historia de Oportunidades: Inicio y cambios del programa*. Mexico City: Fondo de Cultura Económica.

Hernández Romero, Karla. 2016. "How Does Avancemos Work?: Best Practices in the Implementation of Conditional Cash Transfer Programs in Latin America and the Caribbean." Social Protection and Health Division, Technical Note IDB-TN-931,

Inter-American Development Bank. https://publications.iadb.org/en/how-does-av ancemos-work-best-practices-implementation-conditional-cash-transfer-progra ms-latin

Herrera Beltrán, Claudia. 2000. "Fox preservará el Progresa, anuncia equipo de transición." *La Jornada*, July 21. https://www.jornada.com.mx/2000/07/21/018 n1pol.html

Hevia de la Jara, Felipe. 2011. "La difícil articulación entre políticas universales y programas docalizados: Etnografía institucional del programa Bolsa Familia de Brasil." *Gestión y Política Pública* 20 (2): 331–79.

Hicks, Alexander. 1999. *Social Democracy and Welfare Capitalism: A Century of Income Security Politics*. Ithaca: Cornell University Press.

Hirschman, Albert O. 1981. *Essays in Trespassing: Economics to Politics and Beyond*. New York: Cambridge University Press.

Hoddinott, John. 2007. "Social Protection: To Target or Not to Target." *IDS Bulletin* 38 (3): 90–94. https://doi.org/10.1111/j.1759-5436.2007.tb00387.x

Hoffman, Rodolfo. 2013. "Transferências de renda e desigualdade no Brasil (1995–2011)." In *Programa Bolsa Família: Uma década de inclusão e cidadania*, edited by Tereza Campello and Marcelo Côrtes Neri, 207–16. Brasilia: Instituto de Pesquisa Econômica Aplicada.

Holland, Alisha C., and Ben Ross Schneider. 2017. "Easy and Hard Redistribution: The Political Economy of Welfare States in Latin America." *Perspectives on Politics* 15 (4): 988–1006. https://doi.org/10.1017/S1537592717002122

Huber, Evelyne. 1996. "Options for Social Policy in Latin America: Neoliberal versus Social Democratic Models." In *Welfare States in Transition*, edited by Gøsta Esping-Andersen, 141–91. London: SAGE.

Huber, Evelyne. 2005. "Globalization and Social Policy Developments in Latin America." In *Globalization and the Future of the Welfare State*, edited by Miguel Glatzer and Dietrich Rueschemeyer, 75–105. Pittsburgh, PA: University of Pittsburgh Press.

Huber, Evelyne, Thomas Mustillo, and John D. Stephens. 2008. "Politics and Social Spending in Latin America." *Journal of Politics* 70 (2): 420–36. https://doi.org/10.1017/S0022381608080407

Huber, Evelyne, and John D. Stephens. 2001. *Development and Crisis of the Welfare State: Parties and Policies in Global Markets*. Chicago: University of Chicago Press.

Huber, Evelyne, and John D. Stephens. 2012. *Democracy and the Left: Social Policy and Inequality in Latin America*. Chicago: University of Chicago Press.

Hunter, Wendy. 2010. *The Transformation of the Workers' Party in Brazil, 1989–2009*. New York: Cambridge University Press.

Hunter, Wendy. 2014. "Making Citizens: Brazilian Social Policy from Getúlio to Lula." *Journal of Politics in Latin America* 6 (3): 15–37. https://doi.org/10.1177/1866802X1400600302

Hunter, Wendy. 2021. "Diffusion Dynamics: Shaping Social Policy in Latin America's Inclusionary Turn." In *The Inclusionary Turn in Latin American Democra-*

cies, edited by Steven Levitsky, Deborah J. Yashar and Diana Kapiszewski, 93-116. New York: Cambridge University Press. Hunter, Wendy, and Robert Brill. 2016. "'Documents, Please': Advances in Social Protection and Birth Certification in the Developing World." *World Politics* 68 (2): 191–228. https://doi.org/10.1017/S0043887115000465

Hunter, Wendy, and Timothy J. Power. 2007. "Rewarding Lula: Executive Power, Social Policy, and the Brazilian Elections of 2006." *Latin American Politics and Society* 49 (1): 1–30. https://doi.org/10.1111/j.1548-2456.2007.tb00372.x

Hunter, Wendy, and Natasha Borges Sugiyama. 2014. "Transforming Subjects into Citizens: Insights from Brazil's Bolsa Família." *Perspectives on Politics* 12 (4): 829–45. https://doi.org/10.1017/S1537592714002151

IBGE (Instituto Brasileiro de Geografia e Estatística). 2004. "Excesso de peso atinge 38,8 milhões de drasileiros adultos." https://agenciadenoticias.ibge.gov.br/agencia-sala-de-imprensa/2013-agencia-de-noticias/releases/12873-asi-excesso-de-peso-atinge-388-milhoes-de-brasileiros-adultos

IBGE (Instituto Brasileiro de Geografia e Estatística). 2018. "National System of Consumer Price Indexes: Time Series (in Portuguese)." https://ww2.ibge.gov.br/english/estatistica/indicadores/precos/inpc_ipca/defaultseriesHist.shtm

IMAS (Instituto Mixto de Ayuda Social). 2018. "La aprobación de esta ley es un paso más en nuestra ruta para reforzar Avancemos." http://www.imas.go.cr/comunicado/la-aprobacion-de-esta-ley-es-un-paso-mas-en-nuestra-ruta-para-reforzar-avancemos

IMAS (Instituto Mixto de Ayuda Social). 2019. "Exitoso primer depósito a 200 mil beneficiarios del nuevo programa Crecemos." https://www.imas.go.cr/index.php/es/comunicado/exitoso-primer-deposito-200-mil-beneficiarios-del-nuevo-programa-crecemos

IMAS (Instituto Mixto de Ayuda Social). 2020. "Informe anual de labores 2019–2020." https://www.imas.go.cr/sites/default/files/docs/Informe%20Anual%20Juan%20Luis%20Berm%C3%BAdez%20Madriz%20IMAS-MDHIS%202020.pdf

INDEC. 2021. "Precios." June 11. https://www.indec.gob.ar/indec/web/Nivel3-Tema-3-5

INE (Instituto Nacional Electoral). 2019. "Procedentes medidas cautelares contra promoción realizada por servidores de la nación." Comunicado de Prensa 236. https://centralelectoral.ine.mx/2019/08/16/procedentes-medidas-cautelares-promocion-realizada-servidores-la-nacion/

INEC (Instituto de Estadisticas y Censo). 2019. "Pobreza por ingresos se mantiene en 21,0% respecto año anterior." Comunicado de Prensa. https://www.inec.cr/sites/default/files/documetos-biblioteca-virtual/copren-enaho2019_1.pdf

INEC (Instituto de Estadísticas y Censo). 2020. "Inflación." June 1. https://www.inec.cr/economia/indice-de-precios-al-consumidor

Inter-American Development Bank. N.d. "Annual Reports." Accessed January 2, 2019. https://www.iadb.org/en/about-us/annual-reports

IPEA (Instituto de Pesquisa Econômica Aplicada). 2003. "Políticas sociais—

acompanhamento e análise." June 23. http://www.ipea.gov.br/portal/index.php?option=com_content&view=article&id=5769

Jaime, Fernando, and Félix Sabaté. 2013. "Gobernanza multinivel fragmentada en politicas sociales: Respuestas locales implementando la Asignación Universal por Hijo." Latin American Studies Association Conference, Washington, DC.

Jaramillo Molina, Máximo Ernesto. 2019. "¿Una nueva política social? Cambios y continuidades en los programas sociales de la 4T." *Análisis Plural* Segundo Semestre: 137–54.

Jensen, Carsten. 2014. *The Right and the Welfare State*. New York: Oxford University Press.

Jiménez, Arturo Sánchez. 2020. "Garantizados los recursos para Beca Benito Juárez, asegura gobierno." *La Jornada*, May 15, sec. Política. https://www.jornada.com.mx/ultimas/politica/2020/05/15/garantizados-los-recursos-de-beca-benito-juarez-asegura-gobierno-1961.html

Jiménez, Ronulfo. 2014. "Educación pública en Costa Rica: Políticas, resultados y gasto." Análisis 6. Academia de Centroamérica. https://www.academiaca.or.cr/serie-analisis/educacion-publica-costa-rica-politicas-resultados-gasto/

Jones, Damon, and Ioana Elena Marinescu. 2018. "The Labor Market Impacts of Universal and Permanent Cash Transfers: Evidence from the Alaska Permanent Fund." Working Paper 24312. National Bureau of Economic Research.

Kamel, Ali. 2004. "Bolsa-Família, Sem Escola." *O Globo*, September 7. http://www.alikamel.com.br/artigos/bolsa-familia-sem-escola.phpKabeer, Naila. 2014. "The Politics and Practicalities of Universalism: Towards a Citizen-Centered Perspective on Social Protection." *European Journal of Development Research* 26, (3): 338–354.

Kantor, Mora. 2012. "El Proceso de formulación de la Asignación Universal por Hijo y el Plan Jefas y Jefes de Hogar Desocupados en la Argentina: Una perspectiva comparada." Latin American Studies Association Conference, San Francisco, CA.Kaufman, Robert R. 2011. "The Political Left, the Export Boom, and the Populist Temptation." In *The Resurgence of the Latin American Left*, edited by Steven Levitsky and Kenneth Roberts, 93-116. Baltimore: John Hopkins University Press.

Kaufman, Robert R., and Joan M. Nelson. 2004. "Introduction: The Political Challenges of Social Sector Reform." In *Crucial Needs, Weak Incentives: Social Sector Reform, Democratization, and Globalization in Latin America*, edited by Robert R. Kaufman and Joan M. Nelson, 1–19. Baltimore: Johns Hopkins University Press.

Kaufman, Robert R., and Alex Segura-Ubiergo. 2001. "Globalization, Domestic Politics, and Social Spending in Latin America: A Time-Series Cross-Section Analysis, 1973–97." *World Politics* 53 (4): 553–87. https://doi.org/10.1353/wp.2001.0016

Kingstone, Peter. 2018. *The Political Economy of Latin America: Reflections on Neoliberalism and Development after the Commodity Boom*. 2nd ed. New York: Routledge.

Kirchner, Alicia M. 2010. *Políticas sociales del bicentenario: Un modelo nacional y popular, Tomo I*. Buenos Aires: Ministerio de Desarrollo Social.

Korpi, Walter. 1983. *The Democratic Class Struggle*. London: Routledge Kegan & Paul.

Korpi, Walter, and Joakim Palme. 2003. "New Politics and Class Politics in the Context of Austerity and Globalization: Welfare State Regress in 18 Countries, 1975–95." *American Political Science Review* 97 (3): 425–46.

Kugler, Adriana D., and Ingrid Rojas. 2018. "Do CCTs Improve Employment and Earnings in the Very Long-Term? Evidence from Mexico." Working Paper 24248. National Bureau of Economic Research. https://doi.org/10.3386/w24248

La Nación (Argentina). 2005. "Los desafíos de Tabaré Vázquez." *La Nación*, March 3. https://www.lanacion.com.ar/editoriales/los-desafios-de-tabare-vazquez-nid684145

La Nación (Argentina). 2014. "Mauricio Macri mantendría la estatización de YPF y de las AFJP, la Asignación por Hijo y dice que va a 'echar a los fondos buitre.'" *La Nación*, October 16. https://www.lanacion.com.ar/politica/mauricio-macri-mantendria-la-estatizacion-de-ypf-y-de-las-afjp-la-asignacion-por-hijo-y-que-va-a-echar-a-los-fondos-buitre-nid1735972

La Nación (Costa Rica). 2008a. "Zumbado se forja imagen de 'ministro de los pobres.'" *La Nación*, April 16. https://www.nacion.com/el-pais/zumbado-se-forja-imagen-de-ministro-de-los-pobres/PX5A3HOSHBEVJOWJERJOCM7ACM/story/

La Nación (Costa Rica). 2008b. "Colegiales pobres pasan penurias a la espera de beca." *La Nación*, August 20. https://www.nacion.com/el-pais/colegiales-pobres-pasan-penurias-a-la-espera-de-beca/TL6DZREEOJA63HGY7CPYHQSX2I/story/

La Nación (Costa Rica). 2008c. "Desertores tienen beca y alumnos que siguen en aulas, la esperan." *La Nación*, September 28. https://www.nacion.com/el-pais/servicios/desertores-tienen-beca-y-alumnos-que-siguen-en-aulas-la-esperan/KNPBTPYCU5A7FMAB7INDYKYIDE/story/

La Nación (Costa Rica). 2009. "Alumnos de familias acomodadas reciben becas para pobres." *La Nación*, February 12. https://www.nacion.com/el-pais/servicios/alumnos-de-familias-acomodadas-reciben-becas-para-pobres/PDDUG43H7VEIZHX4LWM6RSYPQQ/story/

La Nación (Costa Rica). 2010. "IMAS detecta 6.250 becarios de familias acomodadas." *La Nación*, January 21. https://www.nacion.com/el-pais/servicios/imas-detecta-6-250-becarios-de-familias-acomodadas/DIHOBC5DWNGQNAYDXJLZFHYB2U/story/

La Nación (Costa Rica). 2011. "Avancemos subsidia a jóvenes olvidados por padres con recursos." *La Nación*, February 6. https://www.nacion.com/archivo/avancemos-subsidia-a-jovenes-olvidados-por-padres-con-recursos/CT3BVYMU55AFZAYVG3VYREGDX4/story/

La Nación (Costa Rica). 2012. "Directores ayudan a depurar la lista de becados de

Avancemos." *La Nación*, February 14. https://www.nacion.com/el-pais/servici os/directores-ayudan-a-depurar-la-lista-de-becados-de-avancemos/3MM4H WR4RNDPPJ4OS4FSWBZ3RU/story/

La Verdad. 2020. "Becas AMLO: Aprueban reforma constitucional que garantiza estudiar con beca." *La Verdad Noticias*, April 5. https://laverdadnoticias.com /mexico/Becas-AMLO-Aprueban—reforma-constitucional-que-garantiza-est udiar-con-beca-20200405-0144.html

Lakoff, George. 2016. *Moral Politics: How Liberals and Conservatives Think*. 3rd ed. Chicago: University of Chicago Press.

Lana, Xenia, and Mark Evans. 2004. "Policy Transfer between Developing Countries: The Transfer of the Bolsa-Escola Programme to Ecuador." In *Policy Transfer in Global Perspective*, edited by Mark Evans, 190–210. New York: Routledge.

Lance, Justin Earl. 2014. "Conditional Cash Transfers and the Effect on Recent Murder Rates in Brazil and Mexico." *Latin American Politics and Society* 56 (1): 55–72. https://doi.org/10.1111/j.1548-2456.2014.00221.x

Lavinas, Lena. 2013a. "21st Century Welfare." *New Left Review* 84: 5–40.

Lavinas, Lena. 2013b. "Brazil: The Lost Road to Citizen's Income." In *Citizen's Income and Welfare Regimes in Latin America: From Cash Transfers to Rights*, edited by Rubén M. Lo Vuolo, 29–50. Basingstoke, UK: Palgrave Macmillan.

Layton, Matthew L., and Amy Erica Smith. 2015. "Incorporating Marginal Citizens and Voters: The Conditional Electoral Effects of Targeted Social Assistance in Latin America." *Comparative Political Studies* 48 (7): 854–81. https://doi.org/10 .1177/0010414014565889

Letcher, Hernán, and Julia Strada. 2017. "La metodología del ajuste: Precisiones sobre las propuestas en torno al cálculo de movilidad y análisis sobre los regímenes especiales de jubilación." Buenos Aires: Centro de Política Económica Argentina. https://centrocepa.com.ar/informes/71-la-metodologia-del-ajuste -precisiones-sobre-las-propuestas-en-torno-al-calculo-de-movilidad-y-analis is-sobre-los-regimenes-especiales-de-jubilacion

Letcher, Hernán, and Julia Strada. 2019. "Las transformaciones del programa Progresar bajo la gestión Cambiemos: Desnaturalización y metas de ajuste del 90%." Buenos Aires: Centro de Política Económica Argentina. https://centroce pa.com.ar/informes/236-las-transformaciones-del-programa-progresar-bajo -la-gestion-cambiemos-desnaturalizacion-y-metas-de-ajuste-del-90.html

Levitsky, Steven, and María Victoria Murillo. 2008. "Argentina: From Kirchner to Kirchner." *Journal of Democracy* 19 (2): 16–30. https://doi.org/10.1353/jod.20 08.0030

Levitsky, Steven, and Kenneth M. Roberts. 2011. "Introduction: Latin America's 'Left Turn': A Framework for Analysis." In *The Resurgence of the Latin American Left*, edited by Steven Levitsky and Kenneth M. Roberts, 1–30. Baltimore: Johns Hopkins University Press.

Levy, Santiago. 1991. "Poverty Alleviation in Mexico." Policy, Research, and External Affairs Working Paper 679. World Bank. http://documents.worldbank.org /curated/en/306571468774696697/Poverty-alleviation-in-Mexico

Levy, Santiago. 2006. *Progress against Poverty: Sustaining Mexico's Progresa-Oportunidades Program*. Washington, DC: Brookings Institution Press.
Levy, Santiago. 2008. *Good Intentions, Bad Outcomes: Social Policy, Informality, and Economic Growth in Mexico*. Washington, DC: Brookings Institution Press.
Levy, Santiago, and Evelyne Rodríguez. 2004. "El Programa de Educación, Salud y Alimentación, Progresa—Programa de Desarrollo Humano Oportunidades (2003)." In *Ensayos Sobre El Desarrollo Económico y Social de México*, edited by Santiago Levy, 181–379. Mexico City: Fondo de Cultura Económica..
Licio, Elaine Cristina, Lucio R. Rennó, and Henrique Carlos de O. de Castro. 2009. "Bolsa Família e voto na eleição presidencial de 2006: Em busca do elo perdido." *Opinião Pública* 15 (1): 31–54. https://doi.org/10.1590/S0104-62762009000100002
Lieberman, Evan S. 2005. "Nested Analysis as a Mixed-Method Strategy for Comparative Research." *American Political Science Review* 99 (3): 435–52.
Lindero, Scarlett. 2020. "Servidores de la Nación violan la ley pero no pueden ser sancionados." *Cuestione*, January 3. https://cuestione.com/nacional/servidores-de-la-nacion-violan-la-ley-pero-no-pueden-ser-sancionados/
Lindert, Kathy. 2014. "Conditional Cash Transfers (CCTs): Social Safety Net Core Course." World Bank, December. http://www.worldbank.org/content/dam/Worldbank/Event/social-protection/Lindert%20-%20CCTs%20.pdf
Lindert, Kathy, Anja Linder, Jason Hobbs, and Benedicte de la Briere. 2007. "The Nuts and Bolts of Brazil's Bolsa Familia Program: Implementing Conditional Cash Transfers in a Decentralized Context." Social Policy Working Paper 0709. World Bank. http://documents.worldbank.org/curated/en/972261468231296002/The-nuts-and-bolts-of-Brazils-bolsa-familia-program-implementing-conditional-cash-transfers-in-a-decentralized-context
Lindert, Kathy, Emmanuel Skoufias, and Joseph Shapiro. 2006. "Redistributing Income to the Poor and the Rich: Public Transfers in Latin America and the Caribbean." Social Policy Discussion Paper 0605. World Bank. http://documents.worldbank.org/curated/en/534671468044934128/Redistributing-income-to-the-poor-and-the-rich-public-transfers-in-Latin-America-and-the-Caribbean
Lindert, Kathy, and Vanina Vincensini. 2010. "Social Policy, Perceptions and the Press: An Analysis of the Media's Treatment of Conditional Cash Transfers in Brazil." Social Policy Discussion Paper 70613. World Bank. http://documents.worldbank.org/curated/en/312121468013876967/Brazil-Social-policy-perceptions-and-the-press-an-analysis-of-the-medias-treatment-of-conditional-cash-transfers-in-Brazil
Linz, Juan J., and Alfred C. Stepan. 1996. "Toward Consolidated Democracies." *Journal of Democracy* 7 (2): 14–33. https://doi.org/10.1353/jod.1996.0031
Lodola, Germán. 2005. "Protesta popular y redes clientelares en la Argentina: El reparto federal del plan trabajar (1996–2001)." *Desarrollo Económico* 44 (176): 515–36. https://doi.org/10.2307/3655866
López-Calva, Luis F., and Nora Lustig, eds. 2010. *Declining Inequality in Latin America: A Decade of Progress?* Washington, DC: Brookings Institution Press.

Lo Vuolo, Rubén M. 1995. "La economía política del ingreso ciudadano." In *Contra la exclusion: La propuesta del ingreso ciudadano*, edited by Rubén M. Lo Vuolo and Alberto Barbeito, 109–68. Buenos Aires: CIEPP.

Lo Vuolo, Rubén M. 2008. "Why Basic Income Is Better Than Renewed Policy Promises for Latin American Informal Security Regimes." Basic Income Earth Network Congress, Dublin, Ireland. https://basicincome.org/bien/pdf/dublin08/1diiilovuololabourmarketsinlatinambi.pdf

Lo Vuolo, Rubén M., ed. 2013a. *Citizen's Income and Welfare Regimes in Latin America: From Cash Transfers to Rights*. Basingstoke, UK: Palgrave Macmillan.

Lo Vuolo, Rubén M. 2013b. "Epilogue." In *Citizen's Income and Welfare Regimes in Latin America: From Cash Transfers to Rights*, edited by Rubén M. Lo Vuolo, 259–66. Basingstoke, UK: Palgrave Macmillan.

Lo Vuolo, Rubén M., and Alberto C. Barbeito, eds. 1995. *Contra la exclusion: La propuesta del ingreso ciudadano*. Buenos Aires: CIEPP.

Luccisano, Lucy, and Laura Macdonald. 2014. "Mexico and Social Provision by the Federal Government and the Federal District: Obstacles and Openings to a Social Protection Floor." *Global Social Policy* 14 (3): 333–51. https://doi.org/10.1177/1468018114539692

Luna, Juan Pablo, and Cristóbal Rovira Kaltwasser, eds. 2014. "Profiling the Electorate: Ideology and Attitudes of Rightwing Voters." In *The Resilience of the Latin American Right*, edited by Juan Pablo Luna and Cristóbal Rovira Kaltwasser, 48–74. Baltimore: Johns Hopkins University Press.

Lustig, Nora. 2011. "Scholars Who Became Practitioners: The Influence of Research on the Design, Evaluation and Political Survival of Mexico's Anti-Poverty Program." Scholars, Practitioners, and Inter-American Relations Conference, Los Angeles, CA.

Lustig, Nora. 2014. "Scholars Who Became Practitioners: The Influence of Research on the Design, Evaluation, and Political Survival of Mexico's Antipoverty Program." In *Scholars, Policymakers, and International Affairs: Finding Common Cause*, edited by Abraham F. Lowenthal and Mariano E. Bertucci, 105–18. Baltimore: Johns Hopkins University Press.

Lustig, Nora, Luis F. Lopez-Calva, and Eduardo Ortiz-Juarez. 2013. "Declining Inequality in Latin America in the 2000s: The Cases of Argentina, Brazil, and Mexico." *World Development* 44 (April): 129–41. https://doi.org/10.1016/j.worlddev.2012.09.013

Macaulay, Fiona, and Guy Burton. 2003. "PT Never Again? Failure (and Success) in the PT's State Government in Espirito Santo and the Federal District." In *Radicals in Power: The Workers' Party and Experiments in Urban Democracy in Brazil*, edited by Gianpaolo Baiocchi, 131–54. New York: Zed Books.

Madeiro, Carlos. 2017. "Com redução de 543 mil benefícios em 1 mês, Bolsa Família tem maior corte da história." *UOL.Com*, November 8. https://noticias.uol.com.br/cotidiano/ultimas-noticias/2017/08/11/bolsa-familia-reduz-543-mil-beneficios-em-1-mes-programa-tem-maior-corte-da-historia.htm

Madeiro, Carlos. 2020a. "Governo Bolsonaro reduz em 75% reingressos ao Bolsa

Família." *UOL.com*, February 15. https://noticias.uol.com.br/cotidiano/ultimas-noticias/2020/02/15/bolsona-familia-governo-reingressos.htm

Madeiro, Carlos. 2020b. "Governo corta 158 mil do Bolsa Família em meio a COVID-19; 61% são do NE." *UOL.com*, March 20. https://noticias.uol.com.br/politica/ultimas-noticias/2020/03/20/governo-corta-158-mil-do-bolsa-familia-em-meio-ao-covid-19-61-sao-do-ne.htm

Madrid, Raúl L. 2003. *Retiring the State: The Politics of Pension Privatization in Latin America and Beyond*. Stanford, CA: Stanford University Press.

Madrid, Raúl L. 2010. "The Origins of the Two Lefts in Latin America." *Political Science Quarterly* 125 (4): 587–609. https://doi.org/10.1002/j.1538-165X.2010.tb00686.x

Madrid, Raúl L. 2011. "Bolivia: Origins and Policies of the Movimiento al Socialismo." In *The Resurgence of the Latin American Left*, edited by Steven Levitsky and Kenneth M. Roberts, 239–59. Baltimore: Johns Hopkins University Press.

Madrid, Raúl L., Wendy Hunter, and Kurt Weyland. 2010. "The Policies and Performance of the Contestatory and Moderate Left." In *Leftist Governments in Latin America: Successes and Shortcomings*, edited by Kurt Weyland, Raúl L. Madrid, and Wendy Hunter, 140–80. New York: Cambridge University Press.

Mahon, James E., Jr., Marcelo Bergman, and Cynthia Arnson. 2015. "Introduction." In *Progressive Tax Reform and Equality in Latin America*, edited by James E. Mahon Jr., Marcelo Bergman, and Cynthia Arnson, 1–29. Washington, DC: Woodrow Wilson Center.

Mainwaring, Scott. 1999. *Rethinking Party Systems in the Third Wave of Democratization: The Case of Brazil*. Stanford, CA: Stanford University Press.

Mainwaring, Scott, and Aníbal Pérez-Liñán. 2013. *Democracies and Dictatorships in Latin America: Emergence, Survival, and Fall*. New York: Cambridge University Press.

Mainwaring, Scott, and Timothy R. Scully. 2003. "The Diversity of Christian Democracy in Latin America." In *Christian Democracy in Latin America: Electoral Competition and Regime Conflicts*, edited by Scott Mainwaring and Timothy R. Scully, 30–63. Stanford, CA: Stanford University Press.

Manacorda, Marco, Edward Miguel, and Andrea Vigorito. 2011. "Government Transfers and Political Support." *American Economic Journal: Applied Economics* 3 (3): 1–28. https://doi.org/10.1257/app.3.3.1

Maluccio, John, and Rafael Flores. 2005. "Impact Evaluation of a Conditional Cash Transfer Program: The Nicaraguan Red de Protección Social." *Research Report 141*. International Food Policy Research Institute. https://www.ifpri.org/publication/impact-evaluation-conditional-cash-transfer-program

Marchionni, Mariana, and Maria Edo. 2017. "Condicionalidades educativas en la AUH: Diagnóstico y alternativas." In *Análisis y propuestas de mejoras para ampliar la Asignación Universal por Hijo 2017*, edited by Oscar Cetrángolo and Javier Curcio, 272–304. Buenos Aires: UNICEF/ANSES.

Marco Navarro, Flavia. 2012. "El Bono Juancito Pinto del Estado Plurinacional de Bolivia: Programas de transferencias monetarias e infancia." División de Desarrollo Social LC/W.492. CEPAL. https://www.cepal.org/es/publicaciones/4005-bono-juancito-pinto-estado-plurinacional-bolivia-programas-transferencias

Mariz, Renata. 2016. "Corte no Bolsa Família pode chegar a 10% dos beneficiários." *O Globo*, May 16. https://oglobo.globo.com/brasil/corte-no-bolsa-familia-pode-chegar-10-dos-beneficiarios-19318455

Martin, Christian W. 2010. "Interdependence and Political Ideology: The Conditional Diffusion of Cigarette Taxation in U.S. States." *World Political Science* 6 (1): 1–25. https://doi.org/10.2202/1935-6226.1087

Martínez Franzoni, Juliana. 2008. "Welfare Regimes in Latin America: Capturing Constellations of Markets, Families, and Policies." *Latin American Politics and Society* 50 (2): 67–100. https://doi.org/10.1111/j.1548-2456.2008.00013.x

Martínez Franzoni, Juliana. 2013. "Nicaragua." Sistemas de Protección Social en América Latina y el Caribe, LC/W.530. CEPAL. https://www.cepal.org/en/publications/4059-social-protection-systems-latin-america-and-caribbean-nicaragua

Martínez Franzoni, Juliana, and Diego Sánchez-Ancochea. 2013. *Good Jobs and Social Services: How Costa Rica Achieved the Elusive Double Incorporation*. Basingstoke, UK: Palgrave Macmillan.

Martínez Franzoni, Juliana, and Diego Sánchez-Ancochea. 2016. *The Quest for Universal Social Policy in the South: Actors, Ideas and Architectures*. New York: Cambridge University Press.

Martínez Franzoni, Juliana, and Koen Voorend. 2011. "Actors and Ideas behind CCTs in Chile, Costa Rica and El Salvador." *Global Social Policy* 11 (2–3): 279–98. https://doi.org/10.1177/1468018111421296

Martínez Vargas, Thamara. 2020. "Gasto público en becas escolares: Análisis de programas prioritarios." Centro de Investigación Económica y Presupuestaria. https://ciep.mx/gasto-publico-en-becas-escolares-analisis-de-programas-prioritarios/

Masse, Fátima, and Mariana Olvera. 2019. "Diagnóstico IMCO: La política social en México, sin rumbo ni destino cierto." Instituto Mexicano para la Competitividad. https://imco.org.mx/temas/diagnostico-imco-la-politica-social-mexico-sin-rumbo-destino-cierto/

Mata B., Alonso. 2009. "Gobierno desiste de dar beca a 40.000 colegiales pobres." *La Nación (Costa Rica)*, September 21. http://wvw.nacion.com/ln_ee/2009/septiembre/21/pais2094861.html

Mata Blanco, Esteban. 2008. "Zumbado renuncia al Ministerio de Vivienda." *La Nación (Costa Rica)*, August 7. https://www.nacion.com/el-pais/zumbado-renuncia-al-ministerio-de-vivienda/IFFA6DBAFZAYZE2WZU2YVU7UGQ/story/

Mata Hidalgo, Catherine, and Juan Diego Trejos Solórzano. 2018. "Panorama de la inversión social pública 2017 en un contexto de crisis fiscal." Ponencia para el Informe Estado de la Nación. Estado de la Nación. http://repositorio.conare.ac.cr/handle/20.500.12337/2970?show=fullMatos, Kelly. 2016. "Novo Ministro do Desenvolvimento defende Pente-fino no Bolsa Família." GZH, May 17.

https://gauchazh.clicrbs.com.br/politica/noticia/2016/05/novo-ministro-do-d esenvolvimento-defende-pente-finono-bolsa-familia-5803338.html

MC (Ministério da Cidadania). 2017. "Ministro destaca aprimoramento da gestão de benefícios em audiência pública na câmara)." October 31, http://mds.gov.br /area-de-imprensa/noticias/2017/outubro/ministro-destaca-aprimoramento -dagestao-de-beneficios-em-audiencia-publica-na-camara

MCCI (Mexicanos Contra la Corrupción y la Impunidad). 2019. "Jóvenes Construyendo El Futuro: Un programa con datos improbables, incompletos e inverificables." Comunicado de Prensa. https://contralacorrupcion.mx/jcf-datos/

McGuire, James W. 2013. "Conditional Cash Transfers in Bolivia: Origins, Impact and Universality." International Studies Association Conference, San Francisco, CA. http://jmcguire.faculty.wesleyan.edu/files/2013/08/McGuire2013cBolivian CCTs.pdf

McLeod, Darryl, and Nora Lustig. 2011. "Inequality and Poverty under Latin America's New Left Regimes." Working Paper 2008. Society for the Study of Economic Inequality. http://www.ecineq.org/milano/WP/ECINEQ2011-208.pdf

MDSA (Ministério do Desenvolvimento Social e Agrário). 2016. "Pente-Fino no Bolsa Família encontra irregularidades em 1,1 milhão de benefícios." http:// mds.gov.br/area-de-imprensa/noticias/2016/novembro/pente-fino-no-bolsa -familia-encontra-irregularidades-em-1-1-milhao-de-beneficios

Medinaceli, Mauricio, and Leila Mokrani. 2010. "Impacto de los bonos financiados con la renta petrolera." *Umbrales* 20: 223–63.

Melo, Marcus André. 2007. "Political Competition Can Be Positive: Embedding Cash Transfer Programmes in Brazil." In *Development Success: Statecraft in the South*, edited by Anthony Bebbington and Willy McCourt, 30–51. Basingstoke, UK: Palgrave Macmillan.

Melo, Marcus André. 2008. "Unexpected Successes, Unanticipated Failures: Social Policy from Cardoso to Lula." In *Democratic Brazil Revisited*, edited by Peter Kingstone and Timothy J. Power, 161–84. Pittsburgh, PA: University of Pittsburgh Press.

Melo, Marcus Andre, Njuguna Ng'ethe, and James Manor. 2012. *Against the Odds: Politicians, Institutions and the Struggle against Poverty*. New York: Oxford University Press.

Meltzer, Allan H., and Scott F. Richard. 1981. "A Rational Theory of the Size of Government." *Journal of Political Economy* 89 (5): 914–27. https://doi.org/doi.org /10.1086/261013

Méndez, Enrique, and Andrea Becerril. 2006. "AMLO desconoce recuento parcial y, advierte que no aceptará imposición." *La Jornada*, August 10. https://www.jo rnada.com.mx/2006/08/10/index.php?section=politica&article=008n1pol

Menna Barreto, Marcelo. 2019. "Bolsonaro reduz R$ 2,5 bilhões do Bolsa Família." *Extra Classe*, December 2, sec. Política. https://www.extraclasse.org.br/politica /2019/12/bolsonaro-reduz-r-25-bilhoes-do-bolsa-familia/

Mesa-Lago, Carmelo. 1978. *Social Security in Latin America: Pressure Groups, Stratification, and Inequality*. Pittsburgh, PA: University of Pittsburgh Press.

Mesa-Lago, Carmelo. 1990. *Ascent to Bankruptcy: Financing Social Security in Latin America*. Pittsburgh, PA: University of Pittsburgh Press.

Mesa-Lago, Carmelo. 2008. *Reassembling Social Security: A Survey of Pensions and Health Care Reforms in Latin America*. New York: Oxford University Press.

Mettler, Suzanne. 2002. "Bringing the State Back in to Civic Engagement: Policy Feedback Effects of the G.I. Bill for World War II Veterans." *American Political Science Review* 96 (2): 351–65. https://doi.org/10.1017/S0003055402000217

México ¿Cómo Vamos? 2020. "Semáforo nacional: Pobreza laboral." https://mexico comovamos.mx/

Meza-Cordero, Jaime A., Maurice Kugler, Michaela Gulemetova, Danelly Salas-Ocampo, César Rodríguez-Barrantes, Verónica Campos-Barrantes, and Raquel Barrientos. 2015. "Apoyo técnico para la revisión y evaluación del programa de transferencia monetaria Avancemos del Instituto Mixto de Ayuda Social (IMAS) para contribuir a la reducción de la deserción y el abandono escolar: Informe final de evaluación." UNICEF/IMPAQ International. https://www.uni cef.org/evaldatabase/files/Informe_Final_Evaluacion_AVANCEMOS_CostaRi ca_2015-001.pdf

Milenio. 2019. "Estudiantes alistan protesta contra AMLO por falta de becas," June 25. https://www.milenio.com/politica/falta-becas-estudiantes-alistan-protestas -amlo

Misiones Online. 2009. "El macro comenzará el pago de la Asignación Universal por Hijo a los DNI terminados en 0 el 1° de diciembre." *Misiones Online*, November 27. https://misionesonline.net/2009/11/27/el-macro-comenzara-el -pago-de-la-asignacion-universal-por-hijo-a-los-dni-terminados-en-0-el-1-de -diciembre/

MNR (Movimiento Nacionalista Revolucionario). 2002. "Un plan de emergencia que nace de una visión de Bolivia." http://americo.usal.es/oir/opal/Document os/Bolivia/MNR/ProgramaGobierno2002–2007MNR.pdf

Molina-Millan, Teresa, Tania Barham, Karen Macours, John A. Maluccio, and Marco Stampini. 2016. "Long-Term Impacts of Conditional Cash Transfers in Latin America: Review of the Evidence." Working Paper 732. Inter-American Development Bank. https://doi.org/10.18235/0000470

Molinar Horcasitas, Juan, and Jeffrey A. Weldon. 1994. "Electoral Determinants and Consequences of National Solidarity." In *Transforming State-Society Relations in Mexico: The National Solidarity Strategy*, edited by Wayne Cornelius, Ann L. Craig, and Jonathan Fox, 123–41. La Jolla, CA: Center for U.S.-Mexican Studies.

Moore, Charity. 2008. "Assessing Honduras? CCT Programme PRAF, Programa de Asignación Familiar: Expected and Unexpected Realities." Country Study 15. International Policy Centre for Inclusive Growth. https://ideas.repec.org/p/ipc /cstudy/15.html

Moore, Charity. 2009. "Nicaragua's Red de Protección Social: An Exemplary but Short-Lived Conditional Cash Transfer Programme." Country Study 17. International Policy Centre for Inclusive Growth. https://www.cepal.org/en/publica tions/4059-social-protection-systems-latin-america-and-caribbean-nicaragua

Moore, Charity. 2010. "The Political Economy of Social Protection in Honduras and Nicaragua." In *Conditional Cash Transfers in Latin America*, edited by Michelle Adato and John Hoddinott, 101–26. Baltimore: Johns Hopkins University Press.

Morais de Sá e Silva, Michelle. 2017. *Poverty Reduction, Education, and the Global Diffusion of Conditional Cash Transfers*. Basingstoke, UK: Palgrave Macmillan.

Morales Ramos, Roxana, and Andrea Cubero Alvarado. 2005. "Evaluación de la política social de combate a la pobreza de la administración del Dr. Abel Pacheco de la Espriella (2002–2005)." *Economía y Sociedad* 10 (28): 49–65.

Mudde, Cas. 2004. "The Populist Zeitgeist." *Government and Opposition* 39 (4): 541–63.

Müller, Katharina. 2009. "Contested Universalism: From Bonosol to Renta Dignidad in Bolivia." *International Journal of Social Welfare* 18 (2): 163–72. https://doi.org/10.1111/j.1468-2397.2008.00579.x

Murillo, María Victoria. 1999. "Recovering Political Dynamics: Teachers' Unions and the Decentralization of Education in Argentina and Mexico." *Journal of Interamerican Studies and World Affairs* 41 (1): 31–57. https://doi.org/10.2307/166226

Murillo, María Victoria, and Cecilia Martínez-Gallardo. 2007. "Political Competition and Policy Adoption: Market Reforms in Latin American Public Utilities." *American Journal of Political Science* 51 (1): 120–39.

Murillo, María Victoria, Virginia Oliveros, and Milan Vaishnav. 2010. "Dataset on Political Ideology of Presidents and Parties in Latin America." http://mariavictoriamurillo.com/data/

Murillo, María Victoria, Virginia Oliveros, and Milan Vaishnav. 2011. "Economic Constraints and Presidential Agency." In *The Resurgence of the Latin American Left*, edited by Steven Levitsky and Kenneth M. Roberts, 52–70. Baltimore: Johns Hopkins University Press.

Murray, Charles. 2006. *In Our Hands: A Plan to Replace the Welfare State*. Washington, DC: American Enterprise Institute Press.

Mussa, Michael. 2002. *Argentina and the Fund: From Triumph to Tragedy*. Washington, DC: Peterson Institute for International Economics.

Nelson, Joan M. 2007. "Elections, Democracy, and Social Services." *Studies in Comparative International Development* 41 (4): 79–97. https://doi.org/10.1007/BF02800472

Newman, John, Steen Jorgensen, and Menno Pradhan. 1991. "How Did Workers Benefit from Bolivia's Emergency Social Fund?" *World Bank Economic Review* 5 (2): 367–93. https://doi.org/10.1093/wber/5.2.367

Newsweek Staff. 2005. "Saving Grace." *Newsweek*, July 3. https://www.newsweek.com/saving-grace-121407

Newsweek Staff. 2009. "Brazil's Lula: The Most Popular Politician on Earth." *Newsweek*, September 12. https://www.newsweek.com/brazils-lula-most-popular-politician-earth-79355

Niedzwiecki, Sara. 2018. *Uneven Social Policies: The Politics of Subnational Variation in Latin America*. New York: Cambridge University Press.

Niedzwiecki, Sara, and Jennifer Pribble. 2017. "Social Policies and Center-Right Governments in Argentina and Chile." *Latin American Politics and Society* 59 (3): 72–97. https://doi.org/10.1111/laps.12027

Nieto, Francisco, and Ricardo Gómez R. 2012. "AMLO se compromete a mantener 'Oportunidades.'" *El Universal*, June 7.

Noël, Alain, and Jean-Philippe Thérien. 2008. *Left and Right in Global Politics*. New York: Cambridge University Press.

Novacovsky, Irene, and Claudia Sobrón. 1999. "Propuesta de un programa de transferencia directa de ingresos para La Argentina: Ingreso para el Desarrollo Humano." In *De igual a igual: El desafío del estado ante los nuevos problemas sociales*, edited by Jorge Carpio and Irene Novacovsky, 228–40. Buenos Aires: SIEMPRO/Secretaria de Desarrollo Social.

Núñez González, Leonardo, and Katia Guzmán Martínez. 2019. "Ni censo ni de bienestar." *Nexos*, May 21. https://anticorrupcion.nexos.com.mx/?p=1643

Obarrio, Mariano. 2016. "El gobierno anunció medidas sociales por $30.000 millones." *La Nación* (Argentina), April 17. https://www.lanacion.com.ar/politica/el-gobierno-anuncio-medidas-sociales-por-30000-millones-nid1890117

Observatorio Argentinos por la Educación. 2019. "Educación secundaria: Mejoras perceptibles, aunque insuficientes." Observatorio Argentinos por la Educación. https://cms.argentinosporlaeducacion.org/media/reports/ArgxEduc_Informe_Secundaria_Abril_2019.pdf

Observatorio de la Educación Básica Argentina. 2012. "Presentación de resultados. Informe de eesultados: Módulo del programa Asignación Universal Por Hijo (AUH)." March 21. https://es.scribd.com/presentation/87217707/Presentacion-AUH-1

Ocampo, José Antonio. 2004. "Latin America's Growth and Equity Frustrations during Structural Reforms." *Journal of Economic Perspectives* 18 (2): 67–88. https://doi.org/10.1257/0895330041371349

OECD (Organisation for Economic Co-operation and Development). 2016. *PISA 2015 Results (Vol. I): Excellence and Equity in Education*. Paris: OECD.

OECD (Organisation for Economic Co-operation and Development). 2018. "Revenue Statistics—Latin American Countries: Comparative Tables." https://stats.oecd.org/Index.aspx?DataSetCode=RSLACT

O Estado de S. Paulo. 2001a. "PT nega boicote ao Ministério da Educação." *O Estado de S. Paulo*, August 13. https://politica.estadao.com.br/noticias/geral,pt-nega-boicote-ao-ministerio-da-educacao,20010813p39307

O Estado de S. Paulo. 2001b. "Lula chama malan de cínico." *O Estado de S. Paulo*, September 6. https://politica.estadao.com.br/noticias/geral,lula-chama-malan-de-cinico,20010906p39765

O Estado de S. Paulo. 2001c. "Governo mantém valor do benefício da Bolsa-Escola." *O Estado de S. Paulo*, November 21. https://politica.estadao.com.br/noticias/geral,governo-mantem-valor-do-beneficio-da-bolsa-escola,20011121p41210

OEBA (Observatorio de la Educación Básica Argentina). 2012. "Informe de resultados: Módulo del programa Asignación Universal por Hijo." Centro de Estudios en Políticas Públicas, Universidad de Buenos Aires.

Oliveira de Castro, Henrique Carlos de, Maria Inez Machado Telles Walter, Cora Maria Bender de Santana, and Michelle Conceição Stephanou. 2009. "Percepções sobre o programa Bolsa Família na sociedade brasileira." *Opinião Pública* 15 (2): 333–55. https://doi.org/10.1590/S0104-62762009000200003

Olmos, Javier. 2018. "Propone Albores subir apoyo de Prospera a mil 500 pesos." *Diario de Juárez*, June 16. http://diario.mx/Local/2018-06-16_81d42c04/propone-albores-subir-apoyo-de-prospera-a-mil-500-pesos-/

Onofre, Renato. 2020. "Ministro Marco Aurélio suspende cortes no Bolsa Família no nordeste." *Folha de S. Paulo*, March 23. https://www1.folha.uol.com.br/mercado/2020/03/ministro-marco-aurelio-suspende-cortes-no-bolsa-familia-no-nordeste.shtml

Osorio Gonnet, Cecilia. 2018. *¿Aprendiendo o emulando? Cómo se difunded las políticas sociales en América Latina*. Santiago, Chile: LOM Ediciones.

Osorio Gonnet, Cecilia. 2019. "A Comparative Analysis of the Adoption of Conditional Cash Transfers Programs in Latin America." *Journal of Comparative Policy Analysis: Research and Practice* 21 (4): 385–401. https://doi.org/10.1080/13876988.2018.1491671

OSPE-B (Observatorio Social de Políticas Educativas de Bolivia). 2011. "Evaluación de resultados del programa Bono 'Juancito Pinto.'" CARE/Plan Internacional Inc./DVV International Regional Andina. https://dds.cepal.org/redesoc/publicacion?id=1491

Oviedo, Ana Maria, Susana M. Sanchez, Kathy Lindert, and J. Humberto Lopez. 2015. "Costa Rica's Development: From Good to Better." Systematic Country Diagnosis 97489. World Bank. http://documents.worldbank.org/curated/en/847271468190746362/Costa-Rica-s-development-from-good-to-better-systematic-country-diagnostic

Paiva, Luis Henrique, Fábio Veras Soares, Flavio Cireno, Iara Azevedo Vitelli Viana, and Ana Clara Duran. 2016. "The Effects of Conditionality Monitoring on Educational Outcomes: Evidence from Brazil's Bolsa Família Programme." Working Paper 144. International Policy Centre for Inclusive Growth. https://ideas.repec.org/p/ipc/wpaper/144.html

Pardo, Marcia. 2003. "Reseña de programas sociales para la superación de la pobreza en América Latina." Estudios Estadísticos y Prospectivos 20. CEPAL. https://www.cepal.org/es/publicaciones/4731-resena-programas-sociales-la-superacion-la-pobreza-america-latina

Patú, Gustavo. 2013. "Bolsa Família faz dez anos; Exame de paternidade aponta Petistas, Tucanos e Neoliberais do Banco Mundial." *Dinheiro Público & Cia* (blog), September 8. https://dinheiropublico.blogfolha.uol.com.br/2013/09/08/bolsa-familia-faz-dez-anos-exame-de-paternidade-aponta-petistas-tucanos-e-neoliberais-do-banco-mundial/

Paulics, Veronika. 2005. "Disseminação de inovações em gestão local." Instituto Pólis. http://www.polis.org.br/uploads/742/742.pdf

Paus, Eva. 2005. *Foreign Investment, Development, and Globalization: Can Costa Rica Become Ireland?* Basingstoke, UK: Palgrave Macmillan.

Paz Arauco, Verónica, George Gray Molina, Ernesto Yañéz Aguilar, and Wilson

Jiménez Pozo. 2013. "Explaining Low Redistributive Impact in Bolivia." *Public Finance Review* 42 (3): 326–45. https://doi.org/10.1177/1091142113496133

Peck, Jamie, and Nik Theodore. 2015. *Fast Policy: Experimental Statecraft at the Thresholds of Neoliberalism*. Minneapolis: University of Minnesota Press.

Peduzzi, Pedro. 2018. "Bolsa Família: Problema em cadastro bloqueia ou cancela 2 milhões de benefícios." *Agência Brasil*, January 4. https://agenciabrasil.ebc.com.br/geral/noticia/2018-01/bolsa-familia-problema-em-cadastro-bloqueia-ou-cancela-2-milhoes-de-beneficios.

Penfold-Becerra, Michael. 2007. "Clientelism and Social Funds: Evidence from Chávez's Misiones." *Latin American Politics and Society* 49 (4): 63–84. https://doi.org/10.1111/j.1548-2456.2007.tb00392.x

Pereira, Anthony W. 2015. "Bolsa Família and Democracy in Brazil." *Third World Quarterly* 36 (9): 1682–99. https://doi.org/10.1080/01436597.2015.1059730

Pereira, Felipe. 2019. "Governo vai continuar Pente Fino e quer Bolsa Família com porta de saída." *UOL.com*, January 3. Accessed September 15, 2020. https://noticias.uol.com.br/politica/ultimas-noticias/2019/01/03/governo-vai-continuar-pente-fino-e-quer-bolsa-familia-com-porta-de-saida.htm

Pérez-Muñoz, Cristian. 2017. "What is Wrong with Conditional Cash Transfer Programs?" *Journal of Social Philosophy* 48 (4): 440–60. https://doi.org/10.1111/josp.12215

Pierson, Paul. 1996. "The New Politics of the Welfare State." *World Politics* 48 (2): 143–79. https://doi.org/10.1353/wp.1996.0004

Prengaman, Peter, Saraj DiLorenzo, and Daniel Trielli. 2017. "Millions Return to Poverty in Brazil, Eroding 'Boom' Decade." *Associated Press*, October 23. https://www.apnews.com/89afd8d964984eb69678129e7d4a16cc/

Presidencia de Argentina. 2009. *Decreto 1602/2009 que establece la Asignación Universal por Hijo*. https://www.educ.ar/recursos/129165/decreto-16022009-asignacion-universal-por-hijo

Presidencia de Bolivia. 2006. *Decreto Supremo N° 28.899*. https://www.minedu.gob.bo/files/ministerio-educacion/Creacion-Unidad-Ejecutora-DSN-28899.pdf

Presidencia de Costa Rica. 2006. *Decreto 33154-MP-MIDEPLAN-MEP-MTSS-MIVAH*. https://cgrfiles.cgr.go.cr/publico/jaguar/USI/normativa/Decretos/DE-33154.doc

Presidencia Uruguay. 2005. "Visita de estado del presidente de la República Oriental del Uruguay, Tabaré Vazquez, a La Repúublica Federativa del Brasil: Comunicado Conjunto." http://archivo.presidencia.gub.uy/_web/noticias/2005/04/URUGUAY-BRASIL-010405.pdf

Pribble, Jennifer. 2013. *Welfare and Party Politics in Latin America*. New York: Cambridge University Press.

Pritchett, Lant. 2012. "Impact Evaluation and Political Economy: What Does the 'Conditional' in 'Conditional Cash Transfers' Accomplish?" Center For Global Development, January 12. https://www.cgdev.org/blog/impact-evaluation-and-political-economy-what-does-%E2%80%9Cconditional%E2%80%9D-%E2%80%9Cconditional-cash-transfers%E2%80%9D

Pritchett, Lant. 2013. *The Rebirth of Education: Schooling Ain't Learning*. Washington, DC: Center for Global Development.

Programa Estado de la Nación. 2017. *Sexto informe estado de la educación*. San José, Costa Rica: Servicios Gráficos.

Prospera. 2018. "Información de PROSPERA para directoras, directores y docentes de educación básica y media superior, ciclo escolar 2018–2019." http://www.gob.mx/prospera/documentos/informacion-de-prospera-para-directoras-directores-y-docentes-de-educacion-basica-y-media-superior-ciclo-escolar-2018-2019

Przeworski, Adam, Michael E. Alvarez, José Antonio Cheibub, and Fernando Limongi. 2000. *Democracy and Development: Political Institutions and Well-Being in the World, 1950–1990*. Cambridge: Cambridge University Press.

Quiroga, María Virginia, and Lucía Constanza Juncos Castillo. 2020. "Políticas sociales y nuevos gobiernos en Argentina y Brasil: Un balance a partir de los programas Asignación Universal por Hijo y Bolsa Família." *Polis* (Santiago) 19 (55): 282–308. http://dx.doi.org/10.32735/s0718-6568/2020-n55-1452

Ramos Menar, Braulio, Dante Ayaviri Nina, Gabith Quispe Fernández, and Fortunato Escobar Mamani. 2017. "Las políticas sociales en la reducción de la pobreza y la mejora del bienestar social en Bolivia." *Revista de Investigaciones Altoandinas* 19 (2): 165–78. https://doi.org/10.18271/ria.2017.275

Reid, Michael. 2007. *Forgotten Continent: The Battle for Latin America's Soul*. New Haven, CT: Yale University Press.

Reimers, Fernando, Carol DeShano Da Silva, and Ernesto Trevino. 2006. "Where is the 'Education' in Conditional Cash Transfers in Education?" Institute for Statistics Working Paper 4. UNESCO. http://uis.unesco.org/sites/default/files/documents/where-is-the-education-in-conditional-cash-transfers-in-education-06-en_0.pdf

Remmer, Karen L. 2012. "The Rise of Leftist–Populist Governance in Latin America: The Roots of Electoral Change." *Comparative Political Studies* 45 (8): 947–72. https://doi.org/10.1177/0010414011428595

Repetto, Fabián, and Gala Díaz Langou. 2010. "Desafíos y enseñanzas de la Asignación Universal por Hijo para protección social a un año de su creación." Documento de Políticas Públicas, Recomendación 88. CIPPEC. https://www.cippec.org/publicacion/desafios-y-ensenanzas-de-la-asignacion-universal-por-hijo-para-proteccion-social-a-un-ano-de-su-creacion/

Repetto, Fabián, Gala Díaz Langou, and Vanesa Marazzi. 2009. "¿Hacia un sistema de protección social integral? El ingreso para la niñez es sólo la punta del ovillo." Documento de Políticas Públicas, Análisis 67. CIPPEC. https://www.cippec.org/publicacion/hacia-un-sistema-de-proteccion-social-integral-el-ingreso-para-la-ninez-es-solo-la-punta-del-ovillo/

Repetto, Fabián, and Fernanda Potenza Dal Masetto. 2011. "Protección social en la Argentina." Serie Políticas Sociales 174. CEPAL. https://repositorio.cepal.org//handle/11362/6185

Repretel Costa Rica. 2014. *Sistema de becas Avancemos modificó montos que se darán a cada estudiante*. https://www.youtube.com/watch?v=2Vg-1oTonls

Resende, Thiago. 2020a. "Governo usa verba de aposentadoria e pensões para pagar 13º do Bolsa Família." *Folha de S. Paulo*, January 7. https://www1.folha.uol.com.br/mercado/2020/01/governo-usa-verba-de-aposentadoria-e-pensoes-para-pagar-13o-do-bolsa-familia.shtml

Resende, Thiago. 2020b. "Bolsonaro trava Bolsa Família em cidades pobres e fila chega a 1 milhão." *Folha de S. Paulo*, February 10, sec. Mercado. https://www1.folha.uol.com.br/mercado/2020/02/bolsonaro-trava-bolsa-familia-em-cidades-pobres-e-fila-chega-a-1-milhao.shtml

Resende, Thiago. 2020c. "Há um ano, governo já sabia da falta de dinheiro para o Bolsa Família." *Folha de S. Paulo*, February 26, sec. Mercado. https://www1.folha.uol.com.br/mercado/2020/02/ha-um-ano-governo-ja-sabia-da-falta-de-dinheiro-para-o-bolsa-familia.shtml

Reygadas, Luis, and Fernando Filgueira. 2010. "Inequality and the Incorporation Crisis: The Left's Social Policy Toolkit." In *Latin America's Left Turns: Politics, Policies, and Trajectories of Change*, edited by Maxwell A. Cameron and Eric Hershberg, 171–91. Boulder, CO: Lynne Rienner.

Ribeiro, Gustavo. 2019. "Can Bolsonaro 'Steal' the Brazilian Northeast from Lula?" *Brazilian Report*, April 11. https://brazilian.report/power/2019/04/11/bolsonaro-northeast-lula-bolsa-familia/

Rivera, Astrid. 2019. "AMLO borra programas sociales de Calderón y Peña." *El Universal*, March 16. https://www.eluniversal.com.mx/nacion/amlo-borra-programas-sociales-de-calderon-y-pena

Roberts, Kenneth M. 1995. "Neoliberalism and the Transformation of Populism in Latin America: The Peruvian Case." *World Politics* 48 (1): 82–116. https://doi.org/10.1353/wp.1995.0004

Robertson, Laura, Phyllis Mushati, Jeffrey W. Eaton, Lovemore Dumba, Gideon Mavise, Jeremiah Makoni, Christina Schumacher, et al. 2013. "Effects of Unconditional and Conditional Cash Transfers on Child Health and Development in Zimbabwe: A Cluster-Randomised Trial." *Lancet* 381 (9874): 1283–92. https://doi.org/10.1016/S0140–6736(12)62168–0

Robles, Marcos, Marcela G. Rubio, and Marco Stampini. 2019. "Have Cash Transfers Succeeded in Reaching the Poor in Latin America and the Caribbean?" *Development Policy Review* 37 (S2): O85–139. https://doi.org/10.1111/dpr.12365

Rocha, Sonia. 2013. *Transferencia de renda no Brasil: O fim da pobreza*. Rio de Janeiro: Elsevier.

Rodrigues, Douglas. 2020. "PT pede auditoria no Bolsa Família por suposto desfavorecimento ao nordeste." *Poder360*, March 5. https://www.poder360.com.br/governo/pt-pede-auditoria-no-bolsa-familia-por-suposto-desfavorecimento-ao-nordeste/

Rodríguez-Castelán, Carlos. 2017. "Conditionality as Targeting? Participation and Distributional Effects of Conditional Cash Transfers." Policy Research Working Paper 7940. World Bank. http://documents.worldbank.org/curated/en/612891484142967946/Conditionality-as-targeting-participation-and-distributional-effects-of-conditional-cash-transfers.

Rodríguez Chaves, Evelyn. 2017. "Lo que no se dice del Fonabe." *La Nación* (Costa Rica), April 4. https://www.nacion.com/opinion/foros/lo-que-no-se-dice-del-fonabe/MCH3LGGF5VAURCCJDZE46UCVP4/story/

Rodríguez-Clare, Andrés. 2001. "Costa Rica's Development Strategy Based on Human Capital and Technology: How It Got There, the Impact of Intel, and Lessons for Other Countries." *Journal of Human Development* 2 (2): 311–24. https://doi.org/10.1080/14649880120067301

Román, Isabel. 2010. "Sustentabilidad de los programas de transferencias condicionadas: La experiencia del Instituto Mixto de Ayuda Social y 'Avancemos' en Costa Rica." Serie Políticas Sociales 160. CEPAL. https://repositorio.cepal.org//handle/11362/6179

Román Vega, Isabel. 2012. "Costa Rica." Sistemas de Protección Social en América Latina y el Caribe LC/W.509. CEPAL. https://www.cepal.org/en/publications/4038-social-protection-systems-latin-america-and-caribbean-costa-rica.

Rosenberg, Tina. 2011. "To Beat Back Poverty, Pay the Poor." *Opinionator* (blog), January 3. https://opinionator.blogs.nytimes.com/2011/01/03/to-beat-back-poverty-pay-the-poor/

Rossi, Federico M. 2013. "Juggling Multiple Agendas: The Struggle of Trade Unions against National, Continental, and International Neoliberalism in Argentina." In *Transnational Activism and National Movements in Latin America*, edited by Eduardo Silva, 141–60. New York: Routledge.

Rothstein, Bo. 2018. "UBI: A Bad Idea for the Welfare State." In *Basic Income and the Left: A European Debate*, 103–9. London: Social Europe Edition.

Rudra, Nita. 2008. *Globalization and the Race to the Bottom in Developing Countries: Who Really Gets Hurt?* New York: Cambridge University Press.

Russell, Benjamin. 2019. "What AMLO's Anti-Poverty Overhaul Says about His Government." *Americas Quarterly*, February 25. https://www.americasquarterly.org/article/what-amlos-anti-poverty-overhaul-says-about-his-government/

Sacco, Eva, Lionel Stiglitz, Alejandra Scarano, Felix Schmidt, Julia Strada, and Hernán Letcher. 2019. "Los impactos del ajuste económico en las políticas de niñez y adolescencia, 2016–2019." Buenos Aires: Centro de Política Económica Argentina. https://centrocepa.com.ar/informes/231-la-emergencia-social-que-nunca-se-ejecuto-analisis-de-las-partidas-presupuestarias-previstas-en-la-ley-de-emergencia-social-y-su-implementacion-2016–2019.html

Safatle, Claudia, João Borges, and Ribamar Oliveira. 2016. *Anatomia de um desastre*. São Paulo: Portfolio-Penguin.

Sakamoto, Felipe. 2018. "Lula acerta sobre corte de Temer no Bolsa Família, mas programa cresceu." *Agência Pública*, September 27. https://apublica.org/2018/08/truco-lula-acerta-sobre-corte-de-temer-no-bolsa-familia-mas-programa-cresceu/

Salvia, Agustín, Bianca Musante, and Alejandro Mendoza Jaramillo. 2013. "Análisis de impacto de la AUH en materia de inseguridad alimentaria y déficit educativo." Observatorio de la Deuda Social Argentina, Universidad Católica Argentina. http://wadmin.uca.edu.ar/public/ckeditor/AUH_integrado_03.pdf

Salvia, Agustín, Ianina Tuñón, and Santiago Poy Piñeiro. 2015. "Asignación Universal por Hijo para la potección social: Impacto sobre el bienestar económico y el desarrollo humano de la infancia." *Población & Sociedad* 22 (2): 101–34.

Sánchez Jiménez, Arturo. 2020. "Garantizados los recursos para Beca "Benito Juárez, asegura Gobierno." La Jornada, May 15. https://www.jornada.com.mx/ultimas/politica/2020/05/15/garantizados-los-recursos-de-beca-benito-juarez-asegura-gobierno-1961.html

Sánchez Talanquer, Mariano. 2020. "Mexico 2019: Personalistic Politics and Neoliberalism from the Left." *Revista de Ciencia Política* (Santiago) 40 (2): 401–30. https://doi.org/10.4067/S0718-090X2020005000113

Sandbrook, Richard, Marc Edelman, Patrick Heller, and Judith Teichman. 2007. *Social Democracy in the Global Periphery: Origins, Challenges, Prospects.* New York: Cambridge University Press.

Sauma, Pablo. 2013. "Análisis de la suficiencia de los montos de la transferencia de Avancemos." Unpublished memorándum.

Sauma, Pablo, and Juan Diego Trejos Solórzano. 2014. "Reducir la pobreza en Costa Rica es posible: Propuestas para la acción." Serie Cuadernos para el Desarrollo Humano I-2014. UNDP. http://nacionesunidas.or.cr/recursos/reducir-la-pobreza-en-costa-rica-es-posible-propuestas-para-la-accion

Scartascini, Carlos, Cesi Cruz, and Philip Keefer. 2018. "The Database of Political Institutions 2017 (DPI2017)." Inter-American Development Bank. https://doi.org/10.18235/0001027

Schady, Norbert R. 2000. "The Political Economy of Expenditures by the Peruvian Social Fund (FONCODES), 1991–95." *American Political Science Review* 94 (2): 289–304. https://doi.org/10.2307/2586013

Schady, Norbert, and Maria Caridad Araujo. 2008. "Cash Transfers, Conditions, and School Enrollment in Ecuador." *Economía* 8 (2): 43–77. https://doi.org/10.1596/1813-9450-3930

Schurmann, Anna T. 2009. "Review of the Bangladesh Female Secondary School Stipend Project Using a Social Exclusion Framework." *Journal of Health, Population, and Nutrition* 27 (4): 505–17.

Schwartzman, Simon. 2005. "Education-Oriented Social Programs in Brazil: The Impact of Bolsa Escola." Global Conference on Education Research in Developing Countries, Prague, Czech Republic. http://www.schwartzman.org.br/simon/pdf/bolsa_escola_eng.pdf

Seawright, Jason. 2016. *Multi-Method Social Science: Combining Qualitative and Quantitative Tools.* New York: Cambridge University Press.

Seawright, Jason, and John Gerring. 2008. "Case Selection Techniques in Case Study Research: A Menu of Qualitative and Quantitative Options." *Political Research Quarterly* 61 (2): 294–308. https://doi.org/10.1177/1065912907313077

SEDLAC (Socio-Economic Database for Latin America and the Caribbean). 2018. *Socio-Economic Database for Latin America and the Caribbean.* http://www.cedlas.econo.unlp.edu.ar/wp/en/estadisticas/sedlac/estadisticas/

Segura-Ubiergo, Alex. 2007. *The Political Economy of the Welfare State in Latin*

America: Globalization, Democracy, and Development. New York: Cambridge University Press.

Senado Notícias. 2020. "Senadores criticam decisão de ministro do TCU de suspender ampliação do BPC." *Senado Notícias*, March 16. https://www12.senado .leg.br/noticias/materias/2020/03/16/senadores-criticam-decisao-de-ministro -do-tcu-de-suspender-ampliacao-do-bpc

Simmons, Beth A., Frank Dobbin, and Geoffrey Garrett, eds. 2008. *The Global Diffusion of Markets and Democracy.* Cambridge: Cambridge University Press.

Simmons, Beth A., and Zachary Elkins. 2004. "The Globalization of Liberalization: Policy Diffusion in the International Political Economy." *American Political Science Review* 98 (1): 171–89. https://doi.org/10.1017/S0003055404001078

Simpson, Joshua P. 2018. "Do Donors Matter Most? An Analysis of Conditional Cash Transfer Adoption in Sub-Saharan Africa." *Global Social Policy* 18 (2): 143–68. https://doi.org/10.1177/1468018117741447

Siri, Gabriel. 2000. "Employment and Social Investment Funds in Latin America." Socio-Economic Technical Paper 7. International Labor Office. http://www.ilo .int/wcmsp5/groups/public/—-ed_emp/—-emp_policy/—-invest/documents /publication/wcms_asist_7591.pdf

Slipczuk, Martín. 2017. "Claves del proyecto de reforma previsional que aprobó el congreso." *Chequeado.com*, December 18. https://chequeado.com/el-explicador/claves- del-proyecto-de-reforma-previsional-que-se-trata-hoy-en-el-congreso/

Soares, Fábio Veras. 2012. "Bolsa Familia y Oportunidades: su evolución en perspectiva comparativa." In *Pobreza, transferencias condicionadas y sociedad*, edited by Mercedes González de la Rocha and Agustín Escobar Latapí, 311–39. Mexico City: Centro de Estudios Superiores en Antropología Social.

Soares, Fábio Veras, Rafael Perez Ribas, and Rafael Guerreiro Osório. 2010. "Evaluating the Impact of Brazil's Bolsa Família: Cash Transfer Programmes in Comparative Perspective." *Latin American Research Review* 45 (2): 173–90. https:// doi.org/10.1353/lar.2010.0017

Soares, Gláucio Ary Dillon, and Sonia Luiza Terron. 2008. "Dois Lulas: A geografia eleitoral da reeleição (Explorando conceitos, métodos e técnicas de análise geoespacial)." *Opinião Pública* 14 (2): 269–301. https://doi.org/10.1590/ S0104-62762008000200001

Soares, Sergei Suarez Dillon. 2012. "Bolsa Família, Its Design, Its Impacts and Possibilities for the Future." Working Papers 89. International Policy Centre for Inclusive Growth. https://ideas.repec.org/p/ipc/wpaper/89.html

Soares, Sergei, Rafael Osorio, Fábio Veras Soares, Marcelo Medeiros, and Eduardo Zepeda. 2009. "Conditional Cash Transfers in Brazil, Chile and Mexico: Impacts upon Inequality." *Estudios Económicos* (numero extraordinario): 207–24.

Solt, Frederick. 2016. "The Standardized World Income Inequality Database." *Social Science Quarterly* 97 (5): 1267–81. https://doi.org/10.1111/ssqu.12295

Soss, Joe. 1999. "Lessons of Welfare: Policy Design, Political Learning, and Political Action." *American Political Science Review* 93 (2): 363–80. https://doi.org/10.23 07/2585401

Stampini, Marco, and Leopoldo Tornarolli. 2012. "The Growth of Conditional Cash Transfers in Latin America and the Caribbean: Did They Go Too Far?" Policy Brief 185. Inter-American Development Bank. http://publications.iadb.org/handle/11319/1448

Standing, Guy. 2008. "How Cash Transfers Promote the Case for Basic Income." *Basic Income Studies* 3 (1): 1–30.

Starke, Peter. 2013. "Qualitative Methods for the Study of Policy Diffusion: Challenges and Available Solutions." *Policy Studies Journal* 41 (4): 561–82. https://doi.org/10.1111/psj.12032

Stein, Ernesto, Mariano Tommasi, Koldo Echebarría, Eduardo Lora, and Mark Payne. 2006. *The Politics of Policies: Economic and Social Progress in Latin America, 2006 Report.* Washington, DC: Inter-American Development Bank.

Stephens, John D. 1979. *The Transition from Capitalism to Socialism.* London: Macmillan.

Stern, Andy. 2016. *Raising the Floor: How a Universal Basic Income Can Renew Our Economy and Rebuild the American Dream.* New York: PublicAffairs.

Straschnoy, Mora. 2011. "Asignación Universal por Hijo para protección social y nuevo régimen de Asignaciones Familiares: Un análisis comparativo de los casos de Argentina y Uruguay." *Cátedra Paralela* 8: 111–28.

Straschnoy, Mora. 2015. "¿Para qué y por qué se implementan las condicionalidades en la política social argentina? Un análisis de las experiencias del Ingreso de Desarrollo Humano, el Programa Familias por la Inclusión Social y la Asignación Universal por Hijo." *Debate Público: Reflexión de Trabajo Social* 5 (9): 127–40.

Sugiyama, Natasha Borges. 2008. "Theories of Policy Diffusion: Social Sector Reform in Brazil." *Comparative Political Studies* 41 (2): 193–216. https://doi.org/10.1177/0010414007300916

Sugiyama, Natasha Borges. 2011. "The Diffusion of Conditional Cash Transfer Programs in the Americas." *Global Social Policy* 11 (2–3): 250–78. https://doi.org/10.1177/1468018111421295

Sugiyama, Natasha Borges. 2012a. "Bottom-Up Policy Diffusion: National Emulation of a Conditional Cash Transfer Program in Brazil." *Publius* 42 (1): 25–51. https://doi.org/10.1093/publius/pjr019

Sugiyama, Natasha Borges. 2012b. *Diffusion of Good Government: Social Sector Reforms in Brazil.* Notre Dame, IN: University of Notre Dame Press.

Sugiyama, Natasha Borges, and Wendy Hunter. 2013. "Whither Clientelism? Good Governance and Brazil's Bolsa Família Program." *Comparative Politics* 46 (1): 43–62. https://doi.org/10.5129/001041513807709365

Suplicy, Eduardo Matarazzo. 2004. *Renda de cidadania: A saída é pela porta.* 3rd ed. São Paulo: Cortez Editora.

Suplicy, Eduardo Matarazzo. 2006. "Citizen's Basic Income: The Answer is Blowing in the Wind." Discussion Paper 152. U.S. Basic Income Guarantee Network. https://usbig.net/papers/152-Suplicy-blowin.pdf

Suplicy, Eduardo Matarazzo. 2007. "Citizen's Basic Income." Special Report. Latin

America Program, Woodrow Wilson International Center for Scholars. https://www.wilsoncenter.org/sites/default/files/LAP_CitizensBasicIncome.pdf

Suplicy, Eduardo Matarazzo, and Cristovam Buarque. 1997. "Garantia de Renda Mínima para Erradicar a Pobreza: O debate e a experiência brasileiros." *Estudos Avançados* 11 (30): 79–93. https://doi.org/10.1590/S0103-40141997000200007

Szafranko, Agustín. 2019. "La pobreza alcanzó al 40,8% de los argentinos en el tercer trimestre, según datos de la UCA." Cronista, May 12. https://www.cronista.com/economia-politica/La-pobreza-alcanzo-al-40-8-de-los-argentinos-en-el-tercer-trimestre-segun-datos-de-la-UCA-20191205-0051.html http://www.ciepp.org.ar/images/ciepp/docstrabajo/doc%2071.pdf

Tarricone, Manuel. 2018. "Macri: 'Quiero trabajar para que (. . .) la Asignación no sólo continúe, sino que se extienda a todos, incluyendo a los hijos de monotributistas.'" *Chequeado.com*, December 7. https://chequeado.com/ultimas-noticias/macri-quiero-trabajar-para-que-la-asignacion-no-solo-continue-sino-que-se-extienda-a-todos-incluyendo-a-los-hijos-de-monotributistas-2018/

Tavares de Almeida, Maria Hermínia. 2005. "The Social Policies of Lula's Administration." *Novos Estudos—CEBRAP* 1 (SE): 1–11.

Teichman, Judith. 2008. "Redistributive Conflict and Social Policy in Latin America." *World Development* 36 (3): 446–60. https://doi.org/10.1016/j.worlddev.2007.04.010

TEJPF (Tribunal Electoral del Poder Judicial de la Federació). 2019. "Procedimiento especial sancionador." SRE-PSC-71/2019. https://www.te.gob.mx/salasreg/ejecutoria/sentencias/especializada/SRE-PSC-0071-2019.pdf

Tendler, Judith. 2000. "Why are Social Funds So Popular?" In *Local Dynamics in an Era of Globalization: 21st Century Catalysts for Development*, edited by Simon J. Evenett, Weiping Wu, and Shahid Yusuf, 114–29. New York: Oxford University Press.

Tepperman, Jonathan. 2017. *The Fix: How Countries Use Crises to Solve the World's Worst Problems*. New York: Tim Duggan Books.

Thomé, Débora. 2013. *O Bolsa Família e a social-democracia*. Rio de Janeiro: Fundação Getulio Vargas.

Timmons, Jeffrey F. 2005. "The Fiscal Contract: States, Taxes, and Public Services." *World Politics* 57 (4): 530–67. https://doi.org/10.1353/wp.2006.0015

Toledo, Marcelo. 2017. "Bolsonaro visita festa do peão e critica Bolsa Família e legislação ambiental." *Folha de S. Paulo*, August 26. https://www1.folha.uol.com.br/poder/2017/08/1913378-na-festa-do-peao-bolsonaro-critica-bolsa-familia-e-legislacao-ambiental.shtml

Tomazelli, Idiana. 2020. "Nordeste fica só com 3% das concessões do Bolsa Família." *O Estado de S. Paulo*, March 5. https://economia.estadao.com.br/noticias/geral,nordeste-fica-so-com-3-das-concessoes-do-bolsa-familia,70003220401

Tomazini, Carla. 2019. "Beyond Consensus: Ideas and Advocacy Coalitions around Cash Transfer Programs in Brazil and Mexico." *Critical Policy Studies* 13 (1): 23–42. https://doi.org/10.1080/19460171.2017.1352529

Trejos Solórzano, Juan Diego. 2009. "Programas selectivos y gasto social: Situación durante 2008, evolución reciente y perspectivas futuras." Ponencia para el Informe Estado de la Nación. Estado de la Nación. https://estadonacion.or.cr/files/biblioteca_virtual/015/Trejos_2009.pdf

Trejos Solórzano, Juan Diego. 2012. "Pobreza, desigualdad y oportunidades: Una visión de largo plazo." Serie de Divulgación Económica 16. Insituto de Investigaciones en Ciencias Económicas, Universidad de Costa Rica. http://www.iice.ucr.ac.cr/series/serie_16.pdf

Trujillo, Lucía, and Martín Retamozo. 2019. "Políticas contra la pobreza en Argentina (2002–2015): Alcances, limitaciones y desafíos." *Reflexiones* 98 (1): 89–110. https://doi.org/10.15517/rr.v98i1.33004

Tsebelis, George. 2002. *Veto Players: How Political Institutions Work*. Princeton, NJ: Princeton University Press.

Tutu, Desmond. 2006. "The Role of Social Transfers in. Fighting Poverty and Promoting Development." Presented at the Economic Policy Research Institute, Capetown, South Africa, November 2.

UIS (UNESCO Institute for Statistics). 2017. "UIS Statistics." UNESCO. http://data.uis.unesco.org/

UNDOC (United Nations Office on Drugs and Crime). 2018. "United Nations Surveys on Crime Trends and the Operations of Criminal Justice Systems (UN-CTS)." https://www.unodc.org/unodc/en/data-and-analysis/United-Nations-Surveys-on-Crime-Trends-and-the-Operations-of-Criminal-Justice-Systems.html

UNDP (United Nations Development Programme). 2007. *El Estado Del Estado En Bolivia: Informe Nacional Sobre Desarrollo Humano En Bolivia*. La Paz, Bolivia: UNDP.

UNDP (United Nations Development Programme). 2016. "Brazilian Triangular Cooperation in Social Protection: Contribution to the 2030 Agenda." Development Impact Group. New York. https://www.undp.org/content/undp/en/home/librarypage/development-impact/Brazilian_triangular_cooperation.html

UNESCO (United Nations Educational, Scientific and Cultural Organization). 2016. *Informe de Resultados TERCE: Logros de Aprendizaje*. Santiago, Chile. https://unesdoc.unesco.org/ark:/48223/pf0000243532

UNICEF (United Nations Children's Fund). 2018. "Child Labour Data." 2018. https://data.unicef.org/topic/child-protection/child-labour/

UNICEF (United Nations Children's Fund), ANSES (Administración Nacional de la Seguridad Social), Ministerio de Desarrollo Social de la Nación (Argentina), Universidad de Buenos Aires, and CEDLAS (Center for Distributive, Labor and Social Studies). 2017. *Análisis y Propuestas de Mejoras Para Ampliar La Asignación Universal Por Hijo 2017*. Buenos Aires: UNICEF/ANSES.

Un1ón Jalisco. 2019. "Retraso en pago de Becas Benito Juárez causa molestia y dudas," May 19. https://www.unionjalisco.mx/articulo/2019/05/23/educacion/retraso-en-pago-de-becas-benito-juarez-causa-molestia-y-dudas

U.S. Department of Labor. 2006. "U.S. Department of Labor's 2005 Findings on the Worst Forms of Child Labor." Bureau of International Labor Affairs, U.S.

Department of Labor. https://www.dol.gov/sites/dolgov/files/ILAB/child_labor_reports/tda2005/tda2005.pdf
U.S. Department of Labor. 2018. "U.S. Department of Labor's 2017 Findings on the Worst Forms of Child Labor." Bureau of International Labor Affairs, U.S. Department of Labor. https://www.dol.gov/sites/dolgov/files/ILAB/legacy/files/ChildLaborReport_Book.pdf
Valencia Lomelí, Enrique, and Rodolfo Aguirre Reveles. 1998. "Discursos, acciones y controversias de la política gubernamental frente a la pobreza." In *Los rostros de la pobreza: El debate, Tomo I*, edited by Luis Rigoberto Gallardo Gómez and Joaquín Osorio Goicoechea, 21–93. Mexico City: Editorial Limusa.
Valfré, Vinícius, and Adriana Fernandes. 2020. "Bolsa Família já tem fila de 3,5 milhões de pessoas." *O Estado de S. Paulo*, February 18. https://politica.estadao.com.br/noticias/geral,fila-do-bolsa-familia-ja-tem-3-5-milhoes-de-pessoas-municipios-voltam-a-dar-cesta-basica,70003201822
Van der Veen, Robert J., and Philippe Van Parijs. 2006. "A Capitalist Road to Communism." *Basic Income Studies* 1 (1): 1–23. https://doi.org/10.1007/BF00239129
Van Parijs, Philippe. 2013. "The Universal Basic Income: Why Utopian Thinking Matters, and How Sociologists Can Contribute to It." *Politics & Society* 41 (2): 171–82. https://doi.org/10.1177/0032329213483106
Van Parijs, Philippe. 2018. "Basic Income and the Left: A European Debate." In *Basic Income and the Left: A European Debate*, edited by Philippe Van Parijs, 1–4. London: Social Europe Edition.
Van Parijs, Philippe, and Yannick Vanderborght. 2017. *Basic Income: A Radical Proposal for a Free Society and a Sane Economy*. Cambridge: Harvard University Press.
Van Thienen, Josefina. 2015. "La implementación de las políticas sociales en Argentina: Un análisis exploratorio de las causas de los niveles de centralización y concentración." Licenciatura, Victoria, Argentina: Universidad de San Andrés. http://repositorio.udesa.edu.ar/jspui/bitstream/10908/12019/1/%5BP%5D%5BW%5D%20T.L.%20Pol.%20Van%20Thienen,%20Josefina.pdf
Varoufakis, Yanis. 2016. "The Universal Right to Capital Income." *Project Syndicate*, October 31. https://www.project-syndicate.org/commentary/basic-income-funded-by-capital-income-by-yanis-varoufakis-2016-10
Vega, Andrea. 2019. "'Ya no me llega el apoyo, es un dolpe duro': Familias relatan cómo les afectó la eliminación de Prospera." *Animal Político*, August 28, sec. Animal Politico. https://www.animalpolitico.com/2019/08/becas-prospera-beneficiarios-familias/
Villalobos Álvarez, María Lourdes. 2014. "El planeamiento, ejecución y evaluación de las transferencias monetarias condicionadas: Orígenes y transformaciones del programa Avancemos, Costa Rica." Instituto de Investigaciones en Ciencias Económicas, Universidad de Costa Rica.
Villalobos, Geysel. 2016. "Fonabe: ¿Beneficio o penitencia?" *La Nación* (Costa Rica), April 1. https://www.nacion.com/opinion/foros/fonabe-beneficio-o-penitencia/RGN5PNIWDBHTLEVXNGHVCEFSTA/story/

Villarreal F., Evelyn, and Steffan Gómez A. 2010. "Costa Rica 2009: Enfrentando la crisis internacional en plena campaña electoral." *Revista de Ciencia Política* (Universidad Católica de Chile) 30 (2): 275–96. https://doi.org/10.4067/S0718 -090X2010000200006

Víquez, Diego. 2010. "Estratificación social y movilidad social ascendente: Implicaciones para la convivencia democrática y la cohesión social." In *Costa Rica en tiempo preelectoral: Cohesión social, reforma del estado y descentralización. retos y perspectivas desde diversos actores*, edited by Yahaira Ceciliano, 29–42. San Joséa: FLACSCO.

Walker, Jack L. 1969. "The Diffusion of Innovations among the American States." *American Political Science Review* 63 (3): 880–99. https://doi.org/10.2307/195 4434

Waltenberg, Fábio D. 2013. "Are Latin Americans—Brazilians in Particular—Willing to Support an Unconditional Citizen's Income?" In *Citizen's Income and Welfare Regimes in Latin America: From Cash Transfers to Rights*, edited by Rubén M. Lo Vuolo, 141–67. Basingstoke, UK: Palgrave Macmillan.

Weitz-Shapiro, Rebecca. 2006. "Partisanship and Protest: The Politics of Workfare Distribution in Argentina." *Latin American Research Review* 41 (3): 122–47. https://doi.org/10.1353/lar.2006.0051

Weyland, Kurt. 2004. "Neoliberalism and Democracy in Latin America: A Mixed Record." *Latin American Politics and Society* 46 (1): 135–57.

Weyland, Kurt. 2006. *Bounded Rationality and Policy Diffusion: Social Sector Reform in Latin America*. Princeton, NJ: Princeton University Press.

Weyland, Kurt. 2009. "The Rise of Latin America's Two Lefts: Insights from Rentier State Theory." *Comparative Politics* 41 (2): 145–64. https://doi.org/10.5129/001 041509X12911362971918

Weyland, Kurt. 2010. "The Performance of Leftist Governments in Latin America: Conceptual and Theoretical Issues." In *Leftist Governments in Latin America: Successes and Shortcomings*, edited by Kurt Weyland, Raúl L. Madrid, and Wendy Hunter, 1–27. New York: Cambridge University Press.

Weyland, Kurt. 2013. "The Threat from the Populist Left." *Journal of Democracy* 24 (3): 18–32. https://doi.org/10.1353/jod.2013.0045

Weyland, Kurt, Raúl L. Madrid, and Wendy Hunter, eds. 2010. *Leftist Governments in Latin America: Successes and Shortcomings*. New York: Cambridge University Press.

Wiesehomeier, Nina, and Kenneth Benoit. 2009. "Presidents, Parties, and Policy Competition." *Journal of Politics* 71 (4): 1435–47. https://doi.org/10.1017/S0022 381609990193

Williamson, John, ed. 1990. *Latin American Adjustment: How Much Has Happened?* Washington, DC: Peterson Institute for International Economics.

Wilson, Robin. 2018. "Universal Basic Income: A Disarmingly Simple Idea—and Fad." In *Basic Income and the Left: A European Debate*, 61–66. London: Social Europe Edition.

World Bank. 2001. "Brazil—Eradicating Child Labor in Brazil." 21858-BR. World

Bank. http://documents.worldbank.org/curated/en/233561468770341412/Brazil-Eradicating-child-labor-in-Brazil

World Bank. 2005. "Argentina—Sources of Growth: Seeking Sustained Economic Growth with Social Equity." 32553-AR. World Bank. http://documents.worldbank.org/curated/en/500031468003029334/Argentina-Sources-of-growth-seeking-sustained-economic-growth-with-social-equity

World Bank. 2006. "Basic Education in Bolivia : Challenges for 2006–2010." 35073-BO. World Bank. http://documents.worldbank.org/curated/en/571371468208459467/Basic-Education-in-Bolivia-challenges-for-2006-2010

World Bank. 2020. "World Development Indicators." October 10. http://datatopics.worldbank.org/world-development-indicators/

Yanes, Pablo. 2013. "Targeting and Conditionalities in Mexico: The End of a Cash Transfer Model?" In *Citizen's Income and Welfare Regimes in Latin America: From Cash Transfers to Rights*, edited by Rubén Lo Vuolo, 67–86. Basingstoke, UK: Palgrave Macmillan.

Yang, Andrew. 2018. *The War on Normal People: The Truth about America's Disappearing Jobs and Why Universal Basic Income Is Our Future*. New York: Hachette Books.

Yasbek, Maria Carmelita. 2004. "O programa Fome Zero no contexto das políticas sociais brasileiras." *São Paulo Em Perspectiva* 18 (2): 104–12. https://doi.org/10.1590/S0102-88392004000200011

Yaschine, Iliana. 1999. "The Changing Anti-Poverty Agenda: What Can the Mexican Case Tell Us?" *IDS Bulletin* 30 (2): 47–60. https://doi.org/10.1111/j.1759-5436.1999.mp30002006.x

Yaschine, Iliana. 2015. *¿Oportunidades? Política social y movilidad intergeneracional en México*. Mexico City: El Colegio de México.Yaschine, Iliana, and Mónica E. Orozco. 2010. "The Evolving Anti-Poverty Agenda in Mexico: The Political Economy of Progresa and Oportunidades." In *Conditional Cash Transfers in Latin America*, edited by Michelle Adato and John Hoddinott, 55–79. Baltimore: Johns Hopkins University Press.

YouTube JSerra2010. 2010. *Lançamento do programa Bolsa Família—2003*. https://www.youtube.com/watch?v=Xz80IwOY9DY

YouTube Tony Show. 2016. *Cristovão Buarque faz duras crticias ao modelo de Bolsa familia aplicado pelo PT*. https://www.youtube.com/watch?v=eik6_r3EVC8

Zambrana, Gilmar. 2010. "Educación y movilidad social en Bolivia." Fundación INESAD. https://www.inesad.edu.bo/bcde2010/contributed/d13_42.pdf

Zamora, Daniel. 2017. "The Case against a Basic Income." *Jacobin*, December 28. http://jacobinmag.com/2017/12/universal-basic-income-inequality-work

Zaga Szenker, Daniel. 2009. "Programa Familias por la Inclusión Social: Un análisis comparado." Documento de Trabajo 171. CIEPP.

Zedillo, Ernesto. 2009. "Keynote Address: A Look at PROGRESA's Genesis." The Origins, Implementation, and Spread of Conditional Cash Transfer Programs in Latin America Conference, University of Texas at Austin, 17 April. Zucco, Cesar. 2008. "The President's 'New' Constituency: Lula and the Pragmatic Vote in Brazil's 2006 Presidential Elections." *Journal of Latin American Studies* 40 (1): 29–49. https://doi.org/10.1017/S0022216X07003628

Zucco, Cesar. 2013. "When Payouts Pay Off: Conditional Cash Transfers and Voting Behavior in Brazil 2002–10." *American Journal of Political Science* 57 (4): 810–22. https://doi.org/10.1111/ajps.12026

Zucco, Cesar. 2015. "The Impacts of Conditional Cash Transfers in Four Presidential Elections (2002–2014)." *Brazilian Political Science Review* 9 (1): 135–49. https://doi.org/10.1590/1981-38212014000200006

Zucco, Cesar, and Timothy J. Power. 2013. "Bolsa Família and the Shift in Lula's Electoral Base, 2002–2006: A Reply to Bohn." *Latin American Research Review* 48 (2): 3–24. https://doi.org/10.1353/lar.2013.0018.

Zylberkan, Mariana. 2020. "Fila do Bolsa Família vai de zero a 490 mil no 1º ano do governo Bolsonaro." *VEJA*, January 24. https://veja.abril.com.br/politica/fila-do-bolsa-familia-vai-de-zero-a-490-mil-no-1o-ano-do-governo-bolsonaro/

Interviews

Amadeo, Eduardo. Argentina's secretary of social development during the Menem administration and member of the Argentine Congress's Pension and Social Security Commission when AUH was adopted. Buenos Aires, Argentina, October 2012.

Antezana, Marcelo. Bolivian senator for the opposition Plan Progress for Bolivia/National Convergence (PPB-CN) party and critic of the implementation of Bono Juancito Pinto. La Paz, Bolivia, November 2012.

Apaza, Pablo. Coordinator of social policy, including cash transfer programs, for the city of El Alto. El Alto, Bolivia, November 2012.

Arias, Oscar. President of Costa Rica responsible for launching Avancemos. San José, Costa Rica, June 2013.

Barahona, Manuel. Economics professor specializing in social policy at Costa Rica's Universidad Nacional and part of the technical team that designed Avancemos. Heredia, Costa Rica, May 2013.

Bertanou, Fabio. Specialist on labor markets and social protection at the International Labor Office's (ILO) Argentina office who has researched Asignación Universal por Hijo. Buenos Aires, Argentina, September 2012.

Cordero, Juan Manuel. Costa Rica's vice-minister of labor and social security during the Chinchilla administration. San José, Costa Rica, June 2013.

Garnier, Leonardo. Costa Rica's education minister during the Arias and Chinchilla administrations. San José, Costa Rica, June 2013.

Gasparini, Leonardo. Director of the Center of Distributive, Labor and Social Studies (CEDLAS) at the National University of La Plata and expert on conditional cash transfer programs in Latin America. La Plata, Argentina, October 2012.

Golbert, Laura. Social policy researcher at think tank Center for the Study of State and Society (CEDES) who has researched Asignación Universal por Hijo. Buenos Aires, Argentina, October 2012.

Hernani-Limarino, Werner. Executive director at the think tank Fundación URU who has researched Bono Juancito Pinto. La Paz, Bolivia, October 2012.

Herrera, Rosibel. Coordinator of Avancemos at Costa Rica's Mixed Institute for Social Assistance (IMAS) during the Chinchilla administration. San José, Costa Rica, May 2013.

Li, José Antonio. Executive president of Costa Rica's Mixed Institute for Social Assistance (IMAS), the institution in charge of Avancemos, during 2007–10. San José, Costa Rica, May 2013.

Lo Valvo, Ezequiel. Manager of planning at the National Social Security Administration (ANSES) when AUH was enacted. Buenos Aires, Argentina, October 2012.

Lo Vuolo, Rubén. Academic director and principal researcher at the think tank Interdisciplinary Center for the Study of Public Policies (CIEPP) and long-time proponent of universal basic income in Argentina. Buenos Aires, Argentina, September 2012.

Meave, Erick. Economist specializing in social policy at the Bolivian Planning Ministry's Social and Economic Policy Analysis Unit (UDAPE) when Bono Juancito Pinto was enacted. La Paz, Bolivia, October 2012.

Morales, María José. Member of the Avancemos technical team during 2006–08 who later evaluated the program for the Latin American Faculty of Social Sciences (FLACSO). San José, Costa Rica, May 2013.

Murillo, Orlando. Education economist who has worked for the Bolivian Education Ministry and was coordinator of the Bolivian Educational Policy Observatory (OSPE-B), an education think tank responsible an early evaluation of Bono Juancito Pinto. La Paz, Bolivia, October 2012.

Novakovsky, Irene. Coordinator of the Argentine Social Development Ministry's Systems for the Monitoring and Evaluation of Social Policies (SIEMPRO) during the Menem and de la Rúa administrations and an early proponent of conditional cash transfers in the country. Buenos Aires, Argentina, October 2012.

Paz Arauco, Verónica. Coordinator of the Bolivian National Human Development Report at the United Nations Development Programme (UNDP) and a Bolivian representative for the Commitment to Equity project. La Paz, Bolivia, November 2012.

Repetto, Fabián. Director of the social protection program at the think tank Center for the Implementation of Public Policies for Equity and Growth (CIPPEC) who has researched cash transfer proposals in Argentina including Asignación Universal por Hijo. Buenos Aires, Argentina, September 2012.

Roca, Emilia. Undersecretary of social security policy at the Labor and Social Security Ministry during the Fernández de Kirchner administration when AUH was enacted. Buenos Aires, Argentina, October 2012.

Rofman, Rafael. Lead Specialist in social protection at the Human Development Department of the World Bank's Regional Office for Latin America. Buenos Aires, Argentina, September 2012.

Sauma, Pablo. Economics professor specializing in social policy, poverty, and inequality at Universidad de Costa Rica and part of the technical team that designed Avancemos. San José, Costa Rica, May 2013.

Trejos, Juan Diego. Economics professor specializing in social policy, poverty, and inequality at Universidad de Costa Rica and part of the technical team that designed Avancemos. San José, Costa Rica, May 2013.

Valverde, Carla. Member of the Avancemos technical team during the program's 2008–09 expansion. San José, Costa Rica, May 2013.

Vargas, Olga Sonia. Coordinator of Avancemos at Costa Rica's Mixed Institute for Social Assistance (IMAS), the institution in charge of the program, until 2012. San José, Costa Rica, May 2013.

Vinocur, Pablo. Argentina's secretary of social policy during the de la Rúa administration and director of the Human Development graduate program at the Latin American Faculty of Social Sciences (FLACSO). Buenos Aires, Argentina, October 2012.

Víquez, Diego. Executive president of Costa Rica's Mixed Institute for Social Assistance (IMAS), the institution in charge of Avancemos, during the program's 2006–07 launch. San José, Costa Rica, May 2013.

Yáñez, Ernesto. Former vice-president of Bolivia's Central Bank who has researched Bono Juancito Pinto. La Paz, Bolivia, October 2012.

INDEX

Administración Nacional de la Seguridad Social (ANSES), 162–63
Africa-Brazil Cooperation Program on Social Development, 128
aguinaldo, 152, 178, 180
Alemán, Arnoldo, 40
Alianza para el Trabajo, la Justicia y la Educación, 156
Alliance for Work, Justice and Education, 156
Alvarado, Carlos, 176–77
AMLO (López Obrador, Andrés Manuel), 176, 182–86, 194–95
AMLO Scholarships, 183
Animas, Leticia, 183
ANSES (Administración Nacional de la Seguridad Social), 162–63
Arias, Oscar, 17, 29, 154–61, 165, 190–91
Asignación por Embarazo, 154–55
Asignación Universal por Hijo, 40, 130, 136, 153–57, 160–63, 165–66, 177–78
Asignaciones Familiares (Uruguay), 154
assistencialismo, 11, 18, 37, 43–45, 67, 73, 76, 156–57, 171, 176, 182–83, 185, 195
AUH (Asignación Universal por Hijo), 40, 130, 136, 153–57, 160–63, 165–66, 177–78
Avancemos, 29, 129, 135–38, 140–44, 163, 165–66, 176–77

Barbeito, Alberto, 158
basic income cct; conditionality enforcement of, 4–5, 64–66, 69, 82–83, 86–89, 151–52, 163; diffusion of, 1–4, 16–17, 45–46, 121–22, 126–29, 166, 171; stipend structure of, 2–3, 5, 62–63, 70, 85, 87, 89–90, 112–14, 116–17, 130, 133, 145–46, 154, 159, 172, 183–85; targeting of, 2, 4–5, 17, 63, 68–70, 86–87, 90–91, 95, 114, 130, 132, 137–38, 145, 150–51, 154, 169, 171, 179, 182
basic income movement, 70, 77–80, 82, 90–91, 158, 172
Beca Escolar (Ecuador), 126
Becas AMLO, 183
Becas para el Bienestar Benito Juárez, 183
Benito Juárez Well-Being Scholarships, 183
BID (Banco Interamericano de Desarrollo), 6, 16, 26, 28–30, 37, 44, 61, 119–26, 134, 135, 140, 148, 158–59, 165–66, 173
BJA (Bono Juana Azurduy), 145, 152
BJP (Bono Juancito Pinto), 39, 129–30, 135–36, 144–46, 149–53, 163, 165–66
Bolivia; gas nationalization, 145, 149–50; military of, 149, 151
Bolivian Fiscal Petroleum Deposits, 149
Bolsa Alimentação, 55–57, 59, 63, 69
Bolsa Escola (subnational), 51–53, 126
Bolsa Escola Federal, 24, 38, 47, 52, 54–56, 58–59, 61, 63, 69, 95, 117
Bolsa Família; adoption of, 25, 38–39, 53–62; conditionality enforcement of, 2, 64–66, 82, 91, 117; design of, 4, 60–64, 86–90, 113–15; diffusion of, 1–4, 16–17, 45–46, 121–22, 126–29, 166, 171; expansion of, 62–64
Bolsonaro, Jair, 18, 175, 179–182, 195
Bono de Desarrollo Humano, 126
Bono Educación, 148
Bono Esperanza, 39, 148–49
Bono Juana Azurduy, 145, 152
Bono Juancito Pinto, 39, 129–30, 135–36, 144–46, 149–53, 163, 165–66
Bono Salud, 148
Bono Solidario (Bonosol), 125–26, 148, 150
Bonosol, 125–26, 148, 150

263

Brasil Sém Miseria, 62
Brazil Learning Initiative for a World without Poverty, 128
Brazil Without Misery, 62
Brazil, Northeast, 46, 57, 67, 179–82, 195
Brazilian Social Democratic Party (PSDB), 51, 53–55, 60
Buarque, Cristovam, 49–53, 56, 58, 61, 65–66, 689, 71–73, 78, 126
Buenos Aires, 154

Cadastro Único, 55, 60
Caja Costarricense del Seguro Social (CCSS), 138, 144
Caldera, Rafael, 40
Camargo, José Márcio, 38, 50
Carazo, Rodrigo, 142
Cárdenas, Cuauhtémoc, 38, 77
Cardoso, Fernando Henrique, 24, 38–39, 47, 49–60, 62, 65–66, 68, 70, 73, 84
Carrió, Elisa, 40, 161
Cartão Alimentação, 57, 59–61, 63
Castañeda, Jorge, 14
CCSS (National Health Service, Costa Rica), 138, 144
cct; basic income; see basic income cct; see Bolsa Familia; evaluation of, 37, 76–77, 90, 122–23, 125, 139, 141, 159, 189; human capital; see human capital cct; see Progresa/ Oportunuidades; models of, 4–6, 84–91, 95, 112–17, 123–29, 166, 169, 171–72; popular backlash against, 2, 4–5, 17, 22, 48, 51, 54, 64–66, 68, 69–70, 73, 82–83, 85, 87–88, 91, 95–96, 113, 117, 122, 126–27, 130, 133, 151, 154, 160, 163, 165, 169, 171–73, 189; relationship to universal basic income, 67, 84; retrenchment, 176, 177–8; subnational, 1, 38–39, 49–54, 56, 126, 148–49, 154; surveys on, 67, 82
cct adoption; Argentina, 25, 39–40, 153–161; Bolivia, 144–52; Brazil, 25, 38–39, 53–62; Colombia, 25, 125; Costa Rica, 136–142, 176–77; determinants of, 22–27, 31–34; Ecuador, 125–26; Honduras, 25, 125; Mexico, 25, 37–38. 73–77; Nicaragua, 125; role of diffusion in; see cct diffusion; role of economic crisis in, 25, 125–26, 154, 165; role of ideology in, 23, 31–36, 44–45; role of inequality, 24; role of political competition in, 23–24, 33–34

cct cancellation; Argentina, 161; Costa Rica, 29, 139–140; Mexico, 183–84; Nicaragua, 40, 170–71; Venezuela, 40, 170–71
cct conditionality; and beneficiary exclusion, 69–70, 79, in Brazil, 2, 64–66, 82, 91, 117; effectiveness of, 3–4, 84–85; lax enforcement of, 2, 4–5, 17, 22, 48, 51, 54, 64–66, 68, 69–70, 73, 82–83, 85, 87–88, 91, 95–96, 113, 117, 122, 126–27, 130, 133, 151, 154, 160, 163, 165, 169, 171–73, 189; in Mexico, 2, 88–89
cct coverage; determinants of, 17, 98–112; effect of ideology on, 17, 98–100, 103–12, 119–20, 172; levels of, 3, 13, 17–18, 48, 62–63, 76–77, 87–88, 95–100, 103–12, 119, 127, 130, 137, 141–42, 146, 155, 162–63, 172, 176–78, 187
cct design; human capital versus basic income, 4–6, 84–91, 95, 112–17, 123–29, 166, 169, 171–72; index, 113–14, 117–18; Mexico versus Brazil, 2, 4, 17, 69–70, 86–91, 113–14, 169, 171
cct diffusion, 1–2, 8, 22, 25–27, 31–34, 101, 119, 170; horizontal, 120, 123–24, 126–29, 172; mechanisms of, 120–21; of Brazilian program, 1–4, 16–17, 45–46, 121–22, 126–29, 166, 171; of Mexican cct, 6, 17, 122–26, 140, 166, 172; role of ideology in, 6, 120–24, 129, 166, 170–172; role of IFIs in, 6, 17, 26, 35–36, 42, 44, 47, 56, 61, 119–22, 124–26, 128, 140, 145, 148, 154, 158–60, 165–66, 171–72, 174; to Africa, 127–29; vertical, 120, 123–26, 172; two-track, 6, 122–29, 133–34, 166
cct effects; on child labor, 12, 77, 188; on education, 12, 139, 188–89; on inequality, 12; on politics, 13, 35, 49, 67, 101, 121–22, 171; on poverty (long-term), 12–13, 188–89; on poverty (short-term), 12
cct targeting; of basic income cct, 4–5, 17, 63, 68–70, 86–87, 90–91, 95, 114, 130, 132, 137–38, 145, 150–51, 154, 169, 171, 179, 182; of human capital cct, 2, 4–5, 17, 69, 76, 86–87, 90–91,95, 114, 130, 132, 137, 142, 159, 169, 171; errors of exclusion, 59, 86, 181; errors of inclusion, 63, 86, 181
Censo del Bienestar, 185–86, 195
center, attitudes on redistribution, 41–42
Chávez, Hugo, 7, 14–15, 21, 40
child labor, cct effects on, 12, 77, 188

Children's Mission, 126
Chile Solidario, 29, 125–26, 140, 148
Chinchilla, Laura, 142
Christmas bonus, 152, 178, 180
Citizens' Action Party (PAC), 136, 175–76
Ciudadanía Porteña, 154
clientelism, 11, 18, 37, 43–45, 67, 73, 76, 156–57, 171, 176, 182–83, 185, 195
Clinton, Hilary, 181
Cole, George D. H., 80
Collor de Melo, Fernando, 49
Colom, Alvaro, 115
commodities; boom, 12, 15, 25, 39, 149, 157; bust, 175
communism, 7, 14
CONAPO (Consejo Nacional de Población), 73
conditional cash transfer. *See* cct
Consejo Nacional de Población, 73
Correa, Rafael, 15
COVID-19, 182
Crecemos, 177

da Silva, Luiz Inácio Lula, 5–6, 16–18, 22, 37–39, 45, 46–50, 54–68, 69–71, 73, 84–85, 95–96, 117, 120–22, 125–128, 134, 149, 168, 169, 171–75, 194–95
Database of Political Institutions, 31, 101
Dataset on Political Ideology of Presidents and Parties in Latin America, 7, 9, 16, 28–29, 35, 98, 114, 130
de la Rúa, Fernando, 156, 158
debt crisis, 10, 14–15, 42–43, 73–74, 136, 138–39, 159
del Val, Enrique, 76
Democratic Party (United States), 80–81
Department for International Development (United Kingdom), 128
DFA (Department for International Development, United Kingdom), 128
Diffusion. *See* cct diffusion
Dignity Income (Renta Dignidad), 145, 148, 152
Duhalde, Eduardo, 156, 159, 165

economic crisis; 1980s, 10, 14–15, 42–43, 73–74, 136, 138–39, 159; 2010s commodity bust, 175; Argentina, 156, 158–59; Colombia, 25, 125; Ecuador, 125; global financial, 25, 141–42, 154, 161, 165, 177; 25, 74; Tequila Crisis, 25, 74

Education Attainment Dataset, 30, 101
Education Bonus (Bono Educación), 148
education; access to, 12, 34–35, 41–42, 71–75, 121, 135–36, 138–39, 145–47, 157–58, 183–84, 186–87, 189, 192; effects of ccts on, 12, 139, 188–89; quality of, 12–13, 18, 135, 169–70, 189–194, 196; spending on, 135–36, 138, 192
El Alto, 39, 145, 148, 164–65
emergency social funds, 43–44, 148; in Bolivia, 148, clientelism in, 43–44
errors, in targeting of ccts, 59, 82, 86, 181
Ethical Family Income, 29
event history analysis, 31, 34, 170

Familias (Familias por la Inclusión Social), 159–162, 164–66
Familias en Acción, 25, 125
Familias por la Inclusión Social, 159–162, 164–66
Families for Social Inclusion Program, 159–162, 164–66
Families in Action, 25, 125
Family Allowance Program, Phase 2 (PRAF-II, Honduras), 25, 36–37, 125
Family Allowances (Asignaciones Familiares, Uruguay), 154
Family Scholarship (Brazil). *See* Bolsa Família
Farabundo Martí Front for National Liberation, 115–16
Federal School Scholarship (Brazil). *See* Bolsa Escola Federal
Fernández de Kirchner, Cristina, 17, 22, 39–40, 130, 153–54, 159–163, 165–66, 173, 177
FMLN (Farabundo Martí Front for National Liberation), 115–16
FODESAF (Social Development and Family Allowance Fund), 138–39
Fome Zero, 45, 47, 50, 55–62, 66, 84, 117, 121
FONABE (National Scholarship Fund), 144, 177
Fondo de Desarrollo y Asignaciones Familiares, 138–39
Fondo Nacional de Becas (Costa Rica), 144, 177
Fox, Vicente, 77
Frente Farabundo Martí para la Liberación Nacional, 115–16
Frente Nacional contra la Pobreza, 158
Frente para la Victoria, 39

266 INDEX

Friedman, Milton, 80, 82
Front for Victory, 39

Galbraith, John Kenneth, 80–81
Gas War (Bolivia), 148
globalization, 5, 7–8, 170
Gómez de León, José, 73–75
Graziano da Silva, José, 57, 59, 61
Guaranteed Minimum Income Program (Brazil), 50, 54

Hamon, Benoit, 81
Hayek, Friedrich, 80
Health Bonus (Bono Salud), 148
Hirschman, Albert O., 194
Hope Bonus (Bono Esperanza), 39, 148–49
Hoyos, Luis Alfonso, 125
Huber, Evelyne, 43–44
human capital cct; conditionality enforcement, 2, 4–5, 69, 73, 86–89, 143–44; diffusion of, 17, 26–27, 122–26, 140, 166, 172, stipend structure, 2–3, 5, 70, 85, 87, 89–90, 112–14, 130, 138, 142, 145, 172, 176; targeting, 2, 4–5, 17, 69, 76, 86–87, 90–91, 95, 114, 130, 132, 137, 142, 159, 169, 171
human capital theory, 71–73
Human Development Bonus (Bono de Desarrollo Humano), 126

IDB (Inter-American Development Bank), 6, 16, 26, 28–30, 37, 44, 61, 119–126, 134, 135, 140, 148, 158–59, 165–66, 173
  IDH (Ingreso para el Desarrollo Humano), 158–60, 164, 166
  IFIs (international financial institutions), 22, 27, 29–30, 32–37, 39, 42–45, 47, 56, 59–60, 120–26, 128, 134, 140, 150, 154, 159, 165–66, 172–74
  IFPRI (International Food Policy Research Institute), 76–77, 125
Iglesias, Enrique, 61, 125
IMAS (Instituto Mixto de Desarrollo Social), 138, 140, 142, 144, 177
IMF (International Monetary Fund), 125
import substitution industrialization, 24, 43, 156
income floor. *See* universal basic income
Income for Human Development (Ingreso para el Desarrollo Humano), 158–60, 164, 166

INEGI (Instituto Nacional de Estadística y Geografía), 185
inequality, cct effects on, 12
informality, 10, 24, 43, 79, 84, 132–33, 156, 158, 161, 188
Ingreso Ético Familiar, 29
Ingreso para el Desarrollo Humano, 158–60, 164, 166
Institutional Revolutionary Party (PRI), 23, 37, 70. 76–77
Instituto Nacional de Estadística y Geografía, 185
Inter-American Development Bank, 6, 16, 26, 28–30, 37, 44, 61, 119–126, 134, 135, 140, 148, 158–59, 165–66, 173
international financial institutions, 22, 27, 29–30, 32–37, 39, 42–45, 47, 56, 59–60, 120–26, 128, 134, 140, 150, 154, 159, 165–66, 172–74
International Food Policy Research Institute, 76–77, 125
International Monetary Fund, 125
ISI (import substitution industrialization), 24, 43, 156

Jefes y Jefas, 156–57, 159–61, 165
Johnson, Lyndon B., 81
Jóvenes Construyendo el Futuro, 184
Jóvenes Escribiendo el Futuro, 184
Juana Azurduy Bonus (Bono Juana Azurduy), 145, 152
Juancito Pinto Bonus (Bono Juancito Pinto), 39, 129–30, 135–36, 144–46, 149–53, 163, 165–66
Justicialist Party, 39, 155–57, 159

King, Jr., Martin Luther, 81
Kirchner, Alicia, 40, 159
Kirchner, Cristina Fernández de, 17, 22, 39–40, 130, 153–54, 159–163, 165–66, 173, 177
Kirchner, Néstor, 39–40, 157, 159–60, 165

labor informality, 10, 24, 43, 79, 84, 132–33, 156, 158, 161, 188
labor unions, 47, 82, 156, 158, 170, 192–94
Labour Party (United Kingdom), 80
left; attitudes on redistribution, 21–23, 42–44; effects on social indicators, 4–5, 8, 15, 173; initial opposition to ccts, 37–44; moderate, 15, 104, 107; opposition to ccts, 37–44, 47, 50–51, 55–56, 159; popu-

list, 15, 104, 107; radical, 15, 104, 107; social democratic, 15, 104, 107
Let's Advance (Avancemos), 29, 129, 135–38, 140–44, 163, 165–66, 176–77
Let's Grow (Crecemos), 177
Let's Make Progress (Progresar), 155, 177–78
Let's Overcome (Superémonos), 29, 37, 139
Levy, Santiago, 38, 61, 70–76, 124–25, 172
Lo Vuolo, Rubén, 158
López Obrador, Andrés Manuel, 176, 182–86, 194–95
Lost Decade, 10, 14–15, 42–43, 73–74, 136, 138–39, 159
Luiz Inácio Lula da Silva. *See* Lula
Lula, 5–6, 16–18, 22, 37–39, 45, 46–50, 54–68, 69–71, 73, 84–85, 95–96, 117, 120–22, 125–128, 134, 149, 168, 169, 171–75, 194–95; opposition of ccts, 38–39, 49–50, 55–56, 66, 169; promotion of ccts, 46, 66, 120, 122, 126–28, 166, 172

Macri, Mauricio, 175, 177–78
Magalhães Teixeira, José Roberto, 51, 54
Mahuad, Jamil, 126
market reform, 2, 6–7, 10, 14, 22, 24, 35, 37, 40, 42–45, 48, 50, 70–71, 73–75, 84, 90, 121, 126, 129, 148, 151, 156, 159, 171–72, 174, 194
MAS (Movimiento al Socialismo), 149, 151
McGovern, George, 81
MDB (Movement for Brazilian Democracy), 175, 182
MDS (Ministry for Social Development, Brazil), 61–62, 65, 128
Meade, James, 80
Menem, Carlos, 156, 158, 161, 164, 166
Milner, Dennis and Mabel, 80
Ministério do Desenvolvimento Social e Combate à Fome, 61–62, 65, 128
Ministry for Social Development and the Fight Against Hunger, 61–62, 65, 128
misiones (Venezuela), 40
Missão Criança, 126
missions (Venezuela), 40
Mixed Institute for Social Assistance, 138, 140, 142, 144, 177
Moctezuma, Esteban, 76
monotributistas, 177–78
Morales, Evo, 15, 17, 39, 130, 144–52, 154, 165–66, 173

MORENA (National Regeneration Movement), 175
Movement for Brazilian Democracy (MDB), 175, 182
Movement toward Socialism (MAS), 149, 151
Movimento Democrático Brasileiro (MDB), 175, 182
Movimiento al Socialismo (MAS), 149, 151
Movimiento Regeneración Nacional (MORENA), 175
multilateral banks, 22, 27, 29–30, 32–37, 39, 42–45, 47, 56, 59–60, 120–26, 128, 134, 140, 150, 154, 159, 165–66, 172–74
Murray, Charles, 82

National Action Party (PAN), 37, 70, 76–77
National Front Against Poverty (FRENAPO), 158
National Health Service (Costa Rica), 138, 144
National Institute of Statistics and Geography (INEGI), 185
National Population Council (CONAPO), 73
National Regeneration Movement (MORENA), 175
National Scholarship Fund (FONABE), 144, 177
National Social Security Administration (ANSES), 162–63
National Solidarity Program (PRONASOL), 37, 73–76
National Union of Education Workers (SNTE), 193
nationalization; gas (Bolivia), 149; pensions (Argentina), 160–62
neoliberal bottom, 5–6, 8, 74
neoliberalism, 2, 6–7, 10, 14, 22, 24, 35, 37, 40, 42–45, 48, 50, 70–71, 73–75, 84, 90, 121, 126, 129, 148, 151, 156, 159, 171–72, 174, 194
Nixon, Richard M., 81
Non-contributory and Social Protection Programmes Database, 3, 48, 88, 97–99, 114, 130, 137, 146, 155
Novacovsky, Irene, 158
Nutrition Card (Cartão Alimentação), 57, 59–61, 63
Nutrition Scholarship (Bolsa Alimentação), 55–57, 59, 63, 69

OECD (Organization for Economic Cooperation and Development), 31, 191–92

Operação Pente Fino, 179–81
Operation Fine-Tooth Comb, 179–81
Oportunidades. *See* Progresa/Oportunidades
Oportunities (Oportunidadades). *See* Progresa/Oportunidades
opportunity costs, of remaining in school versus working, 2, 5, 69, 71, 89, 133, 138, 142–43, 147, 158–59, 172
Organization for Economic Cooperation and Development (OECD), 31, 191–92
Ortega, Daniel, 40

PAC (Citizens' Action Party), 136, 175–76
Pacheco, Abel, 140
Paes de Barros, Ricardo, 61
Palocci, Antonio, 60
PAN (National Action Party), 37, 70, 76–77
pandemic, COVID-19, 182
Partido Acción Ciudadana (PAC), 136, 175–76
Partido Acción Nacional (PAN), 37, 70, 76–77
Partido da Social-Democracia Brasileira (PSDB), 51, 53–55, 60
Partido de la Revolución Democrática (PRD), 37–38, 76–77
Partido dos Trabalhadores (PT), 23–24, 38–39, 46–47, 49–58, 61, 65–67, 84, 176, 179–82, 195
Partido Justicialista (Justicialist Party, Peronist Party), 39, 155–57, 159
Partido Revolucionario Institucional (PRI), 23, 37, 70. 76–77
Party of the Democratic Revolution (PRD), 37–38, 76–77
pensions; contributory, 2, 10, 39–40, 155–56, 160–62, 165, 178, 181; diffusion, 26, 174; non-contributory, 37–38, 77, 141, 145, 148–49, 152, 184; privatization, 161
Perillo, Marconi, 60
Perón, Juan Domingo, 155
Peronists, 39, 155–57, 159
PETI (Programa for Erradication of Child Labor), 54, 56
PGRM (Guaranteed Minimum Income Program, Brazil), 50, 54
Piñera, Sebastián, 29
piqueteros, 158
PISA (Programme for International Student Assessment), 191–92
Plan Escudo, 141–42
Plan Familias (Familias por la Inclusión Social), 159–162, 164–66

Plan Trabajar, 156
Porteña Citizenship (Ciudadanía Porteña), 154
poverty; cct effects on long-term, 12–13, 188–89; poverty, cct effects on short-term, 12
power resource theory, 21, 23–24, 29, 45
PRAF-II (Family Allowance Program, Phase 2), 25, 36–37, 125
PRD (Party of the Democratic Revolution), 37–38, 76–77
Pregnancy Allowance (Asignación por Embarazo), 154–55
PRI (Institutional Revolutionary Party), 23, 37, 70, 76–77
Pritchett, Lant, 190
privatization, Bolivia, 148
PRO (Republican Proposal), 175
Programa de Garantia de Renda Mínima (PGRM), 50, 54
Programa for Erradication of Child Labor (PETI), 54, 56
Programa de Asignación Familiar II (PRAF-II), 25, 36–37, 125
Programa de Erradicação do Trabalho Infantil (PETI), 54, 56
Programa Familias por la Inclusión Social, 159–162, 164–66
Programa Jefes y Jefas de Hogar Desempleados, 156–57, 159–61, 165
Programa Nacional de Solidaridad (PRONASOL), 37, 73–76
Programme for International Student Assessment, 191–92
Progresa. *See* Progresa/Oportunidades
Progresa/Oportunidades; adoption, 25, 37–38, 73–77; cancellation of, 183–84; design of, 2–3, 69–70, 73–75, 86–90, 113–15, 171–72, diffusion of, 17, 26–27, 122–26, 140, 166, 172; expansion, 75–77
Progresar (Argentina), 155, 177–78
PRONASOL, 37, 73–76
Propuesta Republicana (PRO), 175
Prospera. *See* Progresa/Oportunidades
PSDB (Brazilian Social Democratic Party), 51, 53–55, 60
PT (Workers' Party), 23–24, 38–39, 46–47, 49–58, 61, 65–67, 84, 176, 179–82, 195

Quiroga, Jorge "Tuto", 39, 148, 164

race to the bottom, 5–6, 8, 74
Red de Protección Social (RPS), 40, 125

Renta Dignidad, 145, 148, 152
Republican Proposal (PRO), 175
right; attitudes on redistribution, 41–42; initial support of ccts, 25, 41–42, 121–22
Rodríguez, Miguel Angel, 139
Rojas, Carlos, 74–76
Rousseff, Dilma, 46–48, 62–63, 66–67, 69–70, 171, 175, 179, 181, 194
RPS (Red de Protección Social), 40, 125

Saca, Antonio, 116
Salinas de Gortari, Carlos, 73
Samuelson, Paul, 81
Sánchez de Lozada, Gonzálo, 39, 148, 164
School Scholarship (Bolsa Escola), 24, 38, 47, 52, 54–56, 58–59, 61, 63, 69, 95, 117
School Scholarship (Beca Escolar), 126
Secretaría de Desarrollo Social, 74, 75–76
SEDESOL (Social Development Ministry, Mexico), 74, 75–76
SEDLAC (Socio-Economic Database for Latin America the Caribbean), 30, 87–88, 97, 100, 130
Seguro de Capacitación y Empleo, 159
Serra, José, 55–56
Servants of the Nation, 185–86
Servidores de la Nación, 185–86
Shield Plan (Plan Escudo), 141–42
Sindicato Nacional de Trabajadores de la Educación (SNTE), 193
Single Registry (Cadastro Único), 55, 60
SNTE (Sindicato Nacional de Trabajadores de la Educación), 193
Sobrón, Claudia, 158
social democracy, 4, 66, 122, 132, 138, 194
Social Development and Family Allowance Fund (FODESAF), 138–39
Social Development Ministry (Brazil), 61–62, 65, 128
Social Development Ministry (Mexico), 74, 75–76
social policy, Latin American model, 10, 22, 43, 174
Social Protection Network, 40, 125
Socio-Economic Database for Latin America the Caribbean, 30, 87–88, 97, 100, 130
Solidarity Bonus, 125–26, 148, 150
Solís, Guillermo, 175–76
Solís, Ottón, 136, 165
Souza, Paulo Renato, 53, 55

Standardized World Income Inequality Database, 30, 100
Superémonos, 29, 37, 139
Suplicy, Eduardo, 38, 49–53, 56–58, 66–68, 69, 71, 73, 77–78, 83–84, 166, 171–72
SWIID (Standardized World Income Inequality Database), 30, 100
Székely, Miguel, 140

targeting, errors of, 59, 82, 86, 181
taxation, 25, 31, 33, 50, 68, 81, 83–84, 102, 104, 149, 162, 177–79, 188
teachers' unions, 47, 82, 156, 158, 170, 192–94
technocrats, 36, 44, 61, 70, 73–76, 78, 90, 109, 121, 124, 128–29, 140, 150, 158, 165, 172
Temer, Michel, 175, 179, 181
TERCE (Third Comparative Regional and Explicative), 190–91
Terra, Osmar, 179–80
Third Comparative Regional and Explicative Exam, 190–91
thirteenth monthly benefit, 152, 178, 180
Thomé, Déborah, 2, 68
To Progress (Progresa). *See* Progresa/Oportunidadesu
Tobin, James, 81
Training and Employment Insurance, 159

UBI. *See* universal basic income
Unemployed Heads of Households Program, 156–57, 159–61, 165
UNESCO (United Nations Educational, Scientific and Cultural Organization), 190
UNICEF (United Nations Children's Fund), 52, 128, 141
unions, 47, 82, 156, 158, 170, 192–94
United Nations Children's Fund, 52, 128, 141
United Nations Educational, Scientific and Cultural Organization, 190
universal basic income; movement, 70, 77–80, 82, 90–91, 158, 172; policy, 3–4, 16–18, 40, 48, 50, 62, 67–71, 78, 116, 120, 122, 127, 145, 149, 154, 161–62, 165–66, 171–73, 184; pros and cons, 78–80; support from left, 80–82, 166, 171; support from right, 82
Universal Child Allowance (AUH), 40, 130, 136, 153–57, 160–63, 165–66, 177–78
Universalism, 4–5, 61, 67–68, 82, 145–46, 151–53, 170, 173

Van Parijs, Philippe, 78, 84
Varoufakis, Yannis, 80
Vázquez Mota, Josefina, 77
Vázquez, Tabaré, 154

Washington Consensus, 2, 6–7, 10, 14, 22, 24, 35, 37, 40, 42–45, 48, 50, 70–71, 73–75, 84, 90, 121, 126, 129, 148, 151, 156, 159, 171–72, 174, 194
welfare regime, 10, 43, 131–32, 138, 174
welfare retrenchment, 22, 174
Well-Being Census, 185–86, 195
Wolfensohn, James, 61, 125
Work Plan, 156
Workers' Party (PT), 23–24, 38–39, 46–47, 49–58, 61, 65–67, 84, 176, 179–82, 195
World Bank, 6, 16, 26, 29–31, 37, 44, 54, 59, 61, 70, 73, 86, 119–26, 128, 134, 135, 145, 148, 150, 156

World Development Indicators, 30–31, 102

Yacimientos Petrolíferos Fiscales Bolivianos, 149
Yang, Andrew, 81
Yaschine, Iliana, 12, 124, 188–89
Youths Building the Future (Jóvenes Construyendo el Futuro), 184
Youths Writing the Future (Jóvenes Escribiendo el Futuro), 184
YPFP (Yacimientos Petrolíferos Fiscales Bolivianos), 149

Zedillo, Ernesto, 37, 70–71, 73–74, 76, 109
Zero Hunger (Fome Zero), 45, 47, 50, 55–62, 66, 84, 117, 121
Zumbado, Fernando, 140–41